INTERNAL SECURITY

Issues, Challenges, Threats & Linkages

DR. B. RAMASWAMY
DR. SASIKALA PUSHPA
DR. SR. V.A. MARY

PRABHAT
EXAMS

Publisher

PRABHAT EXAMS

Imprint of Prabhat Prakashan Pvt. Ltd.

4/19 Asaf Ali Road, New Delhi–110 002

Ph. 23289555 • 23289666 • 23289777 • Helpline/ 7827007777

e-mail: prabhatbooks@gmail.com • Website: www.prabhatexam.com

Price

Five Hundred Ninety Five Rupees

ISBN 978-93-5266-682-9

Printed at

Sita Fine Arts, Delhi

INTERNAL SECURITY

by Dr. B. Ramaswamy, Dr. Sasikala Pushpa and Dr. Sr. V.A. Mary

ISBN 978-93-5266-682-9

₹ 595.00

Preface

India is facing too many challenges to its internal security. The level and possibility of threats are multifaceted, varied and massive. It is the only country in the world which faces so many threats, with so much intensity, simultaneously. In general, more than 50 per cent of India is said to be getting impacted by one or other of these perils, which are not merely 'law and order' issues. They have growing external aspect falsifying traditional understanding that internal security risks are set off mainly by internal sources. They pose a threat to the body politic like a 'cancer'. The state of mediocre internal security condition is not due to India's adverse strategic scenario but also due to frail internal security system, specifically its criminal justice system. In this perspective, the article contends that if suitable measures are not adopted, the threats may bring about the gradual degradation of the Indian State. It proposes renewed set of policies and procedures in political, economic, socio-cultural, military and diplomatic ground.

Insofar as the internal security scenario in India is concerned, we need to first take into account that the Indian society consists of distinct ethnic groups, cultures, languages and religious values. These are both asset and a challenge to the nation. Although the country's national integrity remains primarily protected, we do have some disputes arising from the social and economic inequalities amongst the section of our society. Religious fundamentalism is also an area of trouble that needs to be confronted.

For example, in the current scenario, the overall condition in J&K is well controlled by the Indian security forces and the situation is showing distinct signs of improvement. Our effort is to make certain that the 'moral hegemony' achieved by the Army is upheld and the condition in J&K improves further. Our policy of 'Iron Fist and Velvet Glove' is yielding profits. Our emphasis is on carrying out surgical and professional campaigns built on hard intelligence, that cause minimum trouble to the local population. Preserving human rights is one of the foundations of our anti-terrorist campaigns and our record is worth emulating. The upsurge for peace signals that the general public is sick and tired of violence and is looking for a peaceful restoration of normalcy. Violence intensities have witnessed a severe decline in comparison to the corresponding period of 2007. This can largely be accredited to an efficient counter terrorism network in the hinterland. The upsurge in tourism and other normalcy signs are a demonstration of the objectives of the general Kashmiri public for a peaceful and affluent life. The polls to the State Assembly planned later this year will be a significant benchmark in J&K's return to normalcy.

Moreover, on account of the persistent endeavours of the Security Forces, the security scenario in the North Eastern States of the nation has demonstrated a considerable improvement over the past few months. A wider section of the state today is free of violence and there has been restoration of normalcy. The peaceful handling of elections in Meghalaya, Nagaland and Tripura, with a very high voter turnout, is suggestive of the considerable improvement towards normalcy in the territory. Popularly elected democratic regimes are in authority in all the states. The speed of development activities and tourism are picking momentum, which are positive signs. Persistent operational pressure and influence by the Security Forces has caused in the surrender of a large number of terrorists along with their armaments to various organizations. On the whole, we witness that progressively more groups are willing to become legally committed to a 'Suspension of Operations' agreement with the Government, which is a very encouraging development.

Naxalism. In the broader internal security context, Naxal violence presents a noteworthy challenge. The Army is keeping a close watch at the different trends and developments. Accordingly, we have been influential in better equipping police and paramilitary forces like the CRPF, PAC and Reserve Police Battalions across the nation by offering advice and training in anti-Naxal operations, anti-IED Operations and 'Training of Trainers'. We are providing aid in the formation of Counter Terrorism Schools and in the investigation of vicious episodes to help the police and the PMF to devise an operational mechanism. The Army, nonetheless, asserts it to be a socio-economic issue which must be managed by the states utilizing the Police and Paramilitary Forces.

As India's anti-terror endeavour is yet far detached from the worldwide sophistication levels, it has been projected that by 2020, a considerable 6 per cent of the worldwide acquisition in homeland security (HLS) will be from India. That is immense. Technology has to and will play an ever-increasing part in the whole ambit of security constituents – counter-terrorism, border security, immigration, entry and exit point monitoring. In India, the central government and state governments have predominantly been engaged in offering security whereas the private sector's part has been minimal. Taking into account the huge monetary and infrastructure requirements, there is a huge scope for corporates to play a part in the internal security sector. They can create crucial technologies for the nation's exclusive challenges, supply advanced equipment and safeguard timely execution of a variety of security solutions.

While India's internal security issues may appear comparable to those of other countries, India's geography – 7,000 km of coast and 15,000 km land border – large population, social and political emergencies, dated security and scrutiny technological tools present specific challenges. A federal mechanism with multi and regional party set-up also brings up the task of centre and state co-ordination. Given the limitations, succeeding governments encounter a daunting task in recognizing and preventing security threats.

The terrorist activity has been a cause of concern for India for a long time. The origin of a large number of terrorist activities has been internal, with motives varying from Marxism to ethnicity. The Ministry of Home Affairs has barred 35 organizations across the nation under The Unlawful Activities (Prevention) Act, 1967. In the course of the most recent couple of decades, the emergence of terrorist groups in our neighbouring nations has progressively turned into a source of danger to our internal security. Terrorists across the world have intensified the use of IEDs, the advancement of which continues to perplex investigation authorities. Ammonium nitrate, a substance which is mainly utilized in composts, is also utilized as a primary component in powerful IEDs for carrying out assaults, including the Mumbai attacks. There is urgent need to shield the supply-chain of ammonium nitrate, requiring coordinated endeavours from the government, associations and individual. India is being under consistent threat of terror and cyber-attacks and hostile groups have also formed front organizations in cities. Terrorism in 2012 has taken up different facets and is considerably unique in relation to its form a decade back. Terrorists are impersonal, occasionally using advanced weapons and machineries which are considered to be the domain of security forces. The transformation of an insignificant criminal into a terrorist utilizing advanced technology and weapons – as witnessed in 26/11 terror attack convict Kasab's case – is suggestive of their formidable training capacity.

These new aspects of the dangers India confronts require exceptionally agile security administration. Our state reactions are adapting to coordinate the speed with which things are evolving. Post Kargil, a few measures were set up to boost border security. The occasions of 26/11 Mumbai assault in 2008 compelled the security agencies to look further into what is required to secure the country from internal and external dangers. After three years, the security circumstances in Indian cities has advanced but remains challenging. We will require quick enforcement of manpower and technologies not merely to safeguard urban areas but also to make certain that India's growth rate proceeds at over 8 per cent per annum. Numerous terrorist episodes over the recent few years all over the globe point to the regularly expanding possibility of utilization of Chemical, Biological, Radiological and Nuclear (CBRN) materials by non-state actors. Although the establishment of the National Disaster Management Authority (NDMA) will offer the organizational and coordination process at the national, state, district and local stages for disaster response and mitigation, India's readiness for such an assault remains at a budding phase. There are no accounting practices in operation to account for ammonium nitrate delivered in the nation. Domestic buyers must endorse lawful utilization and suppliers must keep records and report theft or loss of ammonium nitrate to the established order. Terrorists are capable of adopting novel and distinctive styles of terror assaults as demonstrated by the utilization of a magnetic explosive device to target an Israel embassy car in a high security zone in New Delhi, injuring four individuals. The National Security Guard (NSG) Chief has confessed that sticky bombs have turned into a more genuine matter of worry for the security forces in comparison to IEDs. These easy-to-use devices are gradually turning into a favoured option for many terror groups in other nations as well.

The cyber domain – the fourth security measurement after air, land and ocean – offers its own exclusive arrangement of difficulties. As stated by an answer given in the Parliament by the legislature, 117 websites were hacked between January and June in 2011. In 2010, as indicated by reports from Canada and US, a few Ministry of Defence websites and that of India's driving group of experts, the Institute for Defence Studies and Analyses (IDSA) were likewise hacked.

The Indian Computer Emergency Response Team (CERT–In) conducted an investigation on the web server records of the hacked websites and recommended particular steps and countermeasures to cover the present vulnerabilities and reinforce the security of these websites. As proposed by these measurements, government websites getting hacked is turning out to be quite a regular event demonstrating the way that the foundation which powers imperative websites was exceptionally delicate. Then again, cyber threat actors are substantially more advanced and systematized than they are given credit for. In numerous instances evidently, hacking is part of the games played by spying and sabotage agencies from different nations. India needs to move from responsive to preventive technique which would be the cause of noteworthy IT and management effort. Technology has to and will play a growing part in the entire ambit of security mechanisms – counter-terrorism, border security, immigration, entry and exit point monitoring. More than 40 nations have effectively embraced biometrics while 12 to 13 nations require biometrics for permitting visa.

India has unique technologies and methods that do not essentially interoperate ideally. That is a major shortcoming. There are similarly a lot of cases purportedly demonstrating that foreigners from neighbouring nations are effortlessly ready to get some sort of identity cards which instantaneously and unlawfully, transform them into Indian citizens.

The MHA's NATGRID activity, the development of a knowledge database intended to merge and make accessible information assembled by existing security and law enforcement organizations, will end up being an important connection in India's intelligence set-up. In fact the strength of the databases to be coordinated would require to be propped up. The CCTNS proposal of the MHA, to expedite storage, transfer and sharing of data and information between police stations, their state headquarters and the Central Police institutions will see huge advantages accumulating as its utilization goes up. However, data inputs have to be validated in a few layers before approval is accorded. It must be taken into account that whatever system is approved, properly or wrongly, will be there for quite a while.

It might be noticed that in India, the central government and state governments have principally been engaged in delivering security whereas the part played by private division has been minimal. To aid the assets at the administration's disposition though, the proactive engagement of private citizens and institutions in alleviating such dangers is gaining ever-increasing support. Taking into account the immense financial and infrastructure requirements, there is an extensive potential for corporates to assume a part in the internal security area. They can create crucial technologies for the nation's exclusive difficulties, supply advanced equipment and guarantee timely execution of an assortment of security solutions. In the end, in the domain of internal security, one who makes efficient utilization of the cutting-edge technology would gain the upper hand over the other, be it the terrorist organizations or the government.

AUTHORS

Contents

Chapter one

Internal Security: An Introductory Overview

Introduction

Internal Security is intended to secure the country from the numerous dangers it faces. This requires the devotion of representatives, for the most part government ones, in extensive employments that range from aeronautics and border security to crisis reaction, from cybersecurity analyst to chemical facility inspector. The customary perspective of security concentrated on the use of power at the state level and was therefore a genuinely narrow view, relying on military security. It is presently commonly recognized that there is more to security than absolutely military components. The present meaning of security recognizes political, monetary, environmental, social and human among different strands that effect the idea of security. In the most common relationships, the concern for security of the lowermost common denominator of each society, specifically the 'human being', has brought about the advancement of the idea of 'human security', which concentrates on the person. Hence, the definition of security is undeniably expansive – and is identified with the ability of the state to execute the task of securing the interest of its general population. This formulation pay attention to the times of Chanakya and Arthashastra. Numerous significant aspects of human advancement relate similarly to individual's security: roughly characterized as individuals' flexibility from dread and freedom from desire in a general sense. Employing a human security attempt offers opportunity chance to analyse several issues in an explanatory way. Human security correlates to much more than safety from hostility and crime. The human security method was initiated in the 1994 global Human Development Report (HDR), which resulted in a range of literature and plans forming on the idea. In 2012, the General Assembly (GA) assumed a general description of the concept. The human security approach expands the range of security analysis and policy from regional security to the security of individuals. The 2012 GA Resolution emphasizes upon the part played by 'Member States in identifying and addressing widespread and cross-cutting challenges to survival, livelihood and dignity of their people'. Put differently, threat(s) to – and values under threat in – individual's lives are the significant basis of a human security report. The 1994 HDR emphasized upon two key elements of human security: 'freedom from fear' and 'freedom from want'. These liberties, from the preamble to the Universal Declaration of Human Rights, are component of the four human liberties that President Franklin D. Roosevelt prominently brought up in a speech in 1941. He was pressing for a world set up on: freedom of speech and expression, freedom of worship, freedom from want and freedom from fear. Ensuing debate in the 1990s incorporated the liberty 'to live in dignity'. The 1994 HDR was more precise, keep a record of seven crucial aspects of human security: Economic, Food, Health, Environment, Personal, Community and Political.

In the words of Kofi Annan…

- 'We must also broaden our view of what is meant by peace and security. Peace means much more than the absence of war. Human security can no longer be understood in purely military terms. Rather, it must encompass economic development, social justice, environmental protection, democratization, disarmament, and respect for human rights and the rule of law'.
- 'The demands we face also reflect a growing consensus that collective security can no longer be narrowly defined as the absence of armed conflict, be it between or within States. Gross abuses of human rights, the large-scale displacement of civilian populations, international terrorism, the AIDS pandemic, drug and arms trafficking and environmental disasters present a direct threat to human security, forcing us to adopt a much more coordinated approach to a range of issues'.
- 'Human security, in its broadest sense, embraces far more than the absence of violent conflict. It encompasses human rights, good governance, access to education and health care and ensuring that each individual has opportunities and choices to fulfill his or her potential. Every step in this direction is also a step towards reducing poverty, achieving economic growth and preventing conflict. Freedom from want, freedom from fear, and the freedom of future generations to inherit a healthy natural environment – these are the interrelated building blocks of human – and therefore national security'.

Internal Security vs. External Security

Internal Security is the security of a nation inside its boundaries. This fundamentally suggests upkeep of peace and law enforcement inside the nation while maintaining the sovereignty of the state. External security is the safety against hostility by a foreign nation. Giving external security is exclusively the duty of the military of the nation, while internal security comes under the domain of the police, which can be upheld by armed police force, if needed. In the Indian scenario, the Ministry of Home Affairs (MHA) has the nodal obligation for safeguarding the internal security in the nation and external security comes under the purview of Ministry of Defense.

Internal Security Divisions of Ministry Home Affairs, Govt. of India

Division-I: This division manage matters identifying with internal security and law enforcement, including anti-national and subversive exercises of different groups/extremist agencies, policy and functional issues on terrorism, security approvals, monitoring of ISI movements and Home Secretary-level dialogues with Pakistan on terrorism and drug trafficking as a component of the composite dialogue process.

Division-II: This division manages all the issues concerning the Arms Act 1959, Arms Rules 1962, Explosive Substances Act 1908 and other related issues; letters of demand for shared legitimate assistance in criminal issues; National Security Act, 1980 and portrayals thereunder; organization of Narcotics Control Bureau; offering central assistance to victims of terror, communal and naxal aggression; issues identifying with breach of privilege of MPs, etc.

Main Purposes of Internal Secuity

The major objectives of internal security are as follows:

- To safeguard territorial integrity and help defend autonomy within the region of the country.
- To maintain law enforcement, peace and serenity within the country.
- To defend the principle of rule of law and equality before law.
- To guarantee right to freedom as ensured by the constitution.
- Aims at peaceful coexistence and communal accord.

Non-Traditional Security Issues

'They are defined as challenges to the survival and well-being of peoples and states that arise primarily out of nonmilitary sources'.

– Professor Mely Caballero-Anthony (Secretary General, Consortium on Non-Traditional Security Studies in Asia)

Generally, non-customary security refers to those dangers which are originated by the non-state actors. These are difficulties to the survival of the state and welfare of individuals that emerge principally out of nonmilitary sources, for example, environmental change, cross-border environmental degradation and resource depletion and infectious diseases.

The contrast between conventional and non-conventional security dangers is not so impervious now as it seemed in the last century. The conventional concept of security envisions the utilization of military measures to manage the dangers to the harmony, territorial uprightness and autonomy of a state. Presently, a level of 'permeability' has developed.

Features/characteristics of non-traditional security

I. Non-military in nature.

II. Transnational in scope-neither absolutely local nor purely interstate.

III. Transmitted quickly because of the globalization and communication revolution.

Non-Traditional Security Issues India should Worry About

a. ***Food Security:*** 'When all people, at all times, have physical and economic access to sufficient, safe and nutritious food to meet their dietary needs and food preferences for an active and healthy life' (UN definition).

   India's populace is still developing and will not settle until 2050/2060. Positioned among least developed countries when it comes to the issues of malnutrition and stunning. We can gain from nations in Latin America, who have embraced short and long-term policy decisions, classified as consumer, producer and trade-orientated strategic methods to national food security. The comprehensive approach incorporates political exchange of ideas at national levels as well as intergovernmental levels including the different government divisions to successfully execute PDS. Community-based Management of Acute Malnutrition (CMAM) programme depending upon the micro-planning basis at the district level of Rajasthan can be recreated.

b. ***Climate Change and Environment Pollution***: India's progress trajectory has had to struggle with growing environmental difficulties.

Ex-Indian cities are positioned among the most contaminated urban areas in the globe. An effective example of Netherlands and France based on increasing taxes on contaminating inputs which are then put in sustainable infrastructural improvement instead of simply raising the revenue can be implemented. India's National Action Plan on Climate Change (NAPCC) issue of lack of transparency can be managed through Brazilian model including a ranging number of participants under the umbrella unit Inter-Ministerial Committee on Climate Change (CIM).

c. ***Water Scarcity and Contamination:*** With an immense populace, there is burden on rare water assets regardless of having plenty of rain. Unsustainable water harvesting structure: Denmark model which emphasizes on collaborating research organizations append to national colleges in which the administration awarded grants to catch up on clean water technologies. Coordinated effort with Israel in water technology can open new water conservation procedure.

d. ***Energy Security Issues:*** India is an energy-craving country with high GDP growth rate and high reliance on the imported petroleum from the volatile Middle East. Laws similar to Tunisia's 'energy conservation system' law need to be approved which depends on the National Fund for Energy Management to boost renewable energy deal and improve skills competence in the sector. Adopting the Chinese model can be of great help centred on searching for alternatives beyond its neighbourhood and imports fuel from all around utilizing a combination of economic diplomatic tools, and several other financial incentives.

e. ***Public Health Issues:*** Inadequate health infrastructure, high out-of-pocket expenses. Ex-Gorakhpur BRB Hospital case, which resulted in the casualty of several children. 'Chilean Model' built on Explicit Guarantees and Universal Access (AUGE) programme, which promises to offering universal health care for all populations made through its two-tier system of Public Health care should be embraced.

f. ***Disasters:*** Management of regular floods, droughts, landslides and cyclones need a 360-degree preparation mechanism. For example, disaster management model for Bihar, Assam floods and urban floods like in Chennai and Mumbai can be adopted from Japan.

g. ***International Terrorism:*** In the words of Bruce Hoffman, International terrorism could be defined as 'Deliberate creation and exploitation of fear through violence or threat of violence in pursuit of political change'. International terrorism in India is spreading its wings in India through state-funded terrorism by Pakistan through separatist movement in Kashmir valley and the insurgency in Nagaland, Manipur. As per UNESCO, 'Violence begins from the mind', therefore orchestrating minds of people by turning them away from the culture of violence and instilling in them the culture of peace is required. India should raise its voice at the international platform to bring consensus among the world fraternity on the definition of the terrorism. India should collaborate with Israel for effective surveillance and spying mechanism on the borders.

h. ***Illegal Migration:*** To stop unlawful immigration activities from its borders such as Bangladeshi illegal immigrants, recent issue related to Rohingya Muslims, etc., India should encourage legal immigration through redefining citizenship act, reforming laws following the US immigration laws. India should develop bilateral cooperation mechanism among neighbouring countries to have documentation of illegal immigrants and to have an appropriate solution.

i. ***Organized Crimes—National and Transnational:*** India need to make major changes to prevailing legislations to tackle the use of counterfeit currency and finding the connections between terrorists and underworld, for example, the Mumbai terror attack. Terrorist organizations such as the Shining Path (Peru) also take advantage of the organized crime set-up with the intention of establishing a highly effective drugs smuggling network to fund their terrorist operations and nationwide and worldwide crimes such as piracy, smuggling and drugs. Necessary reforms need to be made in substantive laws, investigative mechanism, and police establishment. India need to localize its counter-terror programs similar to the comprehensive programme like Brazil's Pronasci to associate a lot of elements that were the factors triggering violence in the nation, developing local frameworks, gun-free zones and promoting the civic culture to bring down violence.

j. ***Human Security Issues:*** It is the combination of risks related to war, genocide and the shift of people. At the least, human security implies liberty from violence and from the concern of violence. The emphasis should be on early deterrence to reduce the effects of insecurity, to bring forth long-term solutions.

k. ***Poverty:*** In India, the main factors responsible for poverty include: poor agriculture, growing population, the gap between the rich and the poor, corruption and black money, etc. Farmers must get all amenities for irrigation and should be adequately trained and educated. Steps must be taken to make agriculture profitable. Family planning schemes should be initiated and more and more industries should be established to meet the requirements of our nation. Corruption must be brought to an end and our offices should function efficiently.

l. ***Nuclear Security Issues:*** There is a need to reform the legal architecture for radioactive materials. Lack of universal coverage and implementation of the code of conduct along with unsecured and open facilities present a security issue. Cradle-to-grave control mechanism on radioactive resources remain weak and tracking radioactive sources is a major issue. For example, the Goiânia accident, Brazil when in the late 1980s, a widely publicized incident in Brazil emphasized on the significance of properly safeguarding dangerous radiological substance. Similarly issues related to a rogue country like North Korea having a nuclear arsenal pose danger to the world. There is a need to devise effective nuclear policy in view of the possibility of non-state actors taking control of nuclear weapons in future because of uncertainty in the international scenario. There is a need to strengthen the role of the International Atomic Energy Agency (IAEA), embracing India's stand of absolute nuclear disarmament, expand universal coverage for the code of conduct and increase voluntary actions.

m. ***Proliferation of Chemical and Biological Weapons:*** Utilization of chemical and biological weapons is another issue of concern among the world community. In Syrian Civil War, these weapons caused a great havoc. The Vietnam War also witnessed the use of Agent Orange by USA. To tackle this menace, there is a need to further strengthen Chemical Weapons Convention (1992), the Biological

Weapons Convention (1975) and export control regime.

n. *Economic Security Issues:* Economic security is the state of having a steady pay or different resources to sustain a way of life now and in the predictable future. Black money, high cash to GDP ratio, counterfeit currency, trade imbalance are the major obstacles in the path of economic security. The counter measures to be adopted to manage these issues involve facilitating the rapid deployment of civilian technologies, increasing the tax base and reducing import through indignation.

o. *Religious Extremism:* Religious extremism 'describes faith-based actions that are deliberate attempts to cause harm to other people'. The factors causing extremism involve personal causes, religious doctrines and fundamentalism, an abomination of sexuality and a response to gender equality, broken families, social causes and reactions to multiculturalism, secularization, disordered civic life and poor governance, a negative reaction to a dominant culture and modernism and sectarianism and faith schools, etc. Challenges arising due to religious extremism include day to day riots, for example, Shamali riots and Saharanpur riots. Remedies involve (1) religious cure, that is, rather than giving severe punishments to extremists, intellectual debates must be held with them and they must be suitably counselled to reach a solution, (2) social cure where youths must be engaged in constructive work, (3) media to provide a platform where all scholars can gather to debate and discuss religious matters to avoid a confrontation over individual differences. Legal Cure: In the attempts to contain extremism, a legal cure is necessary. This refers to making laws in relation to extremist activities, amending the Religious Unity Act and laws related to terrorism.

p. *Information Security Issues:* It is the condition of being secured against the unapproved utilization of information, specifically electronic data. Difficulties include confidentiality, privacy and data theft/cyber-attack. For example, Stuxnet like attack which can disable the imperative infrastructure is part of cyber terrorism; WannaCry, a crypto-ransomware can disrupt public life reliant on digital infrastructure; A weak IT Act which has turned out to be redundant due to non-abuse and age-old cyber laws. Absence of awareness and the culture of cybersecurity at the personal and institutional level. Absence of trained and qualified workforce to execute the countermeasures. Cures of such issues involve protection of critical information infrastructure through public-private relationship; synchronizing the National Legal Regime with the International Legal Regime. For example, the U.S.-India Cyber Relationship Framework, establishing national cyber-security architecture could be of significant help in dealing with the issue of information security. A National Cyber Security Agency (NCSA) could be established to analyse the kind of cyber threats and react to resolve them appropriately. Acts similar to Singapore's proposed Cyber Security Bill will present a significant safety measure to crucial infrastructure.

□□□

Chapter two

Major Issues and Challenges to Internal Security

While India is progressively considered as a rising world power, it remains a nation plagued by interior issues. India is today an amazing investigation in contrasts. Universal gurus have anticipated a 'global power shift', with a 'transfer of power from West to East', and some have just anointed India as one of the 'great powers' of the nearby future. One prominent economist observes that, 'a simple back-of-the-envelope calculation shows that by 2030 India will have a per-capita income of $20,000, which will place us in the category of industrialized nations'. All of this seems very true. However, there is another India to which the nation's vaunting privileged and much of the world is paying no heed to. It is an India of relentless destitution for millions, expanding rural distress, mass suicides by ruined farmers, prolonged and widespread malnutrition, and vast developmental dislodgments that rebuff the poor. It is an India in which administration is noticeable by its absence or is experienced only in its most careless, insensitive and oppressive indications. It must be clear that the strains between these 'two Indias' are loaded with political and security dangers, and that the dynamism and development of the first is possibly endangered by the stagnation, inertial resistance, and vicious response of the second. It is within the setting of this entrenched and underlying friction that endangers to India's internal security should be assessed.

Some of the major threats to internal security of India are:

- Communalism,
- Regionalism and Interstate disputes
- Hinterland terrorism—international and domestic
- Jammu and Kashmir Militancy
- Border management insurgency in northeast
- Left wing extremism/Naxalism
- Organized crime and its nexus with terrorism
- Caste and ethnic tensions
- Cyber-crime and cyber security
- Maritime security issues
- Drug and Human Trafficking
- ***Jammu & Kashmir Problem:*** The issue has been with us since independence despite the fact that Pakistan has no lawful case. The leader of this former princely state choose to accede to India. According to the Independence Act, the rulers of the princely states were given the option to join either India or Pakistan. Pakistan has been questioning the lawfulness of the accession

signed by the then J&K ruler, Maharaja Hari Singh. The early wavering of the Maharaja to accede to either India or Pakistan and the one-sided Indian offer to discover the desires of the general population of the state has given Pakistan a reason to challenge the lawfulness of the accession. It has been making all its efforts for the last 56 years to seize this state. It has not possessed the power to accomplish its goal through wars with India. Hence, it has begun a proxy war since 1989. Engaging in a proxy war suits the Pakistani plans of draining India. Unfortunately, the shortcomings of the state and of the administrative frameworks have provided Pakistan with chances to take advantage of the confused situation. More intrigued by sustaining their administration than governing the state, its rulers have been misusing provincial and religious differences. Anti-national forces flourished in this scenario and Pakistan has missed no chance to help and support them. Throughout the years, it has. it has succeeded in building a professional Pakistan base in the state. Baffled in their endeavours to achieve power through democratic means, some political leaders joined the anti-India front, more as a pressure tactics on the Indian government than on ideological grounds. In a state, where the overwhelming populace was in opposition to communal politics at the time of partition, the extremist powers have figured out how to penetrate into the secular policy. The numerous major issues of the general population need to be addressed. It is not a coincidence that Pakistan's endeavours to destabilize the condition in the state met some success just when our own political blunder furnished it with a chance to intercede, as in 1965 and again in 1989. One of Pakistan's major aims is to partition the polity on communal lines.

The approach of the Pakistani military leadership is probably not going to change in the near future. In any case, that does not imply that Pakistan ought to be permitted to set the Kashmir agenda. Attempts will have to be made on all fronts to recapture the activity on both political and strategic fronts. The made in the declarations by the Cabinet Committee on Security on October 22 are steps in the right direction; however, the ground scenario does not rationalize over-optimism. There are probably going to be many high and low points on this long torturous road to peace in Jammu and Kashmir.

- ***Communal Disharmony:*** Our multi-ethnic and multi-lingual democracy frequently discovers conflicts of interests. The decreased tolerance ensues out of voracity for power and desire to enslave different groups.

  The instances of Assam revolts in 2012 and the more recent Muzaffarnagar communal riots further enhanced the contempt, mistrust and division between communities. The most aggravating communal conflict occurred in Muzaffarnagar and its adjoining territories in Western U.P. in 2013 where more than 50 individuals lost their lives and about 50,000 were dislodged.

  In most cases, the politician uses this as a dishonest tool to partition the vote bank for their own self-centred interests, without understanding the harm that it causes to our democratic establishment.

  In the vast majority of these states, the activating factors for communal episodes were insignificant in nature and could have been stopped early on by successful, expeditious and impartial administrative activity. It is fundamental for all district organizations to set up an early warning mechanism for prompt recognition of communal issues.

- ***Insurgency in North East States:*** The seven states of Northeast India, known as the seven sisters, were chiefly occupied by the tribals when India merged these states into its union; there was widespread outrage, opposition and unwillingness to accept India as their nation.

NE states are linked with Indian territory, merely by a narrow strip of land called the Siliguri corridor in West Bengal and the dissimilarities in culture, customs and disposition of the general population are extremely stark.

Few states such as Nagaland wanted absolute Independence, while original occupants of most states, including Assam and Manipur raised demand for more notable self-rule.

The partition and demarcation of state boundaries was done indiscriminately, and adequate importance was not given to ethnicity, which often causes cultural clashes.

The current conflicts in Assam and episodes of barricading the Manipur highway by Naga extremists is occurring as a result of a difference between the apparent/acknowledged and genuine state boundaries.

- *Cyber Warfare and Web Espionage:* One domain in which awareness is, at best, indistinct is Cyber Warfare. The annual Virtual Criminology Report of 2007, put forward by McAfee, cautioned that international cyber espionage was considered to be the biggest single challenge to national security in 2008. It asserted that around 120 plus nations were already on the web espionage activities. Main targets incorporate crucial national infrastructure network systems with electricity, air traffic control, financial markets and Government computer networks becoming the dominant focal point of espionage. Reports propose that the USA, Russia and China gained significant ability in this area. The Indian Armed Forces are progressively putting resources in networked operations, both independently and a joint form. As a result, we cannot afford to be helpless to cyber-attacks. Information Technology is our nation's known asset and it would be to our greatest advantage to use this quality in building up an impressive 'hostile' and at the same time 'defensive' cyber warfare capacity. Channelling the gene pool accessible in academia, private industry and the younger generation of capable people is vital.
- *Left Wing Extremism/Naxalism:* Making a start in Naxalbari in West Bengal and Telangana in Andhra Pradesh in the 1970s, the Naxalite activities has since expanded to several states: Bihar, Jharkhand, Madhya Pradesh, Chhattisgarh and Orissa. The underlying basis for the upsurge in Left radicalism is the incompetence of the states to address the numerous authentic complaints of the individuals. The gap between the impractical anticipations, fuelled by populist expression, and their genuine accomplishment has expanded and not diminished over the years. The younger generation is no more eager to bear inactively with injustice and embarrassment without a battle. The hostility of the irate young fellow against the predominant unwarranted socio-economic system is overflowing. The older generation is not insensitive to them. An educational mechanism which brings out unemployable young boys and girls has not been of assistance. Burden on land resources has made the task of survival on agriculture more troublesome.

Insensitive district administrations, particularly in the rural areas, an obstructed legal framework and out-dated approaches have exacerbated the issue. The land disputes have increased significantly, but the land records and the legal framework to settle them is in disorder. There is a feeling of dissatisfaction and outrage. The most noticeable among the groups that have mushroomed in the current years are the People's War Group (PWG) and the Marxist Communist Centre (MCC). However, it is not belief and progressive enthusiasm that is driving them. For several people, joining these groups is the lone means of survival. Extortion is their chief activity. Enormous funds adding up to hundreds of crores of rupees are being extracted by them. What they cannot get through legal methods they achieve through arms and explosives. Their strategies are the same as the guerrillas and terrorists, that is, generate terror and extort money. However, they are not secessionists. Their objective is to oust what they consider an unfair socio-economic system. However, they are in no rush to accomplish their ideological points as long as they can extract enough money. Immoral politicians, policemen and government officials work hand in hand with these groups. A mutually gainful approach is advantageous to all of them. Nobody knows about the amount of money which goes to the extremists or other beneficiaries. The actual victims are the very individuals for whom the radicals are pursuing this war against the state. The Red corridoı (colour of communist flag) has now expanded across 13–14 states of our nation.

The major causes of this drive gaining such extraordinary momentum are governance discrepancy in all affected regions, poverty, unemployment, mistreatment of poor by the rich, mafias' activities, Naxal leaders exploiting naive, uneducated tribals, absence of development in terms of providing basic amenities and infrastructure, politician–naxal leaders relationship, assistance from nations favouring communist ideology such as China and Nepal, etc.

- ***Cross Border Issues:*** With regards to internal security, India face challenges from various quarters including the movement of large numbers of immigrants, both legal and illegal, particularly from Bangladesh (illegal) and Nepal (legal), creates some constant troubles. These migrant influxes disrupt accomplished population equations crosswise over wide swathes of Indian Territory, and have added to a lot of political unsteadiness and occasional violence.

Each one of these nations, barring the Maldives, have likewise, now and again, been utilized as operational bases,, centres of facilitation, or safe havens, or as sources of material support, for extremist and terrorist factions functioning on Indian soil. Bangladesh and Bhutan, at one time, gave place of refuge to various extremist factions working in India's Northeast, however the issue was brought to an end in Bhutan in 2003 and, since 2009, Bangladesh has also worked with assurance to stop these extremist groups against using its soil to carry out anti-India activities.

Myanmar remains a vital safe place of refuge for such groups even now, generally on the grounds that the Government there does not practice adequate control over some of its own defiant domains, and because of expanding Chinese intervention. Maldives is additionally rising as a budding source of Islamist terrorist aid, assembly and action China has turned out to be one of the most crucial sources for unlawful transportation of small arms to extremist groupings in India's northeast, and through them, to the Maoists also. Nepal and Bangladesh remain vital passages for the movement of huge amounts of fake Indian money that are supplied into India by Pakistan's intelligence agencies.

Major Security Threats to India

As India endeavours to rise as a solid provincial power it faces tough security challenges in the New Year, which may cause deterrents in its advancement. The most daunting of these originates from terrorism, in both its outer and internal aspects—the trans-national and home-produced, against which India has since long ago waged a determined battle. The former stems from Pakistan, which confronted an identity crisis after Partition. It tried to make up for its decreasing customary military clout after 1971 through a mission for nuclear parity and deterrence.

It also followed the alternative of unbalanced power, through utilization of non-state performers, first amid the Khalistan movement in east Punjab and after that in Jammu and Kashmir. The Lashkar-e-Taiba (LeT) or 'Army of the Pure', established in 1990 by Hafez Mohd Saeed and Zafar Iqbal in Kunar, Afghanistan began working from Muridke, close to Lahore, with expanding state support. Despite the fact that its essential focus for militant activities was the Kashmir Valley in the beginning, its acknowledged objective now stretches out to destabilizing different parts of India.

While the United States and International/NATO forces pull out from Afghanistan, Pakistan's Inter-Services Intelligence Directorate (ISI) could ascribe another role for the LeT there, as found in the current assault on the Indian Consulate in Herat. Indian consular bases and developmental assistance officials there will remain targets in the immediate future.

India has been in the ideological line of sight of al-Qaeda and its subsidiaries. Both Osama-bin-Laden and Ayman-al-Zawahiri spoke of a 'Zionist-Crusader alliance' which was expanded after 9/11, to a 'Zionist-Crusader-Hindu alliance' when al-Qaeda entered into associations with Pakistan-based militant organizations like the Harkat-ul-Mujahideen (HuM) and Lashkar-e-Taiba (LeT).

In a video which appeared on 04 September 2014, al-Qaeda chief Zawahiri declared creation of al-Qaeda in the Indian Subcontinent (AQIS). He warned to 'liberate our brothers' in Myanmar, Kashmir, Bangladesh 'from injustice and oppression'. One goal of this presentation could be envisioned to compete for leadership, impact and lawfulness with the Islamic State (IS) in Iraq and Syria, however as the suicide bomb assault near the Wagah border, inside Pakistan in 2 November 2014 revealed, it brought the phantom of an AQIS danger that much close to India. The Burdwan blasts in 2 October 2014 uncovered a threatening linkage creating with the Jamaat-ul-Mujahideen Bangladesh (JMB), for probable terrorist activities in West Bengal and Bangladesh. This brings another point of view to the delicate security circumstances in Bangladesh, which has been tormented by firearm running trails and linkages to resentful militant groups of our North Eastern extremists.

Till recently, India has not let al-Qaeda establish its base though newly persuaded Indian jihadists have begun looking for worldwide affiliations. The Tanzim Islahul Muslimeen (TIM) was created in 1985 after the communal unrests in Maharashtra. Its message discovered significance among young individuals of the Students Islamic Movement of India (SIMI), established in Aligarh, Uttar Pradesh in April 1977. SIMI was disqualified in 2001 but its adherents reorganized under Indian Mujahideen (IM), which was effective in plotting and executing a few bombings between 2002 and 2008, with strategic assistance from across the border. IM operated through various systems — the Azamgarh module in Uttar Pradesh, recruits in Beed, Maharashtra and Bhatkal in Karnataka. Two different modules appeared later, one from

Pune in 2009 and the other from Darbhanga in 2011. IM sleeper cells have been observed to be active additionally in Hyderabad and Ranchi. In spite of recent arrests of some of its important pioneers, IM remains a conceivably capable troublesome power.

In spite of all their complaints, discontent and resentment against the Government, Indian Muslims have avoided from malicious pan-Islamic ideologies supported by jihadi terrorist organizations until now. Nevertheless, even as AQIS turns out to be progressively involved in India, it could endeavour to take advantage of the originating discontent among youthful Islamists in India.

China's quickly expanding clout as a noteworthy force in our region have a direct bearing on India's geo-political space. In the close term, the power differential with India, with regards to its economic and military capability will broaden. Long-standing differences on the Line of Actual Control (LAC) are probably not going to be settled rapidly yet India must quicken upgradation of its border infrastructure, setting up military operational ideas and capacities to stop enormous invasions from the north, while nuancing the stance of political exchanges with China in a regulated manner.

On the inner front, left wing radicalism in the purported Naxalite corridor, reaching out to five/six States — Jharkhand, Bihar, Odisha, Andhra Pradesh/Telangana and Maharashtra — represents the most genuine risk. In 2014, there was a declining pattern of casualties, though hostility persisted. A combination of power-driven and development-oriented methodology by the authorities has not diminished its capacity to carry out intermittent assaults resulting in high fatalities among the security forces.

The essential aspects of our policy to tackle these threats in the near term should be facilitating police transformations, plugging manpower deficiencies, boosting rapid response capabilities and equipment modernization.

Overview

Since the dawn of independence, India has confronted large number of security difficulties to its nationhood—both outside and interior - and to its development as a deservingly critical player in the global order. Situated in one of the most security and politically focused regions of the world, and with some hostile neighbours, sharing almost 7000 km of operational international borders with seven countries, and a coastline traversing more than 15000 km, India's outer security challenges are undeniably challenging. External threats, in the present progressively troubled world, are in no way, unique in their orientation and impact. India's internal security concerns, since decades, have also been noticeably sponsored and to a great extent impacted by external machinations and stratagem. In any case, it is also an acknowledged reality that, up till now, external and internal challenges do overlap flawlessly, apart from having manifold in their intensity. Irregular and proxy wars are part of this new dynamic.

In the course of last 70 years, India's core disputes have varied from Pakistan-devised and supported insurrection, terrorist activities in Jammu and Kashmir and other Indian states, frequent internal conflict in some of India's restless North Eastern (NE) states including Assam. Also, diligent endeavours by Pakistan's infamous spy agency, the Inter-Services Intelligence (ISI), to incite communal discord in Punjab and fuel 'Khalistani' separatism, rising Naxal-Maoist Left Wing Extremism (LWE) challenges in India's hinterland, random sectarian, communal and language tensions, organized crime, money laundering, drug trafficking and now cyber-driven offences are the critical internal security threats standing up to the Indian state. However, there can be no denying the fact that since the past 2 years or so there has also been an increase in unwanted right wing radical propensities among some extreme elements inside India.

Internal Security has numerous components and apart from external impacts affecting it, there exist certain basic aspects which, traditionally, impacted its shapes in the Indian perspective. India is home to numerous beliefs and sub beliefs, cultures, castes, dialects, regions, traditions and its diversity, though exceptionally beautiful, is for sure mind boggling. By conservative evaluations, around 1660 languages (22 official) and dialects are spoken in India and around 3000 castes and sub-castes and virtually all known world religions exist in India, making it, indeed, a miniature model of the world. Indisputably, India's typical strength lies in this decent variety, however, it also lends itself to major internal conflict when incited both from internal or external influences. The other country conceived from the womb of Mother India since the parent country's fierce partition in 1947, Pakistan, remains fanatically anti-India, vilely interfering in India's internal matters, fuelling terrorism not only in Jammu & Kashmir (J&K) but in some different states also besides attempting to introduce separatist sentiments in some states of India, notably Punjab, Assam and in Naxal-Maoist tormented regions. Pakistan's persistent mischief inside India has unfavourably affected India's internal security health—an aspect which consecutive Indian governments have tended to belittle regardless of wars with Pakistan in 1947-48, 1965, 1971 and the 1999 Kargil dispute. Mediocre and unresponsive administration in some states, particularly those reeking in poverty and caste divisions, also lend themselves to unfavourable inner clashes within the country. One of the main causes prompting the appalling growth of LWE can be clearly ascribed to this factor troubling the country apart from different facets which lend themselves to the development in LWE. A few politicians of adjustable ideological types, catering to their regional vote banks pander to electoral communal mobilization by instigating fictitious divides, and fuel the flames of regionalism a and separatism for temporary benefits. That the general population of India, through whom an imperceptible yet an unceasing strand symbolizing 'Unity in Diversity' runs, have spoiled such deceitful objectives of some politicians, consistently , is the redeeming quality. India is currently a youth-predominant country, with more than 65 per cent of its populace being under 35 years, which makes India into an exceptionally optimistic society. A large number of youth look for suitable employment opportunity, better living standards and a million aspirations of theirs are yet to be realized. Besides any deferrals on such key societal issues naturally adds to monetary and social dissatisfactions which may prompt serious law and order issues. Moreover, this may cause the youth to deviate from the path of righteousness to anti-national organizations under the influence of international terror, smuggling networks, etc. The subtleties of some of the genuine internal security threats and recommended national reaction to contain/manage/dispose of the internal conflicts within India are described briefly in the succeeding sections.

Since the last numerous years, the phenomenon of terrorism has been a dangerously expanding curse of the advanced age. One of the countries worst impacted by it has been India on account of its neighbour, Pakistan, having adopted terrorism as an augmentation of state strategy to destabilize India. In J&K as well as in other Indian states too, Pakistan has been fanatically seeking its anti-India, though myopic strategies, of stimulating terror and unrest. As globally acknowledged after the 9/11 terror assaults in the US homeland, Pakistan is the origin of most terror exercises across the world. Nevertheless, currently Pakistan is also experiencing extreme terror activity executed by those very 'terror tanzeems' it had raised to accomplish its deceitful objectives in neighbouring India and Afghanistan. Unfortunately, Pakistan until now declines to see reason with radicalism even pervading its official foundation while its sensible common society diminishes quickly. Being a nuclear armed 'failing state' combined with ascend in radicalism that influences Pakistan is an indicator of grave dangers for India. As we cannot anticipate to discover any significant variations in Pakistan's exceedingly anti-India policies, it is significantly vital for the Indian security authorities to take into consideration all security and terror circumstances which may trouble India from its ceaselessly contentious western neighbour, now being generously backed by its mentor, China. It does not require explanation that Pakistan is an intermediary for China, against India. India's security outfit will also need to stay alert from dangers originating from universal Islamic jihadi organization like Al Qaida, the Taliban in the Af-Pak region and now, alarmingly also from Daesh also known as Islamic State or IS. Despite the fact that Indian Muslim youth have stayed unaffected from their despicable forms of publicity, yet a few seem to have been influenced within the country and thus there is a need to monitor the movement of Muslim youth to the Middle East. Intelligence agencies need to keep a close watch over social media channels which endeavour to manipulate/ recruit Muslim youth for terrorist exercises as represented by ISIS websites. That these universal jihadi organizations will team up their exercises in the Indian subcontinent with Pakistani based so-called non-state characters like the Lashkar-e-Taiyabba, Jaish-e-Mohd, Hizb-ul-Mujahideen among numerous other terror 'tanzeems' in Pakistan, remains a particular and grave possibility. As the security organs of the country further streamline their working by synergistic effort and embrace better counter-terror capacity building, the central government needs to expediently attempt extra measures to additionally fortify our counter-terror and response systems. Every political groups in India must avoid politicizing terror and a nationwide agreement among all these political parties must be reached on the national policy and measures to be embraced to battle terror. Furthermore, with regards to the country's resolve, India must make hard-hitting preventive strike plans on terrorist set up in POK and elsewhere in Pakistan, whenever it is required. In addition, India must doggedly attempt to consistently improve its intelligence gathering, analysis and dissemination machinery—both HUMINT and TECHINT. Pakistan must be made to understand, both through discourse and, in case of failure, by prompt and effective dynamic reactions, that terrorism against India will not pay. Harsh action against all aboriginal separatist leadership must be taken if they consistently indulge in anti-national or any sort of secessionist exercises. India must never be viewed as a soft state, either by countries hostile to us and, importantly, by its own inhabitants. India needs to raise the expenses for Pakistan at whatever point it indulges in anti-India operations. Moreover, Pakistan must be made aware that till date, India has not taken advantage of Pakistan's many fault-lines and India's calculated restraint is not India's permanent course of action!

The former Chinese Communist Party head, Mao Tse Tung, had compactly noticed that 'Revolutionary Warfare is never confined within the bounds of military action because its purpose is to destroy an existing society and its institutions and to replace them with a completely new structure'. Among the internal security dangers troubling India, an alarmingly escalating is LWE commonly termed as the Naxal-Maoist threat.

The LWE menace presently extend over to nearly 200 districts spread over 16 states with a wide area of land running across the heart of the Indian hinterland from the Nepal-Bihar border to the Karnataka and Kerala borders, in a south west alignment, generally alluded to as 'The Red Corridor'. That these radicals have firmly declared their intent to seize control in India by extended war against the Indian state must be taken into consideration by our security foundation. It is also well known that a portion of the territories in this 'Red Corridor' are totally deprived of any legislative control and the LWE units refer to these as 'liberated zones'. That Naxal-Maoists have cross border connections with some neighbouring nations aggravates the gravity of this escalating risk to India. To free the country of LWE, it will be judicious to assess the causes behind the development of this menace in India. These are, an absence of an obvious national policy in battling indigenous insurrections, poor intelligence competency at the grassroots level, ill-equipped, inadequately trained and inadequately inspired police staff and central police organizations (CPOs). Most importantly, a total disregard of locally noteworthy development programs in the LWE invaded regions has added to the LWE issues. That most state governments have not executed the different constitutional forest and land ceiling laws in these territories, instituted as early as in 1955, to shield the essential privileges of tribals and the deprived in rural regions has aggravated and fuelled LWE. Hence, even some knowledgeable youth have been attracted to this drive both on idealism and sentimental ideas of battling for 'the have-nots' against a brutal, immoral and inconsiderate system. One of the major causative components for the development of Naxal-Maoism is, that since independence, the benefits of growth have not streamed down to the tremendous marginalized segments of Indian society. The ever-increasing inequalities among the various sections in our society is viewed by the poor as abusive to their fundamental rights and such sentiments subsequently get the deprived fall into the trap of the Naxal-Maoists. It is likewise a verifiable truth that few local leaders from various political administrations keep up general contacts with these rebels, in their constituencies, in their constituencies, to gain electoral advantages—something which is surely dishonourable. Intelligence reports similarly suggest that LWE is gradually yet assuredly expanding its influence to urban areas and the National Capital Region which has a fair amount of industry, trade unions and so forth. In this manner jobless youth in these territories and some industrial workforces are being influenced by the LWE philosophy—each of these developments indicate numerous future issues emerging for the Indian state. To simply ascribe the expansion of LWE in the regressive areas of the nation to solely socio-economic components will be fairly oversimplified. As of now, the Maoists-Naxals have unequivocally declined any peace negotiations with the administration and are indulging in the ghastliest forms of brutality against the police services but also against innocent civilians and lower level state government functionaries. Hence, the principal responsibility of the state should be to confront these brutal cadres of the Naxals-Maoists head-on, kill/arrest whatever number as could be expected under the circumstances without inflicting any substantial indirect loss to regular citizens, villagers and furthermore those among these radicals who wish to surrender to the state. The declared strategy of 'Clear, Hold and Build' is extremely workable given there is collaboration in the will and activity between the political and security components of the country at the state and central government levels, and, significantly among the adjoining states where Maoists by and large escape to after executing their ghastly acts. Endeavours to hone our intelligence expertise at the grassroots level in the LWE invaded areas should be carried out. In spite of the fact that it is the declared policy of the legislature not to utilize the Army against own civilians; however, based on hard intelligence inputs, small units of Special Forces could be utilized for executing quick strikes on the LWE leadership, in combination with utilizing helicopters and drones of the Air Force. In addition, the Indian Army should impart training to CPOs and state police workforces in special operations missions including fighting through ambushes, night and stealth operations, bomb diffusing and IED neutralization missions.

A foremost security concern for the Indian government—with regard to both discrete external and internal aspects —is India's extremely strategic state of J&K. Since J&K's tumultuous accession to the Union of India in Oct 1947, the state's association with its parent country has been a roller coaster ride. Pakistan's misdemeanours in this state, persisting so far, resulting in four wars with India has made Pakistan realize that it cannot seize J&K by force. Hence, it devised a well-conceived methodology to destabilize India by inciting terror, fuelling separatism within the state and indulging in frequent ceasefire breaches along the line of control and the international border. 'Bleeding India by a thousand cuts', whose initiator was Gen Zia-ul-Haq, has transformed as the declared Pak policy. Emotional bonding of the general public of the Kashmir Valley, particularly the youth (different to populace in the Jammu, Ladakh area and Muslims other than Sunnis) with its parent country poses a grave challenge. The present agitation in the Valley in which several adolescents including, unfortunately, school kids have been persuaded to join the stone pelters is a genuine setback to normalcy in the Valley. The separatist leaders in the Hurriyat, on direct orders from their lords in the Pakistani establishment, are engaging in spreading hatred against India amongst the Kashmiri youth in the Valley that needs to be dealt with firm hand. These separatist leaders must be detained, as per the law, for their rebellious endeavours and imprisoned outside the state. Cosy house-arrests in Srinagar barely dissuade them from their anti-national operations. The government must not permit them ever to have a meeting with their handlers in the Pak High Commission in New Delhi from where they get their commands and financial allowances. The security establishment in J&K must keep a close watch on the conduct of all secessionists and their Pak and ISIS flag waving units. As we allow democratic means of expressing dissension in the Valley, rebellious exercises must be crushed with an iron hand. The distinct and first ever trial of absolutely dissimilar parties, the People's Democratic Party (PDP) and the Bhartiya Janata Party (BJP) in the state coalition government, must be made to prevail in the bigger interests of the state and the country. In case of failure of Mehbooba Mufti's government to control the declining law and order situation in J&K, enforcing President's Rule for 6 months as a minimum is the solution—sooner the better. It must be explicitly communicated to Pakistan that J&K is an internal issue for India and the only matter still unresolved by the baggage of history is the reunion of POK/ Gilgit Baltistan into J&K. India must hold talks with the Kashmiri 'awam (excluding the hard-core Hurriyat leaders) and make attempts to persuade them that their future and Sufi heredity is secure within the comprehensiveness of the Indian Union and not in a terror and radicalized state like Pakistan. We may also recall that earlier , whenever some Kashmiri separatist leaders advocated for peace and moderation, they were killed by Pak's notorious agency ISI. The present condition in the Kashmir Valley being somewhat dismal requires the individual consideration of PM Modi. A blend of firmness in re-building normalcy, trailed by a recuperating touch with authentic and liberal economic development packages for the state in the end is the only answer. In the meantime, our intelligence agencies must keep a close watch on the growing number of Wahabi-oriented madrassas whose numbers are increasing in the Valley driven by Saudi funds. India needs to send moderate Islamic leaders/ Ulemas to the Valley to appease and convince the Kashmiri youth to follow the right path before Salafi extremism overpowers them.

Consistently named as a 'distant frontier', NE India's psychological closeness to the parent country has not reduced to the extent as it should have since 1947. NE India is the only region in South Asia which is geologically and strategically surrounded by Nepal, China, Bhutan, Myanmar and Bangladesh. It is joined to the Indian hinterland by a thin strip of land, namely the 'Siliguri Corridor' in West Bengal. The NE states constitutes 7.9 per cent of the country's geological territory but only 3.8 per cent of the national populace. Nearly 70 per cent of this populace dwells in its largest state, Assam and the Brahmaputra Valley while the rest of the populace dwells in the other six states. This area contains more than 160 scheduled tribes and over 400 other tribal/sub tribal groups and communities with primarily a rural economy. Despite the fact that most Indians,, including of the establishment, allude in general collectively to the seven states of the NE, it must be taken into account that each of the states is unique in relation to each other with decent variety in its ethnicity as well as security dynamics. Imperatively, it is fundamental for the Indian state to mull over as to why, even after 60 years of extended endeavours by New Delhi, there has not been a successful resolution of conflict in this region barring the state of Mizoram. Most NE researchers and security experts opine that this key area experiences an assortment of shortages. These include a basic needs deficit, an infrastructure deficit, a resources deficit, a governance deficit and, significantly, a deficit of comprehension between the region and the rest of the country.

This region is perfect as a land passage to the East Asian countries with enormous yet unused economic potential. Despite being land, resource and water surplus, this area remains to a great extent under-developed notwithstanding the fact that general militancy has significantly declined in the region, though Assam, Nagaland and Manipur still have security issues that need attention. Another aspect which hinders the arrival of normalcy to the region is the progressive and considerable nexus between numerous extremist groups and the drug mafias. Moreover, China's covert presence and its association to some anti-India rebellious groups, both in Nagaland (the NSCN-Khaplang faction) and Manipur also have added to political uncertainty in the region. Economic development, efficient and corrupt-free administration and the rebuilding of peace will go a great distance in making India's NE states develop to their maximum capacity and bringing them completely into the national mainstream. As peace-talks and cease-fire agreements are managed by the Centre with different warring tribes every once in a while, Indian Army, Assam Rifles and the local police must not weaken their counter-insurgency activities and further expand their intelligence capacity building in the entire NE region. The security forces must guarantee that while carrying out their missions, they show zero-tolerance with regards to human rights violations. The Indian Army has constantly taken appreciative stance in this regard. The youth of this area are exceptionally talented, physically strong and highly enthusiastic and the Centre must contact them with responsibility and compassion—that will be beneficial for both the region and the nation. Moreover, as India now 'Acts East', this area's economic growth and India's foreign policy commitments with the neighbouring countries, in collaboration, can prove considerably beneficial.

In general, the Centre must take firm innovative political initiatives which are helpful in addressing the numerous inherent socio-economic issues of northeast region. We must open up receptive channels of correspondence with the different guerrilla groups to arrive at mutually agreeable solutions. With an approachable administration in Bangladesh, India must exploit the most part of secure condition which prevails in the NE.

A country like India, with its colossal diversity, as expressed above in the preliminary remarks of this article, is essentially facing a dangerous state of affairs that may spell disaster if certain financial political objectives are not fulfilled by either governments or society. In this manner, ethno-religious-ideological fault lines, which exist in India, must be managed with a feeling of impartiality and adjust for all factions of Indian society. Rough-riding the way of life of minorities leads to more alienation and consequently, more security problems for the nation. Harsh treatment of the minorities' lifestyle results in more estrangement and thus, greater security issues for the country. Indian leaders, of every single political class, must never ignore this fundamental issue and recognize as well as practice comprehensiveness and secularism. The concept of India and its assurance must never be relinquished at the altar of sectarianism and for securing electoral gains. India's internal security disputes, of all sorts, call for that. By any standard, India today remains at the cusp of turning into a world power to count on. We should not lose the India moment. Let us, adorned by progressive leadership, cooperation amongst all institutions and the individuals, and driven by determined execution, re-invigorate the India Story as never before.

India's Internal Security Compulsions

India's security is affected by proceedings in South Asia due to chronological, geographical and demographic constraints. Time has been an observer to the vanishing of convergence of interests and concerted effort ingrained in generic colonial experience of the South Asian nations. The greatest task for the South Asian nations has been the national union into their new individualities, which produced its own external and internal dynamics due to multiple nature of their social orders. This has been demonstrated with the disintegration of Pakistan and formation of Bangladesh. It is contended that mutual mistrust is not found in a similar extent and way amongst all the nations in the sub-continent and is deep between India and Pakistan. This distrust affects the relationship of India with Pakistan as well as other nations of the region and the relationship amongst the different nations of the region is also affected as a result. The region has seen four noteworthy battles and a few military conflicts. Indo-Pak crisis with regards to nuclear tests conducted by both of them and the low intensity conflict over Kashmir are regarded as a trouble spot. Frictions between pluralist elected leaderships and unitary type of non-pluralist leaderships in the sub-continent further increases the inequalities and tensions. The scenario has led to engagement of extra regional powers in South Asian disputes, thus making the situation multifaceted and making matters worse for intra-regional relations.

South Asia comprises seven sovereign nations, with more than one-sixth of world's populace and a large number of ethnic, religious and semantic groups is the area of ethnic and religious aggression which is demonstrated in various nations in its nature and inferences. The ethnic, religious and semantic intersection has affected internal political growth in each state as well as inter-state associations. The borders between neighbouring countries are not natural both geologically and ethnically. Hence, social strains are bound to have an impact extending across the border among different countries. Conventional relationships of friendship and interaction amongst individuals have become challenging provisions for aiding and abetting subversion, terrorism and rebellions. The regional geopolitical scenario is probably going to stay unstable, which in combination with fundamental, political and security conflicts within South Asia will keep on influencing our internal security. Social tensions especially in the ethnic and religious field because of its transborder character will continue to be the key areas to exploit for our adversaries. Muslim extremism and demographic invasion are its major evidence. The requirement to transform the closeness between South Asian neighbours into a suitable economic and security relationship for common advantage cannot be overemphasized.

South Asia is unlike other projecting mass of land constricted to an area or even a continent. The Northern ranges connect it with the 'heart lands' of Central Asia and China, while the Southern Peninsula meets the Indian Ocean and puts it in a position to administer the sea routes from Mallaca straits to South Atlantic around the South African rim. In the west it lays on the Middle East, with which it holds historic trade and social ties and in the East it connects Yunan province of China and Myanmar, a natural overpass to South East Asia, with close demographic and social ties with India's North East. Multi continental measurement of South Asia is a reality, whose progression keep on influencing nations in South Asia.

Two of the three main narcotic centres of the globe, the Golden Crescent in the North West and the Golden Triangle in the East have made South Asia susceptible against drug trafficking combination of extensive accessibility of man-portable weapons, unlawful monetary supplies through narcotic exchange and cross border relationship for smuggling and terrorist operations has made the region violence and conflict prone.

Our security is susceptible to dangers, strains and disputes emanating both from indigenous and exogenous sources. Internal security circumstances in India should be inspected in this context.

The local dynamics of India's internal security are manifested in its socio-political setting, the main attribute of which is its variety. It is reflected in the diversity of its communities and castes, races and ethnic groups, languages and dialects, religious convictions and traditions and conventions, with various exhibitions of culture, all working in a dynamic domain. In this way, our internal security situation will keep on being intricate and diverse. While issues will inherently lay on domestic roots yet external aspects will play a noteworthy part in augmenting these. The external powers in combination with internal powers of conflict will attempt to aggravate our security issues. Dangers due to terrorism, narcotics and drugs, small arms expansion, voids in energy demand and information warfare seem just round the corner. Preserving the internal security will accordingly be one of the biggest challenges confronting the nation.

The British abused the decent variety in the Indian culture to isolate it on communal and religious lines. On attaining autonomy, in view of the colonial experience, our political administration decided on integration as a foundation stone of its policy. This was to be accomplished through economic development along with nation formation through cultural and social association, as these associations were viewed as durable and stronger instead of political integration. Nevertheless, in later years since late sixties, our second generation of political authority dismiss federalism from mind and political integration became the main driving force. In the financial and development field, membership was given short shift and central planning and control of assets left the states helpless before the

Central Government. Step by step, state became all-pervading in the political, economic and even in social and cultural domains.

On freedom the Indian state acquired just the physical base comprising the region and individuals, the state and its democratic establishments needed to give the cohesiveness to weld India into a nation state. Although we have succeeded to a great extent, yet there are disappointments in this regard. In certain regions, there is a conflicting scenario to a state of violence and the contending groups have turned into the objectives of security. In straightforward terms, a reciprocal condition of insecurity exists between these groups and the state and terrorism, rebellion and hostility are merely its physical symbols. In the same way, issues of ethno-nationalism and individuality are result of our inability to incorporate various sections of the Indian social order.

The state policy of secularism came under risk in 1960s when the politicians began influencing emotional feelings of communities and words majority and minority were officially brought in and recognized in politics and vote banks of groups on communal and religious category were made. Awkward treatment of Babri Masjid issue and failure of legislature to avert its demolition led to communalism entering as a key component in the disintegration of the society and the country. The uncovering of Mandal Commission Report added to the disintegration. The net outcome of all these and similar exercises for getting vote was a divide and blow to strengthening of the Indian society two decades after freedom. The atmosphere of unity and secularism was disrupted.

Ethno-communal discords in our nation are an outcome of uneven monetary development and unfulfilled desires of individuals, which forms a sense of hardship. This might be mostly because of modernization itself, aftereffect of socio-economic advancements and changes and literacy and knowledge, leading to what is seen to be uneven economic prosperity. The underlying driver is social and monetary instability. On the off chance that there is just and justifiable distribution of economic and developmental advantages individuals feel satisfied. It is the lack of this fulfilment that propels affected groups to affirm themselves and the principal target is the legislature both local and central. In such a state of opposition the enunciation of group interests in itself leads to political mobilization of the ethnic populations as does its mistreatment. Since the vast majority of such groups are rural and land asset based, any pressure on the land due to population increase or migration further enhances the economic burden. Educated jobless populace further add to the economic and social pressures. The sum total of it is the mobilization of the general population in the form of ethno-nationalism.

Trans-border immigration from Bangladesh is a critical aspect for the troubles in Assam and other regions of the Northeast. The fact that Bangladesh immigrants are a cause of communal and ethnic conflict was well witnessed by the Assam agitation and consequent proceedings. There are approximately 15 to 18 million unlawful Bangladeshi migrants in India, who have spread to all the North Eastern States with most of them living in Assam. A fair share of these assessed to be 3 to 5 million have reached to the next eastern states of Bihar and West Bengal and in the North to Delhi and elsewhere. The invasion is probably going to continue unless checked and those identified by now are deported. Their transgression into land and offering cheap workers is a cause of social and economic uncertainty for local communities and a reason for strain and viciousness. The issue is not only escalating but getting more unpredictable. We must reinforce our immigration controls and there is a need to devise an immigration policy and create a system resembling the Immigration and Naturalization Service on the lines that exist in USA.

The electoral politics since eighties have brought about dispersion of both the state and political affairs, the institutions of legislature have been weakened and politics have lost their ideological and ethical moorings. While on one hand it has prompted expansion of the social base of legislative issues, then again due to bad politics it has resulted in politicization and exacerbation of all issues. Democratic independence and electoral politics have resulted in turmoil and instability. More than any other single factor, the misuse of diversities has brought about breakdown of the cohesiveness of the general public, created insecurity of social identity, promoted religious revivalism in its fundamentalist shape, intensified ethnicity and broadened the gap between the sub national factions and nationalism. The trademark of the deformation of the system is political feasibility. In the economic and progressive field it has led to confusion, undermining of the system, tolerance and misconducts with corruption as the natural effect.

Information Technology (IT) has reformed combat and in the internal security domain it has offered ways to the underworld to extend their reach for criminal exercises without straightforward physical involvement. Pak ISI has utilized it to the full effect by connecting with the Mumbai underworld. Our reactions must be swifter and in view of the developing technological inputs. This demands modernizing educational stages in the security forces and building up a technological temper. Likewise, liberalization of economy has brought about emphasis of financial discrepancies as advantages have not reached the masses. This will undoubtedly build social and financial strains.. The other component of liberalization of the economy is that in our regressive regions like Bihar and the North East both liberalization and privatization are probably not going to succeed due to the absence of necessary infrastructure and adequately proficient administrative system. Assuming any, it will add to the dissatisfaction.

Social researchers consider that frail states in the third world have a higher level of apprehension with internally produced dangers to security because they have not possessed the capacity to make domestic, political and social awareness of ample strength to eradicate extensive scale utilization of power as a noteworthy component in the political existence of the nation. This has likewise been our experience in India. While the state has reacted sufficiently to external dangers, its reactions to internal difficulties have been absolutely inadequate. Our internal shortcomings and insecurity has empowered external dangers and represent a genuine threat to national security.

China is a significant component in India's security concerns and tempers its association with some of its neighbours. Chinese interests in the territory have to be watched in the long term standpoint. In the wake of getting rid of the historical and strategic safeguard between India and China by seizure of Tibet, the Chinese turned to providing financial aid, arms and sanctuaries to Naga, Mizo and Meitei fanatics. This was followed by military infringements finishing in the combat in 1962. Chinese one-sided retreat after the 1962 border combat was a ploy for psychological control of India. Since then China has craftily pursued an approach of tactical control of India by territorial alliances and equipping India's neighbours Myanmar, Bangladesh and Pakistan. In the same way, India's technological and military modernization has been efficiently neutralized by technological and weaponries transfers to Pakistan in the nuclear and missile domain. The policy is devised with the intention to build indirect threats to India and in this ploy utilize Pakistan, India's primary foe as a forefront surrogate..

In the internal security domain, Chinese interference in the North East and support to rebels should remain a point of continuous attention by us. Merely the approach may be different: on the off chance that you can do it by proxy (Pakistan and Bangladesh), then stay away from direct involvement. This provides you the comprehensive choices tactically and diplomatically. Both Issac Swu and Muivah, the extremists from the National Socialist Council of Nagaland (NSCN), made visits to the Chinese embassy officials in Geneva and reports have been received of Chinese offer to set up their bases in Yunan. We must always keep in mind the Chinese intention of destabilizing India, for example, the coordinating bureau was established by the Chinese and Pakistanis in 1969 to organize training, funding and arming of guerrillas in the North East. Whatsoever the Chinese intent to help rebel groups, but its dimensions have extended with greater sophistication and it remains to be a feasible low cost alternative. The possibility for Chinese deviousness is there. Talk of stabilization of relations without making any efforts towards settling the border dispute brings Chinese intentions under suspicion.

Pakistan with regards to its hostility to India position throughout the years has been utilizing state-sponsored terrorism as an essential tool of its foreign policy. The challenge emanating from ISI is genuine and grave and its main objective is to sabotage India's internal security: India's public democratic system, judiciary and socio-political scenario gives anti-India agencies comprehensive opportunities to take advantage of controversial political issues and local conflicts. Pakistan with the intention of executing its outrageous designs has utilized ISI for insurgent activities by stimulating communal instabilities and carrying out terrorist activities. It helps in infiltration of militants and mercenaries and induction of armaments and explosives into India. Hizb-ul-Mujahideen (HUM), Lashker-e-Toiba (LET) and Jammu and Kashmir Islamic Front have extended their activities to Delhi, Gujarat, Haryana, Maharashtra, U.P. and Punjab. ISI agents have also trained transborder operators and couriers for trafficking of arms and ammunition via Punjab, J & K, Gujarat and Rajasthan. It has also set up surveillance networks in various parts of the nation. After Punjab and J&K, it has now increased its exercises in the North East using the regional rebellions to its advantages. Pakistan has set up bases in Nepal, Bangladesh, Sri Lanka and the Middle East, the with the intention of encompassing of India. This together with the increase in Islamic Terrorism at the international level with its epicentre in Central Asian Republic, Afghanistan and Pakistan is probably going to have continual impact on India's internal security.

ISI is progressively focusing on the minority group in the Southern states to undermine their loyalty, while Karnataka and Kerala have turned out to be prone to smuggling, Tamil Nadu and Andhra Pradesh have been targeted for rebellion. Communal strife in various sections of Tamil Nadu and bomb blasts in Madras and Coimbatore provide evidence of ISI involvement. The detention of ISI agent Mohammed Inshtiyaq Ahmed alias Mohammed Saleem Junaid in 1998, busted its intend to expand ISI/Laskhar-e-Toiba network in India. In the same way, revealing of Deendar Anjuman with its connections with Hizabul Deendar Anjuman of Pakistan which was in charge of church blasts in Goa, Andhra Pradesh and Karnataka during July 2000 is an obvious warning of the expansion of fundamentalist Islam and subversive activities through its network.

The appointment of former ISI Chief Lt. Gen. Javed Nasir as chairman of Pakistan's Sri Gurdwara Prabandhak Committee (SGPC) without a doubt delineates Pakistan's intention to resuscitate Sikh Militancy. His policy is to cause disputes between the SGPC and Sikhs based abroad by blaming the

SGPC for misusing offerings made in Pakistan Gurdwaras and not expending on its maintenance. At the same time, ISI agents in Pak missions abroad have been instigating Sikh emigrant community to go to India for troublemaking activities. The submission of Babar Khalsa International (BKI) associates in September 1999 disclosed ISI plans that BKI unit of Germany had been made contact to send influenced youth to India for devising explosions in Punjab, U.P., Delhi and Haryana. Khalistan Commando Force (KCF) and Khalistan Zindabad Force (KZF) other than BKI are being specifically targeted by the ISI.

In the North East, the Siliguri corridor with its permeable borders along Bangladesh and Nepal has become a key medium for ISI destabilizing activities. The swelling of madarsas along the Indo-Nepal and Indo-Bangladesh borders is a strategy devised by ISI with the support of like-minded elements in Bangladesh to increase undermining activities in the North East. The Muslim areas have turned into breeding ground for mafia, smugglers, gunrunning, hawala transactions, narco-trafficking, inflow of fake Indian money and terrorist operations. Bangladesh has also turned into a nodal point for freightage of arms and ammo procured by the Northeast rebels from the arms market in South East Asia. ISI is giving aid for storage and freight through fundamentalist establishments like JEI of Bangladesh, Quami Madarsas and Islamic NGO's under its sponsorship. A few components amongst Bangladesh administration are also suspected to involve in the plot with the ISI. The detention of four Hizb-ul-Mujahideen (HUM) operatives in Guwahati in July 1999 uncovered Pak ISI's strategies of infiltrating trained activists in the North East to bring every single Muslim organization under one roof and building up a collusion between Muslim fanatics and the North East radicals to enhance the insurgency and agitate communal and ethnic partition. ISI has effectively settled connections with the North East radicals Bodo Security Force, NSCN (IM) ULFA, PLA, United National Liberation Front (UNLF) and Muslim fanatics organizations like Muslim Liberation Tigers of Assam (MLTA) and Muslim United Liberal Front of Assam (MULFA). Presence of huge number of illegitimate Bangladeshi Muslims offer a fertile support base for destabilizing operations. The expansion of communal agencies like Students Islamic Movement of India (SIMI), Students Islamic, Sevak Sangh (ISS) and All India Mili Council provides stimulus to Pan-Islamic thoughts, which is susceptible to misuse by Pakistan.

Drug trafficking has a straightforward connection with terrorism. The Golden Crescent is a chief source of hashish and heroin for the West, which is trafficked through the Indo-Pak border. The ISI has been exploiting these instituted avenues for trafficking of arms and ammunition, which has imparted terrorism more strength. In a dialogue with Washington Post (12 September 1994), Nawaz Sharif specified ISI plans to utilize drug money to help militancy. Additional confirmation of it is offered by Altaf Gauhar in his article in 'Politics and Business' dated 28 September 1994, giving particulars of how money amassed from drug trade was used to fund Afghan war and that Gen Zia considered it in 'national interest' Generals Mirza Afzal Beg and K. M Arif both affirmed of donations to Pakistan Army for the war in Afghanistan. CIA report 'Heroin in Pakistan, sowing the wind' substantiates the utilization of drug money by Pak intelligence agencies to fund terrorist activities in Kashmir and Punjab.

The above-mentioned facts make it clear that the Pakistani authorities have been pursuing an organized proxy war against India with undermining and terrorism as the main ammunitions. The objective is to destabilize India by straightforward undermining and access into the secular Indian social order.

While we must control the extremist elements under Pak ISI influence with iron hand but it must not prompt estrangement of our immense minority of Muslims. In this setting, the authorities must be aware of the point that post 1992 there has been estrangement of the Indian Muslims, and it is a direct result of this that ISI could undermine the allegiances of some of the Indian Muslims and set up front organizations across the nation leading to 1993 bomb blasts, serial explosions in the capital region in 1997 and the Coimbatore explosions in 1998.

Similarly, the radicalized Deobandi Schools of Pakistan and the Ahl-e-Hadis Islam of Saudi origin are continually eyeing at the Indian Islam which is vulnerable to get influenced by both the extremist group.. The need is for promoting Indian Islamic practices set up and spread by Dar-ul-uloom in Deoband. State institutions need to play a main part by comprehending it and furthering Islamic traditions. This is the principal assurance against undermining of Islam by the extremists.

Magnitudes of drug trafficking and narco terrorism spread much beyond trafficking and smuggling. It weakens monetary security of India by creating black money, hawala transactions, money laundering and most of all presence of large cash economy facilitates cross border terrorist operations and formation of connections with the underworld as benefits can be directed through the hawala channels. Pakistan, specifically the ISI has comprehended the massive harming capability of money laundering, hawala and fake currency to maintain the destabilizing activities. Pakistan has methodically abetted and encouraged narcotic trade to finance terrorist organizations and the underworld to weaken our financial system and economy. Pakistan National Development Finance Corporation in 1992 had assessed that black money economy of Pakistan acquired US$ 32.5 billion per annum from farming , production and trafficking of illegitimate narcotics from the Golden Crescent, which delivers 75% of all heroin provided to Western Europe and half of that which goes to USA. India is being utilized as a passage route for drugs to Europe and America, the alternate routes being through Nepal and CIS nations. The amount of narcotics valued at ₹ 5000 crores are being trafficked every year through India.

The Golden triangle yields more than 1000 tons of opium which is processed into very high level heroin. The ineffective surveillance and enforcement mechanisms results in very little amount of it being seized in the Northeast. A clear sign of the probable illegitimate narcotic trade in the North East is the high occurrence of drug addiction and exploitation in Manipur, Mizoram, Assam and Arunachal Pradesh. In the same way, accessible Indo-Nepal border is the major source of Hashish.

The procedure of money laundering assists in detaching the black money from any organization with its criminal base and long sequence of transactions renders it difficult to trace the location of the original source. Cash is then propelled through banking networks by means of gifts, donations and trade accounts. This also aids in evading the tax and is well manipulated by expert facilitators like chartered accountants, auditors, lawyers and traders. Since majority of service sector (almost 50% of GNP) is susceptible to tax evasion, it expedites legalizing of black money. Hawala with its ease, pace and indistinctness has made it appealing even to the immigrants due to tiresome procedures and deferrals in our banking system. Money laundering, evading of income tax and hawala are supplementary to each other.

Drug money procured from shipments abroad by the ISI and its partners collected from drug pushing cartels is propelled through different positions and made accessible to its underworld connections in Gulf and different nations, from where it travels through banking and different channels to Islamic fundamentalist organizations over the whole nation. Unless our Foreign Exchange administration, Narcotic Control and money laundering administrations are made more sensitive to the risk, the impact of narco terrorism mongering will not be curbed. In the same way, our implementation of Visa regime related to Pakistan guests needs a fresh evaluation as a larger number of Pakistani guests do not return and remain untraced, which helps Pakistani motives. The contention in Jammu and Kashmir has its discrete external and internal limitations. Kashmir was, is and shall remain the focal point of Pakistan's India policy as both, an anti-India stance and Kashmir are fundamental cause for its identity. Nuclearization of both the nations in 1998 may result in a balance of nuclear deterrence and in this manner stability in the nuclear domain, however, it is probably not going to stop Pakistan from proceeding with the proxy war as was demonstrated by the Kargil incursions and consequent escalation in militancy. The sole impediment to proxy war is to make its cost restrictive for Pakistan.

The other main component influencing Indo-Pak strife over Kashmir is the Islamization of Pakistan since Zia's term and Pakistan claiming the responsibility of leading the Islamic resurgence in the region. Within the comprehensive aim of Islamization of the area, conquest of Afghanistan followed by Kashmir are her prompt vital objectives. We provided them the chance and encouraged Pak plans by leaving Afghanistan completely to it, thereby leaving it entirely on Pakistan where all its planning for the proxy war went on unchallenged. Islamization of Pakistan and its Pan-Islamic inclination has impacted its strategic belief. In the words of Gen Aslam Beg, it has given Pakistan territorial strength and tactical opportunities.

The external dimensions of the Kashmir issue have extended past a bilateral conflict due to nuclearization of the subcontinent and the growing transnational aspects of terrorism. The world community will not allow intensification of the situation into a customary clash of high intensity, where risk of a nuclear confrontation or exchange at any stage is probable to happen (as was witnessed in the Kargil conflict. From global point of view, the peril is genuine, as both India and Pakistan are outside the universal nuclear control regimes. Concurrently, the global powers are concerned about the fact that the Pak Army, ISI and Muslim fundamental organizations have been following their own organized plan. Hence, the peril of a runaway strike and nuclear weapons being secretly handed over to Islamic terrorists is genuine.

The proxy war has three noteworthy aspects external (requiring activity in the diplomatic domain), internal (within J&K), and the third of Pakistan's undermining motifs on the rest of the nation. Each of the three zones are essential for crushing the Pakistani outline of Pan-Islamic extension and terrorism. Endeavours in the diplomatic field to contain and decrease the impact of cross-border terrorism supported by Pakistan have had a positive reaction from the world community. These must be maintained and strengthened. Exceptional endeavour to look for the cooperation of China and South and Central Asian nations is required.

Internally, the main subverting elements are demographic spread of Muslims past their conventional zones, fundamentalism and alienation of the general population. Any further emigration of the minority group and their being targets will bring about development of Muslim dominated territories, which suits Pakistan's strategy. It is easier to nip in the bud than to restore or reverse it. With Islamization of the proxy war and its prominent supporter being Pakistani and foreign Islamic guerrillas, the course of action unmistakably is to change the mixed demography in J&K from Kashmir valley to Kargil, Doda to Gulabgarh and in Poonch, Rajouri and Naushera to Akhnoor along the Chenab River, to make it Islamic. To overwhelm Pakistani ploy it is essential to forestall demographic variations, which will require activity in the political, socio-economic and administrative domain.

With regards to Jammu and Kashmir, fundamentalism is a multi-dimensional event. It has an indigenous, social, cultural and religious substance. The proliferated Wahabi Islam is alien to Kashmiri Muslim's social and cultural spirit. We need to avert its enforcement and strengthen the Sufi culture of Kashmiri. Pakistan's primary purpose will be to misuse the alienation of the Kashmiris. It is similarly critical to counteract Hindu reaction to Muslim fundamentalism.

Both anti India emotion and estrangement of the Kashmiri common people are the combined aspects of Kashmiri recent experience, which unless checked will keep on providing an encouraging atmosphere for Pakistan's plans against India. It has its root in the political affairs of pragmatism played by both the Kashmiri and central leaders. The other feature of estrangement is corruption which has precluded the general population of Jammu & Kashmir advantages of monetary development and genuine engagement in the democratic and developmental process. A blend of political idiocy, defilement and failure of democratic establishments to satisfy individuals' aspiration resulted in dissatisfaction. At the political level, dissatisfaction was blended with protectionism, which segregated the Kashmiris as well as twisted their personality into one of religious authoritarian, susceptible to fundamentalism.

An approach above party political affairs intended at redeeming and consolidating the scenario in the political, socio-economic and religious domains should be the aim. The fundamental chore will be to eradicate the sentimental alienation of the general population of Kashmir Valley and different parts of J & K. In the political domain, it will require obliging the emotion of autonomy and elimination of inter-regional inequalities. The driving principle should be the reinstatement of the regard and trust of all portions of the general population. The other aspect of eliminating the alienation is renewal of the state's economy and the formative process. In the socio-political field, the primary object of contention is fundamentalism, which will require engineering the disintegration of the help base of the Jammat-e-Islami (Kashmir), reversing the communal divide and demographic variations and resuscitating the spirit of Kashmiriyat (the exclusive Kashmiri ethos).

The road ahead in Jammu and Kashmir is dented with obstructions, which must be overwhelmed by an all-encompassing strategy in light of acknowledgment of the political, socio-economic and law and order component of the issue. Restricting it to proxy war will be inviting a catastrophe. The approach must consider the risky components of Islamic terrorism, the misery and hardship of the general population and government structure guaranteed under article 370. The core of conflicting emotions in Jammu and Kashmir must be synchronized with each other and with India's preferences.

The insurrections in the North-East are a manifestation of its social, cultural, ethnic and politico-economic setting and variations in the atmosphere of the region. North-East is an exceedingly diverse zone with high level of ethnic, cultural, linguistic and religious variety. This is reflected in the pattern of contentions, which are fluctuated in their character and causes and the stance of the radical groups, which stay different and regularly evolving. These range from secession to self-governance, crusades against non-natives and migrants, ethnic reconciliation and looking back to their underlying foundations as a response to apparent imposition of Indianness, the common factor is recurring to violence in enunciation and mobilization for the same. Likewise, political development in the North-East is impacted by its different historical experience, social and cultural diversity and distinctiveness prompting socio-political strains and instability, which again brings about agitational approach to deal with issues and violence. Of these, the current phenomenon of ethnic mobilization naturally represents a risk to enemies resulting in a conflict scenario. Inflow of migrants poses monetary, cultural and social intimidations and provides a reason to strife and brutality.

The sensitive feature of our strategies in the North-East has supported the conviction that fomentation and savagery only draw in consideration as our political reactions for the most part took after tumults and revolt which germinated in Nagaland, spread to Mizoram, Manipur, Tripura and Assam. Also there is great exasperation in Arunachal Pradesh and Meghalaya. In the same way, our conviction that disputes run their normal course, thus, defy insurrections with armed power alone and when militancy debilitates, offer transactions and sacred concessions that result in accords, is dubious. These, except for Mizoram have neither put an end to rebellions nor improved the scenario. Rather insurrections in the North-East have flourished while holding their calm stance, a characteristic of the North-East. Regression of rebellions has not brought about its resolution and consolidation of the scenario. The extremist groups have reacted to changing circumstances internally in the politico-social condition and externally in the geo-strategic field to their good fortune, though the state's reactions have been sluggish and disorganized.

The support base of the radicals has moved from rural to urban territories as this is where the material and financial assets are available and Government money being the fundamental source. This has required that their convert presence in population centres must be efficient as well as modern to tap various sources, both private and Government; contractors and Government department payments are the significant targets. Rebellions have learnt by experience that the control of populace and undermining followed by planned demonstrations of savagery and terrorism are remunerating at minimum cost. The focus is on taking advantage of ethnic bonds to impact events in all domains—political, economic, social and cultural. The same inspires rebellions' connections and influence with the legislators, officials and elite in all fields. Insurrection in the North-East will keep on thriving while preserving its subdued posture, with limited periods of high intensity savagery and staying under control for delayed periods. Expanding demonstrations of psychological warfare and subversion and a more noteworthy level of arrangement among the extremist gatherings will be its unmistakable highlights Growing acts of terrorism and rebellion and a greater degree of connivance amongst the insurgent groups will be its exclusive characteristics.

The core of rebellions will remain secessionist and subversive, and traditional for support amongst the general public. The legislator -bureaucrat-elite-guerilla nexus in the North-East especially in the Hill states, unless checked, will keep on providing backing to revolt to accomplish their various objectives and further escalate hardship and estrangement of the general population.

Due to the increasing nexus between Pakistan ISI, the North-East rebellions and the Islamic fundamentalists, the extents of internal security risks to the region have expanded. This must be tackled on a long-term basis.

The contentions in the North-East are based around human dissatisfaction resulting from hardships of different sorts mainly in the socio-economic domains with political articulation, perhaps except for Nagas which is ingrained in their sentiments of being separate with no political, cultural and economic connections with their neighbouring groups. Even this is experiencing a change, while individual's alignment is towards peace, development and economic prosperity, the NSCN (IM) still gives voice to the political viewpoint of independence. The Meitei people sense impoverished in comparison to the hill tribes, because of reservations for the tribals, in the economic and employment fields. In the same way, Assamese feel disadvantaged in comparison people living in other parts of India, as do Bodos in contrast with the Assamese, mainly in the economic domains. Mizoram feels compelled because of its geological area and experience of Mautam (famine) in 1959, again fundamentally the reason is financial hardship. Tribal rebellion in Tripura is due to alienation of tribal land because of Bengalis' incursion resulting in financial and social hardship. The hardship of the general population is further heightened due to extortions, corruption and mismanagement. This is an immediate aftereffect of our approach of drawing in cash when under pressure and to meet the ends of political convenience. Political leaders and officials have consistently utilized their workplaces to redirect formative assets at the cost of genuine development. Defilement, influence through cash and narrow ethnic loyalties have caused most of the politicians and rebellions being persuaded and pushed for narrow parochial gains. This is the principle purpose behind ethnic cleansing, fanatic killings, coercions and criminal exercises of smuggling and drug trafficking. Rebellion in the North East has turned into an industry in which principle purpose is benefit of the individuals in control both through the ballet and bullet. The circumstance is further aggravated by total absence of governance and state machinery being taken control for narrow gains. The situation in Nagaland, Manipur and Tripura is unwarranted.

The solution of disputes in the North East relies on political domains, with main focus on good administration and getting rid of people's sense of poverty. The example of conflict settlement and management appropriate to the circumstances in the North East are Ideal Politik and choice of a cooperative strategy after recognizing the core of poverty in each region. The emphasis has to be on individuals as poverty totally relates to them. In all our efforts till now the emphasis has been on politics and rebellions and the main problem of hardship of individuals is ignored.

In the North East, measures taken in the sccurity domain alone are probably not going to improve the situation. The major emphasis has to be in amending the administration and eliminating the individuals' sense of estrangement due to hardships in the economic and social domains. This needs meticulous focus, recognition and execution.

Pakistan made use of Punjab as a testing ground and as its engagement with J& K grew, it calmed down. Pakistan's seriousness to the Sikh extremist cause was suspicious as a Sikh state on its frontiers was undesirable strategically. Pakistan's ploy was under suspicion in the minds of common Sikhs in Punjab and the concept of Khalistan was neither alluring nor realizable in their minds.

Punjab militancy is to be seen as terrorism and managed principally in the law and order domain. It must not be mistaken for Sikh grievances and political issues like transfer of Chandigarh and river water dispute. The two should be isolated and managed by itself, the former at the administrative and official level with full political support and latter at the political level. Equal importance should be given to manage political issues. To a careful onlooker of Punjab, it should be certain that all through the militancy there was no Hindu-Sikh division albeit customary obligations of solidarity and friendship did come under strain. It will likewise be reasonable to deduce that there never was ever a secessionist movement, its few propagators, mostly based abroad, utilized this policy with fundamentalist overtones to abuse Sikh grievances real and perceived, and government's inactivity and panic emphasized these.

In principle, Punjab terrorism was the result of political clumsiness and drew its strength and authenticity not from any philosophy or religious endorsement but rather from the failures of political establishments, legislature and administration. Its chief aspects were orderliness as disintegrated militant establishments were practicing their own agenda or that of their commanders bringing about in criminalization of the environment. The reactions should have been in the organizational and security domain and so should it be in future.

Left wing extremism is currently restricted to Bihar and Andhra Pradesh with long history of armed agrarian brutality. Naxalites are likewise insignificantly functioning in Maharashtra and Orrisa, while Madhya Pradesh is developing as another focal point of left wing radical savagery. Naxalite groups such as CPI-ML (Peoples War Group) in Andhra Pradesh and Marxist Communist Centre (MCC) the CPI/ML (peoples unity) and CPI/ML (Vinod Mishra Group) in Bihar have been procuring weapons from arms markets in South East Asia and from Pakistan and Afghanistan and have accomplished high level of superiority in the utilization of land mines and technically most modern triggering weapons. PWG linkages which were prior restricted to South American Guerillas and LTTE, have as of late extended to ISI influences and progressively coordinating with militant organizations around the nation.

In Andhra Pradesh, PWG is the prevailing Naxalite group with more than 1500 insurgents and more than 3000 dedicated followers, it has spread its wings to more than two-third of the state, with most astounding brutality being executed in the Telangana territory. It creates significant subsidizes through temporary workers, especially beedi leaf contractors, landlords and business houses. It stalls official development agendas through its own welfare development activities in the forest and rural zones. It has successfully targeted former Home Minister, police officials and police stations.

In contrast to Andhra Pradesh, the naxalite unit in Bihar is more scattered and split between the MCC, CPI-ML (Peoples Unity) and CPI-ML (Vinod Mishra), so is the brutality executed by them. Most naxalite groups are involved in class/caste conflicts under the guise of defending the dalits and backward segments of the social order. Endemic and mindless brutality, mixed with clashes amongst the opponent groups is prevalent in central and South Bihar. Left wing radicals as a part of their ploy to keep general public away from the recent elections caused far-reaching violence and killings. MCC activists held 'Jana Adalats' to penalize those who exercised their rights in elections, the Jana Adalat in Chatra District was conducted in the presence of 2000 people to declare death sentence to a police informer.

Madhya Pradesh has been observing a surge in left wing extremists' operations due to spillover effect of Marxist drive from Andhra Pradesh. The drive is mainly an expansion of PWG activities from Andhra Pradesh and the chief activity is exactions from the Kendu leaf contractors and government employees who are propelled to pay cess. PW in its two noteworthy strikes assassinated the state transport minister and an additional SP in a land mine explosion and over a dozen districts are impacted. Madhya Pradesh MCC in its attempt to extend to new areas has formed border areas committee with its head office at Sarguja to work in conjunction with the UP MCC Area Committee (Sonbhadra) under the general Bihar-UP-MP Simant Regional Committee. In UP MCC is making its essence felt in Mirzapur, Chandauli and Sonbhadra Districts. In West Bengal Left wing fanatics violence has revealed in Midnapore and deliberate endeavours by CPML-PW to extend its impact in bordering territories of Bihar, West Bengal and Orissa are obviously noticeable with the formation of Bihar–Bengal–Orissa border area committee with both an underground and overground mechanism, the regions affected are East Singhbhum (Bihar), Midnapur, Purullia (West Bengal) and Mayurbhanj and Keonjhar (Orissa). The talk of transforming 'Guerilla Zones', areas of maximum operations, into 'Liberated Zones' is normal and CPML-PW and MCC expansionist plans include expanding into new regions to carve out a 'Compact Revolutionary Zone' extending from Nepal through Bihar and the Dandakaranya zone to Andhra Pradesh. This is in consequence of a choice in September 1998 made by them and the Nepal-based CPN (Maoist). In pursuit of this objective MCC has been exchanging visits with associate units from Nepal and articulated solidarity with the individuals' war being pursued by CPN (Maoist). CPML-PW and MCC have also consented to impart training to CPN (Maoist) groups in return of weapons.

The Left wing Extremism must be contained and foiled by a coordinated activity design fusing security and developmental aspects. Trans-state nature of Left Wing Extremist exercises will require facilitated execution and joint activity in the security field.

Fifty years after freedom there is boundless agitation, discontent and clashes among an extensive part of the populace. There are dangers emanating from territorial and social imbalances, which fuel insurgencies and have led to rise of insurgencies, terrorism, sub-patriotism and communalism. Financial disparities have created social strains, urban agitation, rural upsurge and youth disillusionment. Issues of hardship, joblessness, poverty, hunger and nourishment deficiency, absence of lodging, overcrowding, degradation of basic facilities have led to increasing outrage and crime. The issue is deteriorating as rise of populace add to the pressure on demand without corresponding rise in supply. A total of 201 of 535 districts in India are impacted with one type of violence or the other.

Individual security concept extend from confirmation of fundamental human sustenance needs of nourishment and water and protection against elements. In the socio-economic-culture-ethnic groupings, security is conceived around flexibility to rehearse one's principles, without hampered by different groups. To accomplish these individual and group security targets, individuals and groups anticipate security from the Indian country state. The main concentration being the general population and society, their insights are imperative. In general, individuals feel uncertain both at the individual and group level. They believe they are casualties of financial hardship, destitution, lawlessness and negative politics. They are losing confidence in the framework, capacity of law implementation agencies to keep up order and enforce the rule of law, capacity of legal framework to provide justice. The educational infrastructure, health, public distribution system and civic services are on the verge of collapse. The standard of life in rural and urban regions barring the affluent privileged class has deteriorated and the gap between the rich and the poor has widened. In the unstable and insurgency invaded regions general public feel insecure both from radicals and the state. The state's reaction has been to look for greater security powers and more noteworthy militarization of the environment. Propensities to shift away from centralization, as of authority both at the group and gathering level are increasing. advantage and state's advantage is disengaged from that of the and society. Individuals feel that state is missing in zones of their interest and state's interest is isolated from that of the general population and society. In seriously troubled zones, states operational presence is diminishing. We have an enigmatic scenario that both the state and the society are insecure. Since emphasis of internal security is society, therefore, human perspectives of civil society get interconnected, which makes its understanding troublesome and administration complex. The way to managing internal security is to keep the emphasis on individuals and society as these obviously set out the parameters both for strategic framework and administration.

The above interpretations may seem to be inconsiderate and may not be consistently and completely relevant to all regions of our nation but the growing inclinations should be taken insight of. All through the period up to 2025, the internal security scenario is probably going to escalate unless concerted actions are taken and thoroughly considered measures are executed to stop and counter these tendencies. This will require persistent and very well coordinated activities in the political, socio-economic and security contexts. Due consideration should be paid to ruin the plans of our enemies, especially Pakistan to destabilize India through subversion, empowering and inciting fundamentalism and terrorism and inducting arms and drugs into India. Pak designs must be vanquished by strengthening our resilience worked around secularism and practice of democracy in principle, spirit and its constitutional and legal framework. Despite the fact that our democracy and fundamentals of secularism have survived many tempests yet in the near future there is direness to build it up completely as it is just through majority rule government and secularism that we can create a unanimous backing to the national effort. This would chiefly require political knowledge and will get rid of the culture of political appropriateness and deception and supplanting it with cooperation and federalism with responsibility and authority institutionalized. The same holds true in the developmental aspect. Our way to deal with security administration ought to be more holistic and sensitive to individual's feeling and to inclination and to produce reactions to state's endeavours. The political framework needs rearrangement and changes. Individuals are never again content with just portrayal, they also need involvement and genuine empowerment. The diverse components of the general public should be given self-governance and self-sufficiency in their local affairs and their cultural and social identities perceived by selection of indigenous models suited to their genius and conventions. The plan for change must guarantee stability at the centre, states and lower levels in light of consensus and administration decentralized and individuals oriented. The political procedure should be revived with changes in the electoral system and the Peoples Representation Act. The charter of fundamental rights and obligations should be reoriented and strengthened with principal objective of setting up a civil society tuned in to our cultural and conventional esteems. This will require production of another law authorization device responsible to the general population from the grass root level with key objective to serve the general public and be likewise responsible to it at each level. Religion must be an undertaking of individual and the group and not to be a piece of the political framework or process. State must stay impartial and not meddle in its training. Utilization of religion for political purposes and political gatherings with religious introduction ought to be restricted. Religion must be a matter of individual concern and the community and not to be a component of the political system or process. State must stay impartial and not meddle in its practice. Exploiting religion for political objectives and political parties with religious alignment should be debarred.

The planning process for economic advancement ought to have clear introduction of framework creation of infrastructure at the national and central stage and local alignment at the state and lower levels. Creating employment opportunities ought to be part of economic planning, which will require redirecting education to science and technology, vocational training and group work. Rural development and employment guarantee schemes must be of local origin, to meet local prerequisites and to be realized by the community. Civic amenities should be the fundamental area of interest at the local level. The cost of administration should be cut down and government's role in the economic, social and cultural contexts should be lessened. In the economic aspects, government's role ought to be to intervene and adjudge between changing interests and most economic exercises should be left to entrepreneurs, corporations and people within the laid down approach. Government's contribution in the cultural and social aspects should be lessened to the minimum. The proxy war in J& K, uprisings in the NorthEast and prevailing terrorism in Punjab require a commonalty of discernment among national organizations, a national level strategy to settle the situation regional mechanism for execution, keeping in view the local, social, economic, ethnic, religious and political objectives. In the same way, confronting Pak supported terrorism, subversion and trafficking of weapons and narcotics with internal and outer connections requires national level administration. In a similar way, Left Wing Extremism, which goes past state boundaries, demand a general approach, organized action and joint and coordinated method. In the same way, problem of fundamentalism and large-scale migrants requires a national plan to be jointly formulated and actualized. Our reactions in such manner have for the most part been responsive and kept to lawfulness measurements as it were. Our responses with regard to this have, in general, been reactive and confined to law enforcement measurements only. The strategy parameters ought to stretch out past the security (Law and Order) spectrum to grasp political and financial measurements of each of the issues in a comprehensive design, with the aim to lessen individuals hardship and creating a secure and healthy environment. Due to lack of a holistic approach to IS situations, deformations have sneaked in the working of the organization and governance has turned out to be insufficient. The attention is basically on the lawfulness perspectives and the civil face represented by the political and managerial functionaries has suitably retreated, leaving the obligation of fighting the proxy war and insurrections to the security forces. The immeasurably imperative civil face is missing and administration in regions important to the general population is lacking. Lack of clean and responsive organization and powerful administration has intensified our issues in the North East and J & K, both are basic factors in the unstable regions. This has also given rise to noteworthy militarization without a noticeable development in the security situation. Counter insurrection operations accomplished by the SF against militants and rebellions have succeeded more than once to bring circumstance under control but our failure to consolidate the advantages in the political, social and economic aspects brought about the circumstances deteriorating once more.

Indifferent administration brought about further alienating the communities that continue to suffer from hardships.

The destabilizing aspect of the proxy war pursued by Pakistan inside India is very apparent. The objective is to expand the Indian state, its organization and security forces and create unsteadiness. The main organizations are Muslim fundamentalist associations, the criminal class, dissenting elements amongst Muslim populace and radicals. It should be handled as an all India issue, with a multifaceted (political, social, cultural, religious, education and security) and coordinated approach with full participation of the states, with political and social predisposition to secularism. In the security aspect, activities lie in the intelligence and policing domains. Pakistan's proven nexus with the Indian criminal world and terrorists propagated through the profitable and mutually beneficial ways of smuggling, narcotics and arms supply in its all-round dimensions should be handled on long-term basis. This will require upgradation of our own capacity bolstered by modern technology and participation of the neighbours and the international organizations. The North East extremist groups over the recent two decades have acquired strength from their close connections with the politicians, administrators, business group and in specific cases they even have the support of state governments. The politician–administrator–elite–insurgent nexus in the North East unless mercilessly controlled will keep on supporting revolts for mutual advantages. This combined with increasing connections between the ISI, Islamic fundamentalists and the insurrectionary groups have added genuine dimensions to the security dangers in the territory, which requires a coordinated reactions and not through sporadic positioning of SF in the troubled states. The ISI plot can no longer be thwarted through a responsive and defensive strategy.

Administration comes under more prominent pressure in the troubled scenario while great administration contributes significantly towards better administration, terrible or lack of governance puts pressure and genuine limitations on administration of the circumstance. This is apparent from the situation amid the last 11 years at various circumstances in J&K and in various states of the North East. restoring the organization, monetary improvement and security administration are fundamental elements of administration, while great administration is a prime prerequisite all over, it turns into a key component in a bothered domain. In these situations, policy implementation, reviving the administration, economic development and security administration are fundamental elements of administration, while good administration is a prime prerequisite all over, it becomes an important component in a troubled scenario. Since the decisive battle is for the 'hearts and psyches' of the general population and hardship is the core, thus, significant areas of concern for administration are provision of basic civic facilities, public distribution system, health, communications and transportation, lodging and rehabilitation and reclamation and working of the education system. This is the domain where political will and administration is viewed by the general public.

The principal concern should be to set up the trustworthiness and authenticity of the state and its foundations. This must be accomplished by an even minded and implementable strategy, organized approach and an earnest and straightforward usage by credible individuals. Deviations must be settled in a straightforward and just fashion as open observations are imperative. Administration of ethnic and communal clashes and settling them are imperative domains of authority and political administration. Without administration, we unable to protect the environment nor execute policies to expel individuals' hardships. Without administration every single areas suffer, it thus in an important aspect. The Indian State has considered the IS problems just through two facets of the prism, political and lawfulness. The third facet characterized by religious fundamentalism, ethnic brutality, economic differences and hardship is only discussed but seldom at times viewed as hard and persistent. We can no more bear to overlook it especially when globalization and IT can make changes quick, irate and most harming and unanticipated. In the event that reactions to late natural disasters are any sign, the Indian State has too far to go. There is requirement for civil debate and accord on our internal security issues, especially because of coalition government and territorial political stalwarts seeking after their own specific plans. While the magnitudes of our IS threat are well past acute lawfulness and expand to one or the other from of low intensity disputes, politics have deteriorated the lawfulness machinery, law implementation capacity and the legal mechanism to manage such circumstances. TADA may have been politically and officially abused but not to have laws to manage subversion, fear mongering and rebellions is seeking calamity but not to have laws to control subversion, terrorism and insurrections is seeking calamity. Most democracies in the globe have more severe regulations compared to TADA for containing terrorism, subversion and drugs. States apprehensions are unreasonable, for states cannot be self-governing and strong if the country is unsteady. Let us not surge from one extreme to the next. Both the states and the centre must be tough and resilient to insurgency, a fragile centre cannot protect the states from external threats and internal risks. Only a powerful state can secure its citizens. The state must arm itself sufficiently to manage organized crime, subversion, terrorism and danger posed by narcotics. In the same way, political parties cannot allow a state of disorder as it existed in Bihar under the attire of political legitimacy and democracy.

Our reaction to each new IS scenario in the recent history has been an increase in the sorts and number of security forces, Punjab brought forth National Security Guard and the proxy war in J&K to the Rashtriya Rifles. The introduction of other Para Military Forces (PMF) has comparative history, regardless of whether we acknowledge support for their raising. The point to be comprehended is that expansion in numbers and sorts of forces is not a viable replacement for effectiveness. Alongside it there has been redirection of forces raised particularly for border guarding for internal security while on one hand it has made our borders more permeable, especially in the North East, then again a substantial number of various forces with varying capability, ethos and charter handling IS threat has brought about numbers at the cost of cohesiveness and improved capacity. There is requirement for a long term and professional analysis on utilization of forces as counteractive action of intrusion and to check transborder terrorism networks that have a nexus with smugglers and radicals is equally critical as managing the internal components.

Our reaction to internal security has been absolutely that of crisis administration, over-centralization and states renouncing their obligations. Fundamental variations are required in decision-making process, to guarantee independent running of law implementation organizations and a comprehensive strategy consolidating political, economic, socio-cultural and law and order perspectives. This above all will require political resolve. To counter Pakistan plans, there is a pressing need to build up a national point of view of the creating IS circumstance and devise strategies for the same.

Regardless of our disappointments and derailment of the democratic order, India has survived and gained ground because of the versatility of its citizens. The scenario can be recovered by edification of the general public and state working in an ethical and reliable fashion. The key components are great administration and reliable politics.

Role of the Government of India in Internal Security Management

India has been confronting multidimensional internal security risks which involves left wing extremism, an on-going proxy war in Kashmir and rebellion in some northeast regions. The security scenario in the North-Eastern States has started improving. The operations of few militant organizations who continue to be occupied in developing competences are being closely watched. In view of the external connections of some of these insurgent groups, it will be important to stay alert and ready to handle the issue of militancy in the area. The overall security scenario in the Northeast has to a degree balanced out and is under control. Violence intensities have decreased meaningfully as compared to previous years. There is far reaching support for peace by all segments of the social order consequently encouraging progress on developmental plans. Currently, talks/suspension of operation (SoO)/ceasefire is in progress with 15 main groups. The Army, alongside other security powers, has assumed a crucial part in achieving this much needed development. Some of the vital and viable moves made by the government of India are as follows:

North East Division, Ministry of Home Affairs

The northeast division is in charge of matters relating to internal security in the north eastern area. The main concerns being dealt with by the division are as follows:

1. Implementation of the accords.
2. Border conflicts between Assam and its neighbouring states to incorporate Nagaland.
3. Scheme of modernization of the state police.
4. Matters associating to national level, sectoral level and joint working group meeting between India, Bangladesh and Myanmar.
5. Monitoring of the lawfulness circumstance.
6. Surrender and rehabilitation approach.
7. Administration of the unlawful exercises (prevention) act, 1967 and the Armed Forces (Special Powers) Act 1958.
8. Policy of the civic action programme of army/central police establishments.
9. Assessment of suspension of operations/peace talks with different militant groups who shun violence and surrender to the administration.

Ministry of Development of North Eastern Region

The government of India set up a ministry committed exclusively for the advancement of the north east. It is viewed as an impetus in mobilizing attention and endeavours in inducing development in the area which is lacking and is one of the main causes for insurgency. The ministry handles issues concerning the planning, execution and monitoring of development plans and projects to incorporate power, irrigation, roads and communications.

North Eastern Region—Vision 2020

On 2 July 2008, the Prime Minister issued the north eastern region Vision 2020 statement. It defines up the objectives, recognizes the difficulties and proposes implementation methodologies for different areas for peace and prosperity of the area. In order to decipher the goals articulated in the vision document into concrete plans, 17 thematic groups have been formed. The North Eastern Council (NEC) assumed a noteworthy part in delivering the Vision 2020 document. The NEC carries out the following assignments

1. It is an advisory body to the central government and the state governments for monetary and social provision, inter-state transport and communication, power or flood control ventures.
2. It devises and articulates the balanced advancement of the NER regarding cohesive coordinated regional plan, prioritization and location of projects and schemes in the regions. This requires an assessment and appropriate action which is accomplished by the NEC.

Mahatma Gandhi National Rural Employment Guarantee Act 2005

The objective of the Act is to improve the livelihood security of individuals in rural zones by ensuring 100 days of wage-employment in a financial year to a rural household whose grown-up individuals agree to do unskilled manual work. This is a vital step by the legislature for employment, more so in uprising territories in order to guarantee that they do not join the radical groups because of deprivation and unemployment.

Border Area Development Programme

This programme is initiated by the Ministry of Home Affairs (MHA) and includes 17 states bordering Pakistan, China, Myanmar, Bangladesh, Nepal and Bhutan. Along these lines, all the states of the northeast region are secured by this. It works to meet the extraordinary advancement requirements of the individuals who are staying in remote and unreachable regions near the border. It is a 100 per cent subsidized programme by the legislature of India. The gram sabhas of the villages are engaged in the decision making procedure. The programme manages socio-economic and infrastructure advancement of the rural areas. The key development initiatives include pucca road network, electricity, telephone services, safe drinking water, school buildings for the primary education and establishment of community centres. The scheme of the village needs to be coordinated with that of the district to guarantee integration bringing about appropriate and sustainable progress of the remote villages.

Central Police Forces (CPFs) under the Ministry of Home Affairs

The MHA is in charge of the internal security in the nation. It has established seven CPFs to deal with the internal security issues, specifically, Assam Rifles (AR), Border Security Forces (BSF), Central Reserve Police Force (CRPF), Central Industrial Security Force (CISF), Indo-Tibetan Border Police (ITBP), National Security Guard (NSG) and Sashastra Seema Bal (SSB).

1. ***Assam Rifles:*** The Assam Rifles was established in 1835 as the 'Cachar Levy', and was entrusted to safeguard the eastern frontier of Assam stretching out from the Brahmaputra River to Cachar and in addition to execute disciplinary excursions in the hill regions. It is also termed as the friends of the hill people'. Having three inspectorate general headquarters, 9 sector headquarters and 46 battalions across the country, this CPF unit has participated in the two world wars. They endured the worst part of the Chinese invasion and have been associated with Sri Lanka, Jammu & Kashmir, battling rebellion, other than their undertakings in the northeast. The initial draft when the Assam regiment was established was furnished by the Assam Rifles. Till 1965, the Ministry of External Affairs (MEA) governed the operations of Assam Rifles. The name of Assam Rifles was coined after the Second World War. The unit comprises 80 per cent of the officers from the Indian armed forces on deputation and 20 per cent from its own cadre. Though the unit is under the control of

the MHA, the functional control of the force has always been with the army. The MHA has been endeavouring to assume control of the Assam Rifles and bring it under its ambit like the CRPF, BSF, ITBP and different forces. Till now, they have not been effective. The Assam Rifles has a double part of keeping up inner security in the states in the north eastern area and furthermore guarding the Indo-Myanmar Border. The Assam Rifles has a double role of preserving internal security in the states in the north eastern region and also safeguarding the Indo-Myanmar Border. Assam Rifles has been positioned for counter-insurgency operations and furthermore guarding the border. Out of the approved strength of 46 battalions, 31 battalions are assigned the role for counter-insurgency operation and 15 battalions for guarding the border. Currently, all 15 border-guarding contingents are positioned along Indo-Myanmar border on company operating base (COB) approach. The contingents are positioned on all courses of entrance/departure and are checking infiltration, smuggling of arms, ammo, drugs, counterfeit money etc.

2. ***Central Reserve Police Force (CRPF):*** It was brought up in 1939 as the crown delegate's police, and post-independence, rechristened as central reserve police in 1949. Till the time the BSF and ITBP were brought up, the CRPF also guarded the borders. It partook in the operations at Hot Springs in Ladakh preceding 1962 and furthermore participated in the 1965 war. In 2003, a decision was made that all counter insurgency operations in the nation would be dealt with by the CRPF.
   (a) The unit is dealing with an extensive range of duties to incorporate lawfulness and counter insurgency, anti-militancy and anti-terrorism operations. It likewise assumes a key part in helping states in sustaining public order and countering subversive operations of militant groups. The CRPF is an exceptional force for the sort of operations it was trained for i.e. security amid elections, guarding vital installations and establishments to incorporate religious shrines and yatras, dharnas and so on.
   (b) The transfer of the role to counter uprising activities is a quantum leap, particularly, when such a move is undertaken, without any degree of change. The force was not adequately trained to deal with counter insurgency campaigns because of which it has endured and keeps on suffering mass casualties. Nevertheless, the unit is being trained for the counter rebellion role in the prevailing four Jungles/Guerilla Warfare Schools at Silchar (Assam), Hazaribagh (Jharkhand), Sapir (Himachal Pradesh) and Waltham (Uttarakhand).
   (c) The CRPF is less empowered than the civil administration, and subsequently the state police as well. Thus, it is obvious that without the formulation of any strategy or any clear mandate against insurgency, it becomes noticeably troublesome for the CRPF to create the outcomes regardless of it willing to do so. There is a requirement for quality governance in the CRPF which is missing and furthermore regimentation which will give a thrust to the institution. The Government has established counter rebellion and anti-terrorism (CIAT) schools in the states of Assam, Bihar, Chhattisgarh, Jharkhand and Orissa.

3. ***Border Security Force (BSF):*** The BSF was brought up in 1965. Its operational duty is spread more than 6385 km of universal border with Pakistan and Bangladesh. It is also positioned on the line of control (LOC)

in J&K under the operational control of the armed forces.

4. *Sashastra Seema Bal (SSB):* The SSB was established in early 1963 in the aftermath of India-China conflict of 1962 to build up the morale and capacity in the border populace against dangers of subversion, infiltration and disruption from across the border. It has been given the border guarding obligations along the Indo-Nepal and Indo-Bhutan borders and has 25 battalions and 13 battalions positioned, respectively.
5. *Indo-Tibetan Border Police (ITBP):* ITBP was set up in 1962 in the aftermath of India-China war. It is positioned from the northwestern extremity of the Indo-China border up to the tri-junction of India, China and Myanmar.
6. *National Security Guard (NSG):* The NSG was raised in 1984 for specific and high-risk counter hijacking and counter terrorist campaigns. It has special action group (SAG) consisting of army recruits and the special rangers group (SRG) consisting of recruits el drawn from the central police/state police forces.
7. *Central Industrial Security Force (CISF):* The CISF was brought up in 1969 to deliver security cover to public administration divisions to incorporate domestic and international airports and fire protection cover to organizations.

Intelligence Network at the Centre and the States

Intelligence Agencies: The security design at the national level comprises political, executive, intelligence and enforcement components. At the political stage, the Cabinet Committee on Security (CCS) is set up. The administrative component includes the Prime Minister's office, the Ministry of Home Affairs and the Cabinet Secretariat. The intelligence components are spread over various ministries: these includes the Intelligence Bureau (IB) which reports to the Home Minister; the Research and Analysis Wing (RAW) which comes under the Cabinet Secretariat and, therefore, reports to the Prime Minister; and institutions such as Joint Intelligence Committee (JIC), National Technical Research Organization (NTRO) and Aviation Research Centre. (ARC) that report to the National Security Adviser and the National Security Council Secretariat under the NSA which serves the National Security Council. The armed services have their individual intelligence agencies, one each under the army, navy and air force and a parent organization called the Defence Intelligence Agency. There are various organizations that have exclusivity in financial intelligence. The Directorates in the Income Tax, Customs and Central Excise divisions, the Financial Intelligence Unit and the Enforcement Directorate are the organization established for this purpose. The enforcement component of this architecture comprises the central para-military forces such as CRPF, BSF, CISF, ITBP, Assam Rifles, SSB and the NSG. There is no single agency to which these associations report and there is no definite or unified command which can issue instructions to these agencies and organizations.

Multi-Agency Centre (MAC): Some modifications have in reality been achieved after 1 December 2008. The most advantageous shift has been the putting up of the Multi-Agency Centre (MAC) into operation. By an official order issued on 31 December 2008, the MAC was empowered with a more extensive and obligatory membership and another mandate. Every bit of pertinent information or intelligence gathered by one of the participating organizations is conveyed to the table. It is examined and the analysis is imparted with the participating organizations. Another advantageous shift has been the expansion of the reach of MAC to the state capitals and the establishment of the Subsidiary-MAC (S-MAC) in each state capital in which all the organizations working at the state level, particularly the special branch of the state police, are represented. Intelligence sharing at the State Level - The intelligence sharing is done at different levels in the northeast. Every state in the zone has an S-MAC which is associated with the MAC in Delhi. In the state, State Intelligence Bureau (SIB) is the nodal office which is in charge of co-organizing and conduct of weekly meetings with agents of different associations. The unified command structure has the delegates of RAW, SIB in addition to the intelligence organizations of the armed forces, state police and paramilitary forces. This has provided a constrained component of intelligence sharing, which is meeting just the practical prerequisites. Through the MAC-SMAC-State Special Branch network, the Intelligence Bureau possess the capacity to pull more information and intelligence from the state capitals. It has additionally possessed the capacity to push more information and intelligence into the state security framework.

State Administration

Organization Setup: The chief secretary of a state appropriately helped by the district magistrates of each district is in charge of powerful organization of the state with regards to the directions from the state political administration. They, thus, have the state police available to them to guarantee public order and lawfulness which is guaranteed by a system of police stations entrusted with addressing the entire state. Each police station has an assigned jurisdiction and is the lowermost rung at the district level, in charge of guaranteeing internal security and lawfulness. Various such police stations are controlled by an administrator of police with his headquarters at the district level who thus is answerable to the district magistrate. Districts are grouped together in view of their geographic nearness to form a range which is the purview of a Deputy Inspector General of police, which in turn falls under the general ambit of the Director General of Police who is responsible to the Chief Secretary of the state for guaranteeing internal security and lawfulness within the entire state. Far beyond the state police, each state has an additional organization called State Armed Police.

Indian Reserve Battalions (IRBs): In conformity to its name, IRB is an armed reserve accessible at the state level to deal with troublesome law enforcement circumstances, for example, armed robberies, revolts, terrorists and other such internal disruptions including state wide disturbances and low level uprisings which can possibly upset lawfulness. In conformity to its name, IRB is an armed reserve accessible at the state level to deal with troublesome law enforcement circumstances, for example, armed robberies, revolts, terrorists and other such internal disruptions including state wide disturbances and low level uprisings which can possibly upset lawfulness. The Ministry of Home Affairs has assigned 51 IRB's toward the north east, 9 each to Assam, Tripura and Manipur, 7 for Nagaland, 5 each for Arunachal Pradesh and Mizoram, 4 for Meghalaya and 3 for Sikkim. Out of the 51 Battalions, 46 have been raised up until this point. The aim is to organize a well-trained armed police outfit in the states.

There are some procedural safety mechanisms to the police, according to which a policeman cannot arrest or enquire without a warrant, an arrested individual must be sent to court inside 24 hours and broad/multilevel supervision of the police work must be carried out. With regard to control over the police, every police action is available to judicial examination; police is responsible to the chosen delegates and to Quasi-Judicial body like the National Human Rights Commission and is likewise under the control of the District Magistrate.

The Ministry of Home Affairs is executing a plan for the modernization of the state police. all the more so for the new difficulties of the internal security. The Ministry has set every state of the northeastern zone in category 'A', which infers that they will get 100% assistance from the centre to actualize their yearly endorsed plans.

State Police: It is imperative to keep up the civil face of the legislature, even while the armed forces of the union are sent in support of civil authority. The state police are the most obvious symbol of organizational authority and its inability to successfully keep up lawfulness has dissolved the believability of the legislature as well as urged the criminal components to continue with their unlawful exercises with exemption. There has been political intervention in the normal police organization which must be invalidated and the force should remain politically neutral.

With the armed force, and para military working under the armed force (such as the Assam Rifles, for example, in numerous territories), involved forcefully in counter-insurgency activities, the state police in the northeast have practically abandoned their obligation on the terror front. The police in the states in the territory have presumed that it will be the Army or the para military that will do the counter-insurrection operations on the ground which includes making direct move against the agitators.

It has been observed that the police confront a psychological and motivation issue while sent in for in counter insurgency operations. The police workforces are probably going to be a vital part of that very populace to which the guerillas belong to. Moreover, a portion of the sympathizers or the guerillas may even be the friends and relatives of the police who are searching for them. The police personnel and their families may also be a part of the nexus as they need to live and associate in that very community. Hence, at last, a major danger that the policemen need to confront is the risk of retaliations against their families by the rebellions.

It is the police stations which ought to give noteworthy and swift intelligence inputs on internal security, while the state and central intelligence organizations investigate at the large scale level. These police stations are set up in each sub-division of the state in the northeast, with a staff of 15 personnel. In few states, there are hills and the field territories. The hilly regions pose significant issues for the police stations as their zone of duty is immense, the landscape is hostile and villages are numerous. It is likewise to be remembered that they are prepared for criminal examinations and not for counter insurrection and more so against the advanced arms and ammunition which are utilized by the radicals with deadly and intense ethnic political motivation.

Individuals will approach to give the information, in case they have confidence in the police. It, thus, becomes important to thoroughly investigate the working of police stations and deliver changes to make policemen really people friendly. This can only be accomplished by community policing, police reforms and utilization of the most recent technology.

During the counter insurrection operations, the local policeman is supposed to go with the security forces amid an operation as he ought to be the person who provides intelligence and his attendance is needed as per the assemblies of law. Nevertheless, this is not the case, as the policeman is in majority of the cases not accessible because of alternate responsibilities of criminal exercises, not interested in getting involved as he is untrained for counter insurrection operations, unable to cope up with the security forces because of absence of physical wellness and and is also unequipped to manage the guerilla groups. All the official documentation is executed by the police establishments after the operations are finished.

The security forces need overall security of their operations. In reality, even their own troops are on certain occasions not explained of the operation till as late as could reasonably be expected. In case, the police need to be apprised before the operation, then in all possibilities, it will be at the cost of security as they are vulnerable to impart the information with the radical groups being local people of the zone and need to survive. The constabulary is the pillar of our police personnel, forming 87 per cent of the total strength. Enhancing the image of the constabulary is, thus, vital to building open trust. Police constabulary remains the foundation of police. They ought to be imparted better training and instilled with the correct attitude toward the general population. The grassroots information and intelligence accumulation frameworks that have generally been a part of policing have languished or failed into neglect in some places. The role of a cautious and successful beat constable can be essential in checking the exercises of networks, which generally work under radar. A constable's duty is arduous and perilous besides the force is overstretched and performs multifaceted obligations without getting elementary facilities.

There is not a viable replacement for the policeman as he is the gatherer of intelligence, the master of the law, the preventer of the offence, the examiner of the offence and the leading figure of the authority of the state, all combined. In the event that he is not there, it implies that every one of these capacities are not performed. That the inability to perform basic police capacities is the place the spoil started and that is the place the decay lies even today. The police stations to a degree are, today, nearly unconnected islands. However, because of telephones and wireless, and particularly mobile telephones, there is voice network between the police station and senior police officers. Nevertheless, in the hill territories of the north eastern area, communication is a noteworthy issue and in this manner there is very exceptionally constrained correspondence between the police stations and the armed forces. There is no mechanism of data storage, information sharing and accessing information. There is no record of wrongdoings or criminals that can be accessed by a station house officer, aside from the manual records concerning the police station. There is a need for more intensive consideration on the training of cops. This ought to achieve better human advancement. However, considerably more endeavours should be placed in the refresher training or so far as that is concerned in the reorientation of the cutting-edge corps and men as it is they who are the ones whom the individuals from public consistently make contact. It is basic that the abilities of the police are upgraded and there is modification in their conduct and attitude towards the general population. This will influence the police to be more people friendly and a professional unit. There is a need to extend to the general population, a good image of the police drive and their success. In addition, they should be made to comprehend the challenges which the police confront while conducting operations along with their regular obligations to act against the criminal exercises in their area of responsibility. The general populace should understand the trouble which they need to experience by the activities of the police which sometimes are inescapable. Subsequently, there is a need to re-establish the wellness, capacity and team spirit of the state police forces. The profile of the force level in the territory portrays that there is a wide contrast of the public–police ratio in comparison to the task in a rebellion situation.

North East Police Academy (NEPA)

North East Police Academy (NEPA) was set up in 1977 as a regional police training college at Barapani near Shillong. The objective of the college was to conduct police training in the north eastern states. Renamed as NEPA in 1980, it imparts induction and in-service training for the police work force at all levels of the north eastern states. It likewise is a repository of information which relates to the north east issues on policing and internal security. It conducts courses in particular in counter insurgency and jungle warfare, disaster management, border management, management of terrorist activities, etc., besides the basic course for police officers of the north east. It likewise is a repository of information which identifies with the north east issues on policing and internal security. It conducts courses specifically in counter insurrection and jungle warfare, disaster administration, border administration, administration of terrorist exercises, and so forth., other than the fundamental course for cops of the north east.

Ceasefire Agreements and Suspension of Operations

There has been a standard change in combating insurrection in the north eastern states. The centre holds the duty of internal security in the nation. The state governments are in charge of reestablishing lawfulness and furthermore to battle uprising with the police and armed force, have adopted few initiatives to bring normalcy. These initiatives include ceasefire agreements and suspension of operations (SoO) with the guerilla groups who want to give up hostilities. There are two alternatives provided for a ceasefire agreement. Initially, an announcement by a delegate of the governing body, the chief minister of the state is issued for a discourse. For a reaction of this announcement, any radical group which is intent may then plainly or secretly acknowledge the call for the dialogue. For a reaction of this announcement, any radical gathering which is intrigued may then plainly or secretly acknowledge the require the exchange. Moreover, any intrigued guerilla group openly or secretly acknowledge a dialogue and for this situation, the state then reacts to the call. Afterwards, in both the alternatives, these ceasefire accords or SoO are signed between the administration/state and the radical groups or a tripartite deal between the government of India, state government and the guerilla group.

The ceasefire and the SoO don't ensure enduring peace, as there have been issues which were looked by the state establishments. Some of the establishments have utilized this period for combination and redesign of their units, as additionally at the same time execute hostility. The extended ceasefires and deferment of operations, setting up of the assigned camps is probably not going to bring about destroying uprising and furthermore expect previous aggressors staying in the camps to disperse all of a sudden and come to the mainstream. This can likewise prompt a coalition of the eager insurgents bringing about an anti-India activity from within the region. The accords, which are signed, do not tackle the issue of the expanding interfactional dispute. Nonetheless, by presentation of these activities, there has been a descending pattern in the violence. The security forces have possessed the capacity to focus on the counter rebellion operations on those activist groups who have not come up for talks/accords. Each one of these activities are a departure from the AFSPA. There are issues imperiling the peace procedure in view of lacunae's in the accords. The radicals in the camps should not be permitted to leave the assigned camps. Regardless of whether the weapons are saved inside the camps, , there are sufficient accessible outside for them to utilize and complete demonstrations of extortion and other criminal exercises. They along these lines end up becoming genuine extortionists. They cater to the individual requests of the leaders which do not go well with the general population who at some period were in support of the bigger reason for estrangement and improvement. Furthermore, they utilize this period to obtain newcomers, spread their belief systems and assault rival groups and security forces. The moves of these radicals are secured by the groups on some pretext or the other. Moderates can be persuaded without any difficulty and are brought to the camps to the think tank under coercion and intimidated. It is important that legal actions should be taken against the extremists of the camps in case they are engaged with coercion and other unlawful exercises. In addition, the peace talks should not offer freedom to the accused for his cases being disposed of, as there is a requirement for forcing certain limitations. There is a requirement to carry out suitable examination of the cadres and their chiefs before they are permitted to become part of the mainstream. To enable this, individuals should be involved and only through accord and local determining factors they should be permitted to join the mainstream. It is important that the monitoring committee does not end up noticeably hard in their approach with regards to implementing of the ground rules is concerned. In the event that there is any infringement, at that point the responsibility must be settled. According to guidelines, if there is any concern made by the state/central security forces, it must be passed on to the Ministry of Home Affairs quickly on occurrence. It has been observed that a moderate perspective of the same is taken by the ministry.

There have been situations where the police have arrested units while they were endeavouring to extort money from the general public, and all the more so in enormous towns which are miles far from the assigned camps. When defied, the charges are repudiated by the units on the pretext that they were not doing coercion but rather accepting contributions, which is not an infringement of the ceasefire ground rules.

There have been many ceasefire agreements and SoO signed with different groups in the north east. They are detailed as follows:

Ceasefire Agreements

1. NSCN (IM)
2. NSCN (K)
3. NSCN (Khole)

Suspension of Operations

1. Faction of United People's Democratic Solidarity (UPDS)
2. Dima Halam Daogah (Nunisa Group)
3. National Democratic Front of Bodoland (P)
4. Achik National Volunteer Council (ANVC)
5. Kuki National Organization (KNO)
6. United Liberation Front of Assam (ULFA)
7. Dima Halam Daogah (J)
8. Karbi Longri National Liberation Front (KLNLF)
9. United People's Front (UPF)

It is relevant to specify that there is a case which is a test to the implementers of these accords which has been effective and that was the signing of the memorandum of settlement between the Government of India, the state government of Assam and the Bodo Liberation Tigers (BLT) in February 2003, which brought about laying of the arms by the outfit and joining the principal political stream.

Keeping in view the assortment of various ethnic groups, and the resultant complex scenario in the territory, the administration has been available to talks with such groups which firmly shun brutality. Consequently, deferment of operations, agreements have been made with various groups, who have demonstrated readiness to relinquish savagery and look for answers for their issues peacefully within the framework of the Indian Constitution.

Execution of the Ground Rules

It is important that the standard procedures for ceasefire and SoO are upheld by the state government and Government of India. This includes institutional and organizational preparations. Their details are given as follows:

(a) ***State level:*** State level Strategy Group is instituted under the Chief Secretary. The meetings of the group are held once in a month or more frequently if the circumstance so permits. The tasks of the group are as follows:

  (i) Review the security circumstance including security of VIP's, key establishments and so on.

  (ii) Frame methodologies for execution of the ceasefire ground rules, for example, prevailing upon the cadres to occupy the assigned camps.

  (iii) Discuss modalities for executing/ upholding the choices of the Chairman CFMG/CFSB and managing any standoff/potential conflicts between different groups.

  (iv) Consider and propose options to manage the circumstances which are not settled at the level of the Chairman CFMG/CFSB.

  (v) Consider policy options and operational technique to manage the groups which have no SoO/ ceasefire with the Government of India.

(b) ***District Level:*** At the District Level, the district level monitoring group is directed by the Deputy Commissioner of the district involving district SP, Commandant Assam Rifles and the civil society representatives of the Government of India. The task to be executed by the group is as follows:

  (i) The groups will co-ordinate the reaction to any circumstance relating to violation of the ceasefire standard procedures that may develop in the district.

  (ii) It will take all important pro-active measures to defuse any emerging circumstance.

  (iii) The Deputy Commissioner as the chairman of the group will keep the chairman, CFMG/CFSB and Chief Secretary/DGP well aware of any developments relating to infringement of the ceasefire standard procedures.

  (iv) The group will take suitable measures to execute the decisions of the state level strategy group especially identifying with usage of the standard procedures.

(c) ***Unified Headquarters:*** In 1991, the Unified Headquarters were established during Operation Rhino in Assam. This gave the likelihood that the army could work in pair with the civil administration. A number of dialogues were held between them on a regular basis for laying out policy objectives. At the district levels, the civil governance, local military and para military forces got associated with co-coordinating operational issues. This idea, nonetheless, got settled only in 1997 by the Ministry of Home Affairs. There is a coordinated command mechanism in Assam and Manipur. The institutions of these are at Annexure H and J, respectively.

Operations Group

The conditions of reference given to the Operations Group of the Unified Command are as follows:

1. Synergize the counter revolt operations directed by the armed force, central police establishments and state armed police including positioning/repositioning.
2. Decide on modification of the zones of responsibility between the armed force and CPO's.
3. Monitor the procedures of the district level organizing committees.
4. Crisis Management.

Troubles/Limitations looked in Implementation of the Unified Headquarters

There are sure troubles/restrictions which have been experienced throughout the years. These are as given beneath;

Challenges faced in Execution of the Unified Headquarters

There are certain issues/restrictions which have been experienced throughout the years. These are given as follows:

1. ***Sharing of Intelligence:*** It is crucial to share intelligence both vertically and horizontally. Despite the fact that there is an intelligence mechanism, it becomes natural for each organization to provide information to their channels first and afterwards share, which brings about it losing its esteem and by the time it permeates to the ground level, it is no longer actionable intelligence. This is not being guaranteed and is a serious loophole.
2. ***Co-ordination with the CPOs:*** The CPOs have their own plan bringing about getting orders and clearances from their headquarters/institutions to take appropriate actions, thus defeating the very objective of having a Unified Headquarters.
3. ***Statutory Powers:*** There are no statutory powers and is just a coordinating organization.
4. ***Unhealthy Competitions:*** In the conduct of counter-revolt operations, there is a need of cooperation amongst the units, thus, the one upmanship must be controlled. It, hence, becomes important that the offices are made answerable to the chairman of the headquarters. This can be accomplished if the agencies have sufficient responsibility, authority and answerability.
5. ***Organizational:*** The execution and expansion of the guidelines or set of accepted rules and the time of the agreement and SoO is investigated by a joint checking bunch which involves the delegates of administration of India, state government, security forces and the concerned guerilla groups.

For the effectiveness of the Ceasefire's and the SoO, it is important that there is integration between the Ministry of Home Affairs, state governments, security forces and even the eager extremist groups. The lawfulness is a state subject, however the Ministry of Home Affairs gives it the necessary assistance, and be it financial, labour or guidance. State wise security circumstance amid the years 2005–2011 and list of main militant outfits operational in the north east are appended as Annexure K and L, respectively.

Designated Camps

The administration has approved 'designated camps' for guerillas/radical groups who have stopped antagonism and have turned into a party to the ceasefire agreements and SoO. These chosen camps can be characterized as those camps which have been sanctioned and reported by the administration as impermanent residence for individuals from radical gathering that has stopped resentment. The objective of these camps is to keep an eye on these groups and guarantee that they comply with the guidelines to which they are a signatory for ceasefire or SoO. They cannot be intervened by the security forces and the state organization pointlessly. Nevertheless, in some cases due to the absence of participation and keeping a check, a segment of the groups while being in the camps fall back on anti-social activities to incorporate coercion, brutality and even come back to their earlier insurgency mode. A living instance of this is the case of NSCN (IM) which is in a ceasefire agreement mode for the past 14 years. The organization has defied all rules and is running a parallel government. Few of the assigned camps are as follows:

1. *NSCN (IM) in Nagaland:* Mangalmukh (Hebron), which is the headquarters. Lilen Kuki is the training zone and different camps are at Tsemekhutima, Kopamedzu, Phiro, Mukalimi, Salumi, Kudeh, Ghatashi and New Chungtia.
2. *GPRN/NSCN (Khole group):* Khehoi, Sampurre and Kopamedzu
3. *NSCN (Khaplang):* Surohoto and New Phuktong.
4. *NSCN (IM) in Manipur:* There are no camps assigned by the legislature, yet three camps have been identified as operating in Oklong, Buning and Phumching.
5. *All Kuki groups under SoO:* Camps designated to them are at Molvailup, Semasung, Chalap, T. Gamlon, New Phaisat, Akanshu, Nathangjang, Lalon and Mongbung.

Steps to Ensure Success of Designated Camps

There are crucial steps which should be taken at different levels to guarantee that the idea of designated camps is fruitful. These are as follows:

1. It is important that the guerilla groups do not get an opportunity to regroup after the ceasefire and one of the techniques to accomplish this is that there are more number of the camps with a strength not surpassing 100 units in each of these.
2. The spine of the radical gatherings regarding their forces and organizations ought to be broken to incorporate their officers.
3. The foundation of the radical groups with regards to their forces and organizations should be destroyed to involve their commanders.
4. Presently, there are insurgent groups in the ceasefire operandi who still have their camps operating in the neighbouring nations of Myanmar and Bangladesh. This must be investigated by the Government of India by having amiable relations which can guarantee that no aid can be provided to these groups. These camps in the neighbourhood holds the arms and ammo which is being utilized of by the groups even during ceasefire.
5. As far as conceivable these camps ought to be at a sensible separation from each other, so the radicals can't move starting with one assigned camp then onto the next. On the off chance that conceivable, these camps ought to be far from the monetary centre of the state and furthermore the populated territories. This will decrease the odds of coercion and capturing.
6. It should be ensured by the administration to keep these camps at a reasonable distance from each other, so that the movement of radicals from one designated camp to another could be curbed. If possible, these camps should be held far from the economic hub of the state and furthermore the populated territories. This will decrease the options of extortion and kidnapping.
7. The commercial vehicles discover issues in proceeding on the highways and other vital supply routes. It is on these territories that they are troubled by the groups to pay taxes everywhere. Hence, if these camps are shifted away from the highways and supply routes and into the hinterland, the vehicle drivers

will have a trouble-free movement for their business operations.

8. Wherever feasible, the camps should be held in the nearby surrounding or on the way of the camps of the security forces. This will help in keeping an eye on the designated camps and the activities of the groups.

Revised Scheme for Surrender-cum-Rehabilitation of Militants in the North East

The Ministry of Home Affairs, Government of India has embraced a plan for surrender-cum-rehabilitation of insurgents in the north east with the objective to dissuade the ill-conceived youth and uncompromising militants that have gone astray into the groove of militancy and now find themselves trapped in a vicious circle. It also check to ensure that the militants who have laid down arms do not return to militancy. This plan has been reviewed since first April 2005. Copy of the plan is at Annexure. Relevant features of the scheme are as follows:

- It is relevant to those insurgents who surrender with no less than one weapon of the list as specified in Para 5 of the plan. The states have realized the same, however, in special and worthy cases, activists who surrender without arms may likewise be considered for rehabilitation under the plan.
- Militants who surrender under the plan would be in the beginning accommodated in rehabilitation camp where they will be provided training in a trade/ profession of their preference or suitable to their aptitude.
- The prisoners of the camp will now be paid a stipend of ₹ 3500/- every month as against ₹ 2000/- which was chosen earlier according to the plan.
- The prisoner will not remain for more than a time of three years in the camp.
- The organizations which will be engaged in the process of identification and rehabilitation of the surrendered activists are Inspector General (Special Branch), army, central para military force, state police / state administration and a designated NGO.

With regard to surrender policy by the extremists, it influences the authority that there is a loss of the units, weapons and integrity, and in some cases the rehabilitation may turn into an issue. It will likewise destabilize the objective of the unit with the local populace, that it had no solid argument for pursuing insurgency operations. It is vital that the government assesses the insurgents who surrender to determine whether he is useful or not. The focus should be on surrender of the key groups. It has been observed that in few instances of surrender, the arms and ammo deposited at the time of surrender are negligible when contrasted with their level of operations. The net analysis is that these are token surrenders with the plan to discard their guerrilla elements or those elements who want to gain the monetary advantages and lucrative contracts from the government.

The surrender engages that the insurgents are introduced into the mainstream and some of them are set in the rehabilitation camps. The surrender and rehabilitation package as articulated by the legislature has been fruitful to a degree, all the more so after the change which gives more financial support. Nevertheless, does this package suggest that the insurrection is being remunerated? In any case, does this bundle suggest that the insurrection is being remunerated? In case, an individual is being given this sort of monetary and other aid, then why he should not turn into an extremist?

The government has been engaged in ceasefire treaties, suspension of operations, surrender and killing of the radicals in the counter revolt operations. All the above alternatives have their advantages and drawbacks as the consequences differ in the engagement of the government in each situation. In case of a ceasefire or deferment of operations with the extremists, the government needs to work for meeting the demands of the groups who have surrendered arms with a technique for postponing the procedure. In the case of deferral of operations, the objective is to produce a political settlement between the Government and the extremist groups, and once accomplished, the surrender of the units happens. This political settlement is tedious, perhaps the legislature is not interested in settling the requests or has some different reasons.

The Government of India has had a long discontinuance of dangers antagonisms for 14 years with the Nagas but the issue escapes a resolution. The ethnic insurgencies and religious extremism has widespread in almost everywhere in north east which can turn into a piece of worldwide movement and not just an eye on declaration of individuality. It is this worldwide development which appears to be on its course to substitute insurgency. Despite the fact that the Government is engaged in signing of accords, ceasefires and suspension of operations with the groups, the issues are getting intensified.

Recommendations

Few of the proposals which can guarantee that the agreements, dialogues and surrender are effective are as per the following:

1. ***Mutual Consent:*** The agreements are signed after the mutual acknowledgment of the administration and the militant groups. Hence, it becomes obligatory to the extremist groups to cling to the ground rules and in turn the proper monitoring by the government monitoring committees are executed.
2. ***Role of the Government:*** Regardless of the fact that there have been various surrenders and agreements, there is still militancy in the territory. The government authorities delay the negotiations with the objective to destroy the rebellions and once the war exhaustion sets in, treaties are signed whose provisions are seldom executed. This offers relief to the state government but instead it gives a chance to the radical heads to gain power straightforwardly or indirectly. It is, therefore, the responsibility of the legislature to guarantee that the agreements are executed in letter and spirit. The government can embrace actions to discourage the warring groups by taking advantage of ethnic disputes.
3. ***Civil Society:*** There is a requirement to integrate civil society or the subjects to end up plainly a part of the agreement framework. This will build the confidence of the populace in the framework.
4. ***Initiatives to be Taken:*** Government and the military must produce activities to raise awareness of the insurgency and the moves being made to the youngsters in the schools and the universities.
5. ***Development in the Region:*** There is a prerequisite of good administration and capacity building component to convey a conclusion to insurrection which will guarantee advancement in the area.
6. ***Modernization of the police:*** The renovation of the police in all regards is the need of the hour as the insurgents have the most recent technique in terms of arms, communication equipment and are well prepared to accomplish his allocated task.
7. ***Rehabilitation:*** The legislature must guarantee that the surrendered agitators get what they are guaranteed to incorporate rehabilitation otherwise they will return to the insurrection mode There should be a surrender policy in the states affected with insurgency.
8. ***Publicity:*** The Government must advertise

the surrenders which will positively impact the confidence of the general population, raise the spirits of the security forces and create doubts in the minds of the rebels.

9. *Utilization of the Funds:* The Government must guarantee that there is reasonable usage of the vital funds and the same must be examined by the concerned organizations.
10. *Legal Actions:* The legal trial of the detainee must be monitored at every level.

Reimbursement of Security Related Expenditure (SRE)

The Government of India is actualizing a plan for reimbursement of Security Related Expenditure (SRE) for the states genuinely influenced by militancy/ insurgency. It is being executed in every state of the north east region except Mizoram and Sikkim with the intent to provide for the expenditure experienced by the states on different things, including raising of reserve regiments, logistics provided to the central police forces/ army positioned in the state, ex-gratia allowance and complimentary relief to the casualties of fanatic savagery, 75% of the expenses incurred on petrol, oil and lubricants in campaigns and honorarium paid to village guards/village defence committees/home guards positioned for security purposes, expenditure incurred on maintenance of chosen camps established for groups with whom the central government/state governments have become a party to the agreement for SoO, is being recompensed. The compensation per VDP/ VG/SPO which was limited to ₹ 500 every month has been expanded to ₹ 1,500 every month with effect from 08 December 2010.

National Counter Terrorism Centre for India (NCTC)

The devastating Mumbai attacks led by Pakistan-sponsored terrorists in November 2008 made the government realize the consequences of intelligence and operational failures. The home minister then devised a scheme to set up a National Counter Terrorism Centre (NCTC) which will co-ordinate the counter-terrorism endeavours of the centre and the states. Significant features of the NCTC are as follows:

1. The NCTC would operate under the Intelligence Bureau (IB).
2. The intelligence inputs collected of terrorism and related culpability will be examined.
3. Databases will be maintained and the suitable strategies will accordingly be developed.
4. Finally, the NCTC will examine the risk assessments and circulate the same to the centre and state governments.

The NCTC has not received a positive reaction from the states and some of the chief ministers are not in favour of implementing it. Their fundamental resentment is that their opinion was not taken before finalizing the scheme. The establishment has been authorized to arrest suspects and to carry out searches without bringing up the matter with the state governments. There is no legislation over the activities of the intelligence agencies. The government on their part has guaranteed the states that there will be a 'National Standing Council' which will have delegates from the states, yet even this step from the government has not brought any shift in attitude of the opposition. ❑❑❑

Chapter three

Contemporary Security Threats to India

As India endeavours to come out as a formidable regional player it confronts daunting security threats in the New Year, which may bring about hindrances in its advancement. The most intimidating of these threats originates from terrorism, in both its external and internal aspects—the trans-national and home-grown, against which India has long fought a relentless war. The former stems from Pakistan, which encountered an identity crisis after partition. It looked for compensating its declining conventional military prowess after 1971 through a quest for nuclear parity and dissuasion.

It also followed the possibility of disproportionate power, through engaging with non-state actors, initially during the Khalistan movement in east Punjab and then in Jammu & Kashmir. The Lashkar-e-Taiba (LeT) or 'Army of the Pure', established in 1990 by Hafez Mohd. Saeed and Zafar Iqbal in Kunar, Afghanistan began operating from Muridke, near Lahore, with growing state patronage. Although its main emphasis for militant activities was originally the Kashmir Valley, its acknowledged objective now expands to subverting other parts of India.

As the U.S. and international/NATO forces pull back from Afghanistan, Pakistan's Inter-Services Intelligence Directorate (ISI) could allocate another role for the LeT there, as observed in the recent assault on the Indian Consulate in Herat. Indian diplomatic locations and developmental support workers there will remain targets in the anticipated future.

India has been in the ideological line of vision of al-Qaeda and its associates. Both Osama-bin-Laden and Ayman-al-Zawahiri talked about a Zionist-Crusader alliance' which was reached out after 9/11, to a 'Zionist-Crusader-Hindu alliance' when al-Qaeda established links with Pakistan-based militant associations like the Harkat-ul-Mujahideen (HuM) and Lashkar-e-Taiba (LeT).

In a video which surfaced on 4 September 2014, al-Qaeda chief Zawahiri reported creation of al-Qaeda in the Indian Subcontinent (AQIS). He issued threats to 'liberate our brothers' in Myanmar, Kashmir, Bangladesh 'from injustice and oppression'. One goal of this assertion could be planned to contend for management , authority and authenticity with the Islamic State (IS) in Iraq and Syria, but as the suicide bomb assault near the Wagah border, inside Pakistan (2 November 2014) uncovered, it brought the apparition of an AQIS risk that much nearer to India. The Burdwan blasts (2 October 2014) uncovered a forbidding connection developing with the Jamaat-ul-Mujahideen Bangladesh (JMB), for probable terrorist actions in West Bengal and Bangladesh. This conveys another point of view to the delicate security scenario in Bangladesh, which has been blighted by gun running trails and linkages to discontented militant groups of our North Eastern guerillas.

Till recently, India has not offered a fruitful ground to build up an al-Qaeda base though recently new bunch of inspired Indian jihadists have started looking for worldwide affiliations. The Tanzim Islahul Muslimeen (TIM) was established in 1985 after the communal unrests in Maharashtra. Its message created reverberation among youthful individuals from the Students Islamic Movement of India (SIMI), established in Aligarh, Uttar Pradesh in April 1977. SIMI was debarred in 2001 but its followers reorganized under Indian Mujahideen (IM), which was effective in scheming and executing several bombings amid 2002–2008, with logistic assistance from across the border. IM worked through numerous connections —the Azamgarh module in Uttar Pradesh, newcomers in Beed, Maharashtra and Bhatkal in Karnataka. Two different modules turn up later, one from Pune in 2009 and the other from Darbhanga in 2011. IM sleeper cells have been detected likewise in Hyderabad and Ranchi. Regardless of late arrests of some of its noticeable leaders, IM remains a possibly intense troublesome power.

In spite of all their grievances, despondency and outrage against the Government, Indian Muslims have avoided vindictive pan-Islamic beliefs advocated by jihadi terrorist associations till now. Unfortunately, even as AQIS turns out to be progressively intrigued by India, it could attempt to tap the wellsprings of discontent among youthful Islamists in India.

China's rapidly increasing prowess as a noteworthy power in our region encroaches straightforwardly on India's geo-political space. In the immediate term, the power differential with India, with regards to its financial and military capacity, will extend. Long-standing differences on the Line of Actual Control (LAC) are probably not going to be settled rapidly but India must quicken gradation of its border infrastructure, setting up military operational ideas and capacities to dissuade huge invasions from the north, while nuancing the stance of political trades with China in an aligned way.

On the internal front, left wing extremism (LWE) in the alleged Naxalite corridor, reaching out to five/six states—Jharkhand, Bihar, Odisha, Andhra Pradesh/Telangana and Maharashtra—represents the most genuine threat. In 2014, a declining pattern of fatalities was observed, although violence persisted. A blend of power-driven and development-oriented approach by the organization has not diminished its capacity to execute occasional assaults bringing about high casualties among the security forces.

Assisting police changes, stopping labour deficiencies, upgrading fast reaction abilities and hardware modernization ought to be basic features of our procedure to adapt to these dangers in the close term.

Speeding up police reforms, filling manpower shortages, upgrading fast reaction abilities and equipment modernization should be basic features of our approach to meet these dangers in the close term.

Revisiting India's Intelligence and Internal Security

Geologically, India is positioned in the middle of antagonistic Pakistan to its West and not very well disposed Bangladesh, Myanmar and China to its East. Regular terrorist exercises pursued by Pakistan against India have made it fundamental for India to be always watchful and acquire fool-proof intelligence and internal security network. India's new government has given precedence to intelligence in its programme and conceptualized policy building and execution varieties for the nation's safety and security. The regularly expanding security concerns and the more noteworthy dependence on intelligence are the offshoots of a host of causative elements. Novel and complex indications in the kind of security threats, states falling back on low-cost alternative of secretive activities to accomplish their goals, abundance and accessibility of deadly weapons, availability and ease of access of lethal technology, brisk and easy trans-national movement, low effectiveness of traditional security measures, etc., have come to assume an important role in this range of contributive factors. No wonder, intelligence has come to assume a noteworthy part in all methods of contentions. Intelligence might be operative in the twin modes of being hostile and guarded. In the offensive mode, it can provide important inputs for policy articulation and evaluation of enemy strengths and weaknesses on one hand and an ability degrader on the other. In the defensive mode, intelligence assumes the crucial role of envisaging and thwarting security risks. In internal security, it works in a territory-specific and issue-specific way. India is remotely inclined to various vulnerabilities due to numerous factors, geopolitical positioning with antagonistic neighbourhood, long and misleading borders, long sea belt, etc., internally, its communal, caste, linguistic and ethnic financial inequalities, political clashes and turmoil, etc., add to its vulnerability. However, the origin of India's internal security has experienced a radical shift, of late, for the worse. In the traditional breed, the internal risks used to be unsophisticated, in contrast to the external threats which were of an external origin. In the new context, the politico-strategic aims, scheming, accounts, inspiration, etc., of an internal menace are frequently of external origin. Surreptitious in nature, these operations are associated with some household fault-lines which lend them a character and shade of an inward security issue. India has since long been paying the consequences for these remotely sponsored internal security risks. It is an accepted fact in unison that the internal security is the most susceptible fragment of our national security. This reality has been acquiesced by the reports of the Kargil Committee. A few examinations have attempted to evaluate this external factor in India's internal security, and it has been put at as high as 80 per cent probability. This will have disastrous impacts and, to adapt to such a disturbing scenario, what is needed is not intelligence reforms but, as Deborah Barger advocated, intelligence transformation. Our security measures have to be so adjusted as to address the idiosyncrasies of this developing exigencies instead of adjusting them to our comforts.

There are different elements for the change in perspective in the way to deal with the execution of security threats by cross-border organizations. Standard and formal wars are turning increasing expensive and outdated. In such a situation, undercover activity has grown as worthy substitute to numerous countries and organizations. It is an affordable and justifiable onslaught. This belligerent approach is being utilized not only by disproportionate powers too feeble to utilize formal and standard means, but even by real powers. The political teaching endorsed by the US for 'protecting supreme national interests' is yet another facade for this malicious plan. This clandestine plan has cost India deeply till now with about 70,000 human lives including more than 9,000 security work force and untold melancholies and countless losses. The nuclear-empowered Pakistan has reshuffled its huge offensive machinery to undermine India. Pakistan has been attempting to utilize Kashmir as an excuse for jihad for all Muslims throughout the years. The jihadi irregulars have turned into an indispensable part of Pakistani hostile apparatus as demonstrated by the Kargil War. Our reactive principles should be re-visited and evaluated in light of the huge Pak operations which have so far resulted in the demise of more than 12,000 Pakistani terrorists on the Indian soil. Authoritative jihadi Wahhabism is yet another danger aimed at Muslim populace. A considerable populace of Afghanistan and Pakistan has gone under its flurry and frantic endeavours are being made to spread its appendages to India. The superimposition of this traded variation of Islam must be countered ideologically and purposefully. In the North-Eastern Border States, demographic incursion from Bangladesh has turned out so recurrent that the natives are compelled to pitch their territories and flee to different parts. It has brought about an aggregate demographic transformation and has accepted an unyielding proportion. The gravity of the circumstance has developed to the degree of voices, curbed however, in favour of greater Bangladesh, rising both in Assam and Bangladesh this unlawful immigrant populace, surpassing 20 million, is not confined only to the genuinely influenced states like Assam, West Bengal and Bihar, but have discovered new residences in the entire length and breadth of the country. Deceitful political patronages at the involvement of corrupt public authorities have even acquired for these unlawful settlers identity documents building up their lawful presence in the land. The annulment of the IMDT by the Supreme Court of India and the presentation of new guidelines shaped under Foreigners Act have encouraged an easier mobility for this increasing populace. In the North-East India, militant Islamic groups associated to fanatic organizations in Bangladesh effectively shaped over twelve activist outfits with exceedingly evil intentions. The disclosures made by the captured Kari Salim and his associates surely were appalling. It is realized that for strategic reasons, the mentors of these groups in Pakistan and Bangladesh have exhorted their groups not to assault until they are completely developed in their preparation and amiable political scenario. Moreover, a purposeful, crusade intended at the strengthening of the immigrant Muslims in association with local Muslim leaders has begun. Obviously, a vicious rebellion is designed, with weaponry, trained units, tactical supervision and working assets funded from across the border. The rebels in the North-Eastern states have their origins in Bangladesh and Myanmar which is the nourishing factors of insurrections in the North-East. The specific ethno-political atmosphere of this territory is a safe place for the expansion of radical activities. However, another imminent risk to India's internal security is the activities of the CPM (Maoists) in Nepal. This unit, which has known connections with Indian Left-Wing Extremists, has turned out to be stakeholders in Nepal's new power administration. As of now, the disclosures made by the Nepalese Maoists concerning bilateral correlation between the two nations, have been very aggravating. The Maoists in Nepal are alleged to be operating with this plan of removing the monarchy with political backing. Subjecting the purposes of security apprehension to be a cohesive and all-inclusive scrutiny, it is very evident that a considerable challenge lies ahead. As a matter of fact, keeping up a steady vigil over a nation with a populace of more than one billion individuals possessing a landmass of 3 million sq. km and having misleading borders of 15000 sq. km is a formidable task. Clearly, to manage such a highly challenging circumstance demands for a high-calibre intelligence capacity-intelligence seasonably revamped to address the forthcoming difficulties. Upgradation of the weaponry, numerical reinforcing of the security forces and their training, fortifying protective shield for the aimed entities are crucial. What should be of primary interest is intelligence and smart operations. It should be taken into account that what the entire units and brigades with their weaponry and battleships cannot bring out what can be achieved by a few real-time specialists.

Internal Security as an Enormous Threat despite Border Skirmishes

In the current past, an increasing number of events have prompted expanded visibility of this issue as well as signal, what could well be fundamental variation in India's methodology to its security system. Regardless of India's continuing border clashes and confrontations, the reality is that the odds of a full-scale regular war on the Sino-India-Pak stage are less probable in comparison to the internal security threats that are clear, present and growing. With All the media and public talk focusing on India's defence formation, it's easy to lose track of the other segment of India's national security challenge— internal security. This subject does, nonetheless, request centre stage whenever there is a disastrous security breach, as in the awful episode at Paris on 13 November 2015 or the 26 November 2008 incident at Mumbai.

These threats have diverse origins—from across the border threats saturating as uprising at Kashmir and the North East to factions of community decide on military solutions to their problems, as observed in different secessionist and dissident crusades in the North East and Eastern territories, to command acts of terrorism driven by global organizations as was observed in the 26/11 event at Mumbai and finally the societal divisions in a multi-polar masses that now and again breed breakaway thinking.

In the current past, a rising number of incidents have prompted expanded perceivability of this issue as well as indicate, what could well be fundamental variations in India's way to deal with its security process . The first, such initiative was held in early June 2015, with Indian para-commandos seeking aft er and disposing of guerillas/revolts in neighbouring Myanmar. The initial operation unequivocally proclaimed the instance of 'hot pursuit' indicating a preemptive, aggressive and lopsided response to incitement. The second towards the beginning of August 2015, with the government signing a draft of the 'Naga peace accord' with the National Socialist Council of Nagaland. In this manner, conveying to finish an exertion of several decades and several Prime Ministers. It signalled the inclination to deal with such issues not merely as a lawfulness issue. A comprehensive effort that utilized talk, cooperation and negotiation to reach a commonly workable way with shared duties. The third such initiative was taken in September 2015 by Prime Minister Narendra Modi, during his US visit, calling for worldwide consideration regarding the matter of terrorism and encouraging the UN to arrive at a general description of terrorism; accordingly permitting recognition of nations and groups inciting such events In a similar visit he likewise pushed for UN reforms and India holding a seat on the Security Council. Both the efforts, though not a first, indicated India's more visible, comprehensive and emphatic stand on driving worldwide consideration, alignment and momentum to handle the issue of terrorism. The fourth in October 2015, with the politically managed return of two wanted individuals to India—gangster Chotta Rajan from Indonesia and Anup Chetia of the ULFA, from Bangladesh.

What long-term advantages and development would accumulate from these endeavours, covering social involvement in the decision-making process, insistent political sponsorship to drive global coalition, devotion and activity on terrorism and an unbalanced reaction to incitements—remains to be seen, nevertheless arguably it gives off an impression of being a decent beginning as endeavours to rewire its internal security game plan. There is a premonition of change on India's security landscape. While ominous, these occasions and the policy strategy they seem to denote, would have to be managed and supplemented by other 'accelerators' to help drive force towards a more powerful security system and results. Before pondering into possible stimulators, it's vital to see the present security scene in all its degree, scale and intricacy to really comprehend the stage. With the defence services concentrating on across the border threats, it is left to the state and central security organizations, operational and intelligence units, to manage the emergent inner security challenges. While united in objective, there are basic dissimilarities in the way these two organizations are built up and function. Whilst the Defence establishment, consisting of the three working arms, work under the combined central command of the Ministry of Defence, the internal security establishment that reports into the Ministry of Home Affairs is a partitioned house—with the states and their police units having essential charge to keep up lawfulness and the central organizations offering specific support utilizing their paramilitary and intelligence units.

- In this way, considering the 28 states, 7 UTs and a few central organizations (ITBP, BSF, CISF, CRPF, SSB, classified intelligence units and others), constituting of around 2 million workforce at the state level and another million in the central organizations; it is evident that there is considerable investment with regards to workforces. While some would bring up that with 180 police staff deployed per 1 lakh people, the proportion is considerably lower than the developed nations ratio of 225. It likewise demonstrates the possible difficulties of coordination in a non-integrated command structure. The magnitude of the internal security challenge is genuinely enormous. Given the size and extent of the security field—3.2 million square kilometres of territory, 7,500 km of coastline and another 6,000 km of land border, the rising intensity and recurrence of security 'triggers' and the disproportionate power viewpoint—more should be done as a multi-pronged strategy to maintain and accelerate developments in the security scenario. Evolving from discourses with core interest groups, there are some evident 'accelerators' that could help in realizing the premonition of change and that could, after some time, significantly enhance the efficiency of result. Clear Statement of Intent: All effective human and hierarchical activities originate from an unequivocal, obvious, generally acknowledged statement of objective and direction. For this situation, it would imply a national security approach with aides from the states. A play book that would characterize the philosophy and long-term course apart from laying out clear procedures and metrics for determining the strength of the system and viability of its endeavours. While the exact roles of organizations are clear, the strategy would need to lay weight on the collaborative procedure between organizations. Yearly and multiyear strategic plans could rise and fall to suit current strategic requirements, but regularly under the long-term policy course, in this manner guaranteeing aligned endeavours and accumulation of investments and advantages.
- ***Invest in People:*** Presently, the internal security bazaar has a projected expenditure in the range of $12–15 billion and it is increasing in double digits. Huge investments have been set aside and implemented in initiatives like the modernization of police.
- ***Force Modernization Plan, Mega City Policing and Several Other Security Initiatives:*** Apart from investments in equipment and

framework, investment should be made in human capital and procedures. Trained and inspired staff can provide the winning edge—a reality obvious in various agencies. Whilst several security divisions have their own instructional hubs, some of which are genuinely best in class, for many others there is a need to additionally invest in training. Regardless of whether it is the workforce keeping an eye on the area police station or the central armed police forces (CAPFs), training—technical, operational and managerial—is pivotal to remaining applicable and successful. Taking a leaf from the corporate zone, training and skills enhancement has been observed to be advantageous in enhancing viability as well as in upgrading morale and community pride. Operationally, the training inclination would need to traverse from the time a young enlist joins the forces to mid and senior level positions—continuous, tedious and unavoidable. Technology is one domain where the requirement for training is vital. Present growths in correspondence, surveillance, digital and space innovations have taken the game a long way past conventional physical security parameters. Unmistakably a move of this extent would require the current security training centres to be extended and strengthened and in addition team up with private academic and scientific establishments to pull their resources. The present arrangement of sharing training centres amongst organizations and gaining knowledge from the 'Best in Class' needs to be promoted and systematized.

- *Continuity of Policy and Direction:* Standard duration of service in a designation is 2-3 years for security officers and while this turn is sought after, from numerous perspective, it can have a drawback as well—discontinuity prompting unevenness in initiatives. In equipment acquisition it can bring about uneven parts of equipment and technology that do not shape some portion of an all-encompassing framework. A documented longer-term approach route would help keep up consistency and focus over tenure switch leading to more effective results and expansion of effort and investment. A technology guideline for equipment would likewise help establish an all-encompassing framework.
- *Communication and Collaboration:* In a security system that is spread over various operational and intelligence organizations, information sharing, fast and recurrent correspondences and cooperative planning, presume huge significance. While the roles, obligations and zones of operation for different organizations are clearly delineated, the problem lies in working in a unified organized way. On the other hand, take the instance of CAPFs that offer on demand assistance to states. Occasionally, this can turn out to be a long-term exercise, as in the case of certain Maoist-influenced states. A scenario that inquires the primary charter of state and central organizations. In this manner, signalling the requirement for the state to rebuild and fortify its own devices as has been done with remarkable accomplishment by the recent territory of Andhra Pradesh with its anti-rebellion unit the Greyhounds. A unit that has indicated amazing outcomes in the course of last seven years and has been a model for different states to imitate. The present working of the multi agency centre and state multi agency centres need to be extended and quickened to support systemic information gathering and dissemination. Particularly the sharing of significant intelligence in real time—upwards and horizontally—would have quantum variation to event outcomes. Take the instance of coastal security involving

7,500 km of coastline across 13 states. Three tactful organizations are accused of changing roles to protect from coastal threats—coastal police, coast guard and the Indian navy. In addition, there are other state organizations that have a major role to play—Ministry of Shipping and Ministry of Fisheries. Playing off a usual score sheet is crucial to guarantee that all these organizations operate in a harmonized and efficient way.

- *Correspondence between state/state agencies and between state/central agencies:* Both operational and intelligence—It is of major significance. Drawing up cooperative technique maps, strategic plans and hardware acquisition lists would prompt more successful utilization of funds, staff and inventories. Technology could be a great facilitator for information sharing and correspondence; some extremely influential plans in this space, like the National Information Grid, the National Maritime Awareness Grid and the Crime and Criminal Tracking network should be further socialized amongst the units. Collection of multi-point information would lend itself well to huge information analysis and trend recognition.
- *Inclusion of Industry and Community:* Over the last few years, the Defence segment has witnessed consistent policy discussion and review of empowering policy (DPP) as a well as a stage that permits and boosts private industry involvement—bringing about the increasing presence of private players (both India and foreign collaborations) in the high tech domain of defence research and production. Although it is at a slow pace, yet this is a significant step in permitting infusion of private development, investment and technology—all for the improvement of the sector. This is a layout that requires due thought and application in the inner security section as well—even acknowledging that internal security depends less on machines and equipment in contrast to defence. After some time, this would build a comprehensive domain that would permit private undertaking—academia, R&D, production, training—to participate and contribute One idea could be to enlarge the scope of the recent Corporate Social Responsibility (CSR) plan to permit establishments to also make investment into acknowledged security programmes and organizations. This could alleviate the financial burden on the state as well as offer the corporate world another legal and significant opportunity to partake in nation building. Another is to urge industry to concentrate on security equipment together with defence equipment, as a part of the 'Make in India' plan. Community outreach and participation needs to be extended and augmented. Regardless of whether this is by state police with citizen groups or by central organizations with focused attention groups—similar to the case of the Naga Peace Accord. This component of correspondence and incorporation can be an incredible force multiplier and help build strong alliances with the populace who are a noteworthy partner in the security process. An important component of community inclusion is measures taken to enhance welfare and monetary independence. Particularly relevant in the widespread regions which have observed constrained economic advancement and are additionally problem areas for extremist groups. Regardless of whether state funded development, health, and education projects or private industry-driven investments—all assistance in shaping a financially self-reliant community that is impervious to break away thinking.
- *Technology Adoption and Upgradation:* A frequently repeated statement which significantly holds true in contemporary

world is that the domains of national security have long ago moved past the three traditional ones of land, sea and air. The two additional domains, cyber and space, have brought new threats and the old means of conventional warfare will not be adequate to cope with them. There is a requirement to comprehend, integrate, amend and adopt technologies, existing and emerging, to tackle the new threats. Staff will require a training of these technologies on a war footing, not once but recurrently. Rapidly increasing communication and surveillance technologies present additional threats for organizations as we endeavour to manage non-conventional threats. A general technology guideline is significantly required. What technologies will be employed ? What will be secured? What needs to be built up indigenously? The security institution presently needs the equivalent of the DRDO network as in the case of the defence institutions, which are entrusted with the responsibility of building up future generation technologies and equipment. An idea could be to influence the DRDO network and private defence establishment for building appropriate equipment for the security establishment also. India now stays at an articulation point where it can take huge advances to further upgrade and reinforce its internal security procedures. It's a task well initiated but requires auxiliary agents to build impetus and acquire greater efficiency. While the incidences and gravity of security challenges increases, notable incorporation, correspondence, investment in workforce and technology leveraging is the way ahead.

Internal Security Budget of India (2017–2018)

Starting with the spike in budgetary allotment to the Ministry of Home Affairs (MHA) in 2009–2010 following the Mumbai terror attacks of November 2008, the MHA has been observing a consistent increment in its allocations throughout the years. Over the past three years as well, allocations have expanded from ₹ 61,401.78 crore in 2014–2015 to 65,651.10 crore in 2015–2016, and to 73,406.37 crore in 2016–2017. For the forthcoming financial year 2017–2018 as well, this upward trend has continued with allocations reaching ₹ 83,823 crore, an increment of around 11.5 per cent over that of the preceding year. Of the total provisions to the MHA, allocation made under the head 'Police' refer to issues of internal security such as the Central Armed Police Forces (CAPFs), Central Police Organizations (CPOs), border infrastructure, intelligence, disaster and emergency management, etc. The expanded budgetary assignments under the 'Police' head throughout the years reveal the growing concerns over different internal security challenges perturbing the nation as well as a firm determination to manage them. The emphasis, has been to organize these dangers and difficulties and manage them in a determined and persistent manner through security intercessions and development exercises.

One of the genuine internal security risks that the nation has been confronting for over a decade is left wing extremism (LWE). Currently, 106 districts in 10 states are influenced by LWE. Despite the fact that the essential duty of confronting LWE lies with the respective states, the Union government helps them by providing contingents of Central Armed Police Forces to thwart the undermining operations of left wing extremists and preserve public order. In view of the fact that the Central Reserve Police Force (CRPF) is the leading force positioned in the LWE-affected states, the Government of India had, in 2009, approved funds for raising 39 additional battalions of the CRPF. Consequently, the CRPF has been receiving the maximum grant in consecutive budgets since then. In the preceding fiscal year, the unit received ₹ 16,228. 18 crore, which has been enhanced by another ₹ 1635.35 crore to ₹ 17,868.53 crore for 2017–2018. Of the approved 39 contingents, 26 have been brought up till 2016 and the remainder is to be added by 2018–2019. An additional way in which the Union government helps the LWE-influenced state governments is by granting funds for capability building through different security-related expenditure (SRE) plans. Under these plans, the Union government compensates the expenditure incurred by LWE-influenced states in training and operational necessities of the security forces, insurance of police recruits, ex gratia expenditures to the families of civilian or security forces staff killed in LWE violence, reimbursement to surrendered left wing radical cadres under the surrender and rehabilitation policy of the respective states, etc. In the past two financial years, that is, 2015–2016 and 2016–2017 (until 15 November 2016), funds issued to LWE states under these plans were ₹ 258.65 crore and 111.49 crore, respectively. For the forthcoming fiscal year, the monetary allocation under SRE has been fixed at ₹ 1,222 crore, a rise of ₹ 380 crore from the preceding year. Since SRE also involves consumptions incurred by Jammu and Kashmir and insurgency-influenced states in the North East, the increase of almost 45 per cent under this head could be a result of the declining security scenario and the anticipation of a subsequent increase in expenditure under SRE in these states.

Border management is the second field that has seen a considerable increment in budgetary assignments for the fiscal year 2017–2018. The need to efficiently secure the nation's universal borders against intrusion, trafficking and irregular border points has become even more critical following a series of effective invasion endeavours by Pakistani terrorists through the India-Pakistan international border and successive assaults on key establishments in the recent years. These assaults have raised genuine concerns about the viability of the present border administration in foiling such border breaches and has constrained the Union government to embrace measures s to strengthen the India-Pakistan and India-Bangladesh borders specifically. Towards this end, the Union government had chosen to improve surveillance and detection by building trench cum fence hindrances, setting up laser walls along riverine extends, utilizing sensors, cameras and tunnel detection contraptions, building roads and different infrastructures along the borders. The execution of the comprehensive integrated border management systems (CIBMS) along the India-Pakistan border on a pilot basis is a move in this direction. In view of that, ₹ 2,600 crore has been distributed for border substructure, of which 2,355 crore is for capital overheads i.e., expenses on fences, electronic surveillance gadgets, etc. This quantity is, nevertheless, lower than the ₹ 2,490 crore allocated for 2016–2017. One of the reasons for the lower provision could be the under or non-utilization of finances because of different reasons, a reality uncovered by the modified budget of 2016–2017, where the overheads under capital expenses has been reduced to ₹ 1,722.33 crore. Likewise , budgetary assignments for the border guarding forces have been considerably enhanced to increase their strength and effectiveness. Provisions under this sub-head are made for raising extra brigades, training, acquisition of weapons and ammunition, administrative prerequisites, and so forth. The Border Security Force (BSF), which has obligation regarding the India-Pakistan and India-Bangladesh borders, received the maximum amount of ₹ 15,569.11 crore, an expansion of ₹ 917 crores from the earlier year. Moreover, the Land Port Authority of India (LPAI), assigned with the authority to set up and oversee integrated check posts (ICPs), obtained ₹ 300 crore for 2017–2018, an increment of 241 per cent from the previous year. This features the government's dedication towards more noteworthy regional integration by guaranteeing the smooth and proficient cross border movement of people and goods. Similarly, the Border Area Development Programme (BADP), a plan to meet the infrastructural prerequisites of the border individuals, received an upgraded distribution of ₹ 1,100 crore, an expansion of 11 per cent from 2016–2017. The third segment which received a considerable increment in allotments is police modernization and infrastructure. Under police transformation, ₹ 800 crore has been apportioned for transformation of the state police forces. This amount incorporates allowances by the Union government to states to reinforce police substructure in terms of training, weaponry, mobility and correspondence, and the formation of secure police stations. Moreover, it additionally incorporates the formation and maintenance of the crime and criminal network tracking system (CCTNS). Development of projects, both residential and office, for CAPFs and COPs obtained ₹ 4008.06 crore, which showed the seriousness of the Union government to enhance the living and working states of these police associations.

The Intelligence Bureau (IB), which in the last few years has been increasing its strength, has additionally received a fund of ₹ 1,577 crore, an increment of 11 per cent from the earlier year. Most of the overheads, however, will be income expenses demonstrating an expansion in expenditure on salaries and perks of staff. Previously, the IB was operating at a reduced strength with a shortage of around 2000 operatives, as a result of the Mumbai terror attack, voice was raised to reinforce the IB in an exhaustive manner through enhanced recruitments, among other things. The IB has been inducting staff since 2009 but this is yet to reflect precisely in the labour strength since complete induction of agents would only take place after the conclusion of their training. In addition, Delhi Police, the National Emergency Response System for violations against women and national disaster schemes also obtained enhanced budgetary provisions for the fiscal year 2017–2018. The upgraded budgetary provisions for the MHA since 2009 reveal the endeavours of the progressive Union governments to thoroughly renovate the internal security set up of the nation through a progression of measures, for example, capacity formation of security and law enforcement establishments through strength expansion, improved training, cutting-edge weaponry and other substructure, technical upgradation; upgrading intelligence gathering, investigation and dissemination; infrastructure development in violence influenced regions as well as border regions; enhancing reactions to natural disaster and other emergencies and so on. The budgetary distributions for the financial year 2017–18 is a continuation of this procedure. The budgetary provisions for the fiscal year 2017–2018 is a continuation of this procedure. In spite of the fact that the Union government has been making significant budget allocations to the MHA, the ministry's endeavours to produce the desired transformations have, however, shown mixed outcomes till now. While the income expenses have been expanding, the capital costs have seen troughs and peaks in the past four years. This shows that while the concerned associations have been effective in enhancing workforce, they have been unable to develop the proportionate framework required for capacity development, for example, training institutions and laboratories, and acquiring extra vehicles and boats, arms and ammos, computers and surveillance equipment, etc. Endeavours, therefore, must be put to completely utilize the budgetary costs made available to the MHA in order to accomplish a far-reaching transformation of the internal security mechanism of the nation.

The Rohingya Menace to India's Internal Security

A day after Myanmar's armed force asserted that it had found a mass grave holding the corpses of 28 Hindus, including women and children, in violence-impacted Rakhine state, accusing the slayings on Muslim Rohingya radicals. Times Now uncovered that around 300 Rohingya kidnapped 100 Hindus on August 25, killed 92 of them and by force converted the eight surviving ladies to Islam. Around 30,000 Hindus and Buddhists have been dislodged by the savagery. The two consecutive revelations affirmed India's awful apprehensions that Pakistan-based terror groups have gained access to the Rohingya and represent a grave risk to national security. Reports from security organizations suggest the inclusion of some Rohingya in unlawful exercises including fund mobilization through hawala channels, human trafficking and acquiring of fake Indian identity documents. Rohingya with militant foundations have been observed to be operating as far as Jammu, Delhi, Mewat and Hyderabad. Intelligence inputs also warn that the evil plans of the ISI and ISIS incorporate not only utilizing the Rohingya to arouse communal savagery and undermine the Northeast but also a genuine potential of savagery by extremist Rohingya against the nation's Buddhist citizens.

In 2005, the Supreme Court had declared that the Centre had failed its obligation to shield Assam from 'external aggression' because of the IMDT Act, which emboldened widespread illegal immigration from Bangladesh. A recent interview of Himanta Biswa Sarma, the Assam Finance Minister, was quoted as stating: 'Our experience in the Northeast with immigrants has been very bad. Over 30 per cent people are immigrants and as a result, the indigenous people are fast losing their identity... Our monasteries and temples have been encroached upon. We are in very serious trouble when it comes to immigration. So, drawing from my experience in the Northeast, I don't think any more people should be given asylum or refugee status in India'. The uproar for conceding refugee status to the Rohingya likewise does not remain on legitimate grounds as India is not a signatory to the 1951 Convention Relating to the Status of Refugees or the 1967 Protocol Relating to Status of Refugees. Furthermore, Article 19 of the Indian Constitution expresses that the privilege to dwell and settle in, or move unreservedly throughout, any part of the Indian territory is only granted to the citizens of India.

From an absolutely economic perspective, with its issues of populace and meeting their fundamental prerequisites, the nation would be unable to deal with such a noteworthy inundation of illicit migrants. Drawing in more assets to take into account the unlawful foreigners would just serve to deprive genuine Indian nationals, which could bring about social pressures. From the strategic point of view, Myanmar has been broadening cooperation to India in managing radical groups active in the Northeast and encountering drug smuggling and gun-running. With China progressively growing its interests in the territory, it would be unwise on New Delhi's part to set against Yangon by giving shelter to Rohingya terrorists escaping arrest, who have clearly intruded among the illicit migrants in substantial numbers. Despite its reservation on permitting large-scale incursion of unlawful immigrants, India has made a special effort on its part to extend all conceivable humanitarian assistance by hurrying crisis relief material to its responsive neighbour Bangladesh under Operation Insaniyat. The nation just cannot bear to transform more of its states into Assam. India may not construct a partition along its borders but most important obligation is to ensure the privileges of its bonafide citizens and protect them against any type of outside hostility external aggression. It needs to maintain that delicate balance between humanitarian relief and national interests.

On 2 October 2017, Myanmar has offered to take back the large numbers of Rohingya who have fled to Bangladesh in recent weeks. Suu Kyi, who has been severely reprimanded for her inability to intercede in a military onslaught on the Rohingya.

India's Internal Security Priorities for the New Government and Desired Institutional Reforms

Since the Mumbai terrorist assaults on 26 November 2008, the multifaceted nature of internal security risks confronted by the country has increased. Keeping in mind the objective of managing these threats, a collaborative, coordinated institutional methodology in view of the greatest conceivable political consensus and enhanced Centre-State collaboration is required. Moreover, new internal security threats emerging out of contemporary patterns like expanding urbanization, progression of mega cities, demographic shift, rising anticipations of the youth and social media, need to be kept in mind. If not attended to urgently, these issues will become more complex and impossible to deal with.

An immense verbal face-off has been going on in the nation on the type of internal security challenges and the various ways to deal with them. The Group of Ministers Report in 2001 had made a series of suggestions, a large number of which have been actualized. However, we still lack the confidence to handle these threats. Numerous suggestions have been made by different experts and expert organizations. The execution of the proposals has, however, been poor. The political consensus on executing the key suggestions, for example, the setting up of the National Counter-Terrorism Centre has turned out to be elusive.

A. ***Centre-State Relations:*** In the recent years, tense relationships and lack of effectual correspondence between Centre and the States have generated obstacles in addressing issues of internal security positively. There is absence of political consensus on internal security challenges. Accordingly it is prescribed to adopt the following measures:

- ❖ The Prime Minister should hold right from the start of his tenure meetings with the Chief Ministers and political factions to arrive at a political consensus on executing institutional amendments, carrying out suggestions of different committees established by the Government of India and launching a far reaching plan for internal security transformation.
- ❖ The statutory systems like the National Integration Council (NIA), Development Council, etc. should be bolstered to discourse internal security challenges between the Centre and the States.

B. ***Counter-Terrorism:*** The lack of a Central Institution to handle terrorism has brought about a disintegrated approach to terrorism. Hence, it is suggested that:

- ❖ Establish on urgent basis an NCTC like body to combat terrorism. In case the situation demands the need to analyse the prevailing draft and modify it, then go for it.
- ❖ Make the National Intelligence Grid (NATGRID) functional and strengthen national Investigation Agency (NIA).
- ❖ Explore methodologies to control the internal sources for terrorist funding.

C. ***Policing Reforms:***

- ❖ Scarcity of policemen, absence of suitable training and insufficient framework has restrained the efficient working of the Police. Steps required to address these concerns are as follows: Initiate a recruitment campaign and bring the police population proportion to the UN proposed standard of 222 per 100,000 individuals. Comply by it with effective policing and training framework as well as jurisdictional transformations.

- ❖ Provide sufficient legal protection to central police forces for counter terrorism campaigns.

D. ***Border Management:*** Absence of a very well organized approach towards border management has made the nation's borders insecure. The issue is further worsened by feeling of estrangement showed by individuals dwelling along the border zones. To improve the scenario, following proposals are made.

- ❖ Set up a Border Management Commission for figuring out a general vision for border management and formulating plans and policies. A similar commission need to be established for coastal security.
- ❖ Ensure customary visits of central leaders to the border regions and neighbouring nations and connect openly to the general population.

E. ***International Cooperation:*** Terrorist menace has worldwide dimensions. On the political dimension of internal security, following measures need to be adopted:

- ❖ Gain cooperation with different nations in connection with counterterrorism operations
- ❖ Have extradition treaties and accords on criminal issues
- ❖ Get training and skills from different nations

F. ***Research:*** Any long-term workable methodology to tackle internal security threats should be founded on efficient research of the distinctive dimensions of internal security issues. Hence, there is a requirement for establishing research organizations managing issues, for example, ethno-cultural investigations of populations groups, languages, social media and its effect, police and crime, conflict resolution, insurrections etc. Specific research organizations should be established to help devise suitable internal security strategies.

There are different developing issues which require quick and ample consideration. These are detailed as follows:

- Perception management has been the most vulnerable link in India's battle against internal security issues. The government has not possessed the capacity to win the clash of narratives in support of terrorists and counter-narratives against them. To reinforce perception management, a standardized and whole government methodology towards a particular issue should be guaranteed. Counter narratives to the misinformation of the terrorists and insurgents should be built up and popularized.
- The Internet and the social media are expeditiously arising as the fields for contending narratives. Critical advances should be taken against the increasing extremism through them.
- Cyber security transformations should be introduced by upgrading capacities through training and establishment of Cyber forensics.
- Emphasis should be on readiness of huge data, their mining and evaluations. Private segments should be engaged for such activities and most of the proficiency lies beyond the government.
- Half of India will be urbanized by 2050. These urban and peri-urban zones could arise as zones of disharmony, which need consideration through skilled urban policing. Administration of mega cities also present their own issues that need devising a comprehensive strategies to deal with. ❑❑❑

Chapter four

Challenges Posed by Left Wing Extremism/Naxalism

At the beginning of the new millennium, India has not only evolved as an atomic weapons state as well as one of the quickest developing economies on the planet. It is anticipated that except unanticipated cataclysmic events, India would rise as one of the three mainstays of the world economy in the following two decades. With the objective of realizing its maximum potential, India needs to rise above its internal and external threats.

Having confronted four and half wars since freedom, India needed to build up a strong military to overcome any threat to the security of its natives and the territorial integrity of the Union.

Nevertheless, the internal security scenario still remains the chink in the armour of the Republic. Throughout recent decades, left wing extremists has constantly represented a genuine threat to the different states of the union.

Genesis of Naxalism

- The Communist Party of India or CPI was formally established on 25 December 1925 at a conference held in Kanpur. The idea of this party was to initiate communist uprising in India. By 1940s, the communists reinforced their influence over the All India Trade Union Congress but they were politically confronted for their disapproval to the Quit India Movement.
- In 1946, the CPI prevailed to some degree in mobilizing the individuals on the principle of armed battle in Telangana Uprising (1946–1951). Nearly the same time and on same ideological foundation, a militant operation was started in Bengal by the Kisan Sabha (peasants front of Communist Party of India), which is known as Tebhaga Movement.
- Following the Indo-China war (1962), genuine disagreements arised within the CPI as to whether favour India (where the government was Pro-soviet) or China (a socialist country). The conceptual conflict prompted a noteworthy split in CPI and with this, the CPI (Marxist) was conceived in 1964. The parent CPI was considered as a pro-Soviet party whereas the CPI (M) was considered as a pro-Chinese party. The CPI (M) choose to contest elections in West Bengal in 1967. Soon after the election, CPI, CPI(M), Bangla Congress and eight other parties including the All India Forward Block entered into coalition to form a front called the United Front to gain power and displace

congress from authority for the first time in West Bengal.

- A faction of leaders—especially from West Bengal, Odisha, A.P. and Kerala—contradicted the concept of the CPI (M) to become a part of the government. The Government failed to survive long but the difference in principles resulted in a split in CPI (M). The younger members of the party, such as Charu Majumdar, blamed CPI (M) of letting down the revolution. In the mean time, the Naxalbari incident took place.

Naxalbari Incident

- The 'Naxalbari' event was sparked off on 25 May 1967 at Bengai Jote village in Naxalbari, situated in the Siliguri subdivision of the Darjeeling district of West Bengal. In the village, a tribal youth, who had a jurisdictional order to cultivate his land, was assaulted by the goons of local landlords. The tribals countered and declined to part with the land owner's share of their produce and lifted the whole stock from his warehouse. It flared up a ferocious movement. The uprising was driven by the young CPI (M) leaders Charu Majumdar and Kanu Sanyal. To preserve lawfulness, the CPI (M)-led government called for police action against the Naxalites. Police executed the order by opening fire on villagers, which resulted in killing of 9 adults and 2 children.
- It took 72 days to crush the crusade, but the movement succeeded in gaining huge support from the 'communist revolutionaries' which were the parts of the state units of the CPI (M). Thus naxalism was introduced for the first time in India.

First Phase of Numerous Splits

- In 1968, the crusade recurred on a larger basis in the northern regions of Andhra Pradesh. Here the Naxalites took hold of property, lynched landlords and involved in acts of terror. The extremists were confronted with prompt and hard reaction from the state and they were overcome by 1970. In the meantime, in 1969, a movement re-emerged in West Bengal whereby landlords were slayed, property was redistributed and farmers' debts were cancelled. It was likewise quashed within few months. Around the same time, the CPI (Marxist) split, whereby Charu Mujumdar formed the CPI (Marxist-Leninist or ML).
- In 1971, the movement began to lose intensity. In 1972, Mujumdar and other well-known leaders were detained. Mujumdar passed out in custody and this almost finished the Naxalite movement in West Bengal. Nonetheless, the movement turned out to be a motivation for the individuals who were concerned in realizing social justice through savagery.
- After Charu Mujumdar died, the CPI (ML) again split into different groups headed independently by Vinod Mishra, Mahadev Mukherjee, Santosh Rana, Chandra Pulla Reddy, Tarimela Nagi Reddy, Appalsuri and others. Hence, since its inception till late 1980s, the Naxal Movement witnessed various splits and few mergers. But the ideology of Naxalism got a huge boost during this period. During this period, the movement pulled in and inspired a substantial number of youths including the students. Amid this period, just about 200 progressive journals and publications were brought out. During those days, the movement was well supported by China, ideologically, morally, financially and intellectually. At the appropriate time, the Naxal activity spread across various states.

Second Stage of Merger and Reinforcement

In 1980, Kondapalli Seetharamaiah parted from the CPI (ML) and established the Communist Party of India (Marxist-Leninist) (People's War Group, PWG), in the Karimnagar district of Andhra Pradesh. At that time, in 1992, Mupppala Lakshmana Rao (alias Ganapathy) expelled Kondapalli Seetharamaiah and presumed the post of general secretary of the PWG. After that there were noteworthy mergers and strengthening of different Naxalite groups in the nation, most prominent among them is the formation of Maoist Communist Centre of India (MCCI).

Third Stage: Maoist Communist Centre of India (MCCI)

In 2004, the People's War Group, functional in Andhra Pradesh, and MCCI, active in Bihar and adjoining regions, consolidated bringing about the creation of the biggest and most deadly Naxalite unit in India, known as CPI (Maoist). Around then, it had a projected strength of 9,500 undercover armed men and women.

Extent of the Naxalite Problem

- Left Wing Extremism has been recognized as the gravest internal security danger to India, outperforming terrorist developments in Kashmir and the Northeastern uprisings in general effect.
- Presently, it influences no less than 17 states and around 185 out of 602 districts in India. Its major bases are set up in Assam, Andhra Pradesh, Bihar, Chhattisgarh, Jharkhand, Karnataka, Madhya Pradesh, Maharashtra, Odisha, Uttar Pradesh and West Bengal.
- This movement has set up base territories around Dantewada and Bastar districts of Chhattisgarh.
- The number of Naxalites includes 15,000 armed unit and 2 Lakh unarmed unit. A greater part of the armed contingent constituting more than half of the Naxalites is based in Northern Chhattisgarh and Jharkhand.

Factors Responsible for Growth of Naxalism

The Naxal influenced zones are tribal-dominated districts in the interiors of the states where the administrative architecture and improvement has not yet reached. The dissatisfaction among the general public in these zones is on the issues of rights to lands, forests, mining, development and caste-based prejudice. Naxalism is the result of different aspects political and economical in nature as discoursed further.

Political Factors Responsible for Naxalism

- Advent of the movement concurred with the creation of the first United Front Government in West Bengal (1967) with CPI (M) as its principal component. The movement, in this manner, gained growing official backing, exposure and press coverage in those times.
- The movement was affected with the political belief system of Chinese Communist Party and Mao Zedong. They utilized mottos, for example, 'China's path is our path; China's Chairman is our Chairman'. Nevertheless, this conceptual leaning towards China gradually disappeared away. Presently, the Naxalite groups do not hold the same opinions anymore. Nevertheless, their allegiance to Maoism stays as it was before.
- The Naxalbari movement took place as an armed farmers revolution. The indifferent

nature and lack of concern of the political class towards tribals stayed a standout amongst the most vital components that prompted such uprisings. The heartless nature and lack of concern of the political framework towards tribals stayed a standout amongst the most vital components that prompted such uprisings.

- The most critical political factor for ascent of naxalism is the failure of the genuine political authority in India to provide opportunities for organizational uplift to the underprivileged sections of society in the influenced states. There are a few regions where there is definitely no civil government or police.
- The Naxalites function in a vacuum created by administrative and political foundations, advocate for local demands, exploit the dissatisfaction widespread among the abused factions of the population and looks to offer an alternative mechanism of governance that guarantees liberation of these segments from the controls of the exploiter sections through the barrel of gun.

Economic Factors Responsible for Naxalism

- Issue of poverty and monetary disparity and underdevelopment in the naxal influenced territories.
- Skewed dissemination of land and economic development.
- Violation of forest lands and wealth by contractor-politician association.
- Introduction of mining organizations in tribal lands and forests, posturing risk to the livelihood of the tribals.
- Indigenous tribal populace denied of their lands, displaced from their conventional source of livelihood. Globalization blamed to have driven numerous MNCs making advances in tribal zones on account of their resource richness. The advantages of resource exploitation are not imparted to the tribals.
- Well entwined connection between the unlawful mining industry in Chhattisgarh and Jharkhand which brings about a lucrative source of income for the Naxal leadership and units.
- The tribal villages are without any medical amenities or schools and are marred with low literacy and high poverty.
- Tribals and lower castes from India's poorest societies form the Naxalite cadre base. Naxalite movement is backed by the resentments of the tribals and the dalits.

Issues raised by Naxals / Maoists

- *Caste/Gender based exploitation:* This includes exploitation of Adivasi ladies, sexual abuse of ladies residing in Salwa Judum, Recruitment of adolescent girls as special police officers and abuse of low caste females by upper caste men.
- *Religious Minorities:* The Maoists utilize the Babri mosque annihilation, Gujarat uprisings and other such occasions to call up the minorities to join against the right wing Hindus. They give unambiguous support to Kashmiris, Nagas, ULFA and Meiteis.
- *Issues of agrarian community:* The Maoists indicate to the increasing number of peasants committing suicides in Vadarbha, Andhra Pradesh and so on. Their programme incorporates waiving the peasants' loans, reinstatement of farm subsidies, investment in irrigation, legitimate costs of farm produce and ban on multi-national companies.
- *Induced displacement by Development:* Maoists give a top priority to opposition of special economic zone (SEZ) in their

programme. SEZ, from their viewpoint, is a tricky strategy to grab the land of the general population and hand it over to MNCs.

Ideology of Left Wing Violence

The above portrayal clearly expresses that Naxalism emerged as a peasant uprising from Naxalbari in West Bengal. The Naxals are extreme left fanatical communists that back the political philosophy of Maoism. Maoism emerged in China as a kind of Communist theory, drawn from political principles of Mao Zedong. It was broadly employed as the political and military directing principles of the Communist Party of China till 1977–1978. It laid emphasis on the progression of people's social and economic life by building up a an egalitarian society through armed revolution. It was established in the counter colonialist battle and encouraged armed revolution with the intention of achieving political transformation. Naxalism is in reality founded on the principles of Maoism to accomplish a similar transformation in India.

Ideologically, the entire movement of Naxalism/Maoism/Left Wing Extremism (LWE) is a hotchpotch of Marxism, Leninism and Maoism (MLM). This whole movement is for a communist revolution, which they call 'Indian Revolution' to accomplish socialism and thereby achieve the phase of communism. To accomplish this alleged 'Indian Revolution', they would oust the Indian State through armed combat; capture the political power and after that bring in New Democratic Revolution (NDR). They pursue the Theory of Contradiction whereby disagreement between the considerable general population and feudal system can be finished only by the New Democratic Revolution (NDR). The disagreements are as follows:

- Between the idealist standpoint and the materialist viewpoint of the world
- Between labours and middle-class
- Between workforce and capital
- Between feudal system and general masses and so on.

The Maoists party programme incorporated the following:

- To state that Indian Independence in 1947 was a fake independence
- Armed Struggle is the way to take hold of political power by encompassing from countryside to countrywide
- Chinese way of armed struggle has to be pursued.
- Maoist powers of South Asia should be integrated to topple the Indian State
- Women, Dalit, Minority and nationality inquiry is basically a class inquiry
- Boycott of elections
- New democracy will be individuals' democracy. Final objective is to build up a People's Democratic Federal Republics of India.

Stated Purpose of the Naxal Movement

One of the primary objective of the Naxal Movement is to set up a substitutive state mechanism in India by forming a 'red corridor'. The term Red corridor refers to the whole naxal-invaded territories in India including Chhattisgarh, Odisha, Jharkhand, few parts of Andhra Pradesh, Bihar, West Bengal and Maharashtra. Red Corridor almost stretches from India's border with Nepal to the northern borders of Tamil Nadu. Nevertheless, Red Corridor is in reality a contiguous strip that stretches from the southern end of Chhattisgarh to central Jharkhand—the two key realms of naxal violence. Three states, namely, Chhattisgarh, Odisha and Jharkhand provide the naxals scope for easy passage and safe means of access. They are strong around Odisha's densely-forested Naupada district, while have sufficient support ground among the local populace along the Chhattisgarh-Odisha border, right up to Jharkhand's Gumla district.

State Response to Naxalism

Government of India's reaction to Naxalism can be listed briefly as follows:

- Deployment of CPMF, IR, Cobra Battalions and eradication of Naxalites.
- Integrated Action Plan (IAP)
- Modernization of Police Force scheme
- Security Related Expenditure (SRE) scheme, Special Infrastructure Scheme (SIS)
- Training for state police by army, fortified police stations
- Intelligence sharing, inter-state coordination and unified commands
- Assistance in development works, various development programmes and schemes, civil action plans
- No discourse with Naxalites unless they give up violence
- Formulation of surrender policies by state Government

Some of the efforts made by the government to deal with growing Naxal menace have been briefed as follows:

- ***Unified Command:*** In 2006, the Prime Minister supported a planned exertion under a Unified Command structure to discourage Naxalism. He said that a lot of counter measures require synchronization among states—in gathering intelligence, sharing of information and police responses. Subsequently, in 2010, a Unified Command was established in the states of Chhattisgarh, Jharkhand and Odisha, which are the worst-influenced states. Moreover, West Bengal Government has also established Unified Command. The Unified Command will have officials from the security establishment, in addition to civilian bureaucrats representing the civil administration and it will execute meticulously devised anti-LWE measures.
- ***Security-Related Expenditure (SRE) Scheme:*** Under this plan, funds are offered for meeting the recurring expenses with regards to insurance, training and operational requirements of the security forces, rehabilitation of Left Wing Extremist units who surrender in line with the surrender and rehabilitation policy of the state government involved in the operation, community policing, security-related foundation for village defence teams and publicity material.
- ***Special Infrastructure Scheme (SIS):*** This plan tries to take into account the basic foundation gaps for better movement of the police/security forces by renovating existing roads/tracks in unreachable zones, offering secure camping grounds and helipads at vital sites in remote and interior regions, measures to upgrade security in with regard to police stations/outposts situated in risk-prone zones, etc.
- ***Central scheme for aid to civilian casualties/ family of victims of terrorist, communal and Naxal brutality:*** This scheme is devised to support families of victims of terrorist, communal and Naxal carnage. A total of ₹ 3 lakh is delivered to the influenced family under the scheme.
- ***Integrated Action Plan:*** Integrated Action Plan (IAP) is being executed in 82 selected tribal and backward districts for enhanced growth. The objective of this proposal is to offer public infrastructure and services. The activities adopted include establishment of

school buildings, anganwadi centres, drinking water facilities, rural roads, panchayats bhawan or community halls, godowns or PDS shops, livelihood activities, skill development, minor irrigation works, electric lighting, health centres/facilities, ashram schools, toilets, etc.

- *Road Requirement Plan for LWE territories:* The goal is to enhance road connectivity in 34 extremely LWE-impacted districts in eight States, namely, Andhra Pradesh, Bihar, Chhattisgarh, Jharkhand, Madhya Pradesh, Maharashtra, Odisha and Uttar Pradesh.
- *Scheme of Fortified Police Stations:* A total of 400 police stations in nine LWE-impacted states at a unit cost of ₹ 2 crores were approved under this plan.
- *Civic Action Programme:* Under this plan, financial grants are approved to CAPFs to take on civic action in the impacted states. Purpose is to establish means of communication between the local populace and the security forces.

Surrender Policies by State Governments

Naxal-influenced states have likewise reported surrender policies whereby they provide monetary assistance, land and different advantages in lieu of surrender. Nevertheless, there is no effectual intelligence system to recognize Naxal units. Frequently, tribal youths surrender as Naxal units and a significant number of them even join the Naxal crusade to enjoy the welfares.

Saranda Action Plan

The Government has finalized a progressive action strategy in Naxal-affected districts especially in eastern India. The 'Saranda Action Plan', established by the Rural Development Ministry, will be executed primarily in Jharkhand's Naxal-hit Saranda district.

According to the proposal, immediate preference is to assign solar lanterns and bicycles, erection of prefab houses for BPL families under the Indira Awas Yojana and bridges with the assistance of the Army and exclusive water supply—hand pump schemes.

By means of the effective 'Operation Anaconda', the police and security forces have recently freed this dense forest territory from the naxals. Naxal occupied this region for just about 10 years and after Bastar in Chhattisgarh, this was viewed as the second most key Maoist centre in the country.

Roshni

On 8 June 2013, the Rural Development Ministry initiated a new programme called 'Roshni' oriented at the rural/tribal youth.

- *Plan:* A novel skill development scheme called 'ROSHNI' was launched by the Rural Development Ministry in 24 naxal-affected districts. The Ministry for Rural Development initiated this innovative scheme for rural/tribal youth from 24 most critical left-wing extremism impacted districts in the nation.
- *Objective:* To develop the skills of 50,000 youth from 24 chosen naxal-affected regions and provide them placement.
- *Cost:* It was decided that a total expenditure of ₹ 100 crore will be borne jointly by the centre and state governments in the proportion of 75:25 over the next 3 years.
- *Districts Targeted:* Out of twenty-four districts, Six districts each from Jharkhand and Odisha, five from Chhattisgarh, two from Bihar and one each from Andhra Pradesh, Uttar Pradesh, West Bengal, Madhya Pradesh and Maharashtra were chosen. National level agencies are assigned the role for supervision and coordination of the initiative.
- No less than half of the candidates secured under the plan might be ladies and exclusive

endeavours will be made to proactively cover specifically vulnerable tribal groups on a priority basis. Recipients in the age group of 18–35 years with essential aptitude relying on the trade or employment prerequisites are to be chosen according to the participatory identification of poor.

- Training will be conferred through public–private and public-public partnerships. For example, educational institutions, corporate bodies, bodies that train and place for enhanced public service delivery, commercial and not profit training suppliers will be roped in. Four training prototypes with duration ranging from 3 months to 1 year shall be adopted to meet the different needs of youth relying on their entry level capabilities.

Success of A.P. Model in containing Naxalism

The feat of Andhra Pradesh in containing the naxalite issue cannot simply be ascribed to the military one-upmanship the police gained over the Maoists, but to a comprehensive policy covering military strategies upheld by an effective surrender and restoration package, brought into force almost seven years back.

This feat of Andhra Pradesh in counter-insurgency war is sought to be repeated in the naxalite-impacted states in view of the policy on naxalite crusade disclosed by the central government recently. However, simply the repetition of this policy alone might not produce any outcome, as the field level circumstance must be brought under manageable levels, as Andhra Pradesh learnt it through uphill battle.

Before the end of 1990, naxalism had moved into a `strategic hostile' stage in North Telangana, while it was in the `equilibrium' stage in the remaining of the state. The setbacks to security forces were increasing step by step and the state was absolutely reliant on Central Para Military Forces (CPMF), as is the case in Chhattisgarh these days.

It was at this stage; Andhra Pradesh had reclassified the counter techniques. To begin with, the Government needed to reassert its control over territories, which had turned strongholds of Naxalites. A sophisticated intelligence network was the foundation of the counter-insurgency operations.

The methodology of assigning the security of police stations to CPMF and APSP contingents proved to be really effective. The Naxal assaults on police stations were repelled and this enhanced the morale of police forces. At the same time, police were steadily taking control over the affected areas. As the authority of the State was being restated and the police savagely hunted down the naxal dalams, a surrender and rehabilitation policy was devised by the government.

Military Principle

This strategy was grounded on the military principle that if the enemy is encircled from all four sides, his fighting spirit doubles, as there would be no possibility of an escape. But if a side is purposely left open, the fighting capacities would reduce significantly, since his brain would be occupied in discovering the probabilities of an escape.

The viability of this exemplary military principle was proved absolutely certain when Andhra Police progressively gained an upper hand over the naxalites due to this powerful grouping of military as well as surrender strategies. Around 1,848 naxalites (dalam members and above) abandoned their ideology and lay down their arms before the police since 2003.

Aapki Sarkar Aapke Dwar (Aasdwar) Project in Jehanabad District

Aapki Sarkar Aapke Dwar—a spearheading plan with the objective of eliminating Naxal influences through development activities—has appeared as one of the most effective programmes of the state government in Jehanabad district.

Envisaged by the then home secretary H C Sirohy and initiated by the Chief Minister Nitish Kumar at Sikariya village on 21 January 2006, Aapki Sarkar Aapke Dwar (Asdwar) programme has cut down significantly instances of naxalite violence in the area and also won recognition among rural folk, police, academics and social establishments. This is something which is an enormous accomplishment considering that several such projects initiated in the district in the past like the Operation Rakshak and Operation Siddhartha were virtual non-events.

The effectiveness of the programme—both in winning basic praise at different local and state-level platforms and producing exceptional outcomes at the base level lies in its combined development methodology and genuine endeavours of the district administration to preserve the programme despite all odds.

The plan is presently in progress in five naxalite-influenced panchayats of the district, namely Sikariya, Sewanan, Mandebigha, Surungpur—Bhawanichak and Jamuk, all in Jehanabad Sadar block. All villages under these five panchayats have been undergoing a spurt of developmental exercises on a war footing. The state government has launched a liberal package of Welfare programmes under Aasdwar including construction of cement concrete pavements, drains, chaupals and link rods in these panchayats amounting to more than ₹ 29 crores. Construction of buildings for schools and anganwadi centres, culverts and individual toilets are the other works included under the programme.

The general population everywhere appear to have embraced the state's Aasdwar programme in a big way. What is most uncommon is that the administration authorities now move around openly in these rural areas where once every government programme was boycotted by the villagers under intimidations from the banned Naxalite organization, the people's war group (PWG). There was a period specifically during the turbulent 1980s when there was no immediate contact between the government and the general population for quite a long time.

Local people united with the Naxalites in the anticipation that it would reduce deprivation. However, with the changing times, the people appears to have understood that the Aasdwar programme provides all that the naxalites had guaranteed: an end to deprivation , homestead land, drinking water and self-employment opportunities.

Once a feared and unapproachable place, Sikariya is now a place of numerous economic activities—poultry and dairy cultivating, horticulture, bindi and toy-making which brings substantial monthly income to the locals. Moreover, coordinated endeavours are being made by the district rural development organization to train men and women associated with the underprivileged section and encourage entrepreneurship among them.

In the beginning, a minimum of 100 women from the most economically regressive families of Sikariya panchayat have established three self-help groups (SHGs) to increase their income. In the initial stage, 30 women have been provided training in bindi making. The district management is extending financial and marketing assistance to encourage different financial exercises among these ladies.

Nevertheless, this development has not been achieved without a tough opposition from the naxalites. Even in the present situation, the naxalites try to cause disruption to the plan of development initiative taken in the area. But on the account of the exceptional display of unity among the local people for the Aasdwar programme, the naxalites have been left with no choice but to give in to the popular public wish.

❑❑❑

Chapter five

Challenges Posed by the Northeast Insurgency

Introduction

The Ministry of Home affairs established the North East Division to focus on the developmental and security aspects in relation to North Eastern Region in India

Dissimilar to other parts of the nation, the North East holds a significant place from a tactical viewpoint as these states share their boundaries with different nations like Bangladesh, Bhutan, Myanmar and China. The landscape, the state of socioeconomic development and historical factors, for example, dialect/ethnicity, tribal contention, migration, control over local resources and a pervasive feeling of exploitation and estrangement have brought about a delicate security scenario in the North Eastern States. This has given rise to violence and various demands raised by different Indian Insurgent Groups (IIGs).

Northeast India and its History of Oppression

- Northeast India encompasses eight small states (Arunachal Pradesh, Assam, Manipur, Meghalaya, Mizoram, Nagaland, Sikkim and Tripura) in the northeast region of the nation and is specifically well regarded for its primal greenery and diverse tribal cultures, frequently of a historically egalitarian nature. The area itself is tiny, small, comprising scarcely 7.5% of India's landmass and 3.5% of India's populace, but extremely diverse, and home to more than 70 noteworthy communities speaking almost 400 distinct dialects and lingos. Most aboriginal people of the territory have strong cultural and social resemblances with the people of East and Southeast Asia. The term 'Northeast India' itself to a great deal is a post-colonial concept, emerging only after India gained independence in 1947, and the region has undergone suffering for a long period under extremely repressive Indian state administration as well as spatial favouritism in comparison to the rest of India.
- While the region is area is amazingly rich with regard to mineral and natural reserves, including tea, oil, limestone, coal as well as bamboo for papermaking, quite a bit of this has been seized by national and private capital with no advantage to the local population. Development in the territory is frequently never given the priority it merits and the Indian government keeps up an extremely repressive hold over the entire territory. In reality, while the education levels and other

human development indices are keeping pace with the much better developed South Indian states, economic development levels decline at levels identical to poorer Central and North Indian states. The hegemonic treatment administered to the region has brought about various armed nationalist and sub-nationalist extremist movements, resulting in numerous contentions with the Indian state apart from deadly combats with each other. This has brought about severe material conditions for the general population, including human rights abuses, uncertain livelihood, tough working conditions as well as taking advantage of the conflict by capital. Assam (which then included present-day Nagaland, Mizoram and Meghalaya) gradually discovered its place in the provincial state from the 1820s onwards, with the British usurping the region because of it's potential in producing tea and breaking Chinese control on the trade (in fact, Assam is presently the largest tea-producing zone in the world).

- While Arunachal Pradesh and Sikkim weren't a part of British colonial India, Tripura and Manipur were princely states inside the region, but of barely any political importance. However, what happened under the British was an effectual cut off of the area from its customary trading accomplices, including Burma and different parts of Indo-China, and it was the British who concocted the geographical and political term 'Northeast Frontier' to act as a safeguard between their Indian dominion and what is presently known as Southeast Asia. The area assumed an especially essential part in the triumph of the Allied Forces amid World War II, particularly in the various battle theatres of Indo-China.
- Hence, under British expansionism, Northeast India was, apparently, to a great extent insulated from the rest of colonial India and from their customary Southeast Asian trading accomplices. Thus under British expansionism, Northeast India was, one might say, to a great extent confined from whatever is left of frontier India and from their customary Southeast Asian exchanging accomplices.
- After India gained independence in 1947, the territory in fact ended up becoming landlocked, sharing boundaries with Nepal, Bangladesh, Bhutan, Burma and China, further expanding its detachment and bringing about increased spatial bias at the hands of the newly framed Indian state. It was normal for the various tribes within the territory to consider their own future despite India gaining independence and the gruesome partition of the land. The bias administered by the Indian state also generated massive cultural supremacy, and soon numerous developments, for the most part of a cultural-nationalist nature, originated in order to counter Indian state- domination, in addition to ensuring their own rights towards viable self-resolve. While originally peaceful in the 1940s and 1950s, from the 1960s onwards a lot of these movements soon turned into full-scale armed uprising, the most pronounced ones being ULFA (United Liberation Front of Assam), Manipur Peoples Liberation Army (PLA), NSCN (National Socialist Council of Nagalim) and various others. The territory counts around 30 noteworthy radical outfits along with various smaller ones. This has brought about the longstanding, huge and amazingly repressive presence of the Indian military, for the sake of curbing various armed nationalist movements either battling for freedom or more noteworthy self-rule. The historical backdrop of Indian authority in the course of the last 50 years or so in the

territory might not be one of the classical occupation in contrast to say, the Israeli control of Palestine, yet the impacts towards the general population and also misuse of the circumstance by capital and the following arm-twisting of neighbouring nations remains the same. A concise examination of each of these aftermaths is done below.

The Terrorists Operating in India's Seven Northeastern States

- India's northeast has the questionable peculiarity of being home to Asia's longest running extremism. The Nagas under the leadership of A Z Phizo initiated rebellion against the recently framed Indian nation way back in 1956. Since then the Naga uprising has brought forth many comparable dissents over the area that still stays on the fringe of national awareness.
- Each of the seven states in the area presently has some revolt or the other keeping the state occupied, frequently leading and setting the agenda in the particular land territory. Over the most recent decade, no less than 11,000 individuals, including security forces, civilians and militants, have been slain in uprising-related viciousness in the four major states of Assam, Manipur, Nagaland and Tripura.
- Most of these rebellion groups were shaped in the 1980s or early 1990s but each of them is an outcome of prior endeavours to defy the Indian State.
- Except the Naga uprising, the vast majority of the outfits in the northeast have been conceived out of disregard heaped upon by government on these isolated states since Independence. There are other people who view these revolts as only money-making enterprises.

Assam

- In 2003, more than 400 individuals were slaughtered in militant brutality. A large number of militants, around 208 in numbers, were slain while 103 civilians died during the same period. These figures are pretty much with regards to the pattern in 2002 when 445 individuals including 275 militants lost their lives in Assam.
- The United Liberation Front of Asom, formed in 1979, turned into a formidable force to take into account in the late 1980s. It for all intents and purposes ran a parallel government in the state between 1988 and 1990 till the central government decided to clamp down the militants by ordering full-fledged army action.
- The Army pursued Operation Bajrang followed by Operation Rhino. After more than 10 years of initiating these two military operations, ULFA remains active in spite of a split in its ranks and surrender of an extensive number of its units throughout the years.
- The National Democratic Front of Bodoland (NDFB) was constituted by a group of extremist Bodo youth on 3 October 1986 who, similar to their counterparts in ULFA, trust their nationalities can thrive only when outside the Indian State.
- The NDFB is operational in Assam's Bodo-dominated zones adjoining West Bengal and Bhutan. By detonating bombs across the state and in Nagaland, both ULFA and NDFB are bent on proving that they are still a power to figure with in spite of having been expelled from Bhutan last December.
- A minimum of two divisions of the armed force constituting of 20,000 troops and over 10,000 paramilitary personnel in addition to 50,000-odd Assam policemen remain occupied in fighting with ULFA, and to a lesser degree NDFB.

Manipur

- At present, Manipur presents an awful case scenario in the northeast in terms of insurgency. Aside from the reality that there are more radical factions in the state operating in comparison to any other state—no less than seven notorious groups are functional in Manipur—the contentions between these outfits frequently prompts large-scale savagery. Kidnappings and murders are normal in Manipur.
- What concerns the security forces is the parallel government running under militant factions. These extremists extract cash or impose 'taxes' on individuals, government officials and businessmen.
- To operate in the region, the transporters need to pay no less than three prominent militant groups . These groups deliver quick justice, offer protection and command certain zones with impunity. Some of the extremist groups like the Kanglei Yaol Kanba Lup (KYKL) are endeavouring to 'cleanse' Manipuri society by initiating high-profile drives against drug traders, corrupt government authorities and issuing decrees to 'preserve' Manipuri culture.

Nagaland

- Known as the state with the longstanding insurgency in operation, Nagaland gives off an impression of being as normal as any other Indian state in the wake of the ceasefire between the Isak-Muivah groups of the National Socialist Council of Nagaland (NSCN-IM). However, factional combats between the IM group and its rival the S Khaplang-led NSCN (K) has governed the scene in the course of past few years.
- The NSCN (Isiac-Muviah) is viewed as a guide to many factions in the northeast since it helped create these outfits, encouraged and armed them throughout the years. In any case, it has caused strains in the northeast by claiming a 'greater Nagaland' by unifying Naga-inhabited regions spread over different states like Manipur, Assam and Arunachal Pradesh.

Tripura

- Tripura is another leading violence-prone state that has been devastated by murders and kidnappings over the previous decade. Two key radical groups, the National Liberation Front of Tripura and All Tripura Tigers Force have been on the frenzy, slaying and kidnapping individuals with impunity.
- Tripura, which was a princely state prior to independence, has seen a constant decrease in its indigenous population causing the rise in militant activities among the tribals. Tripura has about 10 lakh indigenous tribals who live in miserable conditions in the hilly and often inaccessible terrains of the state.
- The two barred radical factions—the ATTF and the NLFT—have foundations in Bangladesh across the porous international border.

Other States

- Another state in the northeast with insurgency problem is Meghalaya, which has two active insurgent groups. Arunachal Pradesh and Mizoram are comparatively free of militancy but security experts caution that trouble is brewing in Arunachal Pradesh where the NSCN (IM) is making advances in some districts.
- Mizoram is possibly the lone state in the zone which can claim to have deserted insurrection. In fact, the Mizo National Front, which was underground for a long time, signed a benchmark deal in 1986, came over ground and currently runs the state government.

The key militant factions in the northeast which have been proclaimed as 'unlawful organizations' under the Unlawful Activities (Prevention) Act, 1967 include:

Assam

- The United Liberation Front of Asom
- The National Democratic Front of Bodoland

Manipur

- The People's Liberation Army
- The United National Liberation Front
- The People's Revolutionary Party of Kangleipak
- The Kangleipak Communist Party
- The Kanglei Yaol Kanba Lup
- The Manipur People's Liberation Front
- The Revolutionary People's Front

Meghalaya

- The Hynniewtrep National Liberation Council
- The Achik National Volunteer Council

Nagaland

- The National Socialist Council of Nagaland including all factions

Tripura

- The All Tripura Tiger Force
- The National Liberation Front of Tripura

Major Initiatives/Achievements

On 24 March 2012, a three-party deal was signed by the Government of India, Government of Manipur and the United Tribal Liberation Army (UTLA) and Pakan Reunification Army (PRA) under the ambit of Kuki National Organization (KNO). Guidelines for Suspension of Operation (SoO) were set up.

Home Secretary held a summit meeting on 9 April 2012 for chalking out future methodology for fighting militancy in the states of Manipur, Arunachal Pradesh and Nagaland.

Union Home Secretary analysed the execution of Bodo Accord in a meeting held on 18 April 2012 with the chief executive member and members of Bodo Territorial Council (BTC).

Unlawful Activity (Prevention) Tribunal in the matter of NLFT and ATTF of Tripura has affirmed the continuance of ban on NLFT and ATTF under Unlawful Activities (Prevention) Act, 1967 for two years with effective from 3 October 2011. On 30 April 2012, 103 classified UGs of different groups along with their armaments surrendered before the Chief Minister of Manipur in the presence of the State Home Minister, State Chief Secretary, the Director General of Police, Joint Secretary (NE) MHA and Assam Rifles officials at the IGAR (South) headquarter.

Brief of Schemes Administered by NE Division

- ***Reimbursement of security related expenditure (SRE):*** The Central Government is executing a Non-Plan scheme for repayment of Security-related expenditure (SRE) for the states genuinely impacted by militancy/ insurrection. The scheme is being actualized in all States of the territory excluding Mizoram and Sikkim. Under it, the consumption incurred by them on different things, including setting up India Reserve Battalions, logistics provided to the CPFs/Army deployed in the state, ex-gratia grant and complimentary respite to the victims of radical violence, 75% of the expenses incurred on POL (petrol, oil and lubricants) in operations and honorarium, wages for village guards/village defense committees/ home guards deployed for security purposes, expenses incurred on upkeep of assigned camps established for groups with whom the Central Government/State Governments have become legally committed to agreement for suspension of operations, is being repaid.

- *Modernization of state police force (MPF):* The Ministry of Home Affairs is likewise helping the state governments for transformation of state police forces. This non-plan scheme provides assistance, among other things, for obtaining contemporary equipment for surveillance, communications, forensic science laboratories, etc., weaponry, vehicles, computerization, training infrastructure and for building of police infrastructure viz., housing/police stations/outposts/barracks, etc. Under the plan of MPF, all the north eastern states are entitled to receive 100% central aid of their endorsed annual scheme for transformation of Police force.
- *Civic Action Programme in North Eastern States:* Since some of the North Eastern States are impacted by insurrection and militancy, there is a continual requirement to deploy army and other central paramilitary Forces in the territory to battle insurrection. With the intention of taking the local population in confidence and uplift the reputation of armed forces among the common masses, army and central paramilitary forces organize civic action programme. Under this Programme, different welfare/developmental exercises are attempted like conducting medical camps, sanitation drives, sports meets, allocation of study material to kids, minor maintenances of school buildings, roads, bridges, etc. and operating adult education centres, etc.
- *Repatriation of Bru Migrants from Tripura to Mizoram:* A large number of Bru (Reang) families from Western Mizoram migrated to Northern Tripura from October 1997 onwards because of assault on minority Reang tribes by Mizo villagers. About 30,000 of such Bru migrants consisting of 5000 families are sheltered in six relief camps established in Kanchanpur District of Tripura.

  The Governments of Mizoram and Tripura have been receiving grants-in-aid from the Ministry of Home Affairs, respectively, for rehabilitation/resettlement of Brus and for maintenance of Brus lodged in different relief camps. Financial aids of ₹ 9.96 crore and ₹ 7.86 crore were released in the year 2011–2012 and 2012–2013, respectively, to the Government of Mizoram for rehabilitation of Bru families. Further, financial aids of ₹ 29.35 crore and ₹ 6 crore, up to 31 December 2012, was issued in 2011–2012 and 2012–2013, respectively, to Government of Tripura for maintenance of Brus accommodated in different relief camps of Tripura.
- *Helicopter Service in the North Eastern States:* With the intention of providing connectivity to distant territories as additionally to provide air connectivity to the north eastern regions with rest of India, helicopter services are functioning in the six states of Arunachal Pradesh, Meghalaya, Nagaland, Sikkim Tripura and Mizoram under non-plan scheme with grant from the Ministry of Home Affairs. The grant is restricted to 75% if operational cost subsequent to varying recovery from travellers. With the intention of limiting subsidy, yearly ceiling of flying hours for each helicopter has been predetermined. The competent authority has approved the launch of helicopter services as per the details provided further.

  The State Governments are allowed to launch helicopter services beyond the ceiling of flying hours. Nevertheless, the subsidy is limited to flying hours ceiling pre-determined for each sort of helicopter being in operation in these States. Subsequent to adjusting grant from the

Ministry of Home Affairs, the remaining cost of operating helicopter services is borne by the concerned state governments.

- *Advertisement and publicity:* Keeping in view the specific issues of the North East, namely, militancy, infiltration, and perceived feeling of estrangement, Ministry of Home Affairs executes a plan scheme of advertisement and publicity in North Eastern states with a view to put emphasis on the activities being attempted by the government for peace in the territory and furthermore with a view to communicate that 'Peace pays'. Taking into account these objectives, a monthly North East Newsletter featuring the government plans and various developmental endeavours in the North East is published by NE Division in English, Assamese, Manipuri and Bengali languages. Under this plan, several other schemes are likewise taken including the visits of young people of NE States to rest of India and vice versa under the patronage of NYKS, journalist visits to NE States, broadcast of radio jingles and so forth.

Key Factors of Various Conflicts and Insurgencies

- *Political Mobilization by Insurgents:* Most extremist factions in North East earn popular support for their vicious activities alluding to social/ political motives that are crucial to the population being referred to. The political mobilization is thought to be the main indispensable stage of any armed revolution. Furthermore, any uprising is difficult to be pulverized once it is effective in securing the popular social support. The radical factions build a social imaginary in view of genuine or perceived political or ethnic or cultural oppression by other communities. By doing so, they justify the requirement for vicious proclamation of their worries. The radical spearheads likewise exhibit their armed cadres, weapons and financial power in the impacted territories which draws in the jobless youth to join them. The most basic principle of such political mobilization would be that the state management has failed in delivering the essential services to the populace and decent substitutive livelihoods to the youths.
  - ❖ The motivation for political mobilization for NSCN (IM) is the Naga territorial unification and autonomy in view of its own description of independence of Nagas prior to the subjugation of the Naga Territories by the British.
  - ❖ Likewise, ULFA claims mistreatment of Assamese by the colonial rule of New Delhi and mentions that Assamese will get due acknowledgement only when Assam turns into an independent Swadhin Asom. However, very few people agree to this idea in Assam.

In the same way, in Manipur, the dispute that caused political mobilization was the contention that the accession of Manipur in Union of India was a enforced merger by India on a gunpoint, and Manipur was to be an autonomous state after British left India.

Each of the extremist factions asserts that once they get independence from India, they would enhance the general monetary and social states of their target populaces. In light of these political accounts, young people from these territories are motivated to join the armed uprisings.

Without a doubt, a large part of the rural India experiences economic backwardness. This issue is more evident in the North East and LWE-influenced zones that are continuously susceptible to violence. In North East, the backwardness combined with absence of infrastructure makes the states profoundly reliant on centre for their political survival.

- *Porous International Border and Availability of Arms:* The international boundary of India, which is 4,500-kilometre-long, in this territory is porous and has led to easy flow of arms, unlawful immigration and drugs to India. The porous boundary makes it easy for the insurgents to flee to neighbouring nations such as Bhutan, Myanmar and Bangladesh and also set up their underground guerrilla bases. Furthermore, the youth of north east is defenseless against drug addiction because of the thriving drug trade in the alleged Golden Triangle. Certain radical factions such as UNLF, NSCN (IM) and NSCN (K) have been observed to be engaged in drug trade along with the Karens and the Kachins in Myanmar.

  Along these lines, the feasibility factor in north east enables the guerillas to utilize vicious means for political ends. The feasibility hypothesis states that where uprising is substantially reasonable, it will happen. The trouble-free accessibility of arms to insurgents empowers them to support their movements. All the foremost guerrilla units in North East possess AK series of rifles, advanced assault rifles and other weapons and explosives.

- *Tough Geography:* North East India is joined to the Indian terrain by a constricted stretch of land termed Siliguri Corridor. The topographical fragmentation, isolation and the issues in relation to being considered as exterior to India's vision of itself are leading drivers of estrangement in the Northeast.

  Topography and landscape of north east has turned out to be crucial for continuance of extremist drives. Without supportive territory, lightly equipped, highly mobile extremist units cannot support the superiority of the Indian Army. The Northeast region is hilly and difficult to access in view of non-stop rain during the months of April to July, an extremist group once settled, takes a long time to be identified and countered by the state. The known territory enables the radical groups to surprise the Military by strategies of guerrilla combat, inflict casualty and run. The NSCN (IM) operates in the hilly terrain of Manipur and Arunachal Pradesh. They also utilize the hill tracts of Nagaland crossing over into the hilly terrain of Myanmar. The landscape is thickly forested and climate conditions are extreme. In the same manner, the ULFA exploits the less connectivity of districts and thickly forested regions in the Assam-Arunachal Pradesh-Bhutan border.

- *Issue of Governance & AFSPA:* Few of the previous and contemporary policies and issues in regard to governance have also played a part in the worsening of the conflicting scenario in North East India. The seven sisters in addition to Sikkim are inhabited by nearly 40 million people who differ in dialect, race, tribe, caste, religion, and regional legacy. When all of them are grouped under the 'North East' tag, it is likely to portray a 'one shoe fits all' method for this tremendously diverse region. The creation of sixth schedule has originally created several authorities of centre, furthermore an ever increasing number of areas are requesting such autonomous council. This indicates that somewhere the government policy has failed to introduce an authentic process of democratization or autonomy in the territory.

The absence of suitable political actions is also revealed in the imposition of AFSPA (Armed Forces Special Power Act). This act was passed on 18 August 1958, as a transient measure to permit deployment of the armed force to counter an armed secessionist drive the Naga Hills. Presently this act is set up throughout the past five decades and was extended to all the seven states of the Northeast territory in 1972, excluding Mizoram. AFSPA was a chunk of the package of provisions, passed by the central government, to keep hold of control over the Naga regions. Throughout the years, AFSPA has turned into a forceful measure for the central and the state government to act against factors testing the political and territorial integrity of India. It was this act by means of which the Indian armed force was for the first time after independence stationed for an internal dispute.

The significant issues with AFSPA are explained as follows:

1. This act has raised the contention by expediting it on a military level.
2. There are consistent accusations of infringement of human rights by the Indian Amy.
3. AFSPA is inclined to generate lack of concern to Indian armed forces' activities in north east. The followers of a political arrangement have likewise turned away. One of the investigative commissions in 2004 stated that AFSPA has turned into a symbol of tyranny, an object of detestation and an instrument of discernment and arrogance.

Other Factors

- *Ethnic/Factional Violence:* Savagery is rampant in the Northeast, despite the fact that in some states such as Tripura, Meghalaya and Mizoram, it has been dealt with more efficiently. The overwhelming presence of Indian armed force likewise makes them susceptible to future savagery. All north eastern states excluding the Arunachal Pradesh have been dealt with ethnic brutality at one time of another in recent history.
- *Cultural Differences:* The clans of the Northeast are for the most part of Mongoloid stock and they see themselves as unique in relation to the Aryan and Dravidian races of India.
- *Pressure on Land:* This is a blend of different factors, for example, expanding populace, absence of state land reforms, oral conventions of land possession, jhum cultivation, migrant populace, rigorous cultivation, etc. State has not been able to effectively settle these land-related instabilities. In this manner, pressure on land has led to tribal and ethnic 'security dilemmas' in the North East India.
- *Ethnic Security Dilemmas:* North East India is inhabited by multi-ethnic and multi-tribal groups. Dispute emerges when one ethnic group shelters armed members and other group harbours rival arming.
- *Political Corruption:* The political ethnicity of most north east states is loaded with debasement, absence of representation in power hierarchy at the centre, and connection between politicians and rebel groups. The outcome of this is an apprehensive state structure and apprehensive public. Moreover, some of the legislations such as Inner Line Permit and Restricted Area Permit hinder intrusion of outsiders into the territory. The aftereffect of such laws is a 'siege mentality' among the general population. Furthermore, the extortion systems are being operated by the radical factions whereby, each individual needs to pay some part of his/her salary to guerillas.
- *Low quality of Education:* The literacy rate in the states of North East India is quite high. However, the quality of education is inadequate resulting in scarcity of well-qualified individuals to run the issues of these hill states.
- *Transportation and Communication Problems:* The transportation and communication network in North East

is underdeveloped with broken national highways that require repair. The region becomes inaccessible in the monsoon season.

- *Perceived Feelings of Neglect:* The general population of North East India have an apparent feeling of disregard by New Delhi because of their bordering location and cultural dissimilarities.

Bodoland Issue

- The northernmost territory of Assam, which is located on the northern bank of Brahmaputra River, bordering the foothills of Bhutan and Arunachal Pradesh is primarily inhabited by the Bodo individuals and works as the entrance to the entire North Eastern region of India. The individuals of this territory believe that their desires have not been met as far as growth and development are concerned and, subsequently, have been raising demand for a different state of Bodoland, within the Indian Union, to be created by carving out some zone of eight districts, namely, Kokrajhar, Dhubri, Bongaigaon, Barpeta, Nalbari, Kamrup, Darang and Sonitpur of the present State of Assam.
- The Bodos are an ethnic and linguistic society inhabiting the Udalguri and Kokrajhar district of Assam. Among the 18 ethnic sub-groups within the Bodo-Kachari district, they are the largest group.
- The demand for an independent terrain for Bodos has its foundations as back as 1930s when Gurudev Kalicharan Brahma, the then solitary leader of the Bodos presented memorandum to Simon Commission raising demand for a different political establishment for the indigenous and tribal population of Assam. Neither the British India nor the independent India accepted this demand. Another influx of demands arose in 1960s and subsequently in 1980s. The All Bodo Students Union (ABSU) under the leadership of Upendranath Brahma raised demand for Bodoland on 2 March 1987. Bodo Peoples' Action Committee (BPAC), the political wing of the ABSU, was engaged in the movement with an objective to get Assam divided equally between Bodoland and Assam.
- The campaign became fierce and in 1993, the Assam Government became legally committed to a bipartite Bodo agreement with ABSU to form a Bodoland Autonomous Council (BAC) to realize socio-economic objectives of the Bodos. This experimentation turned out unsuccessful due to non-implementation of different conditions of the Accord. It failed within a year. The statehood request was again restored by ABSU in 1996.
- The NDA Government in 2003 signed a second tripartite Bodo Accord with the Assam Government and the Bodo Liberation Tiger (BLT), a militant outfit. By means of this, the Bodos were accorded the Bodoland Territorial Council (BTC), within the State of Assam and offered constitutional security under Sixth Schedule to the said Autonomous organization. The aim of BTC was to satisfy economic, educational and linguistic objectives and the protection of land-rights, socio-cultural and ethnic individuality of the Bodos; and accelerate the infrastructure development in BTC territory. The districts of Kokrajhar, Chirang, Udalguri and Baksa lie under the BTC administrative zone. As per this agreement, the BLT was obliged to surrender all their arms and transformed into Bodoland People's Front (BPF), a political party now ruling the Council.

However, the democratic and unarmed factions of the Bodo groups—the ABSU and the former Coordination Committee for the Bodoland Movement (CCBM) were ignored at the time of signing of the second Bodo treaty despite the fact that they had more public support than the former BLT. Nevertheless, they supported the peace agreement, and this permitted the leaders of the former BLT to hold sway in the constitution of the BTC under the amended provisions of the Sixth Schedule. The Bodoland Territorial Council (BTC) is authorized with legislative, administrative, executive and financial powers over 40 policy zones in the Bodoland Territorial Areas Districts (BTADs) encompassing four districts of Assam.

There are two more organizations active in Bodoland as follows:

- ***National Democratic Front of Bodoland:*** The NDFB, initially known as the Bodo Security Force (BdSF), was established on October 3, 1986. Its specified goal is the fulfilment of a sovereign Bodoland. This was a militant organization involved in several blasts in the zone. Its founder president was Ranjan Daimary, who was handed over by Bangladesh to India in 2010. He was arrested and confined in jail for a certain period and was granted bail in June 2013. This organization had splitted into two factions, namely, NDFB (Progressive) and NDFB (Ranjan Daimary) in 2009.
- ***Bodo National Conference:*** On 19 November 2010, a new umbrella body of the Bodos, called the Bodo National Conference (BNC), was founded at a two-day Bodo National Convention in Kokrajhar. The objective of setting up this body was to provide a general platform for all Bodo organizations – political and non-political – to fight for their common causes and raising the demand for an independent State of Bodoland.

Bodo Territorial Council Act-2003

- Ultimately, a series of rounds of purposeful and meaningful dialogues led the militant groups to surrender with their arms and sign an accord with the government called the Bodo Accord-2003.
- According to the provisions under this agreement, a Bodo Territorial Council (BTC) was set up and the Bodo Territorial Areas Districts (BTAD) was formed under the Sixth Schedule of the Constitution of India.
- The objective behind creating BTAD was to shield the interests of Bodo public and guarantee their proper representation in socio-political decision-making processes in the area.
- The BTAD includes districts of Kokrajhar, Baska, Chirang and Udalguri comprising 35% area of Assam.

Reasons for Frequent Clashes and Riots

- The Bodo Accord looks to secure the privileges of indigenous Bodo individuals, yet in the meantime permits Muslim settlers (both legitimate and illegal) and non-Bodo tribes to openly gain land in the BTAD.
- Bangladeshi illegitimate immigrants have been acquiring documents, like ration cards unlawfully to establish their nationality and purchasing land in the area.
- Non-Bodos and Muslims are of the opinion that Bodos comprising only one-fourth of the total population, should not be authorized to govern and influence three-fourth of the population in the BTAD.
- On the contrary, the Bodos believe that they are the largest tribal community out of the 34 other tribal communities of Assam and, therefore, cannot be ignored, abused and oppressed.
- Several villages with Bodo minority have been incorporated in the BTAD to conserve an adjoining area, that has caused conflict

and the non-Bodos want these to be expelled from the BTAD. Thus, both Bodos and non-Bodos are raising demands to reconsider the Bodo Territorial Council Act-2003. The Bodos believe that their privileges are not being ensured and they might be reduced to a minority in their own motherland. The non-Bodos believe that the Bodos are being given more advantage than they should get.

- The demand for an independent state of Bodoland got reinforced and made stronger again after Telangana was separated from Andhra Pradesh.
- There is a group of Bodo society that is raising demand to get independence from the union of India and form an independent Bodoland. They have an activist group called the National Democratic Front of Bodoland (NDFB).

  NDFB is a secessionist faction that wants freedom and has been accountable for extensive slaying of non-Bodos in the area to generate fear psychosis in the brains of immigrants from outside the state. This militant organization does not believe in peace dialogues with the government.

Therefore, the Bodoland issue has the following major aspects:

- Irreconcilable situation between Bodos and non-Bodos, predominantly Muslims and illegal immigrants.
- Demarcation of the boundary of the Bodo Territorial Areas Districts, as it incorporates territories with Bodo minority that the non-Bodos are protesting.
- Demand for an independent state of Bodoland.
- Demand for freedom from the Union of India to carve out an independent Bodoland.

The Karbi Anglong Issue

- Amongst the 27 administrative districts of Assam, the Karbi Anglong District is the largest. It is located in the central part of the state. In the east, it is surrounded by Golaghat district, in the west by Meghalaya and Morigaon district, in the north by Nagaon and Golaghat district and in the south by N.C. Hills district and Nagaland.
- The villages populated by the Rengma Naga community came under brutal assault. The Karbi People's Liberation Tigers (KPLT) had asked all Rengma Naga individuals to leave the area, but the Rengma Naga refused to move. This incited the militants to attack their villages, slaughter individuals and set houses and granaries ablaze. The KPLT is a separated group of the ethnic extremist Karbi Longri N.C. Hills Liberation Front (KLNLF). The KLNLF is raising demands for a separate State comprising two hill districts—Kabri Anglong and Dima Hasao—and is presently involved in dialogues with the Centre and the State government. After the KLNLF signed the Suspension of Operation accord with the Centre and the Assam government, about 20 cadres of the organization separated and formed the KPLT in 2010. The KPLT has been raising demands for the creation of a Hemprek Kanthim (self-ruled homeland) for the Karbi people. The KLNLF was a breakaway group of the former extremist organization United People's Democratic Solidarity.
- The RNHPF was established in 2012 for the security of the Rengma Nagas from KPLT attacks. The organization has been raising demand for the creation of a regional council for the Rengma Nagas of Karbi Anglong.

The Armed Forces (Special Powers) Act (AFSPA)

Background

On 11 September 1958, the parliament passed the Armed Forces (Special Powers) Act to tackle the northeast issue. It conferred exceptional powers upon the army in troubled zones in the states of Arunachal Pradesh, Assam, Manipur, Meghalaya, Mizoram, Nagaland, and Tripura. The act was initiated in Jammu and Kashmir in 1990 and since 2007 its abrogation has become a uniting factor for all the secessionist groups as also the conventional parties, including the National Conference and the People's Democratic Party.

AFSPA was established to offer army officers and Jawans lawful protection for their activities in troubled zones. This act safeguards every member of the Indian armed forces against prosecution or trial in any criminal or civil court for any act performed by him or her while carrying out his or her duty in a troubled zone. Furthermore, no court or quasi-judicial body can raise objection against the government's decision to announce any territory a troubled region.

The Provisions of AFSPA are very Objectionable

- All that is important for a region of the State to be handed over to the military is for the Governor or the Central Government to report it to be in a 'disturbed and dangerous' situation.
- Even a non-commissioned officer of the military is given the authority, on the mere suspicion of breach of the law or commission of an unlawful activity, to fire upon or else utilize force, even to the resulting of death, against any individual. He can likewise even without having any warrant, arrest any individual and enter and search any premises.
- No trial of anyone indulging in contending to act under AFSPA is likely except with the prior approval of the Government.
- The first inquiry it brings up is: 'Who rules India: The elected representatives or the army?' Another inquiry is 'Why does the army oppose even dilution of the Act to make it more human?' The Justice Verma Commission has reported in clear terms that if a security person rapes a lady, he should be judged under the same act that is applicable to the citizens. Other commissions has also taken a similar stand. In 2005, the Jeevan Reddy Commission asked for the repealing of AFSPA and advocated for including the mandatory clauses in other Acts. Mr. R. N. Ravi, former head of the Intelligence Bureau for the North East, is also of the opinion that AFSPA is the biggest hindrance to harmony in the area. Former Home Secretary Mr. G. K. Pillai has turned out straightforwardly against the Act. These reports are not emotional upheavals. They are issued by people who have acted in the system and are aware of the dynamics of the Act and of administrating the government.
- But the armed force is resisting even this change. What is their basis for suspecting that security people who rape innocent ladies should revel in exemption for the sake of national security? For whose security was the law endorsed, for that of the nation or of the culprits in uniform? At whatever point some change is proposed in the Act, the armed force appears to restrict it and the civilian government caves in under its pressure. For instance, when the Jeevan Commission appointed to investigate into the so-called rape and murder of 30-year old Manorama Devi of Imphal in Manipur detained by the Assam Rifles proposed that the law should be revoked and the clauses that are required should be

incorporated with other All India laws, the government avoided even the publishing of the report. The Hindu obtained it 'unlawfully' and uploaded it on its website. After a report issued by the Verma Commission favoured holding trial for security persons convicted of raping a woman under the civilian law, the Union Law Minister said in an interview on NDTV that there are issues in executing these suggestions. In the course of a TV discussion, another Union minister said that on account of its slow legal procedure the public does not know the penalty meted out by the army. They did not detail the restrictions or the legal action taken. A pursuit of the records illustrates very few instances of trial not to mention punishment. For instance, in the Manorama Devi case, no move has been made yet on the culprits. On 23 December 2005, a bunch of university students moved into a railway compartment at Kokrajhar in Assam, not realizing that armed security persons from Haryana were also the passengers in it. The jawans shut the gates of the compartment and tried to molest the students. Alarmed by their yelling, the Bodo student union halted the train and attempted to take action on the jawans. The police launched fire on them that resulted in casualty of four students. Till today, the culprits have not been booked.

- Many similar instances could be given that have gone unreported or have been suppressed. In a fresh case in Assam, the local individuals caught the jawan, so the army assured prosecution against him. He was imprisoned for three months. Individuals in Jammu and Kashmir talk about several women who have been disregarded yet the military have gone unpunished. Thus, the ladies live with a feeling of disgrace. Some of them affirmed before the Verma Commission and its suggestion comes from their declaration. One is additionally informed that the honour of the armed force is involved and national security requires the law. How does absence of action against rape safeguards the reputation of the army? One can cast doubt on AFSPA even from the security perspective. It was passed in 1958 on a trial basis for six months as a step taken against 'terrorist' groups in the North East. It was put into operation first in Nagaland, in 1980 in Manipur, later in Jammu and Kashmir and over the recent decades expanded to more territories of the North East. What was launched for six months has stayed for over five decades. In 1958, a sole 'terrorist' group was operating in the North East. During the launching of the Act in Manipur, the state had two groups in operations. currently, Manipur has over 20 such organizations, Assam has a minimum number of 15 groups, while Meghalaya has five groups operating, and other States have more groups operating. How does the armed forces clarify this expansion of militant groups notwithstanding the Act? Has it fulfilled its objective?
- One is likewise informed that the armed forces will be unable to sustain in the North East or Jammu and Kashmir in case of repealing the law. This is hard to believe. All over India, the army is positioned without such a law. The individuals requesting its repealing do not ask the army to leave any territory. They merely ask the armed forces to serve the nation under the Constitution without a law that permits exploitation with exemption. There is no motivation why a rapist or murderer should have a different law only because he is from the army. Assume for an instant that all the ladies who they rape are terrorists. On what basis should they be raped? For what reason For what reason they should not be managed under the conventional law? These actions do

not enhance the reputation of the army or the security of India. They just abuse individual's right to live with self-respect and cannot be defended in a democratic nation. Civilians have been nominated to govern the nation. They have an obligation to guarantee that the security forces work under the Constitution. The issues in the North East and in Kashmir should be resolved through a political procedure and not through a law that abuses individuals' entitlement to life and dignity with exemption. They require confidence building measures (CBM) with the intention of moving towards peace with justice.

Sections 3, 4, 6 and 7 of the AFSPA

Critics have frequently bothered at the provisions under Sections 3, 4, 6 and 7 of the AFSPA for being 'draconian.'

- *Section 3:* It sets out the authority which has supremacy to proclaim zones as 'disturbed'. The central and the state governments are these authorities. Hence, the army does not announce the zone as disturbed.
- *Section 4:* It gives the armed force authority to explore premises and make arrests without warrants, to use power even to the degree of causing demise, decimate arms/ammunition dumps, barricades/shelters/hideouts and to stop, search and seize any vehicle.
- *Section 6:* It specifies that arrested individuals and seized property are to be handed over to the police with least possible delay.
- *Section 7:* It provides safety to individuals acting in good faith in their official capacity. Prosecution is allowed only after approval by the central government. These provisions were produced for inspection before a constitution bench of the Supreme Court in a case titled 'Naga People's Movement of Human Rights Vs UOI'. The five-judge bench intricately managed the opposition to the legitimacy of deployment of army in support to civil power. The court had then unequivocally ruled that AFSPA cannot be viewed as a colourable enactment or an extortion on the Constitution.
- It was further stated by the apex court that the conferring of powers vide Section 4 of AFSPA could not be held arbitrary or violative of Article 14, 19 or 21 of the constitution. As a matter of fact, having considered the role and circumstances under which the armed forces have to work, the Supreme Court extended the scope of powers vested vide 4 and 6 of AFSPA in order to incorporate by proposition, the ability to examine the individual arrested.
- It also enabled the military to retain the weapons seized amid the operations in their own custody rather than to hand them over to police specialists.
- The simple fact that the provisions of AFSPA need to be referred in a specific area ex facie establishes that managing the lawfulness situation had gone outside the control of the state government. The army personnel working in those conditions need to appreciate at least comparable powers as the police force if not more extensive ones. Thus, similarly as Section 45 of the CrPC denies arrest of public servants and Section 197 gives exemption against prosecution, Section 7 of the AFSPA gives comparative security to the army personnel, nothing more and nothing less.
- And yet, most adversaries of the AFSPA have decided to either make light of or totally overlook this similarity. On account of J&K, the armed force needs legitimate protection all the more since appropriateness of CrPC is prohibited in the state that works under a different set of laws called the Ranbir Penal Code.

Way Forward

- The renouncement of AFSPA from any zone requires a coordinated perspective of all organs of the state and the Centre. A recommended approach is to change these territories into police regulated zones/police districts as was done for Srinagar primarily without revoking AFSPA. Consequently, as the circumstance improves, while advancing the revocation, an exit policy needs to be worked out for continuous withdrawal of army from the predefined region prompting a smooth transition.
- Lifting the AFSPA can positively be endeavoured yet the provisions of the AFSPA, as an emergency law that authorizes the army—the nation's instrument of final resort—must keep on remaining on the statute books given the progressively violent and indefinite times that the subcontinent is probable to face in coming years.
- When required, it must be employed in small doses. Every nation has to adjust the requirement for a stringent law with the fundamental principles of ensuring human dignity and human rights. Therein lies the test for the national leadership. ❑❑❑

Chapter six

Challenges Posed by Jammu and Kashmir Militancy

Partition and Instrument of Accession of Jammu and Kashmir

The partition of earlier princely province of Kashmir between India and Pakistan since 1947 is to the liking of neither the nations nor the Kashmiris themselves.

Failure to settle on the status of the domain by political courses has resulted in war between India and Pakistan on various occasions, and lighted a revolt that proceeded unabated for decades.

Partition

- When India and Pakistan gained independence from the British administration in 1947, the different princely rulers had the option to join the state of their liking.
- Kashmir under the rule of Maharaja Hari Singh, the Hindu chief of a majority Muslim state sandwiched between the two nations, could not decide which country to join. He endorsed a temporary 'standstill' agreement to continue transport and other services with Pakistan.
- In October 1947, tribals from Pakistan invaded Kashmir, prodded by reports of assaults on Muslims and frustrated by Hari Singh's deferring strategies. The Maharaja sought help from the Indian military.
- India's Governor-General, Lord Mountbatten, was of the opinion that peace would best be restored by Kashmir's joining India on a provisional basis, pending a vote on its decisive status. The Instrument of Accession was signed by Hari Singh that month, surrendering control over foreign and defence policy to India.
- Indian armed forces seized two-thirds of the region, and Pakistan took hold of the northern remainder. China seized eastern regions of the state in the 1950s.

Dispute

- The main source of contention between both India and Pakistan is the quarrel over what came first, whether the Instrument of Accession or the entry of Indian troops. India asserts that Hari Singh signed the deal first, thus legalizing the presence of their troops. Pakistan is unyielding that the Maharaja could not have signed before the arrival of the troops, and that he and India had therefore flouted the 'standstill' accord with Pakistan.

- Pakistan calls for a plebiscite to conclude the status of Kashmir, while Delhi contends that, by voting in consecutive Indian states and national elections, Kashmiris have approved their accession to India. Pakistan quotes various UN resolutions in support of a UN-run referendum, while India maintains its stand on adhering to the Simla Agreement of 1972, which binds the two nations to solve the issue on a state-to-state basis.
- There has been no noteworthy deviation from these stances in the past decades. Moreover, some Kashmiris strive for a third option—independence—which neither India nor Pakistan is prepared to consider.

Line of Control

The Line of Control (LOC) stretches 742 km (460 miles) partitioning Indian- and Pakistan-controlled Kashmir, and acts as part of the existent border between the two nations. The army frontier, which extends through hostile territory, has divided hundreds of families and even partitioned villages and mountains.

- The LOC is established in the ceasefire lines drawn up after the initial India-Pakistan war in 1947–1948. It was formally recognized in 1972, after the conclusion of a third war between India and Pakistan in 1971.
- The LOC has been a minefield between the two nuclear-armed nations since its establishment. Their army have traded gunfire across the line for quite a long time.
- In 2002, India and Pakistan were on the verge of another war after gunmen attacked the Indian parliament in December 2001. Around 1 million soldiers were deployed along the LOC at the peak of emergency.
- In 2004, with the intention of curbing the intrusion of Muslim militants, the Indian army engineers fenced off most of the LOC.
- A ceasefire in 2003 resulted in peace dialogues and improved ties. In 2005, a limited bus service was put into operation to ferry travellers across the LOC from Srinagar, summer capital of Indian Kashmir, to Muzaffarabad, the capital of Pakistani Kashmir.
- After the arrival of a gigantic earthquake in Kashmir in 2005, India and Pakistan decided to open several junctions on the LOC to exchange aid and permit families to meet.

Kashmir Insurgency

- The Kashmiri insurrection, in contrast, grew instantly after partition in 1947, aggravated by the state's denial of the demand for a referendum. The capital punishment of Maqbool Butt of the Jammu and Kashmir Liberation Front (JKLF) in 1984 and the introduction of elections in 1987 against several Muslim contenders aroused the militancy in the area. 'As militancy in the Valley increased, the traditional identity of 'Kashmiriyat' was gradually reconstructed.... [T]he conflict and demands for separatism gradually challenged the secular traditions of the valley.' The split between the Muslims and the Kashmiri Pandits ended up noticeably more noteworthy than at any other time. When Jagmohan, the former Governor of Jammu and Kashmir, pronounced that 'every Muslim in Kashmir is a militant today' and that 'the bullet is the only solution for Kashmir', secularism was completely sabotaged and substituted by militancy, encouraged as it was by Pakistani aid.
- In 1989, armed conflict to Indian regime started in the Kashmir valley. Muslim political parties protested that the 1987 elections to the state's legislative assembly were manipulated against them, and they established militant factions.

- Some groups raised demand for independence of the state of Jammu and Kashmir while others raised demand for union with Pakistan.
- Pakistan gave its 'moral and diplomatic' aid to the movement, demanding the matter to be resolved via a UN-sponsored plebiscite.
- However, the Government of India asserted that Pakistan's aid of the uprising involved training and providing weapons to militant secessionists and repeatedly demanded Pakistan to stop 'cross-border terrorism'.
- During the 1990s, various new militant factions surfaced, most of which maintained radical Islamic perspectives.
- The ideological focus of the development moved from a nationalistic and secularist one to an Islamic one.
- This was to some degree determined by the influx in the Kashmir valley of a significant numbers of Islamic 'Jihadi' fighters who had battled in Afghanistan against the Soviet Union in the 1980s.
- During the time of uprising, Kashmir has transformed—with regards to its politics, dialogue, the nature of the militancy, the level of outer interference and assessments of the potential solutions. However, quite a bit of India's comprehension of Kashmir remains trapped in the constrained bounds of history, and thus India is unable to comprehend the changes, refuses to progress from age-old positions, and declines to search for better approaches to address the contention.
- In 1989, India ended up on the losing side of the Cold War with scarcely a companion in the universal community. All the more in this way, the universal group was adversely inclined towards India with regard to the Kashmir issue. Pakistan was hopeful in the wake of the alliance it had been a part of that had overwhelmed the Soviet Union in the Afghan war and was sure of its capacity and standing in the region. The Kashmiri insurgents, Pakistan and the activists in Kashmir had figured out how to 'internationalize' their cause and garnered noteworthy levels of sympathy for it. India was being put into an unpleasant situation.
- This is no longer the scenario. India is progressively alluded to as a rising power and is viewed as an important balancing power in the South Asian subcontinent. The global community is no more eager to review Kashmir situation or influence a solution; it is aware that India will not be pushed. The emphasis is currently on India and Pakistan arriving at their own solutions, and very little consideration is being given to the desires of the Kashmiris themselves. Moreover, in contrast to the late-1980s, Pakistan is a much-debilitated power now without numerous dependable strategic associates. The general apprehension is that the state is heading for failure due to its imbued encouragement of terrorism. Kashmir is no longer a preferred issue for the global community. There are more important issues that needs addressing.
- Pakistan has obviously failed over Kashmir. In reality, its policy in relation to India in general has turned out badly and has gone wrong terribly. Several elements Pakistan favoured in its intention to 'liberate' Kashmir from India have betrayed it. More importantly, Pakistan has apparently lost the objective of its foreign policy. Conflicting articulations on Kashmir abound, leaving the nation's position befuddling and vague. Such uncertainty points to an understanding among some individuals in Pakistan that it needs to think past Kashmir, and that it is reckless to continue the fight. This has essential ramifications for the contention.

- In India, too, the as well, the talk on Kashmir has changed considerably. The nation's conventional dialogue generally considered the issue as one driven and shaped entirely by Pakistani intervention. Everyone appeared unmindful of the reality that Pakistan had been given the space for this intrusion because of India's conventional mismanagement of Kashmir issue. This standard reasoning was implanted in the media dialogues. Bollywood films and famous composition depicted Kashmir as a terrorism-pervaded terrain that needs to be rinsed of Pakistani operators. It inclined to portray a picture of Kashmiris as followers of terrorism and Pakistan. This belief is experiencing a positive change. Currently, there is a rising understanding about the subtleties of the Kashmir issue and indiscretions the Indian state has committed there. There is a comprehension of the prevalent feeling of estrangement among Kashmiris and a developing acknowledgment that anti-India demonstrations are not essentially pro-Pakistan. There is the awareness that there is a genuine issue in Kashmir that needs a political settlement.
- In recent times, Kashmiri perspectives on Pakistan have changed. Although many individuals in Kashmir never desired it to become a part of Pakistan, there were some individuals who figured they would be in an ideal situation there. Furthermore , in view of the negative perception which several Kashmiris held about India, there was an inclination, even if not so widespread, to view Pakistan with sympathy and profound respect. This perception is changing, because of the existential issues that Pakistan is confronting, the atrocities that Pakistan-sponsored terrorists have conferred in Kashmir, and the general discernment that joining Pakistan may not be the best choice for Kashmir. Thus, there are fewer advocates for Pakistan in the valley at present, and even fewer of them for radicals coming from Pakistan to free Kashmir from Indian oppression.
- Political affairs in Kashmir today is multifarious and more vivacious than ever. Investigators and observers have a tendency to get befuddled while writing about the State principally in light of the fact that they struggle to value the frequently opposing nature of the present political scenario. The general population of Kashmir are figuring out how to talk two differentiating dialects at a time: one of dissidence, and the other of standard issues. Numerous analysts contended that India lost Kashmir amid the dissents against the Amarnath land transfer. similarly, several individuals contended after previous year's elections in Jammu and Kashmir (when more than 62 per cent of the individuals voted in contrast to around 43 per cent in 2002) that the noteworthy plebiscite was the final blow to the separatist politics and 'azadi' opinions in the valley. Both the contentions could not realize the unpredictability of the political issues in Kashmir or value that political undertakings there have changed in a general sense.
- The 'mainstreaming of discord' is another spectacle in modern-day Kashmir. The separatists now are no more impervious. In the contemporary world, secessionist politics and 'azadi' emotions are more refined, more multifaceted than before and acquire many forms, ranging from the All Parties Hurriyat Conference (APHC) to the People's Democratic Party (PDP). The PDP would protest against being called 'pro-azadi', 'separatist' or even 'soft-separatist', reality remains that it walks a very fine line. From one perspective, the self-rule proposal put forward by it requests for more than what the

Constitution of India guarantees the State and is nearer to the platform propositioned by the secessionist leaders (such as Sajjad Lone). On the contrary, the PDP has a political constituency that talks the dialect of both rebellion and 'azadi'. However, the PDP, which has governed the State for three years, is a conventional Kashmiri political party with clear connections to the Indian state. On the opposite side of the gulf, the nonconformist APHC frequently raises administration-related issues. This intersection of customary political limits by the hitherto opposed political groups show the multifaceted nature of Kashmir's new governmental issues.

- The significance of 'azadi' has likewise grown in multifaceted nature in the course of the most recent 20 years, becoming more subtle and growing more shades of interpretations, which numerous experts are unable to perceive. It would be reasonable to state that the yearnings for freedom—the 'azadi' sentiment—were solid in Kashmir when the rebellion started. Nevertheless, 20 years on, this feeling is more refined today; 'azadi' does not generally mean self-assurance in popular phraseology now. 'Azadi' in the present context implies liberty from the fear of militants and security forces, as well as nobility and sense of pride, self-administration, and the absence of New Delhi's apparent political oppression.
- Numerous, multifaceted pathways intended towards rapproachement have emerged. Despite the fact that the India–Pakistan peace process is at present stuck up, the Srinagar–New Delhi conversation is very much alive. There are discussions going on between Jammu and Srinagar and among Muzaffarabad and Srinagar and Jammu. Dealers from the two sides of the State have set up a joint J&K Chamber of Commerce and Industries. While a large number of these 'peace tracks' need to be restored, their very existence demonstrates the essential way in which the contention has been transformed from the time savagery pervaded the State.
- While beyond doubt, its forms have changed in a fundamental manner, it is additionally obvious that both the contention in Kashmir and the contention over Kashmir keep on existing. The stakeholders must be willing to show more resolve and passion to engage each other and find out a solution. Nevertheless, to achieve this, they must first recognize Kashmir's transformation.

Militants in the Kashmir

Over the recent times, they appear to have led the pack, moving the ideological stress of the development from a nationalistic and secularist one to an Islamic one.

Accordingly, some of the factions that were leading the armed insurrection in 1989—specifically, the pro-independence Jammu–Kashmir Liberation Front (JKLF)— paled into insignificance.

Currently, the predominant political propensity among the activists in Kashmir is pro-Pakistani, with an overwhelming emphasis on religion.

Ideological differences

Nevertheless, this may not be altogether valid for the rebel political movement symbolized by the All Parties Hurriyat Conference (APHC), as several of its constituent factions have kept their choices open. Occasionally, such ideological contrasts likewise result in conflict between the factions of the separatist movement. Among the elements that have to a great extent contributed to this shift in the ideological foundation of the armed Kashmiri movement are:

- The overbearing of the Indian security

- Support given to pro-Pakistan factions by Islamabad
- The accessibility of numerous Islamic rebels from Afghanistan
- Restrained activities

Around two dozen armed rebel factions claim to be operational inside the India-regulated Kashmir. Aside from a few noticeable factions, the majority of them are part of an alliance known as the United Jihad Council (UJC).

The UJC has its head office in Pakistan-regulated Kashmir, and is just loosely connected to the Srinagar-based APHC.

The majority of these militant factions are very small in numbers, and want to keep their exercises restricted to a particular part of Jammu or Kashmir.

The different activist factions confront a significant Indian security presence.

As indicated by the figures made available by the Indian military, there are about 125,000 troops and paramilitaries in the Kashmir valley and encompassing zones.

Informal data put the number to be much higher, and Pakistan and the APHC leaders put that number to be over half a million.

Jaish-e-Mohammad

- This is a fast developing group. It came into picture when a previous member of a different rebel group, Maulana Masood Azhar, was set free by the Indian authorities in December 1999 in exchange for the security of passengers of an Indian Airlines plane hijacked by the militants.
- The group has kept on developing and currently appears to have the support of numerous religious institutions in Pakistan.
- India says it was Jaish-e-Mohammad who carried out an assault in the state assembly in Indian-governed Kashmir last October.

Lashkar-e-Toiba

- The armed separatist outfit which has really affected the militant movement as of late is the Lashkar-e-Toiba.
- It is the activist group of Markaz-e-Tawatul Irshad—a religious institution at Muridke in Pakistani Punjab. Lashkar has grown as one of the most noticeable groups that are engaged in militant operations in Kashmir.
- It acquired more backing in view of the part played by it in the 1999 Kargil conflict with India and subsequently by sending its members on suicide missions to explode military cantonments in various parts of Indian-governed Kashmir.
- Lashkar's proclaimed philosophy goes past plainly challenging Indian rule in the northern state of Jammu and Kashmir.
- In a brochure entitled Why Are We Waging Jihad, the group explains its plan as the reclamation of Islamic administration over all parts of India.
- In 2000, its militants executed dubious armed attacks inside the Red Fort in Delhi and endeavoured to assassinate the Mumbai-based hardliner Hindu, the Shiv Sena supremo Bal Thackery.

Operation 'Topac'

- Operation 'Topac', under which Pakistan initiated its proxy war against India, was splendidly imagined and skilfully executed. Pakistan's President, General Zia ul Haq's idea was to misuse the religious slants of the Kashmiri individuals, incite passions on communal and sectarian boundaries, stir up the flames of religious fundamentalism and, all the while, slowly but surely create conditions for instigating a jihad. Before initiating its proxy war in Kashmir, Pakistan also started measures to misuse the discontented sections among the youth of Punjab to wage a war for the creation of a sovereign Sikh state of Khalistan. The goal was to undermine India by creating state of instability in two adjoining forefront Indian states and to bind the Indian security forces, especially the Indian Army, in internal security obligations. It was anticipated that extended work in internal security obligations would debilitate the Indian Army and damage its established superiority over the Pakistan Army. This was to be accomplished through a low-cost alternative, without getting straightforwardly involved.

- The Inter-Services Intelligence (ISI) Directorate of Pakistan was assigned with the obligation of executing the plan. The ISI had acquired tremendous experience in coordinating guerrilla combat in Afghanistan, with sabotage and terrorism as the weapons of choice, while cooperating with the US Central Intelligence Agency (CIA). The ISI had also secretively drawn off about 60 per cent of the small arms, light weapons, ammo and explosives provided to it by the CIA for onward delivery to the Afghan mujahideen. It has been informed that arms and ammunition valued at US$5 billion had been directed into Afghanistan by the US and its partners. Furthermore , the former Soviet Union had provided arms and ammo worth US$5.7 billion. Substantial numbers of these weapons ended up plainly accessible to the ISI for equipping Kashmiri radicals when the Soviet forces pulled back from Afghanistan in 1989. Benefits from the secret sale of openly accessible narcotics from Afghanistan, 'donations from Muslim fanatics in other nations' and benefits from extensive smuggling activities across the Indian border, provided sufficient assets to fund an uprising in J&K. Huge manipulation of elections to the J&K Assembly in March 1987 and the Kashmiri individuals' disappointment with Mr. Farooq Abdullah's professedly debased and inefficient government prompted unconstrained dissent and a call for azadi (independence). Along these lines the circumstance was suitable for exploitation and the ISI, which was prepared and awaiting , ventured in to fan the flames.

The tactical outline of Operation Topac was to initiate a proxy war against India in a staged way. The noticeable features of Pakistan's strategy were as follows:

- Initiate a low-level uprising to restrict communications networks and undermine the police and financial establishments.
- Afterwards, apply direct pressure along the Line of Control (LoC) by extensive disruption and secure access to guerrillas and special forces to carry out assault at crucial targets in rear regions.
- At a suitable stage, utilizing religion as a persuading and uniting aspect, give a push to the jihad to top and, if essential, be prepared to workout the military alternative to liberate J&K.

Government of India's Developmental Initiatives in Kashmir

The Government of India consented to an agreement with the Asian Development Bank (ADB) for a $60 million loan to help enhance urban administrations, including water supply and urban transport framework, in two important cities of Jammu and Kashmir. The loan from the ADB's Ordinary Capital Resources is of 25-year term that includes a grace period of five years.

The Special Industry Initiative J&K (SII J&K) 'Udaan' Scheme is to offer skills and upgrade employability of 40,000 youth over a time of five years in important high development sectors. The programme is focused at offering well-paying employments to the trained labour. The Scheme is being executed by National Skill Development Council (NSDC) and the corporate segment in PPP mode. The Scheme incorporates graduates, post graduates, professional degree holders and three-year engineering diploma holders.

The Government of India presented plan of central grant or subsidy for industrial units in the Jammu & Kashmir with the intention to speed up industrial development in the State.

Key Schemes for J&K

- A security-related expenditure (SRE) scheme for Jammu and Kashmir was launched.
- Special industry initiative (SII in J&K) 'UDAAN', a scheme initiated by the Prime Minister, the NSDC, and the MHA, was launched with the objective of imparting training to 40,000 youth over a period of five years.
- A road infrastructure development program worth ₹ 900 Crore was launched in J & K on the lines of Naxal-affected areas.
- A central initiative was launched for help towards damaged immovable/movable assets during operation by CPMFs and army in Jammu and Kashmir.
- Construction of two-room apartments for Kashmiri migrants, which is funded by the planning commission
- Construction of 200 flats for Kashmiri migrants at Budgam
- Package for return and rehabilitation of Kashmiri migrants
- Cash and ration relief to Kashmiri migrants
- Project 'Himayat' for capacity development and employment of youth

Package Declared by PM for Different Sections of Society

- Centred on the report and suggestions of Working Group-I on 'Confidence building measures across segment of society in the State', an all-inclusive package was declared by the Prime Minister on 25 April, 2008. This incorporates:
- A package for the return and rehabilitation of Kashmiri immigrants who were compelled to leave their homes because of the carnage executed by the militant and terrorist groups in the state and are currently living in Jammu and other different parts of the country;
- One time monetary reimbursement of ₹ 5 lakh to the families of the casualties of militancy in lieu of employment;
- Enhancement of pension to widows of citizens slaughtered in militancy-related savagery;
- Financial help without prejudice for the education of those bereaved in militant brutality;
- A package for 1947 West Pakistan refugees incorporating measures with the intention of expediting admission to their dependants in professional and other educational establishments, bank loans without mortgage for taking up independent work/business exercises, professional training for youth under the Skill development proposals of the Ministry of Labour and Employment;
- Package for 1947 immigrants from PoK adding up to ₹ 49 crore to meet their unsettled requirements with regards to allotment of land and related rehabilitation processes.
- Package for return and rehabilitation of Kashmiri refugees.

Article 370

What is Article 370?

- The state of Jammu & Kashmir is granted a special autonomous status according to Article 370 of the Indian Constitution, which is a 'transitory provision'. Part XXI of the Constitution of India, which deals with 'Temporary, Transitional and Special provisions', accords special status under Article 370 to the state of Jammu and Kashmir. Each one of the provisions of the Indian Constitution which are relevant to different states are not applicable to J&K. For instance, till 1965, J&K had the post of Sadr-e-Riyasat instead of Governor and Prime Minister instead of chief minister.

- Sheikh Abdullah, the then Prime Minister of Jammu & Kashmir appointed by Maharaja Hari Singh and Jawahar Lal Nehru, drafted the provision in 1947by. Sheikh Abdullah had contended that Article 370 should not be set under transient provisions of the Constitution. He wanted 'iron-clad self-rule' for the state, which the centre did not agree to.

Provisions of Article 370

- In accordance with this article, with the exception of defence, foreign affairs, finance and communications, the parliament needs the state government's consensus for applying every other law. Hence, the state's occupants live under a different set of laws, including those identified with citizenship, ownership of property, and fundamental rights, in contrast to other Indians living in different states. On account of this provision, Indian residents from different states cannot buy land or property in Jammu and Kashmir.
- According to this Article, the Centre has no power to announce financial emergency under Article 360 in the state. It can announce emergency in the state just in case of war or external hostility. The Union government can in this way not pronounce emergency on the basis of internal disturbance or imminent threat unless it is made at the demand or with the consensus of the state government.

❑❑❑

Chapter seven

Challenges Posed by Communal Strife and Violence

Introduction

Communal violence engages individuals from two different religious groups activated against each other and conveying the sentiments of hostility, emotional fierceness, abuse, social discrimination and social disregard. The high level of solidity in one group against another is built around tension and polarization. The objectives of assault are the individuals from the 'adversary' group. By and large, there is no initiative in communal riots which could adequately control and contain the riot situation. It could along these lines be said that communal violence is construct fundamentally in light of hatred, enmity and revenge.

Communal violence has expanded in a quantitative and qualitative manner ever since political issues became communalized. Gandhi was its first casualty came after the murder of several individuals in the 1970s and the 1980s. Following demolition of Babri mosque in Ayodhya in December 1992, and bomb explosions in Mumbai in early 1993, communal uprisings in Maharashtra, Tamil Nadu, Bihar, Uttar Pradesh and Kerala have significantly increased.

While few political groups endure ethno-religious communalism, a few others even empower it. Recent cases of this tolerance, detachment to and latent acknowledgment of or even conspiracy of the exercises of religious groups by certain political leaders and some political parties are found in assaults on Christian missionaries and in vicious actions against Christians in Gujarat, Madhya Pradesh and Allahabad.

Crisis of the mid-1970s initiated the pattern of criminal components entering conventional politics. This phenomenon has now firmly established itself in Indian politics to such a degree that religious extremism, casteism and blending of religion and politics have expanded in different dimensions. Political parties and political leaders embrace a sickening sanctimonious attitude in connection to each other as opposed to taking a collective stand against these negative whims influencing our society.

The Hindu associations point the finger at Muslims and Christians for coercively converting Hindus to their religions. Without indulging in the conflict whether conversion or religious transformations were coercive or intentional, it might just be said that raising this issue today is obviously irrational radicalism. Hinduism has been tolerant and assumes all mankind to be one family.

In this way, it must be acknowledged that the doctrine of Hindutva staining Indian politics has nothing to do with the Hindu idea. It is high time that secular political leaders and political parties neglect political and electoral contemplations and denounce and make a move against those religious associations which upset peace and stability through statements and debilitate the solidarity and pluralistic character of India.

Historical Background

- Communalism for sure is a contemporary phenomenon and started with the foundation of British empire in India. All historians and social researchers concur with this. Communal politics is strongly connected with electoral politics and as the foundation of electoral politics enlarged in the twentieth century, communalism and communal viciousness also escalated. The British initiated electoral reforms in the early twentieth century to neutralize the nationalist movement but simultaneously attempted to widen the rift between the Hindus and the Muslims. Separate electorates were a premeditated and malicious approach. It would not be impractical to claim that the introduction of separate electorates had been the notable cause behind the partition of India. Partition was the worst calamity for India and it left everlasting scars on the Indian psyche and fostered a communal mindset.
- Partition was not fundamentally realized by religious disparities but by disagreements between the privileged of the two communities on a power-sharing game plan. The Muslim elites under the leadership of Jinnah called for more representation in the parliament than the Muslim populace justified. The Muslims were one fourth of the populace but Jinnah and his supporters demanded that Muslims be given one-third representation in the parliament. Jinnah was concerned that if Muslims represented in less numbers, the Congress would change the concurred constitutional set up. The Cabinet Mission Plan which was a superior solution to the political mess did not work due to mutual suspicions.
- After the establishment of Pakistan, it was believed that the communal issue had been settled and that independent India would not accede to it. The Indian Constitution not only ensured religious and political rights for the minorities but also pronounced India a secular state (however, the word 'secular' was not utilized as a part of the Constitution until 1975). Prominent leaders such as Jawaharlal Nehru were of the view that the spread of a scientific education would help in cultivating a secular mindset. This turned out to be a short-sighted supposition. As democratic politics without holding a competitive spirit is nothing, communal patterns re-emerged in post-independent India. The post-partition riots persisted up to 1949. The Constitution was set up and implemented in 1950 and the first general elections were held in 1952. No major communal strife happened until 1961 when the Jabalpur riots shook the nation. This was increasingly an outcome of a monetary rivalry between a Hindu and a Muslim bidi manufacturer. Yet, since the incident happened almost immediately after the Partition, it was asserted that Pakistani spies were active in coordinating the riot and that directions were being sought by local Muslims on a hidden transmitter from Pakistan.
- A series of violence erupted especially in the eastern region of India—Rourkela, Jamshedpur and Ranchi—in 1964, 1965 and 1967, in localities where Hindu migrants from the then Eastern Pakistan were being rehabilitated. Hindu communal associations took advantage of their tales of grief to

provoke communal passions. The violence in 1967 in Ranchi occurred on the question of adopting Urdu. The CPI in Ranchi held a demonstration demanding for granting recognition to Urdu as a second language. An assault was carried out at the procession resulting in the eruption of communal riots.

- The Ahmedabad riots took place in 1969 followed by the riots in Bhivandi-Jalgaon in 1970. The Ahmedabad riots jolted the integrity of the country. Over 1,000 persons died. The primary driving force was severe resistance to Indira Gandhi's leftward thrust by the Jan Sangh and the Swatantra Party. The Jan Sangh adopted an aggressive stance and in 1968 that it had passed a resolution to Indianize Muslims. The seriousness of the issue can be assessed from the way that Khan Abdul Ghaffar Khan who was then in India for treatment and Jayaprakash Narayan together founded an association called 'Insani Biradari' (Human Brotherhood) and held a number of conferences to promote communal concord. Similarly, the 1970 Bhivandi-Jalgaon riots were disastrous and were incited by the Shiv Sena which was attempting to build up itself in Maharashtra.
- In the post-Emergency period when Janta Party was in power, communal violence spread again in 1978. The Jan Sangh had joined hands with other socialist parties and formed the Janata Party. The party then took an oath to abide by the guidelines of secularism and Gandhian socialism. But soon socialist leaders like Raj Narain, Madhu Limaye and others put forth the controversy of dual membership and the Jan Sangh leaders declined to step down from the RSS and the Janata Party Government which was led by Morarji Desai came to an end. It was the time when the dual membership controversy was at its peak and thus communal violence spread around at a many places like Jamshedpur, Aligarh and Benaras. But the worst was yet to dawn.
- During the decade of the 80s, the worst in the form of communal violence came to light. A number of riots spread starting with Moradabad in 1980. The Eighties can be termed as the communal decade in the Indian history post-independence. In 1981, after Moradabad, Bihar Sharif was most affected apart from Meerut and Baroda. In the region of Moradabad, the unofficial toll was more than 1000. In Bihar Sharif, Indira Gandhi could not control her tears when she saw a truck filled with a number of dead bodies. The Baroda riots were equally disastrous in terms of loss of life. But Neli in Assam claimed a record death toll of 4,000 people in communal violence which spread out in 1983. A number of village was wiped out. The prominent sufferers were the so-called Bangladeshi Muslims.
- After the Neli riots, other two major riots that broke in 1984 were the Bhivandi-Bombay riots of May and the anti-Sikh riots of November after the assassination of Indira Gandhi. Over 4000 Sikhs lost their lives in Delhi and other parts of India, especially in the state of Uttar Pradesh. In the riots that spread in the regions of Bombay-Bhivandi, the Shiv Sena was primarily indulged. Mr. Bal Thackeray instigated these riots with his anti-Muslim outburst to strengthen the political fortunes of the Shiv Sena which had lost its overwhelming public support. It held on the Hindutva bandwagon to discover its political prospect. The Meenakshipuram conversion of some hundred dalits had encouraged the VHP and the controversy was completely used to advance the appeal of Hindutva forces. Indira Gandhi also allegedly tried to use the VHP to enhance her toothless appeal among the Hindus.

- The Shah Bano controversy in 1985 brought waves in India and Muslim fundamentalists and political leaders used this judgment completely for the maintenance of a Muslim divorcee. This promoted communalism both among Hindus and Muslims. After the Meenakshipuram conversions, the Shah Bano case was the most prominent communal controversy. Both these controversies became potent instrument to intensify communalism in the Eighties. After this, the Babri Masjid-Ram Janmabhoomi controversy came to light. The Rajiv Gandhi Government gave an encouragement to it by altering the law for Muslim divorcees, on the one hand, and by opening the Babri Masjid doors, on the other. A number of riots took place after this — Meerut 1987 and Bhagalpur 1989.
- In 1990, Mr. L. K. Advani took out a Rath Yatra which turned into a blood yatra and over 300 small and big riots occurred that year. It seemed as if communal chauvinism had controlled the middle classes. The BJP strengthened its vote-catching potential by making use of this controversy. The ultimate disaster of the 20th Century communal violence took place in December 1992 when in spite of assurances to the contrary the BJP, the RSS, the VHP and the Bajrang Dal toppled the Babri Masjid. This resulted in the worst riots of post-independence India in places like Mumbai, Surat, Ahmedabad, Kanpur, Delhi etc.
- It can be inferred that communal violence reached its apogee in 1992–93 and nothing worse could occur thereafter, at least in the 20th Century. Let us hope that in the new millennium, religion will not be misused as a political tool and it will become a vital resource for peace rather than a tool for ill-will and dispute.

Order of Communal Riots in country's history One of the first major communal riots that occurred in August 1893 in Mumbai, around a hundred people were killed and 800 suffered injury.

The period between 1921 and 1940 denoted an especially troublesome stage. The 1926 Muharram festivities in Calcutta were for instance defaced by a conflict that resulted in 28 deaths.

India faced its worst communal riots in 1948 during the time of partition. The worst hit areas were Noakhali in Bengal and several villages of Bihar.

The major riots between Hindus and Muslims after the killing of partition in 1947 happened in Jabalpur in Madhya Pradesh in 1961.

- ***1969 Ahmedabad riots:*** Communal riots between Hindus and Muslims exploded in Ahmedabad in 1969, claiming the lives of at least 1,000 people. At the time there was a clash over the leadership of the Congress party between Indira Gandhi and Morarji Desai. There were recommendations that clash was purposely plotted to discredit the chief minister of Gujarat who was a sponsor of Mr. Desai.

  After that, riots occurred in Uttar Pradesh with periodic violence erupting elsewhere.

  Riots between Hindu and Muslim erupted in Jamshedpur and Aligarh in 1979 and in Moradabad in 1980.
- ***1984 Sikh riots:*** The murder of Prime Minister Indira Gandhi on 31 October 1984 ignited riots that went on for 15 days. After several inquiries, eight people were convicted. The politicians and police got away.

  The chaos began at about 6 p.m. shortly after the death of Indira Gandhi was broadcast at the All India Institute of Medical Sciences, Delhi. The news provided the base for a communal massacre that India hadn't quite witnessed since Independence. Chaos reigned on the streets and locality after locality in the capital echoed with the shrieks of the dying and burning people. A fortnight of carnage saw over 2,700 dead and many thousands injured.

'President Zail Singh wanted the army to act, but it didn't. The then prime minister and home minister did not take his calls', recalls Tarlochan Singh, the then Zail Singh's press secretary.

The most affected areas include the ones that had elected Congressmen HKL Bhagat and Sajjan Kumar to the Lok Sabha. Yet nothing happened to them until now.

- *1987 Meerut riots:* The unrest began on 21 May 1987 and went on for two months. The state police directed a probe, but all cases were later withdrawn by the state. The armed personnel accused went scot free.

Like most riots, there exist conflicting versions on what set this one off: burning of mills or a reaction to the carnage by the Provincial Armed Constabulary (PAC) personnel. A majority asserted it was the armed police.

The PAC personnel needed to arrest a man from the Hashimpura area but were disrupted by a mob. When the police tried to force their way in, the crowd became violent. The PAC called in reinforcements and retaliated instantly. About 40 dead bodies were later found floating in the canal near Maliana village. This ignited communal passions and Meerut was soon on fire. Within few hours, over 350 shops in the city and three petrol pumps had been burnt. The two-month-long riots claimed the lives of 350 people, among them prominent residents including a doctor from Hapur and an army captain.

Rationality took the backseat as one set of residents instigated massacres against another. It took some weeks for a 13,000-strong army detachment to reinstate peace in Meerut. The Uttar Pradesh government, under pressure from the Rajiv Gandhi government, pull out hundreds of cases from district courts in Meerut. As a result, there were no convictions. The PAC, having terrorized a large section of Meerut, was the biggest gainer-and justice the biggest loser.

- *1989 Bhagalpur riots:* On 23 October 1989, the month-long clashes triggered by police atrocities began in Bhagalpur. Out Of the 864 cases filed by the police, 535 were closed and most accused acquitted due to lack of evidence.

Following police mayhem in 1989, the silk city of Bhagalpur witnessed massacre and arson, which claimed the lives of over 1,000 people, nearly 50,000 were displaced and 11,500 houses torched.

In the slaughter, an army major gathered 100 men, women and children in a house at Chanderi village and deployed the local police for their protection. The next morning, however, he found the house empty. Four days later, 61 mutilated bodies were found in a nearby pond, among them a live Malika Bano whose right leg had been chopped off. Bano recounted a story that remains to haunt Bhagalpur.

On the night of October 27, a furious gang took over the house from the police, killed the people hiding inside and disposed their bodies in the pond. Of the 864 cases registered by the Bihar Police, charge sheets were filed in only 329 cases. In 100 of these, the accused were proved not guilty due to lack of evidence. Chanderi was no different. Out of the 38 accused, only 16 were convicted and sentenced to rigorous life terms, whereas 22 were acquitted.

The Babri masjid demolition sparked violence between December 1992 and January 1993. The Sri Krishna panel scrutinized 502 witnesses, but no police officer has yet been punished.

- *1992 Mumbai riots:* Just few hours after the demolition of the Babri masjid, Mumbai erupted. For continuous five days in December 1992 and then again for a fortnight in January, the city faced exceptional riots, claiming the lives of 1,788 people and destroying the wealth worth crores of rupees.

  On 25 January 1993, the Maharashtra government constituted the Sri Krishna Commission of Inquiry, which verified the evidence of 502 witnesses and examined 2,903 exhibits. But three years later, on 23 January 1996, the BJP–Shiv Sena government dissolved the commission, only to restore it later under public pressure. The commission finally submitted its report on February 16, 1998. Of the 17 police officers who were formally charged in mid-2001, not one has been arrested so far. Even departmental action has not been initiated against them. In April this year, former city police commissioner R D Tyagi and eight serving police officers accused of killing nine people, were discharged by a Mumbai sessions court.
- *2002 Gujarat riots:* On 27 February 2002, suspected Muslim group attacked a train with activists of the Vishwa Hindu Parishad (VHP) on board who were coming back from the disputed holy site of Ayodhya. The attack left 58 Hindu activists dead. The attack led to major riots, leaving many Muslims dead in Gujarat.

Constitutional Provisions Related to Secularism

The notion of secularism has been clearly as well as indirectly exemplified in the Constitution of India. The most significant modules of secularism as preserved in the Indian constitution are as follows:

- *Preamble:* The word 'secular' did not first occur either in Article 25 or 26 or in any other Article or Preamble of the Constitution. By the Constitution (42nd Amendment) Act, 1976, the Preamble was amended and for the words 'Sovereign Democratic Republic' the words 'Sovereign, socialist, secular, Democratic Republic' were substituted.
- Article 14 guarantees right to equality;
- Article 15 and 16 prohibit any discrimination on the ground of religion, caste, etc.;
- Freedom of speech and expression all other importance freedom of all the citizens are conferred under articles 19 and 21;
- Article 25 to Article 28 confers rights to practice religion;
- Article 44 provides for the directive principle to enact uniform civil laws treating all the citizens as equal.

Among the religious rights, the constitution promises freedom of conscience, freedom to profess, practice and propagate religion and also freedom to establish religious institutions and manage or administer their affairs. The Constitution also pledges religious minorities the right to establish and administer learning institutions of their choice and to protect their script, language and culture.

The above rules and regulations specify that the Constitution of India has tried to build up in India the philosophy of secularism on freedom, equality and tolerance in the field of religion. The Constitution does not form a wall of separation between the state and religion. India does not have a state religion. The state will neither create a religion of its own nor give any special patronage upon any specific religion.

Constitutional Provision Related to Communal Violence

Article 355 of the constitution defines that it shall be responsibility of the Union to protect every State against external violence and internal trouble and to ensure that the Government of every State is carried as per the provisions of Constitution.

Efforts have been made by the successive governments to tackle communal violence in India

Communal clashes have become a distinctive story of communalism in India. They are not caused spontaneously, and they are rarely caused by religious animosity. History shows that the communal violence in India has occurred due to contradictory political interests, which are often connected to economic interests. Till 2002, the successive governments did not take any notable legislative actions, but to tackle the periodic events of communal violence, the UPA government had in 2005 brought forward the 'Communal Violence (Prevention, Control and Rehabilitation of Victims) Bill, 2005'. This bill included measures for prevention and control of communal violence; fast investigation and trials as well as reintegration of victims. This bill could never see the light of the day and the parliamentary standing committee tagged this bill as something, which violates the basic federal principle of the Indian Constitution. After that, the National Advisory committee drafted and brought forward the Prevention of Communal and Targeted Violence (Access to Justice and Reparations) Bill. Recently, the UPA-II government has deferred this bill also.

Prominent features of the Communal Violence Bill 2005

The prominent provision of the above bill was about announcing the Communally Disturbed Area. According to this bill, if the state government thought that communal violence is taking place in one or more areas of the state, which can be a danger to the secular fabric, integrity, unity or internal security of India, then the state government can pronounce that area in question as 'communally disturbed area'. Once it is done, the district magistrate or the competent authority selected by the state government can take measures such as regulating assembly, directing persons to deposit their arms, searching premises and so on to tackle communal violence.

Besides this, the bill also has the provisions to offer double punishment. The bill sanctioned the state government to form special courts to try the offences in relation to communal violence. For restoration, the bill offered creation of Communal Disturbance Relief and Rehabilitation Councils (CDRRC) at national, state and district levels. It also has provisions in which district-level council shall pay at least 20% of total compensation as instant reimbursement to victims.

However, this bill failed to become an act. The most vital reason was that it was more bent towards the post-violence scenario and not about tackling the violence in the first place. Further, there were uncertainties regarding proclaiming the communally disturbed area, and the state government bureaucrats were given extraordinary powers without any accountability. Further some provisions coincided with the Criminal Procedure Code, and some even disturbed the provisions of the constitution and other statutes.

Largely, the 2005 bill was thought to be against the federal principle enshrined in the constitution.

Significant Provisions of the 2011 Bill

The significant provisions of this bill are as described as under:

- It comprises acts which may result in damage to persons or property, if such acts are focused against persons based on their affiliation to any group, and if such an act terminates the secular fabric of the nation. Sexual assault, hate propaganda, torture and organized communal violence included.

- The public officials were made liable to be punished for failing to execute their stated duties in an unbiased manner.
- The responsibilities of the public servants also include duty to provide protection to victims of communal violence.
- There is a rule to form a National Authority for Communal Harmony, Justice, and Reparation (NACHJR) and State Authorities for Communal Harmony, Justice, and Reparation (SACHJRs). These would avert acts of communal violence, provocation to communal violence, comprise the spread of communal violence, and monitor investigations into acts of communal violence.
- Central and state governments were given a free hand to intercept any messages or transmissions if they feel that such communications may lead to communal violence.
- The public servants were made liable to be prosecuted for offences under the bill. The state government would need to grant sanction for such prosecution within 30 days.
- The states are required to form Human Rights Defender of Justice and Reparations' in every district. The Human Rights defender will see that those affected by communal and targeted violence are able to access their rights under existing laws.
- There are provisions of state and district-level authorities for evaluating compensation for victims of communal violence. There are some obligations of the states towards victims, such as the creation of relief camps, guaranteeing proper facilities, medical provisions and clothing for those within such camps, etc.

Why the 2011 Bill has been opposed and on what grounds it has been now deferred by the Government?

The 2011 bill searched for the fundamental changes regarding how the existing system of governance tackles the violence against minorities. The bill has religious minorities at its heart, although it also has provisions for SCs and STs. The major blemishes in the bill are as follows:

- The bill describes that the word 'group' against which communal violence occurs means a linguistic or religious minority. So, what would ensue if there is a communal riot by the minority against the majority? Although a democracy has the duty to protect its minorities from violence, but there are several regions in India where otherwise majorities are minorities and otherwise minorities are majorities. The bill highlights that only minority is vulnerable to communal violence, thus it is anti-majority. Thus, no member of the majority community can ever be a victim. It opens up a huge scope for abuse and would act that they would never be charged under the act.
- Second disagreement is regarding the formation of the National Authority under the bill at the Central level. This has been seen as an effort to limit the jurisdiction of the states as any direction issued to the state authority by the National Authority is binding.
- In the bill, 'hate propaganda' is a crime against minority community and not otherwise. The law brands only members of the majority community guilty and distinguishes on the basis of a religion or caste. The definition of the hostile environment is not clear, to which acts would precisely fall under the ambit of this Act. Therefore, it may also contain a speech, music or video clippings which may have the ability of creating an intimidating,

hostile or offensive environment and who shall have the preference to decide as to which Act qualifies as being intimidating or hostile is left out.

- The bill makes the public servants liable for riots against minorities. It states that if the 'communal and targeted violence' against minorities occurs, it will automatically be thought that the civil servant in charge of law and order has not exercised 'lawful authority vested in him or her under law' and he or she 'shall be guilty of dereliction of duty'.
- It appears to be a welcome move since frequently public servants wait and act as per the orders of their political masters. By making it clearly their own liability, the bill strives to strengthen the civil servant against the politician. But this is only half truth. The remaining half is that the riots are partly conducted by politicians and leaders who may or may not be the part of the government. Communal violence is also a function of socio-economic fabric of a particular town. A civil servant may be extremely successful in conducting his duties at one place and may find himself or herself helpless at another place, just because of many factors. Thus, the provisions of the bill have a prejudice against public officials.

Thus, largely, the bill has many loopholes. In February 2014, the government was pressurized to drop plans to introduce this bill. The highlights from the debate which led to deferral of the bill are as under:

- The bill was largely opposed on the basis that 'Law and Order' is a state subject, and the centre has completely no jurisdiction in bringing such a bill. As per Arun Jaitley of BJP, the bill is entirely beyond the legislative competence of Parliament. This was countered by Kapil Sibal of UPA by saying that if it is a state-sponsored communal activity, then it is not a law and order issue.
- The bill comprises provisions on what type of action should be initiated against state government officials who fail to prevent riots, and provides frameworks for the upkeep of public order. These are exclusively state subjects and this within the domain of the state executive. The opposition claimed that the government is willing to pass this bill just before elections to win the Muslim votes.
- The bill states that only minorities can be targeted during a riot, and that the majority community will never be victims. This rule was amended, but then, it drew censure from chief ministers such as Jayalalithaa, who stated that the bill would give 'unfettered powers' to human rights bodies at the centre and state, letting them to issue orders to the state government.

Grounds of Communal Violence

- Various scholars have tackled the problem of communal violence with different perspectives, assigning different causes and giving different measures to tackle it. The Marxist school relates communalism to economic deprivation and to the class tussle between the haves and the have-not's to attain a monopoly control of the market forces. Political experts consider it as a power struggle. Sociologists see it as a phenomenon of social tensions and relative deprivations. The religious specialists recognize it as a diadem of violent fundamentalists and conformists.
- The class analysis of communalism needs some attention. The explanation is that the economic, social and political scenarios in a society occasionally make such problems and crises for the people that even if they try to come to grips with these crises, they fail

to do so. Without trying to grasp the real causes for this failure, they 'perceive' the other community (numerically much stronger than their own) as the cause of their miseries. Communalism is thus a social truth which is generated and reflected in a biased way.

- After independence, although our government appealed to follow 'socialistic pattern of economy', yet in exercise, the economic development was reliant more on capitalist pattern. In this pattern, on the one hand, the growth has not occurred at a rate where it could solve the problems of poverty, unemployment and insecurity which could check frustration and unhealthy competition for scarce jobs and other economic opportunities, and on the other hand, capitalist growth has generated success only for certain social strata leading to sharp and visible inequality and new social strains and social anxieties.
- Beneficiaries have their expectations soar even higher. They also feel helpless in their newly gained prosperity. Their relative prosperity awakens the social jealousy of those who fail to advance or who decline in power and prestige. The efforts of the government to solve the problems of the religious minorities arouse intense resentment among those prosperous sections of the community who are in numerical majority and who have achieved economic, social and political power through manipulations.
- They think that any increase in social scale of the minority community will intimidate their social domination. Thus, outlooks of suspicion and hostility on the part of both the communities continuously bolster the growth of communalism. Particularly, it (communalism) creates a ready appeal to the urban poor and the rural unemployed whose number has grown quickly as a result of lop-sided economic and social development and large-scale migration to cities.
- The social anger and frustration of these rootless and needy people often find expression in spontaneous violence whenever chances arises. A communal riot offers a good opportunity for this. But this economic analysis is not considered objective by many researchers.

Is Religion Responsible for communalism?

There are scholars who do not accept as true that religion has any role to play in it. Bipin Chandra (1984), for example, states that communalism is neither motivated by religion nor is religion an object of communal politics, even as the communalist bases his politics on religious differences, uses religious identity as an organizing principle, and in the mass phases of communalism uses religion to organize masses.

The religious variance is used to 'mask' non-religious social needs, ambitions and struggles. However, religiosity, i.e., 'too much religion in one's life' or the invasion of religion into areas other than those of personal belief, appears to form a certain receptivity to communal ideology and politics. Moreover, religious conservatism, narrow-mindedness and prejudice in the name of going back to fundamentals tend to divide people whom life and history have bought together. In this respect, different religions have different fundamentals in their structure, rituals and ideological practices which relate to communalism in different ways. Their examination and removal have to be specific to different religions.

Some researchers have offered a multiple-factor method in which they give prominence to several factors together. Ten major factors have been identified in the aetiology of communalism: social, religious, political, economic, legal, psychological, administrative, historical, local and international.

- *The social factors* comprise social customs, typecast images of religious communities, caste and class ego or inequality and religion-based social stratification.
- *The religious factors* comprise decrease in religious rules of tolerance and secular values, narrow and dogmatic religious beliefs, and use of religion for political gains and communal philosophy of religious leaders.
- *The political factors* comprise religion-based politics, religion-dominated political institutions, campaigning in elections based on religious deliberations, political intrusion in religious affairs, provocation or support to agitations by politicians for vested interests, political justification of communal violence, and failure of political leadership; to contain religious feelings.
- *The economic factors* comprise economic abuse and discrimination of minority religious communities, their skewed economic development, insufficient chance in competitive market, nonexpanding economy, displacement and non-absorption of workers of minority religious groups, and the effect of gulf money in instigating religious conflicts; the legal factors include absence of common civil code, special provisions and concessions for some communities in the Constitution, special status of certain states, reservation policy, and special laws for different communities.
- *The psychological factors* comprise social preconceptions, typecast attitudes, distrust, hostility and lethargy against another community, rumour, fear psychosis and misinformation/misinterpretation/misrepresentation by mass media.
- *The administrative factors* comprise deficiency of coordination between the police and other administrative units, ill-equipped and ill-trained police personnel, incompetent working of intelligence agencies, prejudiced policemen and police excesses and inaction.
- *The historical factors* comprise alien attacks, harm to religious institutions, proselytization efforts, divide and rule policy of colonial rulers, partition trauma, past communal riots, old disputes on land, temples and mosques.
- *The local factors* comprise religious demonstrations, slogan raising, false stories, land quarrels, local anti-social elements and group rivalries; and the global factors involve training and financial aid from other countries, other countries' machinations to disunite and weaken India, and support to communal establishments.

Against these tactics, we require a universal approach to recognize the problem of communalism and communal violence. The stress of this approach would be on various factors, differentiating the major from the minor. We can classify these factors in four sub-groups: most conspicuous, chief cooperating, minor aggravating, and apparently inoperative.

Precisely, these factors include communal politics and politicians' backing to religious radicals, preconceptions (which lead to discrimination, avoidance, physical attack and extermination), the development of communal institutions, and conversions and proselytization. Broadly speaking, attention may be dedicated on fanatics, anti-social elements and vested economic interests in generating and fanning violence in the rival communities.

Communal clash is provoked by religious radicals, started by antisocial elements, supported by political activists, sponsored by vested interests and spread by the callous attitude of the police and the administrators. Although these aspects openly cause communal clash, the factor which helps in spreading violence is the ecological layout of a particular city which enables rioters to escape un-apprehended.

There is a feeling of discrimination among Muslims . In reality, the number of Muslims who appear for these jobs is very low. The feeling of discrimination among Muslims is ludicrous and irrational.

The other aspect includes the flow of money from the Gulf and other regions to India. A significant number of Muslims go to the Gulf nations to earn a handsome income and become affluent. These Muslims and the local Sheikhs transfer money to India generously for building mosques, opening madrassas (schools) and for operating charitable Muslim institutions.

This money is, thus, meant to help Muslim fundamentalism. Pakistan is one nation whose rulers always does not like India. This country's power elite have been incessantly interested in generating instability in India. It has now been recognized that Pakistan is actively supporting Muslim terrorists (of Jammu and Kashmir and Punjab) by providing training and military weapons.

These disrupting efforts of Pakistan and other governments have further produced ill-feeling and suspicion among the Hindus against the Muslims. The same can be said about Hindu militants and Hindu organizations in India which encourage antagonistic feelings against the Muslims and Muslim establishments.

Matters like the Ram Janambhoomi–Babri Masjid clash in Ayodhya, the Krishna Janambhoomi and nearby Masjid alteration in Mathura, the clash over Kashi Viswanath temple and its adjoining mosque in Varanasi, and the debatable Masjid in Sambhal claimed to be the temple of Lord Shiva from the days of Prithviraj Chauhan, and events like a Muslim leader giving call for nonattendance of Muslims on Republic Day and the perceiving of January 26, (1987) as a 'black day', have all provoked the ill-feeling between the two communities.

The mass media also occasionally back communal tensions in their own way. Many a time, the news items published in papers are based on hearsay, rumours or wrong interpretations. Such news items further fuels communal feelings. This is what occurred in Ahmedabad in the 1969 unrests when 'Sewak' reported that several Hindu women were stripped and raped by Muslims. Although this report was contradicted the next day, the damage had been done. It provoked the feelings of Hindus and shaped a communal riot.

One of the aspects which has been a bone of contention among Muslims and Hindus in recent years is the Muslim Personal Law. With the verdict of the Apex Court in favour of Shah Bano, and its advice in April 1995 to the government that it should ratify a uniform civil code, the Muslims are of the opinion that their personal law is being interfered with. The politicians also misuse the situation to keep themselves in power.

The BJP, the Vishwa Hindu Parishad, the Shiv Sena and the RSS are the parties which claim to support Hinduism. Likewise, the Muslim League, the Jamait-e-Islami, the Jamait-Ulema-a-Hind, the Majlis-e-Ittehadul Musalmeen and the Majlis-e-Mushawarat utilize Muslims as their vote banks by championing their religious sentiments.

The communal politics in different regions of our country, such as Jammu and Kashmir, Andhra Pradesh, Kerala, Uttar Pradesh, Maharashtra and Bihar, are examples of such behaviour. Politicians charge the social atmosphere with communal passion by their inflammatory speeches, writings and propaganda. They sow the seeds of distrust in the minds of the Muslims, while the Hindus are persuaded that they are unjustly coerced into making astonishing concessions to the Muslims in the economic, social and cultural fields.

They also take undue advantage of the deep religious traditions of both the communities and show differences in their respective practices and rituals. The leaders also try to use economic debates to instil fear and suspicion in the minds of people and prepare their followers to initiate a riot at the least provocation. It has happened in Bhiwandi, Moradabad, Meerut, Ahmedabad, Aligarh and Hyderabad.

Social issues, like large sections of Muslims declining to use family planning measures, also generate suspicion and ill-feeling among the Hindus. A few years ago, leaflets were spread in Pune and Sholapur in Maharashtra by one Hindu organization condemning/debunking the Muslims for not implementing family planning programme and practicing polygyny with the goal to allegedly increase their population and install a Muslim government in India. All this shows how a combination of political, economic, social, religious and administrative factors worsens the situation which leads to communal riots.

Following are some of the important factors responsible for the growth of Communalism in India:

- ***Divide and Rule Policy of the British:*** The British rulers initiated the strategy of 'Divide and Rule' to strengthen their roots while living in India. They separated the people of various communities of India and induced the feeling of distrust among them and hence they sowed the seeds of communalism in India.
- ***Political Institutions:*** Various communal institutions are traced in India which have spread hatred among the people of various religious communities by proliferating, and hence they are the main reason of communalism.
- ***Inertia indifferent Government:*** When the government does not initiate proper action at the proper time, communalism extends its roots among the subjects. Sometimes, the government favours the religion and leave others which create differences.
- ***Ineffective Handling of Communal Riots:*** Occasionally, the state governments have been unsuccessful in curbing the communal riots in their respective states, resulting in spreading the communalism.

Due to the above factors, communalism disturbed India after the Independence and also posed great problems even in the working of Indian political system.

Remedies

- The remedy of constitutional protections to eliminate the chronic malaise of communalism and casteism shall not have anticipated effect unless it is eliminated by society itself.
- Efforts should be made by the progressive citizens to eliminate the communal and caste-based forces from the social, political and electoral process to make these forces inapt. They are to be opposed not to be appeased.
- Communal killing and caste wars should be dealt seriously with new tactics.
- To bring an era of social equity and sarva dharma sambhava, the Indians should not blend religion and caste with politics to accomplish the goal of common brotherhood for the unity and integrity of the nation.

❑❑❑

Chapter eight

Major Linkages Between Development and Spread of Extremism

Important Types of Development

- Economic development includes subject related to employment, income, output, investment and infrastructure development.
- Social development focuses on subjects related to gender equality, women empowerment, no caste and religious differentiation, social protection and social capital.
- Political development relates to political stability, democracy, civil liberties, political rights and so on.
- Administrative development is a term related to good governance, effective and efficient delivery system, transparency, accountability and pro-people governance.
- Human development includes all facets of development, that is, physical, mental and spiritual development. All the above-mentioned developments aim at human progress.

Extremism and Its Meaning

'Extremist' can be defined as 'a person who holds extreme or fanatical political or religious views, especially one who resorts to or advocates extreme action'. It is 'an ideology (particularly in politics or religion), considered to be far outside the mainstream attitudes of a society or to violate common moral standards. Extremism can take many forms, including political, religious and economic'.

If an individual's views on the subjects like politics, religion or social issues are completely against liberal and progressive views of the mainstream, then he/she will be considered among the category of extremists.

Extremism, considering both sides of the political field, is any philosophy or political action that is totally against the laws of a society; or otherwise seen to break common moral rules. In liberal societies, those advocating to replace the democracy with a more authoritarian regime are seen as extremists; in authoritarian societies, those who advocate liberal ideals are seen as extremists by the ruling class or government. Extremism is normally compared with moderation, and extremists with moderates (for example, in contemporary thoughts in Western countries of Islam, or of Islamic political movements, it is usual to lay stress on the difference between extremist and moderate Muslims, and it is also not uncommon to signify difference between extremist Christians and moderate Christians, as in nations such as the United States). Political agendas thought of as extremist often contain those from the far left or far right; as well as radicalism, reactionism, fundamentalism and fanaticism. Extremism is almost invariably used pejoratively; however, it may also sometimes be associated with person(s) who have different view(s) which is not consistent with the prevailing norm(s). It need not necessarily imply that the person is a threat to the society or the government or any other agency.

Definition of Extremism

There exist many definitions of 'extremism' with the changing time.. Following are the observations of definitions by Dr. Peter T. Coleman and Dr. Andrea Bartoli:

- Extremism is a complex process, although its complexity is often hard to detect. Normally, it can be defined as activities (beliefs, attitudes, feelings, actions, strategies) of a character far removed from the ordinary. In conflict settings it manifests as a severe form of conflict engagement. However, the labelling of activities, people, and groups as 'extremist', and the defining of what is 'ordinary' in any setting is always a subjective and political matter. Thus, we suggest that any discussion of extremism be mindful of the following:
- Typically, the same extremist act will be considered by some as just and moral (such as pro-social 'freedom fighting'), and by others as unjust and immoral (antisocial 'terrorism') depending on the observer's values, politics, moral scope and the nature of their relationship with the actor.
- Besides these, one's logic of the moral or immoral nature of a given act of extremism (such as Nelson Mandela's use of guerilla war tactics against the South African Government) may differ as scenarios (leadership, world opinion, crises, historical accounts, etc.) change. Thus, the current and historical context of extremist acts shapes our view of them.
- Power differences are also considered while defining extremism. When in a difficult situation, the conducts of members of low power groups are likely to be viewed as more extreme than similar activities conducted by members of groups advocating the status quo. In addition, extreme acts are more likely to be employed by marginalized people and groups who view more normative forms of conflict engagement as blocked for them or biased. Whereas, dominant groups also commonly employ extreme activities (such as governmental sanctioning of violent paramilitary groups or the attack in Waco by the FBI in the United States).
- Extremist activities often use violent means, although extremist groups will vary in their choice for violent vs. non-violent tactics, in the level of violence they use and in the preferred targets of their violence (from infrastructure to military personnel to civilians to children). Again, low power groups are more likely to use direct, episodic forms of violence (such as suicide bombings), whereas dominant groups are likely to be associated with more structural or institutionalized forms (like the covert use of torture or the informal sanctioning of police brutality).
- Though an individual or group with extremist ideology (such as Hamas and Islamic Jihad) is often viewed as cohesive and consistently evil, it is important to recognize that they may be conflicted or ambivalent psychologically as individuals, and/or comprise a great deal of difference and conflict within their groups. For example, individuals of Hamas may vary considerably in their willingness to negotiate their differences with the Palestinian Authority and, ultimately, with certain factions in Israel.

- Finally, the main problem that extremism poses in conditions of protracted conflict is less the severity of the activities (whereas violence, trauma and escalation are obvious concerns) but more so the closed, fixed, and intolerant nature of extremist attitudes, and their subsequent imperviousness to change.

Radicalism or Extremism

The terms extremism and extremist are almost exonymic, that is, implemented by others to a group rather than by a group labelling itself. Instead of thinking themselves extremist, those labelled as such might pose themselves as, for example, political radicals. There is no political party that calls itself 'right-wing extremist' or 'left-wing extremist', and there is no sect of any religion that calls itself 'extremist' or which calls its doctrine 'extremism'. The term extremist is used to describe groups and individuals who have become radicalized, in some way, even though the term radical originally meant to go to the root of a (social) problem. 'Radical' is a term not usually regarded as pejorative (except perhaps in the United States of America) and, unlike extremist, is sometimes used by groups to describe themselves. The term extremist is frequently used in relation to those who use or advocate violence against the will of society at large, but it is also used by some to describe those who support or use violence to enforce the will of the social body, such as a government or majority constituency. Those described as extremist would in general not accept that what they practice or advocate constitutes violence and would instead speak in terms of acts of 'resistance' or militant action or the use of force. The term violence cannot be considered as value-neutral. Ideology and methodology normally become indistinguishably inculcated under the single term extremism. The belief that there exists a philosophy which can be described as extremism is considered by some to be suspect. Within sociology, several academics who track (and are critical of) extreme right-wing groups have objected to the term extremist, which was popularized by centrist sociologists in the 1960s and 1970s. As per Jerome Himmelstein, 'At best this characterization tells us nothing substantive about the people it labels; at worst it paints a false picture'. The process of labelling a person, group or action as extremist is sometimes claimed to be a method to further a political goal – especially by governments wanting to defend the status quo, or political centrists. In any case, the word extremist – like the term violence – cannot be considered as value-neutral.

Factors that Led to Expansion of Extremism

The following are the factors that led to expansion of terrorism:

- *Jal–Jungle–Jameen:* disruption of age old tribal–forest relationship, violation of traditional land rights, land acquisition without appropriate compensation and rehabilitation
- *Economic:* unemployment, poverty, hunger, lack of basic facilities, persisting inequality
- *Social Discrimination:* untouchability, denial of human rights oppression and abuse of life
- *Political:* lack people's participation in government, political indifference to the excluded section of society
- *Poor Governance and Mal-Administration:* lack of pro-poor policies, problem in implementation, corruption and leakage in the system
- Geographical
- Historical
- Cultural and Ethnic Issues

There exist some development-related aspects which are directly responsible to spread extremism

(1, 2 and 3 have direct link with the cause of the extremism) among the above-mentioned aspects. Political and governance problems only add fuel to the existing tension. Geographical, historical, ethnic problems have their own roots.

Dismantling age-old relationship

- The relationship between tribes and forest is century old. They have born in the lap of nature and nature is the livelihood for them. But modernization and industrialization started destroying natural forest, resulting in loss of basic livelihood for tribes. The forest Act 1927, the forest conservation Act, 1980 and developmental activities like mining, power and infrastructure projects are some of the important interventions in their life and livelihood.
- The Forest Survey of India Report 2003 revealed that about 60% of the forest cover of the country and 63% of the dense forests lie in 187 tribal districts, that is, districts covered by the Fifth and Sixth Schedules to the Constitution. This has many effects which impinge on the condition of adivasis. The commercial and industrial over exploitation of forest produce including timber and minerals create hazards for ecological balance. Adivasis are traditionally aware of the ecological interest of preserving forest cover, and the protection of biodiversity including wildlife conservation for their community life.
- With the advent of industrialization, the tribals became helpless and were deprived of getting the fruits of development. In addition, extreme poverty deteriorated their conditions further.
- Problems like deprivation and poverty are responsible for extremism and radicalization in the tribal areas. Tribals followed extremist ideologies and became vulnerable to extremist ideologues. These people should have been given proper attention and fair share in the economic gains.
- Hence, tribal population became an easy target to influence them with extremist ideology, and poor governance and socio-political factor have given enough room for this ideology to grow and turn in to a Naxalite movement.

Economic factors

- High rate of poverty, want of education and low employment prospects are the major reasons of emergence of extremist groups.
- Economic exploitation leads to a feeling of desperation, and it forces the people to resort to violent means for their survival.
- Marginalized section of the society like Dalits and Adivasis are the sufferers of these economic sufferings and in turn they adopt the extremist path. States like Bihar, Orissa, Madhya Pradesh, Uttar Pradesh and West Bengal have highest rural poverty, and they also account for a high proportion of SC and ST poor.
- Unemployment among the youth is one of the key socio-economic issues of the area that ultimately finds linkages with issues like insecurity and extremism. Minds of the unemployed youth can be manipulated and encouraged to take up the extremist activities in exchange of some economic gain.

Social issues

- Social segregation and banishment in some parts of society cause a feeling of deprivation and frustration among the excluded people, and they mature antagonistic attitude towards the government and the system, causing extremism to grow.
- Dalits proposed to keep the Government allotted TV in the Dalit colony in Senganyam

village, Tamil Nadu. The Panchayat Pradhan got angry and high caste Hindus attacked the Dalit houses and ransacked them in collaboration with the local police.

Political Marginalization

The Constitution through its various articles has ensured the political participation of SCs/STs (dalits and adivasis) through the following three measures: Fundamental Right to equality granted to citizens, abolition of discrimination including untouchability and special provision for their representation in legislature.

The equality in political arena for dalits is compromised in various ways. Untouchability practices and exertion of dominance by 'higher' caste groups were the biggest threats to the exercise of the right to vote without fear or favour. The absence of public buildings to serve as a polling booth near the cluster of dalits prevents this option being exercised on a large scale, even where the local officials are motivated to provide such a booth. Dalit votes are frequently 'captured' en-masse. Both discrimination and dominance affect the exercise of the right to contest elections, which severely circumscribes dalit freedom. The practices, such as threatening dalit aspirants not to contest the election, forcing them to withdraw their candidature if they file their nomination, and assaulting them and their supporters if they persist in their political assertion, are mostly prevalent.

Because of restrictions on civil liberties and political rights, affected groups hold extremist ideology to claim their rights.

Governance Deficit

- In the Indian Constitution, Articles 14, 15 and 16 provide the framework for a harmonious conjuncture of equality as citizens and compensatory discrimination and affirmative action in favour of SCs/STs and the other backward sections in certain areas. The Directive Principles cast an obligation on the State to promote the educational and economic interests of these sections, and social and economic justice and equality. These mandates have been translated into specific policy instruments for social justice.
- For protecting the interests and entitlements of these communities against encroachment by non-eligible persons and neglect by the State, Constitutional and statutory bodies like National/State Commissions have also been created.
- The failure of governance has led to these lapses, which has multiple dimensions and is not confined to the inefficiency of the delivery system only. It is not accidental that tremendously large sections of bureaucracy/technocracy constituting the delivery system come from landowning dominant castes or well-to-do middle classes, with their affection to ownership of property, cultural superiority, purity pollution governed behaviour and a state of mind which rationalizes and asserts their existing position of dominance as compared to others. It affects their attitudes, behaviour and performance. With the passing time, the politics has also been functioning as per this social segment, which constitutes the power structure in rural and urban areas since colonial times. It is this combination of interests and social background that deeply affect governance at all levels.
- The pitiable execution of social sectors in government programmes has been credited to the dearth of mobilization and accountability, the lack of performance appraisal, non-existence of a system of incentives and penalties, understaffing, poor working conditions and large-scale loopholes.

- These disorders can be fixed by introducing improved transparency, greater accountability and streamlining the structures of Government.
- There exist numbers of cases of socio-economic exploitation of these downtrodden sections by the upper class and caste in Indian scenario. For instance, when Dalit people staged a peaceful protest on 7 March 2004 against the molestation of a Dalit girl in Punjab, police opposed and violently lathicharged the community. They were dragged, beaten and even the Dalit women were not spared.
- These types of development paradigms happening since independence have only heightened the prevailing discontent among marginalized sections of society. This is because the development paradigm as conceived by the policy makers has always been imposed on these communities, and therefore it has remained insensitive to their needs and concerns, causing irreparable damage to these sections. The benefits of this paradigm of development have been disproportionately cornered by the dominant sections at the expense of the poor, who have borne most of the costs. Development which is insensitive to the needs of these communities has invariably caused displacement and reduced them to a sub-human existence. In relation to tribes, in particular, it has ended up in destroying their social organization, cultural identity, and resource base and generated multiple conflicts, undermining their communal solidarity, which cumulatively makes them increasingly vulnerable to exploitation.
- Various worrying factors of the socio-economic context that remains in large parts of India today, and that may (and can) contribute to politics such as that of the Naxalite movement or erupt as other forms of violence.

Constitutional and Legal Safeguards for Tribal Population: A Critical Appraisal

The aim of tribal development in India was best defined in Nehru's Tribal Panchsheel. The Nehru's Panchsheel (five point) are as follows:

- People should develop as per there genius or thinking, and we should not impose anything on them. We must try our best to encourage others to follow their own traditional art and culture.
- Tribal right in land and forests should be respected.
- We should make an attempt to train and build up a team of their own people to do the work of administration and development. Some technical people from outside will no doubt be needed, especially in the beginning. However, we should not introduce too many outsiders into tribal territory.
- We should not over administer these areas or overwhelm them with multiplicity of schemes. We should rather work through and not in rivalry to their own social and cultural instructions, and
- We should guide results not by statistics or the amount of money spends but by the quality of human character that is involved.

The policy of the Indian government is totally based on this five-point formula. This formula was later elaborated by Elwin, who highlighted the need for the tribal people to come to terms with their own past avoiding danger of pauperism and without creating a sense of inferiority. Elwin stressed on recognizing the contribution of the tribal people in helping the Indian Society as a whole, so that they may feel as they are the part and parcel of India as any other citizen. Dr. B.S. Guha described the tribal welfare goals in such a manner that 'schemes for tribal welfare must fulfil two essential conditions namely, conformity to the social values and patterns of the people for whom they are intended and the psychological receptivity and ability of the tribal population to absorb them'. Scheme's theoretical perfection or its suitability to people in general must not be considered the criterion for tribal people. Unawareness of these basic factors and incompetence to appreciate them are the main reasons responsible for the failure of many developmental programmes which by themselves are unexceptionable. Dr. Guha further highlighted regarding tribal development that isolation and absence of interaction with other communities are harmful to the people. The opinions given here are motivated by these consideration only and not framed with the purpose, conscious or unconscious of attempting to keep the tribal people as 'museum specimens' as is so often wrongly attributed to the anthropologists. To enable a tribe to hold its traditional value and the mode of life in its natural setting and provide it the chance to develop along its own genius is in contrast to the 'museum specimens' idea. The goal of tribal development is to increase the incomes and strengthen the material aspects of tribal culture through better consumption of the environmental resources, i.e., forests, minerals, flora and fauna, agriculture, animal husbandry, industrial potential as wells as skill of the tribal people.

The aims of tribal development can be categorized into:

1. Long-term objectives
2. Short-term objectives

The long-term objectives include narrowing the gap of development between non-tribals and tribals and improving the quality of life without disturbing their natural habitat.

The short-term objectives are as follows:

1. Abolition of exploitation by all means, by rapid socio-economic development;
2. Refining organizational capabilities; and
3. Building up inner strength of the tribal people.

Tribal development is often likened to rural development. The tribal condition in the country offers a varied picture. Some areas have high tribal people, while some have no tribals. The developmental parameter of each tribe is different and it depends on the inhabitants and their settling conditions. The tribal development scene was critically reviewed on the eve of Fifth Plan. The evaluation of the first Tribal Plan 1974–1979 was also discussed in the report of the working group on tribal development, during the Sixth Plan (1980–1985) under the chairmanship of B.G. Deshmukh. In relation to 'tribal concentrated areas', it was decided to accept an area development approach with focus on a family oriented programme for tribals and for dispersed tribals.

The significant concern of the developers of the Constitution for the upliftment of the SCs, STs and OBCs can be seen by the elaborate constitutional mechanism set-up for their upliftment. Article 17 eliminates untouchability. Article 46 requires the State to promote with special care the educational and economic interests of the weaker sections of the people, and, in particular, of the Scheduled Castes and the Scheduled Tribes, and to protect them from social injustice and all forms of exploitation. Article 335 provides that the claims of the members of the Scheduled Castes and the Scheduled Tribes shall be taken into consideration, consistently with the maintenance of efficiency of administration, in the making of appointments to services and posts in connection with the affairs of the Union or of a State. Article 15(4) proposes the special provisions for their advancement. Article 16(4A) speaks of 'reservation in matters of promotion to any class or classes of posts in the services under the State in favour of SCs/STs, which are not adequately represented in the services under the State'. Article 338 offers a National Commission for the Scheduled Castes and Scheduled Tribes with responsibilities to investigate and monitor all aspects relating to safeguards provided for them, to investigate into specific complaints and to take part and advise on the planning process of their socio-economic development etc. Articles 330 and 332 of the Constitution respectively propose reservation of seats in favour of the Scheduled Castes and the Scheduled Tribes in the House of the People and in the legislative assemblies of the States. In Part IX regarding the Panchayats and Part IXA of the Constitution relating to the Municipalities, reservation for SCs and STs in local bodies has been provided.

In the Constitution, Parts IX and IXA allow the legislature of a State to frame provision for reservation of seats in Panchayat and Municipalities in favour of backward classes of citizens. Article 340 of the Constitution includes appointment of a Commission to investigate the conditions of backward classes. Articles 16(4) and 16(4A) respectively ensure reservation of appointments or posts and in matters of promotion in favour of backward classes not adequately represented in the services under the State. Article 15(4) allows the State to make special provision for the advancement of any socially and educationally backward classes of citizen. In addition to these, there are also other Constitutional provisions for the welfare and socio-economic empowerment of the SC, the STs and other backward classes.

India's population includes 100 million tribal people who have constitutionally been presented via two distinct avenues. The Fifth Schedule is related to an overwhelming majority of India's tribes in nine States, whereas the Sixth Schedule includes areas that are settled in the northeastern States bordering China and Myanmar.

The Sixth Schedule provides tribal communities substantial autonomy. The states of Assam, Tripura, Meghalaya and Mizoram are autonomous regions under the Sixth Schedule. The roles and responsibilities of the Governor and the State have significant limitations, with greater powers devolved locally. The District Council and the Regional Council under the Sixth Schedule have real power to make laws, possibility on the various legislative subjects, receiving grants-in-aids from the Consolidated Fund of India to meet the costs of schemes for development, health care, education, roads and regulatory powers to state control. The fiat regarding devolution, deconcentration and divestment determines the protection of their customs, better economic development and most importantly ethnic security.

The Fifth Schedule of the Constitution of India has special provisions about the Administration and Control of Scheduled Areas and Scheduled Tribes. The governor also holds the power to give directions to the state on the administration of the Scheduled Area of the state. Such areas are to be managed by the governors of the states by appointing tribal advisory councils from among the tribal community of a particular forest reserve or a scheduled area. Unfortunately this has never happened in India. Instead of protection of these forest lands, these have been leased for mining, causing displacement of tribals.

The Fifth Schedule however fails because it has never been applied. Latest parliamentary efforts to provide greater autonomy within the Fifth Schedule have not had the desired results. The 1996, PESA or Panchayats (Extension to the Scheduled Areas) Act should have been a landmark for the tribal communities. It orders the state to decentralize certain political, administrative and fiscal powers to local governments elected by the communities. This became exclusive to the Fifth Schedule areas, to encourage tribal self-government. PESA was meant to benefit not only the majority of tribals but also extended to cover minority non-tribal communities. It guarantees tribes half of the seats in the elected local governments and the seat of the chairperson at all hierarchical levels of the Panchayat system.

The Ninth Schedule

It includes provisions to deal with the impartial distribution of cultivable land by enacting land ceiling laws and distributing surplus land among the landless labourers. Astonishingly, only three states – Jammu and Kashmir, West Bengal and Kerala – have executed this constitutional imperative. It means that 'all the actions taken by the states through the Forest Department in granting mining leases in forests where Adivasis were living in their state are illegal and unlawful and ultravires of the Constitution of India'.

In West Bengal, the Jotedars (land lords) tried very hard to forge the land records and deceive landless farmers. This resulted in an uprising in a village called Naxalbari, in the Darjeeling district of West Bengal.

Any Naxalite movement was prevented in Kerala as the state government had implemented land ceiling in the non-hilly districts.

PESA

It was regarded as the most rational move in the Fifth Schedule areas to guarantee tribal welfare and accountability. But, sadly, it was not properly executed. Over the period of time, tribal people have been denied self-government and rights to their communities' natural resources that should have been provided under the legislation. In its 1997 Samatha decision, the Apex Court ruled that the Fifth Schedule commanded Governors to bar purchase of tribal land for mining activity by any entity that was not state-owned. This judgment attracted opposite reaction from the Ministry of Mines, and subsequent appeals from the Andhra Pradesh government claiming that Samatha would have an adverse effect not only on the mining sector but also on non-agricultural activities especially industrial activity and hence would impact the economic development throughout the country. In response, the Governors were then provided authority in the transfer of Scheduled Tribe land to the government and allotment to non-tribals, altering the balance of power and undermining the stated goal of tribal autonomy.

Forest Right Act, 2006

The Act provides the power to recognize and vest the forest rights and occupation in forest land in forest dwelling Scheduled Tribes and other traditional forest dwellers who have been living in such forests for generations but whose rights could not be recorded.

This Act establishes the right of communities to guard and manage their forests (as does PESA), but only if the state agrees whether a certain region is denoted as Village Forest or Reserved Forest. In this course, many communities are expelled without a proper channel of rehabilitation.

The situation is so pathetic that the then Commissioner for SCs and STs, in his 29th Report, said that 'The criminalization of the entire communities in the tribal areas is the darkest blot on the liberal tradition of our country'.

In an example, around 450 families – totalling up to 3,000 people – from the Baiga and Gond tribes in the Kanha Tiger Reserve were expelled June 2014 and told by the forest department that elephants would be released to trample their homes and crops if they did not leave, said London-based Survival International.

Even the government did not provide them any resettlement or any source of income. Some families received a fraction of the compensation they were expecting, while others received nothing.

The forest department's attempt to dilute the provisions of the Scheduled Tribes and other Traditional Forest Dwellers (Recognition of Forest Rights) Act, also known as Forest Rights Act (FRA),Besides rights over MFP, community rights include rights to pasture, water bodies and diversion of up to one hectare (ha) forestland for community infrastructure like schools.

The Scheduled Castes and Scheduled Tribes (Prevention of Atrocities) Act 1989 is an Indian act which focuses on eliminating atrocities that are occurring against members of the SCs and STs while at the same time providing protection, compensation and rehabilitation to victims.

However, its execution remains very weak and the conviction rates are shockingly low. A national-level method has therefore started in India to recommend amendments and improve its enforcement under the name of The National Coalition for the Strengthening of the PoA Act.

The Land Acquisition Act swaps the Land Acquisition Act of 1894 by instituting new rules for reimbursement as well as resettlement and rehabilitation. The most important characteristic of the Act is that the developers will need the agreement of up to 80 per cent of people whose land is acquired for private projects and of 70 per cent of the landowners in the case of public–private partnership projects. Besides, it provides for compensation as high as four times than the practice now in rural areas and two times in urban areas.

However, industry anxieties regarding land use have not been addressed in these draft rules because it is a state subject. 'Centre will only come out with suggestive guidelines on issues where it does not have a legislative jurisdiction but these are desirable activity under the Land Acquisition Act'.

Future Prospects

It should be known that there are various types of movements, and that calling and treating them generally as unrest, a disruption of law and order, is little more than a rationale for suppressing them by force. It is essential to contextualize the tensions in terms of social, economic and political background and bring back on the agenda the issues of the people – the right to livelihood, the right to life and a dignified and honourable existence. The state itself should feel committed to the democratic and human rights and humane objectives that are inscribed in the Preamble, the Fundamental Rights and Directive Principles of the Constitution. The State has to adhere strictly to the Rule of Law. Indeed, the State has no other authority to rule.

It is crucial for the Government to establish that dissent or expression of displeasure is a positive feature of democracy, that unrest is often the one and only thing that actually puts pressure on the government to make things work and for the government to live up to its own promises. However, the right to protest, even peacefully, is often not recognized by the government, and even non-violent protests are met with severe repression. Greater possibility and space for democratic actions will decrease the scale of unrest, as it would generate confidence in governance and open channels for expression of popular discontent. What is surprising is not the fact of unrest, but the failure of the State to draw right conclusions from it. Although the official policy papers establish that there is a direct correlation between what is termed as extremism and poverty, or take note of the fact that the implementation of all development schemes is ineffective, or point to the deep relationship between tribals and forests, or that the tribals suffer unduly from displacement, the governments have in practice remedied unrest merely as a law and order situation. It is necessary to amend this mindset and bring about congruence between policy and implementation. There will be peace, harmony and social progress only if there is equity, justice and dignity for everyone. ❑❑❑

Chapter nine

Challenges to Internal Security Due to the Roles Played by External State and Non-State Actors

Background

Terrorism is an infringement on the sovereignty of countries. The word 'terrorism' is actually very difficult to explain. According to a Chinese philosopher, it means 'to kill one and frighten a thousand'. In other words, 'terrorism is the indiscriminate use of force to achieve a political aim'. It involves committing outrageous acts with a purpose to ensure a political change. Terrorism is also distinguished by its non-state charter even when terrorists receive military, political, economic and other means of support from states. The purpose of a terrorist act is to wilfully target the innocent with the wild use of violence.

Terrorist groups aim to cause widespread disturbances, fear and intimidation. They use violence or the threat of violence as a tool to publicize their causes, motivating those who might be sympathetic to them and threatening those who do not sympathize. Their goal is to influence government policies and they usually reject existing democratic processes, or even democracy itself, as a tool to achieve their objectives.

Their action is designed to influence the government or an international governmental organization or to threaten the public, or a section of the public; made for the purposes of promoting a political, religious, racial or ideological cause; and it involves or causes:

- severe violence against an individual;
- severe damage to assets;
- a danger to an individual's life;
- a severe health risk and risk associated with safety of the public; or
- severe interference with or disruption to an electronic system.

'Terrorism is the premeditated and unlawful use of violence against a non-combatant population or target having symbolic significance, with an aim of either inducing political change through intimidation and destabilization or destroying a population identified as an enemy' (Forst, 2009).

Terrorism refers to planned, organized and systematic use of violence as a tool of coercion with an aim to fulfil political or religious or ideological purposes.

Terrorism in India has had a long and violent history spreading over many decades. But, in the recent past it has seen a series of strikes in different parts of the country. The last decade has seen lethal strikes on the Indian Parliament on 13 December 2001, synchronized series of attacks in the economic hub of India, Mumbai on 26 November 2008, and the bomb blast in the technology, educational and real estate hub of India, Pune on 13 February 2010. According to the Ministry of Home Affairs (MHA) 2009-2010 Annual Report, 'there are subversive/extremist/terrorist activity in Jammu and Kashmir and various States in the North-Eastern region particularly Assam and Manipur; Left Wing Extremism is concentrated in five or six States but is found at some places in other States also'.

Terrorism can be broadly categorized into two parts:

1. Terrorism associated with external state actors; and
2. Terrorism associated with non-state-state actors

In the Arthashastra, Chanakya has opined that a state could be at risk from four types of threats, namely, internal, external, externally-aided internal and internally-aided external. Out of them, the internal threats should be taken care of quickly, for internal troubles, like the fear of the lurking snake, are far more dangerous as compared to external threats. Thus, the most dangerous enemy is the enemy within, according to Chanakya. This advice of Chanakya holds true even today.

As of now, the major internal security problems in India are:

- Separatism in the state of Jammu and Kashmir
- Insurgency in Northeast India
- Left Wing Extremism
- Hinterland Terrorism

1. ***Terrorism associated with External State Actors:*** When any government directly or indirectly involves in terrorism against its own people or the people of another country, it is called as terrorism by state actors.

   Out of the above, the first and the last are a direct outcome of Pakistani influence, which consists of the ISI and Pak military.

   Support to terrorism can have its extensions in the form of financial support, technical support, arms, training or infrastructural support etc.

2. ***Terrorism associated with Non-State Actors:*** When the government or its agency is not directly or indirectly linked in any manner with any terrorist group, then terror activities of these groups are known as terrorism by Non-state Actors. However in reality, without the support of the government, these groups can't function in any country. So any linkage of the government with these terrorist groups can't be totally ruled out. For instance, Naxalites, LTTE, North East extremists.

   The insurgents in north east get direct or indirect assistance from neighbouring countries of India around its porous north east border. The left wing extremism gets direct and indirect support from Nepal, China and other countries of South East Asia.

Rise of Terrorism in Neighbouring Countries and Threat to India

From historical perspective, India has border disputes with Pakistan, China and Bangladesh. The problem with India is that it is situated on the epicentre of terrorism and handling so many hostile neighbours, all at once. India has faced head to head wars with our neighbours in 1947–48, 1962, 1965, 1971 and 1999. The causes for India's security circles include:

- Nuclear Capabilities of countries like China and Pakistan

- Military domination and String of Pearls strategy of China
- Pakistan's military rule in the guise of the civilian government
- Anti-India feelings in Nepal and Bangladesh
- Suspicion of Sri Lanka in Tamil cause and fishermen issues
- Bhutan's concern to move closer to China
- Illegal immigration from Bangladesh to design ethnic issues in North East

Thus, the whole subject matter can be categorized into the following:

- Contribution of state and non-state actors in Pakistan
- Contribution of state and non-state actors in China
- Contribution of state and non-state actors in Nepal
- Contribution of actors in Bangladesh.
- Contribution of different actors in Pakistan

There is no need to introduce ourselves on the perennial external covert and overt threat from Pakistan to India's internal and external security apparatus. Since its birth, India has fought four wars in 1948, 1965, 1971 and 1998 with this rogue country. As a result of its military inability to challenge India in direct war, India is facing low intensity conflict in J&K, assisted and initiated by Pakistani military, in the North-East and through support to different fringe extremist groups within the country. We also undergo large economic problems due to the rackets of fake currency.

Pakistan is one of India's main causes of worry both on external and internal security fronts. Due to its long-standing strategic partnership with China, it can stretch our armed forces capabilities in the Eastern sector also. The Chi-Pak nexus has resulted in external concerns such as modernization plans of Karakoram highway, development of Gwadar as a naval port and covert assistance in Pakistan's nuclear and missile program. The different state and non-state actors in Pakistan involve:

- Inter-services Intelligence as well as Pak Military
- Islamic terrorist groups such as the Al-Qaeda, Lashkar-e-Toiba, Harkat-ul-Jihad Islami, Jaish-e-Mohammad, the Pakistani Taliban as well as various other Jehadi Tanjims.

The covert activities of these organizations apart from terrorist attacks in different parts of the country involve training and facilitation to armed rebels by ISI in different training camps in Pakistan. Besides Kashmiri militants, ISI has in past and present trained the Sikh Separatists also. In recent times, union government claims that the ISI has been making all efforts to revive the Sikh Militancy to carry out terrorist attacks in Punjab and other regions of the country.

China's Role

Historically, China has offered financial aid, arms and sanctuaries to Naga, Mizo and Meitei extremist's right since the British Era. The military infringement and conflict of 1962, followed by defeat of India has psychologically contained our leaders thereafter. Since then, china has been shrewdly following a policy of strategic containment of India by regional alliances and arming India's neighbours Myanmar, Bangladesh and Pakistan. So far as internal security is concerned, China's interest focuses on North East along with the Left Wing Extremism. The Nagas were the first to take the assistance of Beijing, but China made best use of it. Other groups such as MNF, ULFA, PLA, ATTF and NDFB followed. However, it is difficult to say that the linkage was unilateral. It was a relationship of convenience and an alliance of opportunism between China and Indian militant groups. Both Issac Swu and Muivah have been visiting the Chinese embassy officials in Geneva and there are reports of Chinese offer of basses in Yunan. The Maoist movement received ideological, moral, financial and intellectual support from China.

Nepal's Role

Nepal is amidst political turmoil since the removal of unpopular King Gyanendra. India and Nepal continue to share an open boundary with free exchange of people and currency across the borders. In recent times, the CPN (Maoists) are increasingly becoming formidable political power and this brings new implications for India's internal security, especially in view of their known connections with Indian Left Wing Extremists. Moreover, India's hold in Nepal no more remains the same as in past as the Maoists have been continuously protesting against India, accusing India of poking its nose in internal affairs of Nepal. Thus, Nepal can significantly add to India's Maoist menace by joining hands with the rebels in the red corridors of India. In this way, the unfolding political and security situation in Nepal would have to be closely examined.

Bangladesh's Role

Trans-border migration from Bangladesh has been an important cause for the problems in Assam and other North East regions of India. The fact that Bangladesh immigrants are a source of communal and ethnic tension was well reflected by the Assam agitation and subsequent events. These are estimated to be 15 to 18 million illegal Bangladeshi immigrants in India, who have moved across the North Eastern States with most of them positioned in Assam. In a few states, these illegal immigrants have turned the majorities into minorities. The influx is likely to go on unless checked and those already identified are deported. Their infringement over land and offering cheap labour is a cause of social and economic insecurity for local communities and a cause of tension and violence. The problem is getting more and more complicated. India needs to tighten its immigration controls and there is need for evolving an immigration policy and putting in place a set up similar to the Immigration and Naturalization Service on the lines that exist in the USA.

Militant Outfits Active in India

- The government has taken note of 65 terror groups that are active in the country, out of which a maximum of 34 are in Manipur.
- The list of terrorist groups active in various states underlines that Jammu and Kashmir has five such organizations which include Lashkar-e-Taiba, Hizbul-Mujahideen, Jaish-e-Mohammad, Harkat-e-Mujahideen and Al Badr.
- In the North-east, Assam has 11, Meghalaya four, Tripura two, Nagaland four, Mizoram two and Manipur 34. In the North-east, Assam consists of 11 such groups, Meghalaya four, Tripura two, Nagaland four, Mizoram two and Manipur 34.
- The three militant groups active in Punjab include Babbar Khalsa International, Khalistan Zindabad Force and Khalistan Commando Force.
- Different terrorist groups such as LeT, IM, HM, HuJI, and Al Badr are active in the main land of the country, especially in states like Uttar Pradesh, Maharashtra, Gujarat, Karnataka, Kerala, Rajasthan, Andhra Pradesh and Delhi.

Ministry of Home Affairs has put a ban on the Communist Party of India (Marxist-Leninist) People's War, all its associated formations and front organizations, the Maoist Communist Centre, all its allied formations and front organizations in LWE hit areas.

Important Militant Outfits in India

- ***Lashkar-e-Taiba(LeT):*** It was formed by Hafeez Saeed in the year 1990. It is one of the largest and most active terrorist organizations in south Asia. Its centre of operation is in the regions of Pakistan and Pakistan occupied Kashmir.

- ***Jaish-e-Mohammed (JeM):*** It was founded by Maulana Masood Azhar in March 2000 after a rift within Hazrat-ul-Mujahideen (HUM). JeM as well as LeT has been indicted of Indian Parliament attack in 2001.
- ***Hizb-ul-Mujahideen:*** This outfit came into being in the Kashmir Valley in September 1989 under Master Ahsan Dar as its chief. Of the terrorist outfits presently active in Jammu and Kashmir (J&K), the Hizb-ul-Mujahideen (HM) is the one of the largest, with a cadre base drawn from indigenous and foreign sources. It is one of the most noted terrorist outfits based on its effectiveness in perpetrating violence across the State on a periodic basis. The HM is one of the 32 outfits proscribed under the Prevention of Terrorism Act, 2002.
- ***Students Islamic Movement in India (SIMI):*** The Students Islamic Movement of India (SIMI), proscribed under the Unlawful Activities (Prevention) Act, 1967, is an Islamist fundamentalist organization, which campaigns for the 'liberation of India' by converting it to an Islamic land. The SIMI, an organization of young extremist students has made a declaration of lodging Jihad against India, the purpose of which is to set up Dar-ul-Islam (land of Islam) by either converting everyone to Islam by force or by violence.

  The SIMI was established at Aligarh in the State of Uttar Pradesh on April 25, 1977. Mohammad Ahmadullah Siddiqi, Professor of Journalism and Public Relations at the Western Illinois University Macomb, Illinois, was the founding President of the outfit.

  In 2001, SIMI was banned by the Indian government, when it was found to have involved in terrorist acts.
- ***Indian Mujahideen (IM):*** The most widely known terrorist organization of India is the Indian Mujahideen (IM), an Islamic terrorist group. Due to the organization's close association with the Islamic terrorist groups Lashkar-e-Taiba (LeT) and the Student Islamic Movement of India (SIMI), its initial origins are unclear. However, the first attack connected to the IM was the Varanasi bombing in February 2005. That was followed by the Mumbai train bombings in 2006, serial bombings in Ahmedabad and Delhi in 2008, and the attack on the 'German Bakery' in Pune in 2010.

  Most of these attacks consisted of pressure cooker bombs, bicycle bombs, and car bombs, but occasionally firearms. However, the organization does have a trademark: Before each attack, IM terrorists sent emails to the National Intelligence Agency (NIA) or government departments, in which they communicated the attack's purpose. Then, shortly before the attacks, hackers penetrated Wi-Fi networks to cover their traces and make it more difficult for investigators to recognize them.

  For instance, before the Delhi blasts in 2008, IM members spread messages about the forthcoming event by hacking into an open Wi-Fi in Mumbai, aiming to send the intelligence team to the wrong place. The IM has also been known to use cyberspace to collect knowledge, recruit new personnel, and upset national security by spreading terror and propaganda online. This has been in evidence recently. In August 2014, the IM was accused of assisting the Islamic State with recruitment and propaganda. By providing financial incentives and using YouTube videos as a medium to promote jihadism, the IM is making use of the Internet to attract and persuade poor Indian Muslims to join the fighting in Iraq. By the time of the report, more than 100 young Indian men were reported missing, believed to have visited Middle East to become a part of the Islamic State.

Earlier, the IM was known to be active only within India, targeting territories with strong Islamic ideological bonds, such as Kerala, Karnataka, the north-eastern states bordering Bangladesh and Myanmar, rural areas in Uttar Pradesh, and Jammu & Kashmir. This recent cooperation with the Islamic State suggests the organization is expanding its ties towards the Middle and Far East.

- ***Tehreek-ul-Mujahideen:*** The Tehreek-ul-Mujahideen (TuM) was founded in June 1990 by Yunus Khan, a close comrade of Mohammed Abdullah Tairi, chief of the Jammu and Kashmir Jamaat-e-Ahle-Hadith.

  The TuM works with a purpose to merge the Indian State of Jammu and Kashmir (J&K) with Pakistan and also encourages a pan-Islamist identity. The protection of Asidih community, a small fraction of Sunni Muslims, was an important motivating factor for the outfit in its initial days.

  Since 1995, the ISI began to route funds to the LeT through the TuM.
- ***Sleeper Cell:*** This includes secret agents who get highly specialized training in their home countries and are then provided some violent assignments to assimilate into another country's culture and society. These agents may spend years doing their routine activities while living deep undercover, and then all of a sudden receive orders from their overseas handlers to either execute an act of terrorism or provide assistance to those who want to involve in such acts.

Terrorist Organizations That Have Been Banned

Schedule I - First Schedule (of the UA (P) Act, 1967)

Terrorist Establishments

1. Babbar Khalsa International
2. Khalistan Commando Force
3. Khalistan Zindabad Force
4. International Sikh Youth Federation
5. Lashkar-E-Taiba/Pasban-E-Ahle Hadis
6. Jaish-e-Mohammad/Tahrik-e-Furqan
7. Harkat-ul-Mujahideen/Harkat-ul-Ansar/Harkat-ul-Jehad-e-Islami
8. Hizb-ul-Mujahideen/Hizb-ul-Mujahideen Pir Panjal Regiment
9. Al-Umar-Mujahideen
10. Jammu and Kashmir Islamic Front
11. United Liberation Front of Assam (ULFA)
12. National Democratic Front of Bodoland (NDFB) in Assam
13. People's Liberation Army (PLA)
14. United National Liberation Front (UNLF)
15. People's Revolutionary Party of Kangleipak (PREPAK)
16. Kangleipak Communist Party (KCP)
17. Kanglei Yaol Kanba Lup (KYKL)
18. Manipur People's Liberation Front (MPLF)
19. All Tripura Tiger Force
20. National Liberation Front of Tripura
21. Liberation Tigers of Tamil Eelam (LTTE)
22. Students Islamic Movement of India
23. Deendar Anjuman
24. Communist Party of India (Marxist-Leninist) – People's War, All its formations and front organizations.

25. Maoist Communist Centre (MCC), all its formations and Front Organizations
26. Al Badr
27. Jamiat-ul-Mujahideen
28. Al-Qaida
29. Dukhtaran-E-Millat (DEM)
30. Tamil Nadu Liberation Army (TNLA)
31. Tamil National Retrieval Troops (TNRT)
32. Akhil Bharat Nepali Ekta Samaj (ABNES)
33. Organizations listed in the Schedule to the U.N. Prevention and Suppression ofTerrorism (Implementation of Security Council Resolutions) Order, 2007 made under section 2 of the United Nations (Security Council) Act, 1947 and amended from time to time.
34. Communist Party of India (Maoist) all its formations and front organizations.
35. Indian Mujahideen, all its formations and front organizations.
36. Garo National Liberation Army (GNLA), all its formations and front organizations.

Terrorism associated with Right Wing

- If terrorism has a periodic external threat to India, right wing Hindu fanatics have a more constant danger of destabilizing Indian politics and society. some of the Right Wing activities include Malegaon Blasts, Samjhauta Express bombings and the Ajmer Sharif dargah blast.
- The growth of right wing forces over the past few years puts forth alarming questions about the safety and security of liberal ideals in India. Examples of right wing excess abound. Renowned painter Maqbool Fida Husain was hounded by right wing Hindu forces who finally abandoned his Indian citizenship to live in Dubai and England. He died as lonely man in the latter, far from his friends and home. And, last year, Mumbai University was forced to withdraw the book Such a Long Journey from its syllabus because it contained 'unpalatable' references to the Hindu group Shiv Sena.
- A book release function for the writer and social activist Arundhati Roy, which this writer attended, saw similar right wing hooliganism a few months ago. The moment the Booker Prize winning author mentioned Kashmir, goons rushed to the stage, disrupting her speech and snatching her microphone from her. The attackers reportedly had previous connections with the main Opposition Bhartiya Janata Party and its parent organization Rashtriya Swayamsewak Sangh (RSS).

Methods to Counter Terrorism in India

The November 2008 fatal terrorist assault on Mumbai's hotel district and a spate of bomb attacks (BBC) across India's cities the same year have claimed hundreds of lives and once again put forth questions about India's vulnerability to terrorism. As per the recent report on global terrorism by the U.S. government's National Counter-Terrorism Center, more than one thousand people were killed in India due to terrorist attacks in 2007, ranking India fourth behind only Iraq, Afghanistan, and Pakistan. India, a nation of a billion people, has been facing terrorism since its birth, and presently contends with a variety of regional groups mainly intent on separatism.

Agencies Associated with Fighting Terrorism in India

- A number of intelligence, military, and police organizations within the Indian government play an important role in countering terrorism. These consist of state-run police forces, special security forces to guard airports and other high-profile targets, and paramilitary forces that keep a watch on the borders and help the police when required. These paramilitary groups, like the 165,000-strong Central Reserve Police Force, have been alleged of violating human rights, particularly in Kashmir, where they are especially active. The army often takes part in counterterrorism operations as a last resort, though in Jammu and Kashmir they play a more consistent role. India's closest structural equivalent to the U.S. Department of Homeland Security is the Ministry of Home Affairs, which oversees national police, paramilitaries, and domestic intelligence gathering.

- India has a number of intelligence agencies that keep a watch on terrorist activities. The Research and Analysis Wing (RAW) is the external intelligence agency and the Intelligence Bureau (IB), a division of the Home Affairs Ministry gathers intelligence inside India. A Joint Intelligence Committee analyses intelligence data from RAW and IB as well as from a small number of military intelligence agencies, which often provide tactical information gathered while carrying out counterterrorist operations.
- The IB supervises an inter-agency counterterrorism centre similar to the CIA. The Ministry of External Affairs looks after its own counterterrorism body, much like the U.S. State Department, which oversees diplomatic counterterrorism operations like briefing other nations on suspected Pakistani sponsorship of terrorism in India.
- In the year 2002, India passed the Prevention of Terrorism Act (POTA), expanding the government's powers in fighting terrorism. Some steps, such as the ability to keep terror suspects in custody without bringing them to trial, met with objections, and the law was repealed in 2004 after allegations that officials were abusing their powers. However, after the spate of bombings in recent times, some Indian politicians are demanding to restore the law.
- It is expected that a multi-disciplinary centre on counter-terrorism, led by a senior IB officer, within the IB, be established on the CIA's counter-terrorism centre. Administrators of different agencies responsible for intelligence collection and counter-terrorism operations will work under a common entity and be responsible for joint analysis of the intelligence flowing in from different agencies and coordinated follow-up action.
- In addition, a counter-terrorism unit should be planned in the ministry of external affairs, based on the counter-terrorism division of the US state department. The responsibility of this unit will be to co-ordinate with the various diplomatic aspects of counter-terrorism, such as briefing other countries on Pakistan's sponsorship of terrorism against India, processing requests for extradition and mutual legal assistance, servicing the work of various joint working groups on counter-terrorism which India has set up with a number of countries, etc.

Changes after the 2008 Mumbai Attack

Post the terror attacks in Mumbai in 2008, India had taken many steps in building its counter-terrorism policies by agencies like the Central Bureau of Investigation (CBI), the National Security Guard (NSG) and the National Investigation Agency (NIA). It also took steps to execute the National Intelligence Grid (NATGRID), a system for linking databases in different government departments and Ministries for use by intelligence agencies.

- ***Formation of the National Investigation Agency (NIA):*** It was formed after the enactment of the NIA Act, 2008, and it is assigned, at the national level, to probe and prosecute violations affecting the sovereignty, security and integrity of India, friendly relations with foreign States and offences under Acts enacted to implement international treaties, agreements, conventions and resolutions of the United Nations and other international organizations and for matters connected therewith or incidental thereto.

According to the National Investigation Agency (Manner of Constitution) Rules, 2008, NIA was constituted to provide help to, and seek help from, other intelligence and investigation agencies of the Central Government and State Governments.

- ***Constitution of NATGRID:*** The idea for the constitution of an integrated intelligence unit is to connect databases of several departments and ministries of the Government of India in order to collect wide-ranging patterns of intelligence that can be voluntarily retrieved by multiple agencies. Moreover, it will help identify, capture and prosecute terrorists and help pre-empt terror plots. NATGRID was first conceptualized by former Home Minister P Chidambaram and was approved by the then UPA Government. It was also aimed to identify, capture and prosecute terrorists and help pre-empt terror plots.
- ***Formation of four new NSG Units:*** The problem of inadequate security forces was solved by forming NSG hubs at four places at Mumbai, Kolkata, Chennai and Hyderabad besides Manesar to ensure fastest and more effective reaction to crisis situation.
- ***Solidifying Multi-Agency Centre:*** After the Kargil war in 1999, the Indian government formed the Kargil Review Committee and afterwards constituted a Group of Ministers (GoM) to assess the National Security Apparatus as a whole. The relevant recommendations of the Group of Ministers given in the year 2001 are as follows:

  According to GoM study, Multi Agency Centre (MAC) was formed at Delhi and Subsidiary Multi Agency Centres (SMACs) in different states comprising representatives from various security agencies, for reforming intelligence efforts. Later, Union Home Minister of India assessed the security scenario and issued Multi Agency Centre (functions, powers and duties) order, 2008 on 31 December 2008. MAC-SMAC is working since 2002 and has been re-operationalized with effect from 2009. As a follow up of the above order, 24x7 Control Rooms have been set up at Multi Agency Centre (MAC) at New Delhi and the Subsidiary Multi Agency Centres (SMACs) at State Level and at Headquarters of Intelligence Wings of other agencies to ensure timely sharing of information and better co-ordination between intelligence agencies Daily meetings of Nodal Officers of 25 member agencies are being conducted on every working day. Presently, MAC-SMAC network has 416 nodes spread across the country and connected to MAC HQ at New Delhi. It comprises of 31 SMAC HQs and 32 SSBs located at state capitals. These nodes are connected by 2 Mbps leased lines of BSNL/MTNL. As of March 14, 2013, 362 nodes, out of total 416 have been installed and made functional.

  MAC is a counter terrorism unit whose work is to share terrorism-related inputs on a day-to-day basis.
- Besides the above measures, several other steps have been taken to toughen the coastal security of the Country after 2008 Mumbai attack.
  - The NSG crack commando strength has been increased to 460 personnel each

stationed at select hubs in Mumbai, Chennai, Kolkata and Hyderabad to perform quick and swift counter-terror or counter-hijack operations.

- ❖ The 2008 Mumbai terror attack, which exposed lapses in coastal security, forced the government to accelerate measures to improve both physical and electronic surveillance along the country's 7,516-km-long coastline. There are a total of nine states and four union territories along the coastline.
- ❖ The government moved on several fronts and set up joint operation centres. Vulnerable spots and gaps along the coast were identified and proposals finalized to improve surveillance.
- ❖ Moves were also expedited for comprehensive registration of fishing boats, providing multipurpose national identity cards (MNICs) to the population in coastal villages and biometric cards to fishermen.
- ❖ The government also decided to set up National Command, Control, Communication and Intelligence Network (NC3I) for real-time maritime domain awareness, linking operations rooms of the Navy and Coast Guard.
- ❖ In addition, 46 radar houses along the coast on lighthouses and promontories were proposed as per the first phase of the coastal surveillance network and at least 30 have been made operational.

Legal Context

- *Terrorist and Disruptive Activities (Prevention) Act, 1987 (TADA):* This act was enacted on 3 September 1987 to tackle terrorism. Its provisions are said to be more strict as compared to other. When TADA was formed, it came to be challenged before the Apex Court of the country as being unconstitutional. The Supreme Court of India upheld its constitutional validity on the assumption that those entrusted with such draconic statutory powers would act in good faith and for the public good in the case of Kartar Singh vs State of Punjab (1994). However, there were many instances of misuse of power for collateral purposes. The rigorous provisions contained in the statute came to be abused in the hands of law enforcement officials. TADA lapsed in 1995.
- *The Maharashtra Control of Organized Crime Act, 1999 (MCOCA):* The other main anti-terrorist law in India is The Maharashtra Control of Organized Crime Act, 1999, which was enacted on 24th April 1999. This law was especially formed to tackle rising organized crime in Maharashtra and especially in Mumbai due to the underworld. For example, the definition of a terrorist act is more widely defined in MCOCA than under POTA. MCOCA mention organized crime and what is more, includes `promotion of insurgency' as a terrorist act. Under the Maharashtra law a person is presumed guilty unless he is able to prove his innocence. MCOCA does not stipulate prosecution of police officers found guilty of its misuse.
- *Prevention of Terrorism Act, 2002*

  With the increase in cross-border terrorism and Pakistan's ISI motive to destabilize India, it became really important to devise a special law to deal with terrorist acts. Accordingly, the Prevention of Terrorism Act, 2002 (POTA, 2002), was formed and notified on 28 March 2002.

  The POTA, 2002, clearly describes the terrorist act and the terrorist in Section 3 and awards exceptional powers to the probing authorities under the Act. In the case of People's Union for Civil Liberties vs. Union of India (UOI) (2004) 9 SCC 580, the constitutional validity of the Prevention of Terrorism Act, 2002, was argued. The court said that the Parliament possesses power under Article 248 and entry 97 of list I of the Seventh Schedule of the Constitution of India to legislate the Act. Need for the Act is a matter of policy and the court cannot go into the same.

- However, to guarantee that these powers are not abused and the violation of human rights does not take place, specific safeguards have been built into the Act. Some of these are as follows:
    - No court can take cognizance of any offence under the Act without the previous sanction of the Central Government or, as the case may be, of the State Government.
    - No officer lower in rank than the Deputy Superintendent of Police can investigate offences under the Act.
    - Confession made by a person before a police officer not below the rank of Superintendent of Police is admissible as evidence under the Act provided such person is produced with 48 hours before a magistrate along with his confessional statement.
    - The Act provides for punishment for any officer who exercises powers maliciously or with malafide intentions. It also provides for award of compensation to a person who has been corruptly or maliciously proceeded against under the Act.

The POTA, 2002, is a unique law for the prevention of and for dealing with terrorist actions and clearly describes the terrorist act and the terrorist in Section 3, Sub-Section (1) of the Act. The Act offers the legal outline to empower the hands of the administration in our fight against the menace of terrorism and can and should be applied against such persons and acts as are covered by the provisions of this law and it is not meant as a substitute for action under ordinary criminal laws.

Unlawful Activities (Prevention) Amendment Act

- Unlawful Activities (Prevention) Act was formed in 1967. This act vested the Central Government to pronounce any association unlawful if Central Government thinks that any association is, or has become, an unlawful association. After the association was declared unlawful by the Government of India by notification, the central Government would move to the 'Unlawful Activities (Prevention) Tribunal' within 30 days for the purpose of adjudicating whether or not there is sufficient cause for declaring the association unlawful. The 'Unlawful Activities (Prevention) Tribunal' was consisting of one person, to be appointed by the Central Government; this person must be a judge of a High Court. The act offered numerous penalties and punishments for the people associated with the unlawful establishments. However, India has an array of similar working acts. Lately UAPA has been used as an antiterrorist law as at present we don't have such law enabled in the country.
- In 2008, the government again made a plan to make the law more stringent to tackle terrorism in a more effective manner. The Unlawful Activities (Prevention) Amendment Bill proposed in 2008 aimed at firming up the arrangements for speedy probe, prosecution and trial of cases related terrorism while at the same time protecting against any possible

misuse of such provisions. At that time, a National Investigation Agency Bill was also introduced which inter alia provided for setting up an agency at the Central level with powers to probe terrorism and other crimes having national ramifications across the country.

- In 2010, the nation became the member of the Financial Action Task Force (FATF). FATF is an intergovernmental unit seeking to fight money-laundering and terrorist financing. Being its member, India agreed to adopt legislation to implement these goals by 15 March 2012. The UAPA (Amendment) Bill was introduced in the Lok Sabha on 29 December 2011 to ostensibly comply with FATF's policy. This was the basic reason that the Unlawful Activities (Prevention) Amendment Act, 2012 came in to being.
- The revision in the Unlawful Activities (Prevention) Bill entitles economic offences including circulation of counterfeit currency as terrorist acts.
- The Act also offers extension of period for ban on an association from existing two to five years.
- An individual, group of individuals and an association indulged in counterfeit currency circulation will be covered under the law.
- Other salient characteristics of the amended law consist of expansion of the definition of terrorist act to include acts that involve detention, abduction, threats to kill or injure, or other actions so as to compel an international or inter-governmental organization to comply with some demand.
- The reformed legislation will cover those indulged in procurement of weapons, raising funds for terrorist activities and counterfeiting Indian currency. It would also cover offences by companies, societies or trusts.

NIA Act, 2008 and Special NIA Courts

- National Investigation Agency (NIA) is a federal body constituted by the Indian Government to fight terror in India. It acts as the Central Counter Terrorism Law Enforcement Agency. The agency is vested to deal with terror-related crimes across states without special permission from the states.
- The Agency was formed after the enactment of the National Investigation Agency Act 2008 by the Parliament of India on 31 December 2008.
- NIA was created after the 2008 Mumbai terror attacks as a requirement for a central agency to fight terrorism was realized.
- NIA has concurrent jurisdiction which authorizes the Centre to probe terror attacks in any part of the country, covering offences, including challenge to the country's sovereignty and integrity, bomb blasts, hijacking of aircraft and ships, and attacks on nuclear installations.
- Besides sins of terrorism, it also deals with counterfeit currency, human trafficking, narcotics or drugs, organized crime (extortion mobs and gangs), plane hijacking and violations of atomic energy act and weapons of mass destruction act.
- Many special courts have been notified by the Central Government of India for conducting trial of the cases registered at various police stations of NIA under the NIA Act 2008. Any question about the jurisdiction of these courts is ruled by the Central Government. These are presided over by a judge appointed by the Central Government on the recommendation of the Chief Justice of the High Court with jurisdiction in that region.
- The Apex Court of India has also been empowered to transfer the cases from one

special court to any other special court within or outside the state if the same is in the interest of justice in light of the prevailing circumstances in any particular state. They are empowered with all powers of the court of sessions under Code of Criminal Procedure, 1973 for trial of any offense.

- An appeal from any judgment, sentence or order, not being an interlocutory order, of a Special Court lies to the High Court both on facts and on law. Such an appeal is heard by a bench of two Judges of the High Court.
- At present there are 38 Special NIA Courts. State Governments have also been empowered to appoint one or more such special courts in their states.
- Besides the above domestic laws, against terrorism, India has already endorsed 14 of 19 instruments of UN council resolution on counter terrorism as a measure of the universal legal framework.

National Counter Terrorism Centre (NCTC)

- This agency was constituted as a need felt after the Mumbai attacks of 26/11. It has reportedly been a top priority for former Home Minister P Chidambaram. The NCTC was given a task to scrutinize through intelligence shared by different agencies like the Intelligence Bureau and decide what is needed. It has the authority to conduct searches and arrests in any part of India. The NCTC, to be located within the Intelligence Bureau, will perform counter-terror operations and collect, collate and distribute data on terrorism. The agency will also maintain a data base on terrorist and their associates including their families. The NCTC will also frame a response to terror threats. It is meant to serve as a single and effective point of control and coordination of all counter terrorism measures.
- The Central Government on 3 February 2012 finalized the formation of the anti-terror agency called National Counter Terrorism Centre (NCTC). NCTC will have the authority to conduct operations including arrest, search and seizure. It will get its functional power of search and seizures under the provisions of the UAPA (Unlawful Activities (Prevention) Act. It will work as an integral part of Intelligence bureau.
- The states who opposed the agency alleged that the NCTC was given the right to search and arrest people without keeping the state government, police or anti-terror squad in the loop. In reply, the centre has changed the rules. Now, the senior most police officers in all states – the Director Generals of Police and the chiefs of anti-terror squads of all states – will be members of the Standing Council of the NCTC. They will be kept in loop before the NCTC conducts an operation in their state.

Difference between Terrorism, Insurgency and Naxalism

Terrorism

It is a well-organized and planned use of violence against civilians, armed forces and the nation by some persons or groups to promote a political agenda.

- It can be across the border and against one's own or other country.
- It may or may not have the support of the local people.

Al Qaeda, Harakat ul-Ansar, Harakat-ul-Mujahideen, Jaish-e-Mohammed, etc. are some of the terrorist organizations.

Being a general term, and Naxalism and insurgency are different forms of terrorism.

Insurgency

It is a violent act or rigorous agitation by a group in the form of uprising against a constitutionally formed government.

- It is limited within the national boundary and is directed against one's own elected government.
- It is often run with the support of a section of the local people.

For instance, some of the insurgent groups are National Socialist Council of Nagaland (NSCN), National Liberation Front of Tripura (NLFT), All Tripura Tiger Force (ATTF), United Liberation Front of Assam (ULFA), etc.

Naxalism

Naxalism signifies a particular kind of militant and violent armed struggle by the peasants and tribals against government. Naxalites have created a serious law and order problem before the nation through killings, blasts, extortions and kidnappings.

- It is fundamentally limited to the tribal belts. However, the network of naxalites has broadened to urban India for logistics, finance and manpower through global terrorist links.
- It has voluntary/involuntary rural support.

The People's War Group (PWG), Maoists Communist Centre (MCC), etc. are some of the naxal groups. ❑❑❑

Chapter ten

Challenges to Internal Security Posed by Radiological and Nuclear Terrorism

Nuclear Terrorism

The term nuclear terrorism can be defined as a number of different ways nuclear materials might be exploited as a terrorist method. These tactics may include attacking nuclear plants, purchasing nuclear weapons, or building nuclear arms or otherwise devising ways to disperse radioactive materials.

Article 2 of the International Convention for the Suppression of the Financing of Terrorism defines the offence of nuclear terrorism as follows:

'Any person commits an offence within the meaning of this Convention if that person unlawfully and intentionally:

(a) Possesses radioactive material or makes or possesses a device:
   - ❖ With the intent to cause death or serious bodily injury; or
   - ❖ With the intent to cause substantial damage to property or to the environment.

(b) Uses in any way radioactive material or a device, or uses or damages a nuclear facility in a manner which releases or risks the release of radioactive material:
   - ❖ With the intent to cause death or serious bodily injury; or
   - ❖ With the intent to cause substantial damage to property or to the environment; or
   - ❖ With the intent to compel a natural or legal person, an international organization or a State to do or refrain from doing an act'.

Concept

The concept of nuclear terrorism is possibly among the least understood of all threats emerging with the proliferation of nuclear weapons. The reason for this is that yet no terrorist group is known to have developed, obtained or deployed nuclear weapons. Hence, the intensity of its threat remains debatable. Conventional countries state that nuclear terrorism is too difficult to occur since it would need substantial efforts, expertise and competence on behalf of the perpetrators. This conditional decision, along with the fact that no incidence of nuclear terrorism has been reported, reinforces the observations that while 'biological, chemical and radiological terrorism is likely, nuclear terrorism is improbable'. Some researchers have sidelined nuclear terrorism on the grounds of technical hurdles, internal factors such as geography and politics, and have mocked it as 'an overrated nightmare'.

Nuclear terrorism can be been defined as 'Acts of violence and destruction performed by non-state actors where the means applied are nuclear explosive devices – or threats of such actions – with the purpose of inflicting destruction, creating a condition of fear, getting attention, blackmailing, installing instability, and to affect an audience beyond the victim directly targeted'.

Radiation in various forms exists everywhere. It is assumed to be rarely dangerous. Nuclear and other radioactive materials, or materials that produce radiation above the normal background rate, are generally well protected. However, the likelihood that terrorists or other criminals might attain nuclear or other radioactive materials for mischievous use has become a real danger to global security and has become more acute due to progress in information technology, financial globalization and the better use of such materials for lawful purposes. Generally, nuclear and other radioactive materials used for mischievous aims are attained by unfair means, e.g., smuggled or stolen from nuclear sites and storage facilities.

Main Threats

- The magnitudes of a terrorist organization developing the ability to use nuclear or radiological materials to achieve their goals could be disastrous.
- The world's law enforcement forces must remain ready to tackle the threat presented by terrorists who seek to acquire and use nuclear or radioactive materials.
- Besides this, nuclear or radioactive materials are appearing with increasing frequency in organized and environmental crimes, such as illegal disposal schemes carried out for profit.
- Hazardous levels of radiation could easily spread from one nation to the next. As such, the problems of nuclear or radioactive terrorism affect not just individual countries but entire regions. Additionally, such an occasion would have implications for national security and economic and political stability on a global level. Consequently, the prevention of such incidents is a high priority.

Nuclear Security

Nuclear security includes employing a series of pre-emptive actions to prevent internal and/or external threats directly or indirectly related to nuclear materials, radioactive sources, related facilities or other associated activities. Keeping in view imminent threat, it involves taking countermeasures to trace, delay and prevent illegal acts, as well as administrative and technical measures to minimize the damage caused by accidents.

- ***Landmarks in the Evolution of the Nuclear Security Issue:*** In the late 1960s, cross-border handovers of nuclear materials increased with the inflated use of nuclear energy for peaceful purposes. The goal of nuclear security was to guarantee stability in the supply of nuclear fuel by preventing the illegal seizure of nuclear materials in transit.

  After the fall of the Soviet Union, handling existing nuclear materials and facilities within the former Soviet territory became a priority issue, with stress on disarmament and the protection of and the reduction in the number of nuclear materials and facilities. After the 9/11 attacks in 2001, the possibility of terrorists misusing nuclear materials and facilities became a real threat, and nuclear security was highlighted as a means to combat the threat of nuclear terrorism. Risks of nuclear terrorism and blackmail have increased significantly in recent years mainly because of the following three factors:

- The development and spread of nuclear weapons;

- The expansion of civilian nuclear programmes; and
- The surge in extremist political groups waging campaigns of terror

The mounting threat embraces much of the world. Sloppy or inadequate security for nuclear materials and weapons in one country could be misused to trigger atomic blackmail and terrorism elsewhere. Inadequate security at nuclear facilities also could provide extremists waging a campaign of terror within a nation an opportunity to create a condition of national terror by clutching or harming a civilian nuclear power plant or a research reactor or a laboratory.

Nuclear power stations, research reactors and laboratories are susceptible to actions of damage and blatant terrorist attacks that could lead to the release of dangerous amounts of radioactive materials. Expanding civil commerce in weapons-usable nuclear materials has raised the spectre of theft of plutonium or uranium in significant quantities in plots aimed at political blackmail or terror. There is also a danger of theft of nuclear arms by terrorists.

Potential for Nuclear Terrorism in South Asia

The terrorist group's lethal combination of technology and a renewed determination to achieve political goals has significantly raised the potential for nuclear terrorism. It is imperative that this expanding threat of nuclear blackmail and terror should spur policymakers to concentrate on corrective measures to guarantee stringent security and safety at nuclear installations.

In South Asia, the potential for nuclear terrorism should be a matter of special concern for following factors:

- First, rapid expansion of nuclear programmes in India and Pakistan involving massive investments in the construction and operation of civilian nuclear power plants, research reactor, laboratories and reprocessing and enrichment facilities;
- Another reason is the increasing stockpiles of nuclear fissionable materials, possibly of actual weapons, in each nation; safeguarding them needs special technologies, safety systems and security checks and surveillance;
- A third reason is that both neighbours continue to be wracked by high levels of terrorist activities that pose major political challenges to their national leaders. Indeed, one country or perhaps both lost a leader at the hands of terrorists since 1984;
- A fourth reason is the increasing sophistication of terrorist methods of operation and attack and the increasing availability of portable weapon systems like shoulder-fired rockets that can be used to accurately strike nuclear installations.

Effects of a Nuclear Terrorist Attack

- The attack with the help of a crude nuclear device by a terrorist organization would be shattering. Although the actual yield of such a device is highly variable, but a clever and competent group could design and construct a device which would produce a significant nuclear yield. Even a device with a yield of 1-10 tonnes, small by military standards, could topple large buildings and devastate urban centres. A one tonne nuclear blast, e.g., would theoretically create an overpressure of 3 pounds per square inch, enough to knock down wooden structures at a radius of 65 meters from the centre of the blast.
- A nuclear blast would also generate considerable fallout, potentially contaminating large areas. A one tonne surface detonation would normally result in fallout with gamma radiation levels in excess of 500 rad (radiation dose) to a distance of 30

to 100 meters from the point of the explosion, with lesser amounts settling over a wider area. Larger blasts would result in greater and more widespread contamination.

- In addition to the immediate physical damage due to a nuclear terrorist attack, the psychological, economic and sociological effects of such an attack would be shattering. Unlike natural disasters, a nuclear attack may occur without warning, leaving little chance for preparation. An attack in an urban area would not only kill large numbers of people, it also could render the area virtually uninhabitable for a long period of time. Survivors may have to be relocated; hospitals and shelters would quickly become filled with displaced persons, many of them injured or suffering from radiation exposure. The shock of such an explosion would leave long-lasting psychological and emotional wounds on the survivors. The clean-up task would no doubt rival even the largest efforts undertaken following comparable natural disasters, such as hurricanes, and would require long-term commitments from local, state and federal relief programmes.

Radiological Dispersal Devices

A different type of nuclear terrorism includes the use of a radiological dispersal device. A radiological weapon is used for dispersal of highly radioactive materials over a target area to make the area uninhabitable or to produce casualties. With few exemptions, governments have not installed radiological weapons, in part because the standards set for such weapons by the military are often too difficult to sustain. To deny territory during a military campaign, for example, the Defense Department requires that a radiological weapon produce a dose rate of 1,000 rad per hour over an area of 10 square kilometres. Isotopes apt to produce such levels of radiation typically have relatively short half-lives, and therefore must constantly be replenished.

Iraq thought of using a radiological weapon during its war with Iran, but found it costly and militarily ineffective. But in relation to a terrorist weapon, the performance of the radiological weapon is less important than the disruption and panic that the spread of even small amounts of radioactive materials would cause. In comparison to the exotic, short-lived isotopes that nations would want to use for military objectives, terrorists might be able to employ isotopes commonly found in commercial use. Many such isotopes are sufficiently radioactive to contaminate an unprotected urban area, even when dispersed in small quantities. Such an attack would have a devastating psychological impact on those exposed to the dispersed materials, and would fear increased risks of cancer or genetic defects. A radiological dispersal would also require an expensive environmental clean-up, and would likely leave large areas not suitable to use even if the level of radiation was small.

The production of a radiological weapon is far less complicated than the assembly of a nuclear explosive device, and may be well within a terrorist group's capability, although the managing and spread of highly radioactive materials pose health and safety challenges that a terrorist group might not wish to risk for fear of incapacitation or discovery. The quantity of radioactive elements required for a dispersal device is substantially less than the quantity of plutonium required to build an explosive device. Nor would the terrorist group be limited to plutonium or HEU for source materials; any highly radioactive substance could cause contamination and necessitate an expensive clean-up if dispersed at a large scale.

For example, the accidental contamination of a village in Brazil with an industrial radiation source illustrates the potential for a terrorist organization to hurt an unsuspecting population. In September 1987, a 20 gram mass of cesium-137 chloride was leaked in Goiana, Brazil, a city of about one million inhabitants. The 1,371 curie (Ci), lead-shielded source was primarily traced by scavengers at an abandoned cancer clinic and taken to a junkyard for sale as scrap. Workers broke open the shielding and discovered the shiny, white caesium chloride capsule inside.

The caesium capsule was broken up, and workers took home the pieces and showed them to their friends out of curiosity. Soon after, thirteen people exposed to the deadly caesium fell ill. Of those 13 people, 4 eventually died. By the time authorities in Rio de Janeiro realized what had happened, 249 people were affected by radiation, some receiving doses as high as 1,000 rem, with thousands more, rushing to emergency rooms fearing contamination. To decontaminate the area, 6,000 tonnes of clothing, furniture, dirt and other materials, filling, 3,460 cubic meters, were packed into steel drums and removed away to an abandoned quarry.

Isotopes that have use in a radiological dispersal device have extensive commercial application in industry, medicine and research. These elements are normally unprotected in contrast to fissile materials and are generally easy to access than fissile materials. Isotopes in use for industrial purposes may be vulnerable to loss or theft, given the requirement to transport these materials from one place to other. Owners sometimes lack adequate control over their radioactive sources, which may place these sources at risk of being lost or stolen. For example, an assistant radiographer for a petrochemical company disappeared for almost two weeks with a 41.5 Ci iridium-192 source; he was later arrested for drunk driving while driving the company vehicle containing the source. In another instance, the driver of a truck transporting medical isotopes was apprehended under gunfire by federal officials on charges of kidnapping.

The fall of the former Soviet Union resulted in rise of a lively black market in radioactive isotopes, including long-lived materials that would make impactful sources for crude radiological weapons. As per International Atomic Energy Agency (IAEA) officials, a significant percentage of the confirmed nuclear trafficking incidents reported to the IAEA since 1993 involved some type of radioactive material other than uranium (of any enrichment) or plutonium. While many of these illicit transactions appear to be fraudulent, with the seller trying to convince an unwitting buyer that nuclear explosive materials are being exchanged, the unregulated trafficking of radioactive sources from the former Soviet Union offers new options for terrorists to obtain the materials they need.

Effects of Radiological Dispersion

The prediction of the effects of a radiological weapon is more difficult than the effects of a nuclear explosion. Environmental situations (temperature, time of day, relative humidity and wind conditions) impact the size of the affected area. The type of material and method of dispersion also affects the size of the contaminated area and the level of dispersed radioactivity.

Even low levels of contamination could affect urban population severely. The federal government and many states have implemented protocols to guard citizens against the impacts of radiation in the case of the accidental dispersal of radioactive materials. The threshold concentrations of dispersed radioactive materials set by many of these guidelines that would trigger evacuation, relocation or affect land use are often set far below levels that would cause immediate harm. As a result, these guidelines amplify the disruption and fear that even low levels of dispersed radioactive materials would cause on the affected population.

Dangers of Nuclear Terrorism for India

Terrorist activities in India have also supported the view of their increasing predilection for horrible violence. Each activity raises the bar of lethality in relation to casualties and spread of terror amongst the survivors. Some of the major militant attacks on India include:

- The March 2006 blasts in Varanasi attacks killing at least 15 people; and seven bomb explosions at railway stations and on trains in Mumbai by militants in July 2006 killing more than 180 people.
- In February 2007, two bombs exploded aboard a train heading from India to Pakistan. At least 66 passengers, most of them Pakistanis, were burnt to death giving India-Pakistan diplomatic relations a backseat.
- In May 2008, seven bombs ripped through the crowded streets of Jaipur, killing approximately 63 people; in July 2008, 16 small bombs exploded in Ahmedabad, killing 45 people and wounding 161. Later, the 'Indian Mujahideen' claimed responsibility for the attack of July 2008 and the May attack in Jaipur; 11 bomb blasts that detonated in quick succession killed at least 68 people and injured 335 in Guwahati in October 2008; between 26 November 2008 and 28 November 2008 coordinated bombing and shooting attacks by ten Pakistani gunmen from the Lashkar-e-Taiba (LeT) group killed 166 people in Mumbai. India blames Pakistan-based militants for the attack, and the only surviving gunman confessed they were members of the LeT.

In July 2011, three blasts in Mumbai during the rush hour killed at least 10 people and injured nearly 60 others. Although, these incidents have no direct correlation with terrorists and their penchant for nuclear weapons, yet they highlight the growing level of fatality among the perpetrators of violence. These lethal incidents indicate the changes in the nature of the terror activities perpetrated by the non-state actors. They emphasize the belief that the world has entered into a new era in terms of violence and terror. These pointers direct that now terrorists could seek to demonstrate higher levels of violence with the 'appropriate means'.

Nuclear Terrorism in Indian Scenario

Recently, the matter of nuclear security seems to have overshadowed the political agenda in several parts of the world including India. The threat of a likely nuclear attack by terrorists is gradually looking for attention and permeating concerns within the political leadership as well as the scientific establishment.

Following are the reasons for this emerging concern:

- First, the global discussion on nuclear terrorism after the September 9/11 attacks has considerably influenced India's nuclear security discourse.
- Second, the developing strategic ties between the United States and India has led to emerging concerns of New Delhi being the target of Al Qaida, which considers the US and its allies as primary foes.
- Third, India's rising apprehensions about nuclear terrorism also stems from the political instability prevailing in the nuclear capable country of Pakistan. The prevailing domestic turmoil coupled with terrorist- infested safe havens in several parts of Pakistan portrays it as a dangerous neighbour to India.
- Last, increasing reported incidents of loss of fissile material poses serious concern about a potential atomic attack by terrorists. Since 1993, nine trafficking cases involving uranium ore and low enriched uranium (LEU) have been recorded in India, one in Bangladesh and another in Pakistan.

In August 2001, the West Bengal police confirmed of arresting two men with more than 200 grams of semi-processed uranium. The Indian intelligence sleuths revealed that there is a uranium smuggling gang operating in the region. On 1 May 2000, Mumbai police seized 8.3 kg of uranium, which was termed as depleted but radioactive uranium by the Bhabha Atomic Research Centre (BARC). In April 2005, uranium was seized from Assam, stolen by two men from a government facility from Shillong. In addition, some intelligence reports have also revealed that terrorists are aiming to attack India's nuclear infrastructure. On the eve of the Independence Day in 2006, the BARC was kept under strict vigil with deployment of the elite National Security Guards (NSG) for the first time following inputs of a possible terrorist attack. Fears were doing the rounds over the prospect of the LeT infiltrating a nuclear power plant when reportedly three men were arrested for entering the Narora nuclear power plant with fake IDs in August 2006. Intelligence agencies had information that LeT modules were planning to attack critical installations, possibly nuclear ones, and military targets.

- *Al Qaida and Nuclear Weapons:* The aim of terrorists with apocalyptic outlook is to attain nuclear material or explosives to wreak terror. Many of the terrorist groups designated as Foreign Terrorist Organizations (FTO) by the US State Department worldwide have stated their interest in chemical, biological, radiological, or nuclear (CBRN) capabilities. A September 2006 statement by Al Qaida in Iraq called on scientists to join the struggle in Iraq and produce unconventional weapons against American forces in that country. Amongst terrorist groups, Al Qaida leadership in particular has shown a consistent interest in the development of a nuclear capability and other WMD potential. Former senior Al Qaida operations planner Khalid Shaykh Muhammad (KSM) confirmed in March 2003 that senior Al Qaida leadership – including bin Laden, Ayman al-Zawahiri and Muhammad 'Atif' – believed that attaining a CBRN capability was necessary and that they were intent on developing weapons that could cause large numbers of casualties.

In May 2003, a fatwa was issued by Nasir Bin Hamad Al Fahd, a Saudi cleric, justifying the use of nuclear weapons on infidels. In 'A Treatise on the Legal Status of Using WMD against Infidels', a 25-page fatwa, Fahd states that the Western ban on use of WMD 'was not to protect humanity but to protect themselves and monopolize such weapons'. Fahd also asserted that Americans and the West have killed 10 million Muslims and, therefore, 'If a bomb that killed ten million of them and burned as much of their land as they have burned Muslims land were dropped on them it would be permissible, with no need to mention any other argument'. It is widely believed that the present Al Qaida leadership (in the aftermath of the demise of Al Qaida chief, Osama bin Laden) most likely adheres to this understanding.

Security Structure of the Indian Nuclear Establishment

India's nuclear institution is guarded by sophisticated safety and security measures in place. However, substantial measures still require to be undertaken to boost its safety. Although the Central Industry Security Force (CISF) is in charge for protecting India's nuclear installations, it is 'overburdened with additional responsibilities' and 'stretched too thin'. The government's official website highlights 'CISF is increasingly being called upon to perform important duties beyond its charter such as internal security, airport security and security of highways, election duty, etc.' It also safeguards steel plants, oil refineries, ports and airports and many vital installations.

The CISF's seven training institutions are 'trying to keep the force abreast of the latest trends in threat perception and its management vis-à-vis the technological advancement in the field'. Possibly this accounts for the major security failure involving one or more insiders in the theft of as many as 29 aluminium alloy titanium rings (used in rocket engines) from the high-security ISRO's Liquid Propulsion Systems Centre (LPSC) in Bangalore in February 2004.

Some organizational failures also raise the eyebrows of experts about India's nuclear establishment. For example, in October 2003, a major security breach happened when 18 to 20 computers having highly classified data, including communication codes vital for ensuring secrecy of intragovernmental communications, were stolen from a Delhi office of the DRDO, an integral part of the nuclear-weapons establishment. The codes remained unchanged for nearly nine months after the incident. In September 2004, a senior scientist at the Remote Sensing Applications Centre (RSAC) in Lucknow was imprisoned along with his wife, a former employee at the Centre, for selling classified satellite pictures and data.

Nuclear establishments also face cyber-security and insider threats. There remain doubts about the probable effects of a chartered aircraft full of high explosives crashing into a 'typical Indian reactor building'. Although the CANada Deuterium Uranium (CANDU)-type reactors like the pressurized heavy water reactors (PHWRs) have some safety measures that safeguard them against sabotage, its spent fuel pool is outside the containment building and hence is more vulnerable to sabotage than the boiling water reactor. The two Vodo-Vodyanoi Energetichesky Reactor (VVER)-1000 type plants built by Russia in Koodankulam, Tamil Nadu, may be also intrinsically susceptible to an airliner crashing into it like the World Trade Centre (WTC) attack.

There exist infrastructural flaws within existing plants of this type creating vulnerability to a single blast. The containment erections of long-standing commercial reactors like Tarapur are not as vigorous as those of modern reactors. Hence, it remains a matter of discussion whether they can survive a large airplane crash like the one on the WTC.

It is well known that India's nuclear institution have some of the finest safety and security measures for protecting its nuclear facilities. Every nuclear power plant is surrounded by a double-layer security arrangement with a distance of 1.5 km of sterilized zone from the nuclear facility deployed with sophisticated surveillance systems. Any type of habitation is prohibited in the sterilized zone, which expands up to five km. This sterilized zone is again surrounded by an Emergency Planning Zone (EPZ) extending up to 16 km.

The Nuclear Power Corporation India Ltd. (NPCIL) is a part of the World Association of Nuclear Operators (WANO) that is responsible for conducting peer reviews of all the atomic power stations progressively. But the security is not absolute in any measure. Hence, it is important to carry out regular assessment of the inbuilt safety mechanism in the nuclear installations, and strict application of the personnel reliability programme is vital especially in view of the internal-sabotage risk factor. When there is an issue relating to the protection of India's nuclear power plants, there should be no room for complacency. Within a month after 9/11, New Delhi announced no-fly zone borders around nuclear power plants but these have not been strictly enforced. There is also not much information available on whether anti-aircraft defenses protect these facilities or not, since aircrafts fly over BARC even today.

India's Efforts towards Countering Proliferation of WMDs

India is conscious of the threats posed by proliferation of WMD and their delivery means to its national security and the international order.

On the basis of these aspects, India has taken fundamental steps to tackle the illegal proliferation of WMD. India recognizes the significance of export controls not only for its own national security but also for the international order.

India has thus offered its cooperation to international community to encourage and advance the goals of non-proliferation and international security. Being a responsible nuclear nation having advanced and sensitive nuclear technology and materials, India recognizes the critical importance of careful handling of its nuclear materials and technology right from initial to final stages. Towards that end, India has joined the Convention on the Physical Protection of Nuclear Material (CPPNM) and the Convention on Nuclear Safety (CNS) both of which are directed towards the protection of nuclear facilities and safeguards.

India in November 2004 revealed its first report on measures taken to execute the obligations set by UNSCR 1540. Following September, India acted in a positive way by making an ordinance to amend the 'Unlawful Activities Prevention Act' of 1967, which expanded punishment for any 'unauthorized possession of any bomb, dynamite, or hazardous explosive substance capable of mass destruction or biological or chemical substance of warfare'. Thereafter, India showed consistent adherence to the UNSCR 1540 resolutions by further submitting two more reports to the Security Council in 2006.

Being a responsible nuclear state, India abstains from any illegal nuclear activity involving helping and abetting terrorists. Its motive can be clearly understood from its Weapons of Mass Destruction and their Delivery Systems (Prohibition of Unlawful Activities) Act of 2005 (WMD Act) which criminalizes any transfer of WMD, missiles specially designed for their delivery, and WMD-usable materials, equipment and technologies; or to transfer fissile or radioactive material for use in terrorist acts.

In 2010, the Foreign Trade Act, which has extended the domain of dual-use controls, was passed by the Indian Parliament.

In 2013, with a view to tighten its export control, India had updated Special Chemicals, Organisms, Materials, Equipment and Technologies (SCOMET) list to be on par with the existing NSG and MTCR lists.

Global Efforts to Combat Nuclear Terrorism

- *NSS, 2010:* The first Nuclear Security Summit, held in Washington in 2010 at the initiative of President Obama, was attended by 47 countries and 3 international organizations. The aim of the summit was to improve worldwide nuclear security by enhancing cooperation and to make concrete agreements aimed at better securing nuclear materials and facilities.

  The outcomes of the summit were given in the Washington Work Plan in the form of concrete plans and action points, and the Washington Communiqué, which has commitments and declarations of intent from the participating countries.

  Following are the commitments made in Washington in 2010:

  - Leaders jointly affirmed the seriousness and urgency of the threat posed by nuclear terrorism.
  - The participating nations complied to work to secure all vulnerable nuclear material worldwide.
  - The participating nations complied to shoulder their responsibility for securing nuclear material within their own borders.

- The participating nations complied to work together as an international community to improve nuclear security.

- *NSS, 2012:* After the summit in Washington in 2010, South Korea invited six new countries (Azerbaijan, Denmark, Gabon, Hungary, Lithuania and Romania) and one new international organization (Interpol) to join the NSS.

  In Seoul in 2012, 53 nations attended the second summit, which worked on the goals that had been identified in Washington. New ambitions were added to the Washington Work Plan: the members recognized the requirement to increase synergy between nuclear safety and security and better protect radiological sources from theft and misuse. Radiological sources may not be usable for a nuclear weapon, but they are well suited for making a 'dirty bomb', which can release radiation and cause social upheaval.

  The solid results of the summit were presented in the Seoul Communiqué.

- *NSS, 2014:* The 2014 summit discussed the endeavours of the past four years, identifying which of the aims set out in the Washington Work Plan and the Seoul Communiqué had not been achieved and proposed ways to achieve them.

IAEA Nuclear Security Plan for 2014-2017

The aim of the Nuclear Security Plan for 2014–2017 is to help global efforts by all to attain effective security wherever nuclear and other radioactive material is in use, storage and/or transport, and of associated establishments by helping states, on request, in their determination to meet their national responsibilities and international responsibilities, to diminish risks and to answer appropriately to threats.

For making this a truth, the agency will:

- Help states, on appeal, in their struggles to institute effective and sustainable national nuclear security patterns.
- Work as the focal point for solidifying international cooperation, and for coordination of nuclear security assistance provided by regional and bilateral programmes and other international initiatives.
- Boost global nuclear security struggles by finalizing international guidance in the Nuclear Security Series and, on request, supporting its implementation by states.
- Inspire and help states to observe to relevant international instruments and support States, upon request, in their efforts to adopt implementing national legislation.
- Construct on the progress made during the implementation of the first three Nuclear Security Plans to aid states endure and further improve their national nuclear security regimes.

The Agency's actions in nuclear security started in the 1970s when the Agency started providing ad hoc training courses in physical protection. However, post 11 September 2001, it became clear that to protect both nuclear and other radioactive material from malicious acts, much more is required.

In March 2002, the Agency boarded on its first wide-ranging plan to fight the danger of nuclear terrorism by helping states in boosting their nuclear security. Sanctioned by the IAEA Board of Governors, the first three-year plan described a plan of work encompassing eight activity areas. The accomplishments of the first nuclear security plan were sketched in the Review of the Implementation of the Nuclear Security Plan of Activities: 2002–2005 which was submitted to the Board of Governors and General Conference in September 2005.

In September 2009, the Board of Governors accepted the third Nuclear Security Plan including the period 2010–2013. The Plan constituted upon the achievements of the first and second Plans assessed the threat scenario as it has grown since the formation of the priorities and approach set in 2002, and promoted strengthened international instruments to combat nuclear terrorism.

The new Nuclear Security Plan for 2014–2017 aims to work on seven programme elements, namely:

- Information Collation and Assessment
- External Coordination
- Supporting the Nuclear Security Framework Globally
- Coordinated Research Projects
- Assessment through Self-assessment and/or through Peer Review Missions
- Human Resources Development
- Risk Reduction and Security Improvement

India, Nuclear Security and NSS 2014

It is always believed that India has lot to contribute to the Netherlands Security Summit. It could put in more efforts to meet the criticism that its nuclear programme is opaque, and become more forthcoming about its emergency response systems. It must also clarify why it has not been able to fulfil its earlier obligations to form an independent nuclear regulatory authority and a Centre of Excellence to train workers in nuclear safety and security subjects. It had given US$ 1 million to boost the IAEA as the focal entity to ensure nuclear security. India could add to this contribution, and offer training facilities to IAEA personnel in its Centre of Excellence.

But, India should also propose the extension of nuclear security procedures by endorsing pro-active methods to guarantee nuclear security through a four 'Ds' plan.

In summary, the risk of nuclear terrorism is of low-probability, yet of a high consequence probability. Instead of the efforts to lessen the risk of nuclear terrorism, the subject is still devoid of serious dispute and awareness. Extreme stress on secrecy can hinder a neutral assessment of the risk scenario causing serious problem in reducing the risk. The necessity of the hour is a comprehensive legislation to provide clear directions for effective nuclear disaster management. Though, the Disaster Management Act (DMA), 2005, publicizes certain guidelines, a 'more dedicated policy framework' is required to combat the threat. A more dedicated policy guideline would essentially compose of comprehensive supporting infrastructure capable of delivering expertise and immediate response in coping with the challenge of nuclear terrorism.

Tackling the problem of nuclear terrorism proactively, however, needs a holistic plan that can be outlined within a matrix of four 'Ds', namely, detection, deterrence, defense and disaster management. Clearly, detection is an intelligence task, which needs high-level attention, regular vigilance, technical competence and so on. The deterrence option needs the country sheltering potential nuclear terrorists to be placed on notice, and threatened with condign punishment if any activity of nuclear terrorism is conducted by its terrorists-in-residence. The problem here is that group like al Qaeda has branches in several nations. How can a deterrent bond be established vis-à-vis such an organization? Protection against a nuclear attack is not feasible. Hence, it must be sought within the defence and deterrence matrix. Lastly, disaster management in the post-attack aftermath must include a combination of immediate and longer-term relief, medical assistance, evacuation and rehabilitation methods. Unique methods would be required to deal with radiation casualties. There are many grey areas here such as the first responders getting incapacitated, and the sociological impact on affected societies, of which we have no knowledge or previous experience.

Nuclear Safety Regulatory Authority Bill, 2011

The Nuclear Safety Regulatory Authority Bill is a primary step towards permitting functional sovereignty to the nation's nuclear regulator by dissolving Atomic Energy Regulatory Board (AERB) which is been interrogated for long. The issue gained further importance in the wake of the Fukushima nuclear disaster in Japan. This became more prominence as a threat with hunger for nuclear power on one side and government and nations concerns to tackle events like Fukushima in an Indian scenario.

After Fukushima disaster in Japan, nuclear task force of Japan presented a report to IAEA which clearly demands for more independent autonomous regulator and single decision-making body in such situations for nations. Further, it also makes it clear that leaving such tragedy alone to nuclear technologists may induce less actualizing effort.

It is said that provided the lack of expertise in relation to nuclear subjects outside the DAE system, the AERB has to depend on the scientists and engineers of DAE institutions to serve on its evaluation committees.

It has also been observed that the present structure in AERB cannot take independent objective decisions in relation to standards and safety as it is an adjunct body of the Nuclear Energy establishments. Almost 95% of the members in AERB's review and Advisory Committees are drawn from among retired employees of the DAE, etc.

As a consequence of both Fukushima and such concerns of AERB, the Bill was proposed in September 2011 after a statement by Prime Minister of India following the mishap at Fukushima assuring the Nuclear Regulatory Authority would be made independent and thus more accountable to public in relation to safety and public health concern arising out of nuclear installations.

Scope

- The roles of the NRSA shall be limited only to guarantee the radiation safety and nuclear safety during activities concerning to production, storage, disposal, transport, transfer by sale or otherwise, etc., and in no case shall spread to functions or any matter which the Central Government is required to discharge under the Atomic Energy Act.
- Thus, the NRSA is to keep itself reserved from the sitting and designing facets of the nuclear installations and the nuclear mining. It would remain reliant on Central Government for procuring information on almost all the sectors.
- The role of the NSRA in nuclear emergencies also remains peripheral limited to the extent of apprising National Disaster Management Authority (NDMA) concerning the procedures NDMA should be taking in such situations. There is no specific mandate in the Bill to conduct certain public hearings when it is considering application from the parties in regard to their proposed radiation and nuclear related matters.

Objectives

The Bill offers for the suspension of AERB and creates the Council of Nuclear Safety (Council) and the Nuclear Safety Regulatory Authority (NSRA).

The Council shall include the Prime Minister as its Chairperson and six Cabinet Ministers, Cabinet Secretary, Chairman of the Atomic Energy Commission, and well-known specialists chosen by the central government. It will supervise

NSRA's rules on nuclear safety. The NSRA shall include a Chairperson, two whole-time members and a maximum of four part-time members.

The NSRA is authorized to take procedures to guarantee that the use of nuclear energy is harmless for workers, public and the environment. It may start to:

- Plan and execute guidelines for nuclear safety;
- Direct the central government on nuclear safety and preparedness in emergencies;
- Control grant of approvals for production, storage, transport and use of nuclear material; and
- Inform in the official gazette nuclear accidents under the Civil Liability for Nuclear Damage act.

The Bill prohibits the authority of civil courts in respect of subjects the Authority is empowered to control.

The bill also wishes to penalize the guilty for revealing, stealing or misuse of any information connected to its functioning supervision and control. ❑❑❑

Chapter eleven

Challenges Posed by Cyber Security, Communication Networks, Role of Social Media and Networking Sites

Model of Cyber Security

Cyber security, which is also known as IT security, aims at guarding computers, networks, programmes and data from unintentional or unofficial access, alteration or damage.

The common security goals comprise the following points:

- Availability
- Integrity, which may comprise authenticity and non-repudiation
- Confidentiality

Governments, army, corporations, financial institutions, hospitals and other trades accumulate, process and stock a great deal of trusted information on computers and transfer that data across networks to other computers. With the increasing incidents and sophistication of cyber-attacks, it is important to guard sensitive business and personal information, as well as safeguard national security.

Although advances in technology have provided vast areas of new opportunity and potential sources of efficiency for institution of all sizes, they have also presented unprecedented threats. Cyber security – defined as the protection of systems, networks and data in cyberspace – is a critical issue for all businesses. Cyber security will only become more important as more devices, 'the internet of things', become related to the internet.

Cyber Risks/Threats

Cyber threats may be generally divided into three different areas:

- *Cybercrime:* These types of crimes are done by individuals working alone, or in systematized groups, with the aim of stealing money and data or causing disruption. Cybercrime can take many forms, including the acquisition of credit/debit card data and intellectual property, and impairing the operations of a website or service.
- *Cyber war:* This type of crime is occurs when a nation-state conducts sabotage and espionage against another country to cause disruption or to extract data. This could involve the use of Advanced Persistent Threats (APTs).
- *Cyber terror:* This type of cyber terrorism involves websites dispersing extremist propaganda, hiring terrorists, scheduling

attacks and otherwise sponsoring terrorists' political and social objectives. It also includes the use of hackers by terrorists to debilitate states and governments, much like in Cyber War, with the only difference that this involves a non-state actor. Cyberspace bids a great benefit for the shrouded business of terrorists, making their work murkier than ever to those outside.

Cybercrimes

Cybercrime is a crime conducted by an individual or an organized group with the help of computers, internet, cell phone, other electronic devices, etc.

It has become so widespread that it has now outdone illegal drug trafficking as a criminal moneymaker.

With the advances in cybercrime, somebody's identity is stolen every 3 seconds. Sans a foolproof security package, your unprotected PC can become infected within four minutes of connecting to the Internet.

Those committing these types of crimes employ a number of models, on the basis of their skill-set and goal. Some of the different ways cybercrime can take shape are as follows:

- Theft of personal data
- Copyright infringement
- Fraud
- Child pornography
- Cyberstalking
- Bullying

As can be seen by the recent trend, cybercrime includes a wide range of different attacks, and all of them deserve their own unique approach when it comes to improving our computer's safety and safeguarding ourselves. Symantec draws from all the different interpretations of cybercrime and defines it concisely as 'any crime that is committed using a computer network or hardware device'.

In these crimes, your computer or device may be the catalyst of the crime, the architect of the crime or the target of the crime. The crime may occur on the computer alone in addition to other sites. The broad range of cybercrime can be better understood by dividing it into two overall categories, defined for the purpose of this research as Type I and Type II cybercrime.

Type 1 cybercrime

- It is generally a single event from the viewpoint of the victim. An example of this includes a situation where the victim accidentally downloads a Trojan horse virus, which installs a keystroke logger on his or her machine. The keystroke logger then lets the hacker to steal private data such as internet banking and email passwords.
- Another type ofType 1 cybercrime is phishing. This includes a situation where the victim gets a supposedly valid email (quite often claiming to be a bank or credit card company) with a link that takes one to a hostile website. Once the link is clicked, the PC can then be infected with a virus.
- Hackers usually indulge in Type 1 cybercrime by taking advantage of loopholes in a web browser to place a Trojan horse virus onto the unprotected victims computer.
- Any cybercrime that relates to theft or manipulation of data or services via hacking or viruses, identity theft, and bank or e-commerce is fraud.

Type 2 cybercrime

- Being of much more serious intensity, Type 2 cybercrime includes activities such as cyberstalking and harassment, child predation, extortion, blackmail, stock market manipulation, complex corporate espionage, and planning or carrying out terrorist activities.

- It is usually an ongoing chain of events, including repeated interactions with the target. For instance, the target is communicated in a chat room by someone who, over time, tries to establish a relationship. Eventually, the criminal abuses the relationship to commit a crime. Or, members of a terrorist cell or criminal organization may use hidden messages to communicate in a public forum to plan activities or discuss money laundering locations, for example.
- More often than not, it is conducted with the help of programmes that do not fit under the classification crimeware. For instance, conversations may take place using IM (instant messaging) clients or files may be transferred using FTP.

Crimeware

The software tools employed while committing cybercrime are from time to time regarded as crimeware. Crimeware is software that is:

- employed in the commission of the criminal act
- not generally considered as a desirable software or hardware application
- not involuntarily enabling the crime

Just like cybercrime, the word crimeware includes a wide range of different malicious or potentially malicious software.

On the other hand, it is important to note that not all software used while committing a computer-based or computer-facilitated crime can be regarded as crimeware. For instance, while IM client may be used in conducting a cybercrime, the instant messaging application software itself is not considered crimeware. FTP clients may be used in the commission of crimes; however, they are not considered crimeware.

Crimeware does, however, contain programmes that may be categorized as bots, keystroke loggers, spyware, backdoors and Trojan horses.

Types of malware

Cyber criminals work remotely, which is also known as 'automation at a distance', employing numerous means of attack available, which broadly is categorized under the umbrella term of malware (malicious software). These include:

- ***Viruses***

  Aim: Gain admission to, steal, alter and/or corrupt information and files from a targeted computer system.

  Technique: It is a software programme that can imitate itself and spread from one computer to another by attaching itself to another computer file.
- ***Worms***

  Aim: By abusing weaknesses in operating systems, worms tend to damage networks and often supply payloads which allow remote control of the infected computer.

  Technique: Worms are the types of viruses that are self-replicating and do not require a programme to attach themselves to. Worms continually seek for vulnerabilities and report back to the worm author when weaknesses are traced.
- ***Spyware/Adware***

  Aim: To attain control of your computer and/or to steal personal information without your knowledge.

  Technique: While opening attachments, clicking links or downloading infected software, spyware/adware is installed on your computer.
- ***Trojans***

  Aim: To generate a 'backdoor' on your system by which information can be stolen.

  Technique: A software programme seems to perform one function (for instance, virus removal) but actually acts as something else.

- ***Attack vectors:*** There exist a wide range of attack vectors to cyber criminals which let them to infect computers with malware or to harvest stolen data.
- ***Phishing:*** It is an effort to obtain users' information by camouflaging as a legitimate entity. For example, spoof emails and websites.
- ***Pharming:*** It is a process to redirect a website's traffic to a different, fake website, where the user's information is exploited.
- ***Drive-by:*** This is an opportunistic attack against specific weaknesses within a system.
- ***MITM:*** It is known as 'Man in the middle attack', where a middleman imitates each endpoint and is thus able to manipulate both victims.

Social Engineering

It means psychological manipulation of an individual or group of people into executing actions or divulging confidential information. Pharming and phishing are examples of social engineering.

Cyber Security for Organizations

- An efficient cyber security position should be proportional to the risks faced by each organization, and should be based on the output of a risk assessment.
- Critical Issues – cyber security tackles cyber security challenges faced by the business today and recommends a fully structured tactic to achieving both cyber security and cyber resilience.
- All organizations face one of two types of cyber-attack.
- They will be deliberately attacked due to their high profile and valuable data (or there is some other publicity benefit in a successful attack).
- The attack will be opportunistic, since an automated scan traces the being of exploitable vulnerabilities. Virtually every Internet-facing entity, until it has been specifically tested and secured, will have exploitable vulnerabilities.
- Cyber criminals are indiscriminate. Where there is a weakness, they will try to exploit it. Therefore, all organizations need to understand the cyber threats they face, and safeguard against them.

The Cyber Essentials Scheme

This approach has been constituted by the UK Government to aid businesses tackle with the business-critical issue of cyber security and cyber resilience. It offers a set of controls that organizations can apply to achieve a basic level of cyber security.

ISO 27001 and Cyber Security

- Besides safeguarding your critical assets, customer information and your operating systems, efficient cyber security can also aid organizations win new business by giving assurances of their commitment to cyber security to their supply chain partners, stakeholders and customers.
- For attaining real cyber security, today's institutions need recognize that expensive software alone is not sufficient to guard them from cyber threats. The three fundamental domains of effective cyber security are: people, process and technology.
- ISO 27001 is the well-recognized standard for information security management. It makes the backbone of every intelligent cyber security risk management strategy. Other standards, outlines and practices need ISO 27001 to deliver their specific added value. Implementation of ISO 27001 will assist you in protecting your information assets in cyber space, complying with your regulatory obligations and thriving by assuring your

customers and stakeholders that you are cyber secure.

Cyber Warfare and Cyber Terror vs. Traditional War

- Cyber warfare includes the activities by a nation-state or international group to attack and seek to harm another nation's computers or information networks by, for example, computer viruses or denial-of-service attacks.
- It is noticeably dissimilar from the traditional warfare in which armies, navies and air forces fight one another.
- Cyber war is an efficient way of lodging a protest as it can be fought by anyone using hacking skills against huge institutions, nations or even different civilizations. An individual's malicious software can dismantle computer networks and programmes spread across nations and continents. The modem world's industry, economy, institutions and even other facets of life is supported by computers and associated software. So all these facets of life can be disrupted for prolonged period by cyber-attacks. The individual could be -acting alone; he could be part of a group pursuing its inimical agenda or could be state supported, working to further the plans of the state. The defender fails to differentiate between them or determine the full identity of the attacker or the actual source of attack. So while the cyber enemy may be guessed, definite, pinpointing is nearly impossible.
- Cyber war emerged as the cheapest option among other types of war. It just needs an individual on one computer to originate cyber-attacks. There is no requirement for regular massive cyber armies provided with all the paraphernalia of a conventional war; being trained, sustained and replenished regularly. Unlike in conventional war, where the attacker generally suffers heavy casualties, in Cyber War there is no casualty to the attacker. In this war, it is not the physical might of a soldier, the quality and quantity of equipment, the integration and orchestration of systems, or the strategic genius of a General which is tested. It is only the computer genius and skills – and these too come as easily to gifted teens as to the experts after years of serious study and perseverance. Hence, it is not easy for everyone to be a cyber warrior. Conscription cannot form a Cyber Army – it is by hiring capable people with hunger for such work. In cyber force, there is not much place for officer – soldier hierarchy. Rather it is a team of the like-minded.
- When an individual's PC collapses, it is not easy to confirm whether the failure is a genuine fault or a result of malicious attack. More often than not one seems to believe that his computer system itself is malfunctioning. So it is difficult to recognize if one is under cyber-attack. The nature of attacks is such, for example, hidden Trojans activated on command or at pre-determined time, that one does not know when the actual attack was launched.
- The roots of attack also remain ambiguous. The attacking country or non-state actor can plan his attack via computers located in a third country or even through benign computers based in the country being attacked. These could be the PCs of citizens of the country under attack. Such a tactic presents major dilemma for defender and for the right to computer privacy in democratic societies.

Snowden Revelations

Edward Snowden, an American computer professional, is a former official of the CIA and former contractor for the National Security Agency.

He is charged by the USA for theft of government property, unlawful communication of national defence information and wilful communication of classified communications intelligence.

The information stolen by Edward Snowden about NSA acts is among the most significant seepages in American political history. It exposed that the NSA ran a number of mass-surveillance programmes over its own citizens, including retrieving information stored by some of America's biggest technology companies, often sans individual warrants, and intercepting data from global telephone and internet networks to make a store of information on millions of US citizens, irrespective of whether or not they are 'persons of interest' to the agency.

Snowden has also termed it as 'the largest programme of suspicion less surveillance in human history'. The leaked information also exposed details of Tempora, a programme run by Britain's spy agency, GCHQ, to amass, store and review vast quantities of personal information stolen from global email messages, Facebook posts, internet histories and telephone calls, which Snowden terms as 'probably the most invasive intercept system in the world'.

These revelations have sparked debates over mass surveillance, government secrecy and national security.

NSA Scrutinized Indian Embassy and UN Mission

- Information exposed by Snowden indicates that much of the NSA surveillance was concentrated on India's domestic politics and its strategic and commercial interests.
- The US National Security Agency may have retrieved information from computers within the Indian embassy in Washington and mission at the United Nations in New York as part of a huge clandestine effort to mine electronic data.
- To target India, NSA used two data mining tools, Boundless Informant and Prism, a system permitting the agency easy access to the personal information of non-US nationals from the databases of some of the world's biggest tech companies, including Apple, Google, Microsoft and Yahoo.
- In March 2013, the NSA amassed 6.3bn pieces of information from internet networks in India and 6.2bn pieces of documents from the nation's telephone networks during the same period.
- PRISM is a covert programme sprung in 2007, under which the NSA amasses internet communications of foreign nationals from at least nine major US internet companies.
- The understanding that cyber security should be at the front of national security efforts came to India after the 2010 Commonwealth Games, which uncovered numerous probable vulnerabilities within the country's national critical infrastructure. India wishes to address the goal of achieving a safe and stable cyber environment in an all-inclusive way. Current focus centres on capacity and infrastructure building which will enable establishment of secure and resilient cyberspace that will not only protect the country's networks from criminal activity and espionage but ultimately also from acts of cyber warfare.

Critical Infrastructure (CI)

- Critical infrastructure is the pillar of our country's economy, security and health. We recognize it as the power we use in our houses, the water we drink, the transportation that carries us and the communication systems we depend on to stay in touch with friends and family.

- Critical infrastructure include assets, systems and networks, either physical or virtual, and they are so important to the United States that their destruction would have a devastating effect on security, national economic security, national public health or safety or any combination thereof.
- Security to these infrastructures involves reducing the risk to critical infrastructure by physical means or defense cyber trials to intrusions, attacks or the effects of natural or man-made disasters.
- Various security measures include badge entry at doors, using antivirus software, fencing around buildings and locking computer screens.

Critical Information Infrastructure (CII)

- Around the globe, critical information infrastructure can be widely defined as inculcating those networks which are interrelated, interconnected and interdependent. In India, the strategies would initially comprise information and communications, transportation, energy, finance, technology, law enforcement, security and law enforcement, government, space and sensitive organizations.
- India's new rules are an addition to a legislative recognition under the IT Act 2000, which describes critical information infrastructure as 'those computer resource and incapacitation or description of which, shall have debilitating impact on national security, economy, public health or safety'.
- The rules offer 40 controls for protection of critical information infrastructure across sectors. These are generic and guiding controls, with each individual sector being left to develop their own sector-specific controls.

Threats and Weaknesses to India's Information Infrastructure

- Although the Indian economy is growing, there exist serious security concerns that emerge ahead on the horizon, challenging our extraordinary progress. These apprehensions relate not only to old-fashioned security threats, such as terrorism, communal or sectarian violence, crime and militancy/insurgency but increasingly comprise non-traditional and unconventional threats as well.
- Besides prominent terrorist attacks on our commercial and financial centre – Mumbai – which were carried as an effort to undermine our economic strength, there also have been attacks on our scientific institutes, such as the alleged attack on the Indian Institute of Science (IIS) Bangalore in December 2006.
- Although expertise in science and technology, especially in Information Technology (IT), forms the backbone of our economy, in reality these comprise soft targets, which are highly susceptible to a myriad of threats, fluctuating from physical acts of terrorism to electronic attacks on information assets.

Robust ICT Infrastructure

However, everything has become a reality only in the backdrop of a strong Information and Communication Technology (ICT) infrastructure. During the last decade or so, the government, public sector and private organizations have seen exponential opportunity in the sector and have consequently devoted large capital in building up suitable information infrastructure. This includes submarine undersea cables, satellite transponders or receivers, and massive on-ground, telecom and Internet connectivity.

As businesses develop, there were great demands to develop the infrastructure, which were effectively met from time-to-time. However, we have become increasingly reliant on this infrastructure, and as a result, our susceptibilities have also grown manifold. Today, we are highly susceptible to any disruption, even if it is of a short-term nature, infrastructure and IT development notwithstanding.

The threat scale is extremely broad, from non-state actors conducting cyber-attacks, adversaries waging out information warfare (IW) and deviant individuals exploiting the information superhighway with deadly electronic viruses and worms. It is not under the jurisdiction of this article to delve into technicalities or details of these, but it is pertinent to note that USA, which is the most connected nation in the world and thus most susceptible to IW, has not experienced any major IW attack on its infrastructure.

The world's superpower, the USA, is highly suspicious and has piloted numerous simulation games on its critical information infrastructure, but to date no significant instance of a cyber-attack (or cyber-terrorism) targeting it has been recorded.

This does not mean that threat does not exist. Possibly, non-state players do not currently have the kind of abilities needed to carry out advanced cyber-attacks. However, even in the Indian context, a distraction on any critical information infrastructure, such as the Indian Railways computer network, Reserve Bank's financial network or the National Stock Exchange's system, is likely to incur heavy financial losses as well as result in widespread chaos.

Industrial Espionage

It is recognized that terrorists only use the structure and technology that is freely accessible to plan and coordinate their violent actions. Be it is satellite imagery through Google Earth, terrorist advertising through Jihadist websites or statement through electronic mail and instant messaging, the misuse of ICT infrastructure by terrorist organizations is on the rise. We may levy certain restrictions, but technology is a double-edged sword, and the perpetrators of evil will always find a way of circumventing these checks.

The data from all over the world indicate a rise in cybercrime. With banks getting tech-savvy, networked and offering conveniences like Internet Banking and Any Time Money (ATM), a these white-collar thieves are unleashing cleverer and more lucrative methods of stealing money.

Recently, many gangs stealing money from ATM have been arrested in India's major cities, showing that the threat is not just restricted to foreign countries. In the times of information, where information is power, cyber thieves are not regularly targeting financial networks; they are also stealing information or classified documents. In reality, industrial espionage has taken a new form, with professional hackers coming onto the scene and pilfering secret information from business rivals or sensitive installations.

'Insider' Threat

In India's case, the most threatening risk is that of 'Insider threat'. Several information security examinations have revealed that the greatest information security threat to an institution is not from an adversary or a criminal, but from an insider. The insider can be anyone, a former employee, a disgruntled worker or someone who is just financially motivated. A case related to this is the arrest of three former employees of the BPO, MphasiS BFL, during April 2007 from Pune for allegedly stealing over $350,000 from four Citibank clients. Financial losses aside, the incident had an adverse impact upon the company's credibility and reputation, especially amongst global clients.

Because this was not the first of its kind and provided the media attention that such events attract, the data mining case proved to be a fatal blow to the Indian BPO industry, and it lost several business opportunities during the period. Recently, the naval war room case was also reported where senior officials were implicated of espionage and passing vital national security information. The officers had deceptively used thumb/pen (USB) drives to retrieve information from the computers on the classified networks. Both the BPO and the War Room case highlighted the ease with which employees could access vital information and pass it on to the wrong hands.

Sans adequate information security safeguards, and developments in technology making broadcasting and distribution of information easier, protection of vital information poses a major challenge.

Information Security Installations

India did not face a case of a secretive programmer masquerading a malicious code, a virus or a worm programme on the Internet. In the past decades, strong viruses, such as the Lovebug, Nimda Worm and the Code Red, aided in extensive disorder of the World Wide Web (WWW) and other networks connected to the Internet. Web-based organizations incurred huge losses due to these viruses. Some of the perpetrators were identified and charged under the Computer Fraud and Abuse Act while others were too clever to be nabbed.

To make the systems safe and secure, institutions are considering information security (INFOSEC) more seriously than ever before and executing appropriate strategies. These comprise the employment of INFOSEC technologies, such as Firewalls, Biometrics, Intrusion Detection Systems (IDS), anti-virus programs, logging mechanisms, etc. Technology is further boosted when INFOSEC practices and policies are formed.

Some organizations are embracing the BS 779, ISO 17799 or similar information security mechanisms which are standardized security policies and standards procedures. Organizations are making strict information security practices for employees, and employing dedicated security professionals to enforce these. Finally, it is very vital to have up-to-date legislation. While we have the IT Act providing information security, there are several loopholes and lacunae in the act that need to be plugged. As technology is rapidly evolving, legislation must keep pace in order punishing those who breach security.

Training and Synchronization to meet Information Security Needs

In relation to national security, training and coordination are important to achieve information security. There is a requirement for making sensible effort, maybe on the lines of what the USA has done, in classifying critical information infrastructure and carrying out vulnerability assessment/s. Thereafter, appropriate agencies need to be trained and tasked with relevant directives.

For tackling the problem, the Indian CERT (Computer Emergency Response Team) was established to monitor and react to information security threats. Similarly, cyber cells have been established in many state police departments to combat the rising menace of cybercrime. However, the approach appears to be reactive and is in response to actions of the perpetrators', who would always have the benefit of changing track and outsmarting various security mechanisms. Probably, a lot is happening in the area of information security, but it is in pockets of isolation. A lot more coordination and information sharing between the various agencies involved in information security is imperative.

Develop Idea of National Security

With fluctuating times and threat scenarios, it is vital that we redefine our model of national security and develop it to include new and emerging threats. There is no negating that information infrastructure is highly exposed, but the spectrum of threats is much too broad and may even be impractical, especially in terms of IW and cyber-terrorism.

A realistic trend analysis based on practical know-hows would recognize the real threat and devise the way forward in safeguarding our vital information assets. Finally, unless we protect our information highways, it will be erroneous and misleading for us to claim being an information superpower.

Global Measures on Cyber Security

With the advent of the 21st century, the International law enforcement departments initiated to identify the scope and the threat of the cybercrime, as the widespread prospective for economic damage and disruption was validated by the crippling Mafia Boy attacks on Yahoo, Amazon, eBay and other well-known ecommerce sites in February 2000. This led to creation of cyber squads in many nations including US, UK, Australia, Canada, etc. This step became the backbone to establish specialized organizations for dealing with cyber security and cybercrimes as follows:

- *Australia:* Trusted Information Sharing Network (TISN) for Critical Infrastructure Resilience (CIR).
- *Canada:* Public Safety and Emergency Preparedness Canada (PSEPC)
- *Germany:* Federal Office for Information Security (BSI)
- *New Zealand:* Centre for Critical Infrastructure Protection (CCIP)
- *UK:* National Infrastructure Security Co-ordination Centre (NISCC)
- *US:* Department of Homeland Security (DHS).

Initiatives by the Government of India on Cyber Security

For highlighting the growing threat to information security in India and focus-related actions, Government constituted an Inter Departmental Information Security Task Force (ISTF) with National Security Council as the nodal agency. The Task Force was given the role of studying issues such as:

- National Information Security Threat Perceptions
- Critical Minimum Infrastructure to be protected
- Ways and means of ensuring Information Security including identification of relevant technologies
- Legal procedures required to ensure Information Security
- Awareness, Training and Research in Information Security

As per the commendations of the ISTF, the following major actions have been taken by the government:

- Computer Emergency Response Team (CERT-In) to counter cyber-attacks
- Public Key Infrastructure (PKI) to help in implementation of IT Act and promote use of Digital Signatures
- R&D via the support to premier Academic and Public Sector Institutions.
- Mandatory compliance with ISO 27001
- National Cyber Security Policy 2013

- Empanelment of Security Auditors.
- Nationwide Information Security Education and Awareness Programmes

Indian Computer Emergency Response Team (CERT-in)

For boosting the security of India's Communications and Information Infrastructure by proactive action and effective collaboration, Indian Computer Emergency Response Team (CERT-in) was formed in January 2004.

Cyber Security R&D

Research and development actions are encouraged under this programme through grant-in-aid support to documented autonomous R&D organizations and academic institutions offering to start time-bound projects related to the following areas:

- Cryptography and Cryptanalysis
- Network and Systems Security
- Security Architectures
- Vulnerability Detection and Analysis
- Assurance Technologies
- Monitoring, Surveillance and Forensics

Information Technology (IT) Act, 2000

- The Government of India enacted the Information Technology Act, 2000 (IT Act, 2000), on 9th June 2000 that provided a legal agenda for dealings carried out by means of electronic data interchange and other means of electronic communication, commonly considered as 'electronic commerce', which involve the use of substitutes to paper-based methods of communication and storage of information, to enable electronic filing of documents with the Government agencies.
- Over many years, with some new forms of computer crime, misuse and fraud taking place, there was a need to boost legislation pertaining to information security. Accordingly, the IT Act, 2000 was modified and the Information Technology (Amendment) Act, 2008, was ratified on 5 February 2009 with a view to instil confidence in the users and investors in the area of Information Technology in India.
- This Act added rules to the prevailing Information Technology Act, 2000, to cope with new types of cybercrimes like publicizing sexually explicit material in electronic form, video voyeurism, cyber terrorism, breach of confidentiality and leakage of data by intermediary and e-commerce frauds.

Controller of Certifying Authorities

- The Information Technology Act, 2000, offers the needed legal sacrosanctity to the digital signatures on the basis of asymmetric cryptosystems. The digital signatures are now recognized at par with handwritten signatures and the electronic documents that have been digitally signed are treated at par with paper documents.
- The IT Act affords for the Controller of Certifying Authorities (CCA) to permit and regulate the functioning of Certifying Authorities. The Certifying Authorities (CAs) issue digital signature certificates for electronic validation of users.
- The CCA verifies the public keys of CAs by means of its own private key, which allows users in the cyberspace to authenticate that a given certificate is delivered by a licensed CA. For this purpose, it runs the Root Certifying Authority of India (RCAI). The CCA also maintains the National Repository of Digital

Certificates (NRDC), which contains all the certificates issued by all the CAs within India.

Cyber Appellate Tribunal

- Cyber Appellate Tribunal was constituted under the Information Technology Act under the guidance of Controller of Certifying Authorities (C.C.A.). The primary and the only Cyber Appellate Tribunal in India was formed by the Central Government in agreement with the provisions under Section 48(1) of the Information Technology Act, 2000. The Tribunal, which was known as the Cyber Regulations Appellate Tribunal (C.R.A.T.), started functioning from October 2006.

Industry Initiatives

- To create awareness on cybercrime, NASSCOM has scheduled to present advanced training programmes with due stress on latest trends in usages of cyber forensic tools and methodologies at its Cyber Labs. Cyber Labs, constituted and managed on a public–private partnership approach, can register and probe cybercrimes with the help of the police department and provides training to police officers, prosecutors, military police officers, bank officials and others on cybercrimes.
- These labs over the period have taught over 3,000 sleuths at multiple locations. These law enforcement people will be able to perform various activities like analysing and examining data on hard disks, email tracking, extracting evidence using Internet and mobile phones and on cybercrime-related legislation.
- Media, being the fourth pillar of democracy, has proved to be an important tool in the modern era. It works to fulfil interests, objectives and goals of the state. But irrespective of the degree of independence and impartiality available to the media, in matters of national security and interests, media works as per the nationalistic lines. Yet the rapid expansion and development of social media is a threat to national security and can be used to cause problems by propagating certain ideologies, mobilizing and organizing people.

National Cyber Security Policy, 2013

The National Cyber Security Policy was announced by the Central Government in 2013 to address the apprehensions arising from the cyber world. The 'National Cyber Security Policy' was constituted in consultation with all relevant stakeholders, user entities and public.

- It targets to facilitate creation of secure computing environment and enable acceptable trust and confidence in electronic transactions and also supervising stakeholders' actions for protection of cyber space.
- This Policy document sketches a road-map to produce a framework for comprehensive, collaborative and collective reaction to tackle the issue of cyber security at all levels within the country.
- It identifies the requirement for objectives and tactics that need to be implemented both at the national and international levels.
- The purposes and tactics given in the National Cyber Security Policy together serve as a means to:

(a) Articulate our apprehensions, understanding and primacies for action as well as directed efforts.

(b) Offer confidence and reasonable promise to all stakeholders in the country (government, business, industry and general public) and global community, about the safety, resiliency and safekeeping of cyber space.

(c) Embrace a suitable posturing that can signal our resolution to make determined efforts to effectively monitor, prevent and deal with cybercrime and cyber-attacks.

Prominent Features of the National Cyber Security Policy

In summary, the National Cyber Security Policy aims to cover the following subjects:

- A vision and mission statement intended at building a secure and resilience cyber space for citizens, businesses and Government.
- Allowing goals aimed at reducing national vulnerability to cyber-attacks, averting cyber-attacks and cybercrimes, diminishing response and recover time and effective cybercrime investigation and prosecution.
- Concentrated actions at the level of government, public-private partnership arrangements, cyber security-related technology actions, safeguard of critical information infrastructure and national alerts and advice mechanism, alertness and capacity building and promoting information sharing and cooperation.
- Improving cooperation and coordination between all the stakeholders within the country.
- Objectives and strategies in support of the National cyber security vision and mission.
- Framework and initiatives those can be followed at the Government level, sectoral levels as well as in public-private partnership mode.
- Providing monitoring key trends at the national level such as trends in cyber security compliance, cyber-attacks, cybercrime and cyber infrastructure growth.

Valuation of National Cyber Security Policy

- It sketches the basic purposes and tactics 'to build a secure and resilient cyberspace for citizens, businesses and government'. It also envisions constructing a workforce of 5 lakh professionals skilled in cyber security in five years. However, specialists say the document has been laid out very broadly, and implementation, especially that of creating skilled manpower to handle cyber threats, is a huge issue.
- The cyber security division is not well-organized right now, and there is a requirement to inspire more people to get indulge in cyber security as professionals.
- Government should outline the benchmark to motivate people to work towards cyber security. We require more of security people, we don't require hackers now.
- India has faced a significant surge in the number of cyber security activities in the past 10 years. As per the data from the Indian Computer Emergency Response Team (CERTIn), the number of incidents increased to 62,189 until May 2014 from 23 in 2004.
- For Indian organizations, there has been a 20% surge in average losses as a result of security gaps, while the average cost per event has increased to $414 from $194, according to a recent PwC report. It also added that employee and customer records are top targets of cyber-attacks.
- For any nation that has systems in cyberspace, the formation of national strategy is the first step towards setting up a cyber-security force. This should be followed by expansion of technology and means for executing the security measures and training for personnel to work with this technology within the defined strategy.

National Critical Information Infrastructure Protection Centre (NCIPC)

National Critical Information Infrastructure Protection Centre (NCIPC) works under the aegis of National Technical Research Organization (NTRO). NCIPC is the nodal unit that manages the cyber security jobs related to critical infrastructures in India. NCIPC is expected to set up sectoral Computer Emergency Response Teams (CERTs) and will also mount sensors on critical systems for getting real-time information related to cyber-attack of any kind for arranging a quick response. NCIPC ensure critical infrastructure protection and critical ICT infrastructure protection in India. Sectors whose cyber security falls under NCIPC are as follows: Energy (natural gas, coal, oil and power) Finance and banking Transportation (civil aviation and railways) Space Law enforcement Security Telecom Defense.

NTRO and Intelligence Bureau (IB) would firstly be answerable for security of various government networks. Although NTRO would operate through NCIPC, IB would be normally looking at the physical security of networks. State polices, CBI, NIA, etc. would be responsible for follow-up action, if any intrusions are spotted.

Information Technology (Amendment) Act, 2008

- The Information Technology Act was sanctioned in the year 2000 to provide a fillip to the development of electronic-based transactions, to give legal recognition for e-commerce and e-transactions, to enable e-governance, to avoid computer-based crimes and guarantee security practices and actions in the context of widest possible use of information technology globally.
- The Act offers legal outline to address different types of cybercrimes and recommends punishment also for such crimes.
- The revised Act has spread its net to fight more offences, including cyber terrorism, Wi-Fi hacking, transferring and viewing child pornography, video voyeurism, identity theft and even spam. But at the same time, it permits the government to intercept information and snoop on its citizens.
- The original Act only had one criminal section (Section 66) for cybercrime, and it had wide provisions, but vague. The new Act covers a range of crimes that attracts punishment from a three-year jail term to a life sentence.
- Section 66F details provisions for cyber terrorism and life sentence. It is applicable in cases where Wi-Fi is misused to send terror mail. Any electronic action that goes against the country comes under this section. Online child pornography or child exploitation is a strict no-no under Section 67B, and would attract a prison term of five years for the first offence. Data theft is a criminal offence as well, and cyber law specialists say punishing it would increase India's standing across the globe.
- The IT Act of 2000, the first main effort to standardize cyber transactions, e-commerce and prevent computer-based crimes, was amended after much delay in December 2008, and received Presidential approval in February 2009.
- Named as The Information Technology (Amendment) Act, 2008, it synchronizes various e-services, boosts laws on cyber terrorism, identifies phishing as a crime, and for the first time, identifies child porn as a separate offence.
- With the significant shrink in virtual world, safety of data security and privacy

assumed importance, as did safety of critical information infrastructure for national security. These areas were at risk under the old Act, said experts.

- Opponents say the flip side is that it gives autonomous power to the government to monitor all e-traffic. The information could be exploited, say cyber activists. The central government, though, says safety measures have been put in place to check misuse.
- The other crimes under the Act comprise sending offensive emails and multimedia messages, disseminating sexually explicit material, breach of confidentiality and leakage of data by intermediary, e-commerce frauds such as cheating by personation, commonly known as phishing, and scams on online auction sites.

New Crimes

- Sending offensive emails and multimedia messages
- Data theft
- Child pornography
- Cyber terrorism
- Publishing sexually explicit material in electronic form
- Video voyeurism
- Breach of confidentiality and leakage of data by an intermediary
- Phishing, which is essentially e-fraud via impersonation
- Identity theft and fraud on online auction sites

Prominent Features of the Amended Act

1. The terminology 'digital signature' was replaced with 'electronic signature' to make the Act more technology neutral.
2. A new section has been introduced to outline 'communication device' to mean cell phones, personal digital assistance or combination of both or any other device employed to communicate, send or transmit any text video, audio or image.
3. A completely new provision has been introduced to define cyber cafe as any place from where the entry to the internet is offered by any person in the ordinary course of business to common people.
4. A new explanation has been introduced for intermediary.
5. A new provision (Section 10A) has been introduced to the effect that agreements determined electronically shall not be deemed to be unenforceable completely on the ground that electronic form or means was used.
6. The earlier punishment to pay the damages of ₹ One Crore (given under Section 43 of the earlier Act of 2000) for damage to computer, computer system etc. has been removed, and the concerned parts of the section have been replaced by the words, 'he shall be liable to pay damages by way of compensation to the person so affected'.
7. To safeguard sensitive personal data or information possessed, dealt or handled by a body corporate in a computer resource which such body corporate owns, controls or operates, a new section (Section 43A) has been introduced. If such body corporate is neglectful in executing and keeping reasonable security practices and procedures and thereby causes unfair loss or unfair gain to any person, it shall be liable to pay damages by way of compensation to the person so affected.
8. Sections 66A to 66F have been inserted to Section 66 defining penalty for offences such as lewd electronic message transmissions, identity theft, cheating by impersonation

using computer resource, abuse of privacy and cyber terrorism.

9. Section 67 of the IT Act, 2000, has been revised to minimize the term of imprisonment for publishing or transmitting lewd material in electronic form to three years from five years and raise the fine thereof from ₹ 100,000 to ₹ 500,000. Sections 67A to 67C have also been included. Although Sections 67A and B deal with penal provisions in relation to offences of publishing or transmitting of material containing sexually explicit act and child pornography in electronic form, Section 67C tackles the obligation of an intermediary to preserve and retain such information as may be specified for such duration and in such manner and format as the central government may propose.
10. Section 69 was amended to give power to the state to issue instructions for interception or monitoring of decryption of any information through any computer resource. Further, Sections 69A and B, two new sections, provide power to the state to issue directions for blocking for public access of any information through any computer resource and to approve to monitor and gather traffic data or information through any computer resource for cyber security.
11. Section 79, which exempted intermediaries, was amended such that an intermediary shall not be liable for any third-party information data or communication link made available or hosted by him if:
    (a) The role of the intermediary is restricted to offering access to a communication system over which information made available by third parties is spread or temporarily stored or hosted;
    (b) The intermediary does not start the communication or select the receiver of the transmission and select or modify the information contained in the transmission;
    (c) The intermediary follows due diligence while performing his duties. However, Section 79 will not apply to an intermediary if the intermediary has conspired or abetted or helped or induced whether by threats or promise or otherwise in the commission of the unlawful act or upon receiving actual knowledge or on being notified that any information, data or communication link residing in or connected to a computer resource controlled by it is being used to commit an unlawful act, the intermediary flops to expeditiously eradicate or disable access to that material on that resource without vitiating the evidence in any manner.
12. A provision has been included in Section 81, which outlines that the provisions of the Act shall have overriding effect. This rule also states that nothing contained in the Act shall limit any person from exercising any right conferred under the Copyright Act, 1957.

Section 66A of the IT Act

Section 66A states the penalty for transferring 'offensive' messages through a computer or any other communication device like a mobile phone or a tablet. If convicted, an accused has to face a maximum of three years in jail and a fine.

- ***What is the problem with that?***

  The ambiguity about what is 'offensive'. The term has a very wide meaning and is open to distinctive, varied explanations. It is subjective, and what may be innocuous for one person, may lead to a complaint from someone else and, consequently, an arrest under Section 66A if the police prima facie accepts the latter person's view.

- ***How did the controversy start?***

  The first petition was filed in the court after two girls were arrested in Maharashtra by Thane Police in November 2012 over a Facebook post. The girls commented on the shutdown of Mumbai for the funeral of Shiv Sena chief Bal Thackeray. The arrests sparked outrage from all quarters over the manner in which the cyber law was used.

- ***How frequently has 66A been used?***

  Maximum number of cases of arrest were reported in 2012. Jadavpur University professor Ambikesh Mahapatra was arrested for spreading cartoons on Trinamool Congress chief Mamata Banerjee on Facebook. Activist Aseem Trivedi was arrested for making cartoons ridiculing Parliament and the Constitution to depict their ineffectiveness. Air India employee Mayank Sharma and K V Rao from Mumbai were arrested for allegedly making offensive comments against politicians on their Facebook group.

  Businessman Ravi Srinivasan was also booked by Puducherry police for an allegedly offensive tweet against the son of a former cabinet minister.

- ***What are the grounds for the challenge?***

  Although the aim behind the 2008 revision was to avert the misuse of information technology, particularly through social media, Section 66A provided extremely wide parameters, which permit whimsical interpretations by law enforcement agencies. Most of the words used in the section have not been specifically defined under the Act. The petitions have claimed that it is a potential tool to gag legitimate free speech online, and to curtail freedom of speech and expression guaranteed under the Constitution, going far beyond the scope of 'reasonable restrictions' on that freedom.

- ***What has the court said so far?***

  The Apex Court, in the initial hearing, acknowledged the contention that the provision was 'very widely drafted' and provided arbitrary powers to police officers to make arrests. Nudged by the court, the central government outlined a set of guidelines in January 2013, planned to prevent misuse of the provision. These rules mandated that only senior police personnel could order arrests under this section. The petitioners have, however, maintained that the guidelines could not redeem a provision that was otherwise unconstitutional.

Social Media

- Social Media enables to share and exchange content between users on virtual groups. For example, Facebook, Twitter & Google Plus, etc.
- Social media is the terminology usually specified to web-based tools which permit users to communicate with each other in some way – by exchanging information, opinions, knowledge and interests online. As the name refers, social media includes the building of online communities or networks to encourage participation and engagement.

Social Media vs. Traditional Media

- The traditional media includes prints and broadcasts such as newspapers, magazines, radio broadcasting books, CDs and so on. The social media, which grows hand in hand with technology, embraces the use of Twitter, social networks as well as blogs – using internet as a platform.
- Social media finds its roots from traditional media in aiding the same purpose, similar procedures in collecting information and sharing the same audiences; however, it may

supersede traditional media because of the differences in the freedom of speech, coupled with social networking services authorized to users and the hastened speed broadcasting.

- The goal of new media is very much inspired by traditional media. Both social media and traditional media have the common goal – to keep one informed.
- Although social media has many things in common with traditional media, social media seems to be an 'improved' avtaar of traditional media. Among many differences, a more common one is the level of freedom of speech exercised in new media versus traditional media. Before the print media is distributed to the masses, the editors would have vetted and censored, following strict laws that applies.
- Unquestionably, technology has upgraded almost every aspect of media development. Its loopholes in making censorship across the board available, however, allows netizens to speak up. Yet, this seeming freedom of speech, which is only made available through internet, seems to endorse opposition of various political stances and an eye-opener to liberal views. Especially with people more acceptable of liberal mindsets, freedom of speech is censored in old media will result in technology will gathering more supporters of new media.
- Even as both platforms aim to keep you informed of news, social media has an added advantage that allows users to network. Traditional media has no room for networking. You would have noticed advertisers leaving their contact number. However, they would only be contacted to query about a deal. Seldom would you notice an ad whose purpose is to look for a friend. More importantly, you would not publish your address for snail mails or provide your contact number for interested members of the public to call you. There is no prospect to chat or socialize since everything is publicized. In contrast, based on data gather by the website Pingdom, there are 350 million people on Facebook as of January 2010. Facebook, like Friendster, has not only made social networking easier as users can add friends whom share common interests but has also improved the search for long lost friends. Additionally, there exists a privacy setting which you can adjust to let you provide information to only people whom you want to. This permits you to form a connection with a stranger before committing in a friendship. New media also offers interactive activities such as game communities or internet chat relays. Through these game communities, players can gather teammates for online gaming and establish stronger relationships with strangers. However, chatting alone aids introverts in making friends without having to meet people in the real world.
- Even as these offerings by technology are seemingly helpful, social networking via media has seen a surge in crime rates, often against minors. Paedophiles are actively using social network sites to prey on victims. They become successful in that because they can remain anonymous or adopt false personalities that would not be validated. (William-Thomas, 2009). Possibly, social networking is the only bane of new media which most internet users adopt as reason for new media to succeed traditional media.
- Finally, new media has the advantage in terms of time, that is, event is reported in no time. Publication time varies from the aforementioned methods of gathering and refers to the time it takes for the end product to reach out to the masses. As noted, it takes correspondents, journalists and editors to form an article on the newspaper, making

the course of getting a written article printed very long. Even if the information is ready for distribution, the newsletter has not been printed and thus cannot be distributed. Furthermore once stumbled, it takes half or a day to correct the error and send an apology letter for the mistake or post an article the next day. If a mistake is made on a newspaper article, the journalist has to make an apology letter or a new article for the paper next day, informing readers of the errata. On the other hand, with new media, it just takes the author a click of the button to share any information around the world on the World Wide Web. Although there are precise rules to follow if a reputable site makes an error, it does not take more than a day to have its entry edited on the site. When an error is traced, the author can rectify the same by just pressing 'edit'. In the case of Twitter, you can simply delete your tweet, another name for your entry and post again. The convenience can be experienced when you upload a video on YouTube. After all the tedious filming and editing, all you need to do is to click on your computer screen is the word 'upload'. Similarly for online news articles, a simple click is enough to have it published on a website.

- With the advances in technology and fast-paced life with no time to read newspaper, people around the world are choosing to read news online instead. For example, recall the 2007 Burmese anti-government attacks, had internet not been there, history would have repeated and we would have been misinformed of the total death toll, just like the uprising in 1988 (Sai, 2008). Blogging of pictures taken in Burma via internet allowed traditional media in other countries to cover the attacks. Similarly in today's context, information is instantly available to us with the shortened publication time in new media compared to old media, all thanks to technology.
- The new media and traditional media share common purposes, procedures and target audience. However, they vary in publication time, accessibility to networking and censorship. Both aim to keep their viewers informed and include tiresome processes before getting the end product. They also serve the same target audience, be it electronic or print. However, with the drastic surge in internet users, social media has slight censorship as it is inaccessible with the vast volume of websites, unlike traditional media. Additionally, new media tends disseminate messages faster than traditional media due to the short time needed in posting. To sum up, it provides opportunities for users to socialize and network.
- Roots of new media can be traced back to traditional media, and this new form has definitely improved services and caters to the generations born in the era of technology. They key achievement, if new media is to ever succeed traditional media, is advanced technology in internet. Although social networking through new media has helped in increasing crime rates, it can be eradicated if strict rules are imposed. With technology, social media has definitely exceeded the abilities of traditional media as an advertising alternative and smoothened the process of gathering concrete information for news articles. Ease and flexibility in attaining information has also attracted traditional media followers to shift to new media.

Encouraging Effects of Social Media

- Social networks benefit the businesses in a various ways. Traditional marketing media (radio, TV commercials and print ads) are completely old-fashioned now and demand for thousands of dollars. However, social media helped brands to connect with their targeted customers for free, with the only cost being energy and time. Through Facebook, Twitter, LinkedIn or any other social site you can lower your marketing cost to a significant level.

- Social sites like Twitter, Facebook and LinkedIn have cemented their position as the most viable communication choices for the bloggers, article writers and content developers.
- These social networking sites have provided the writers and bloggers a platform to connect with their tech-savvy clients for sharing expertise and articles. Your audience will further share your articles, blog or expertise in their social circle which further develop your networks of the followers.
- Social networks have eradicated all the communication and interaction barricades, and now one can share his/her perception and thoughts over a variety of matters. Students and specialists are able to share and converse with like-minded people and can ask for the input and outlook on a particular topic.
- Another positive influence of social networking sites is to bond people on a huge dais for the success of some specific objective. This is very vital to bring the positive change in society.

Adverse Effects of Social Media

- One of the negative consequences of social media or network is its addiction. Spending most of time on the social sites can distract the focus and attention from a specific task. It affects the motivational level of the people, especially of the teenagers and students. They mainly depend on technology and the internet instead of learning the practical knowledge and know-how of the everyday life.
- These social networking sites have negative effects on kids if they are allowed to use them. People sharing photos on social media that depicts violence and sex can damage the behaviour of kids and teenagers. It put the negative impact on overall society as these kids and teenagers involve themselves in crime related activities.
- Another negative impact of the social media is that sometimes users share too much information, which may pose threats to them. Even with the tight security settings, your personal information may be retrieved for antisocial purposes. Downloading your videos or pictures and copying your status is an easy task and can be done within few clicks.

Due to the positive effects of social media, drawbacks associated with the same get sidelined. However, no one can underrate the role it has played in the way people can share and communicate with each other.

Main Issues

- Regarding latest occurrences of use of Section 66A of IT Act in November 2012, Shaheen Dhada and Rinu Shrinivasan from Palghar, Maharashtra, had on Facebook criticized the shutdown of Mumbai for the funeral of Shiv Sena chief Bal Thackeray. As per the complaint, the women were arrested for spreading hatred under the Section 66(A) of the IT Act, triggering a countrywide chaos.
- Ravi Srinivasan, a businessman, was arrested by Puducherry police in October for tweeting against Union Finance Minister P. Chidambaram's son Karti Chidambaram. In April, chemistry professor of Jadavpur University, Ambikesh Mahapatra, was arrested by West Bengal police for making a cartoon of Chief Minister Mamata Banerjee and two Trinamool Congress leaders. His neighbour was also arrested for allegedly circulating it.
- Aseem Trivedi, a caricaturist, was also arrested on charges of sedition for exhibiting cartoons

during the Anna Hazare protest in the Bandra-Kurla complex (BKC) in November 2011. The arrest was conducted based on a complaint filed by Amit Katarnayea, a legal consultant for a Mumbai-based NGO. Katarnayea reached the BKC police in December 2011 for filing a complaint against Trivedi's allegedly derogatory sketches, disrespecting the National Emblem and the Parliament. The complainant said that the offending cartoons were shared on social networking sites too, thereby hurting the sentiments of the nation.

Challenges to Internal Security through Communication Networks

- Communication networks denote an interconnection of communicating units (computers, laptops, mobiles, telephones, etc.) to provide the basis for information exchange for all other sectors including voice, data, video and internet connectivity.
- Communication network is different from the computer networks such as LAN, WAN, etc. because they are just one form of the communication networks. Different communication networks are the backbone of much of the critical structure in many sectors today such as civil aviation, shipping, railways, power, nuclear, oil and gas, finance, banking, IT, law enforcement, intelligence agencies, space, defence and government networks. As such, communication systems play an important role with other key internal and external security and emergency preparedness. Furthermore, the communication networks are very much reliant on each other in a very complex form. The downfall of one communication network can affect adversely many sectors.
- Some of the main security assaults by the communication networks and to the communication networks include data theft, fraud, denial of service attacks, hacking, cyber warfare, terrorist and antinational activities. A cyber-attack which can regulate the structure can have devastating effect. The attacks can be done by viruses, malware, Trojans, hacking, network scanning, probing, phishing, etc. Furthermore, the social network attacks can be one of the major sources of attacks in near future because of the volume of users and the amount of personal information shared on these networks.

Types of security threats via the communication networks are as follows:

- ***Network Packet Sniffers***
  - ❖ While sending large information via a network, the information is broken into smaller pieces, which are called network packets. Usually, these packets are transferred as clear text over the networks, that is, information sent across the network is not encoded.
  - ❖ This presents a great security threat of packets being processed and understood by any application that can collect them up off the network. So, a packet sniffer is a software that can easily understand the network packets. The problem is compounded by availability of abundant freeware and shareware packet sniffers poses.
- ***Social Engineering Attacks***
  - ❖ Social engineering denotes to psychological tactics employed to influence people to dent their own online security. These include opening an email attachment, clicking a button, following a link or filling in a form with sensitive personal information.

- All types of spams and methods employed to spread malware use social engineering techniques and target human needs and fears as well as just plain inquisitiveness to get past the caution of being online. These attack methods are collectively called social engineering attacks. These attacks pose a risk to meaningful and often sensitive information related to user account, databases, etc.

- *IP Spoofing*
  - A situation where an outside attacker pretends to be a trusted computer is termed as IP spoofing. This type of attack can be carried out either by using an IP address of targeted network pool or by using an authorized and trusted external IP address.
  - It actually results into injection of data or commands into an existing stream of data passed between a client and server application or a peer-to-peer network association.
- *Phishing*
  - Phishing generally is a method to access someone's personal information for the purpose of identity theft, using fraudulent e-mail messages that seem to be coming from genuine establishments such as banks. These authentic-looking messages/e-mails are encrypted to attract recipients into divulging account data like login details, passwords, credit card numbers, etc.
- *Denial of Service*
  - Regarded as the most popular form of attack, denial of service (DoS) attacks are also among the attacks extremely impossible to eliminate. Hackers consider these types of attacks as trivial as they need so little effort to execute. Because of their ease of implementation and potentially significant damage, DoS attacks deserve special attention. These attacks include the TCP SYN Flood, Ping of Death etc.
  - When this type of attack is simultaneously initiated from many different systems, it is called a distributed denial of service attack (DDoS). DDoS refers to not actually hacking the website, but it is a common way to temporarily bring down websites. DDoS attacks are well-planned ones on Web servers of a website, and on the domain name servers. The aim is to flood the servers with a large number of requests, resulting in the temporary outage of a website or shutdown of the servers. Once this is achieved, the incoming traffic can be forwarded to an intermediate page, where often the culprits of these attacks share their messages clarifying the reason why the website has been targeted.
- *Password Attacks*
  - Password attacks generally mean repeated efforts to track a user account and/or password; these repeated efforts are called brute-force attacks. If this account has sufficient privileges, the attacker can create a back door for future access.
  - These types of attacks can easily be eradicated by not depending on plaintext passwords in the first place. The using OTP or cryptographic authentication can virtually eradicate the chance of password attacks. Passwords should be at least eight characters long and contain uppercase letters, lowercase letters, numbers, and special characters (#, %, $, etc.).
- *Sharing of Delicate Information*
  - Most of the computer crimes that institutions go through are because of

troublesome present or former employees. Essentially, it results into leakage of delicate information to competitors or others that will use it to organization's disadvantage.

- *Man-in-the-Middle Attacks*
  - ❖ These attacks are out by accessing network packets that are traced in the networks. An ISP has the qualities to gain access to all network packets shared from one network and any other network. It can launch such an attack. Executed using network packet sniffers and routing and transport protocols, these attacks carry information theft, control over an ongoing session to gain access to one's internal network resources, traffic analysis to derive information network and its users, denial of service, corruption of transmitted data and introduction of new information into network sessions.
- *Application Layer Attacks*
  - ❖ These attacks are executed by tracing the well-known weaknesses in software that are usually traced on servers, such as send mail, Hypertext Transfer Protocol (HTTP), FTP, etc.
  - ❖ The main problem with application layer attacks is that they often employ ports that are permitted through a firewall. For instance, a TCP port 80. Application layer attacks can never be fully eradicated.
- *Virus and Trojan Horse Applications*
  - ❖ Viruses and Trojan horse applications are the principal weaknesses for end-user computers. Viruses mean mischievous software that is attached to another programme to implement a certain unwanted function on a user's workstation.
  - ❖ A Trojan horse is dissimilar only in that the complete application was carved to look like something else, when in fact it is an attack tool. An example of a Trojan horse is a software programme that runs a game on the user's workstation. While the user is busy playing the game, the Trojan horse mails a copy of itself to every user in the user's address book. Then other users receive the game and enjoy it, thus spreading the Trojan horse.
- *Scareware*
  - ❖ Scareware is fake/rogue security software. There are innumerable versions of malware, with many more being created and used every day.
  - ❖ These are considered profitable for cyber criminals, as many users trust the pop-up warnings suggesting that their system is infected and are attracted into downloading and paying for the special software to protect their system.
- *Spam*
  - ❖ Besides spam into other areas online, traditional email spam still poses a significant problem, especially in business. Workers still require to keep their inboxes free of junk, and advanced systems to filter mails are a necessity in any business to use email efficiently.
  - ❖ This remains one of the biggest threats as the same is used by everyone.
  - ❖ Spammed emails having attachments continue to be a popular tool for cybercriminals, usually taking benefit of vulnerabilities in Office and PDF Reader software to launch defected code from within innocent-looking document formats.
  - ❖ Emails having links to mischievous sites is on increase as a major way of leading new victims to attack sites.

- ***Ransomware***
    - ❖ Ransomware is a type of malware that confines access to the computer system that it infects, and asks a ransom to be funded to the creator of the malware to gain access. Some forms of ransomware encrypt files on the system's hard drive, while some may simply lock the system and show messages intended to lure the user into paying.
    - ❖ Modern ransomware attacks were primarily occurring within Russia, but in recent times, these ransomware attacks have also been carried out in other countries, such as Australia, Germany, and the United States among others.
    - ❖ The 1989 'PC Cyborg' Trojan was known as the first ransomware written by Joseph Popp. Ransomware typically spreads like a conventional computer worm, accessing a system through, for example, a downloaded file or vulnerability in a network service. The programme will then run a payload: such as one that will start to encrypt personal files on the hard drive.
- ***Malvertising***
    - ❖ Malvertising means inserting of mischievous ads onto websites. In many cases, the websites are completely innocent and ignorant of the threat they're posing to their visitors.
- ***Clickjacking***
    - ❖ 'Clickjacking', also known as 'UI redressing', is one of the common types of attacks affecting Facebook users. It uses maliciously formed pages where the true purpose of a button is hidden beneath an opaque layer showing something entirely different.

Clickjacking employs the social engineering tactics to attract new victims and trick them into clicking on the camouflaged links. Clickjacking attacks not only escalate social networking link-spam, they also frequently carry out other actions such as granting access to treasured personal information and even making purchases.

❑❑❑

Chapter twelve

Border Areas Security Challenges and Management

Definition of Border and Its Types

A border refers to a real or artificial line that separates geographic regions. Borders denote political boundaries. They separate countries, states, provinces, counties, cities and towns. A border outlines the region that a particular governing body controls. The government of an area can just make and implement laws inside its borders.

Over time, borders change. Occasionally, the people in one area take over another area by means of violence. While on other occasions, land is traded or sold peacefully. On many occasions, land is parcelled out after a war through international agreements.

Occasionally, borders fall along natural boundaries like rivers or mountain ranges. For instance, the boundary between France and Spain follows the crest of the Pyrenees Mountains. For part of its length, the boundary between the United States and Mexico follows a river called the Rio Grande. The borders of four countries divide Africa's Lake Chad: Niger, Chad, Cameroon and Nigeria.

Borders—specifically national borders—impact travel and migration. People can often move freely inside the borders of their own countries, but may not be permitted to cross into a neighbouring country.

Three distinct sets of borders at the global levels are:

1. Land borders
2. Maritime boundaries
3. Airspace

Protection of Borders

A number of countries have some kind of military or law-enforcement presence along their borders. Countries safeguard their borders for many reasons. One is to ensure protection from invaders. This is particularly true in regions where two or more countries have fought over the same land for several years. Cambodia and Thailand, for instance, have disputed the territory of the Preah Vihear Temple for over a century. Cambodian and Thai military units are placed along the border near Preah Vihear Temple, and skirmishes usually result in deaths on either side.

Borders sometimes serve as an essential tool to keep the citizens inside. Many governments with these 'closed borders' are not democratic. Besides North Korea, nations like Myanmar and Cuba hardly permit their citizens to cross their borders.

Borders can also be used to safeguard resources. On some occasions, the borders of U.S. congressional districts ensure protection of ethnic, religious or economic communities. Citizens inside these borders usually vote as a unit on the basis of shared political beliefs. The region's representative in the U.S. House of Representatives must be aware of the interests inside his or her district's borders. The concerns of a representative from the urban area of St. Louis, Missouri, for example, are less likely to be issues affecting farmers than a representative from rural Missouri, which is dominated by agriculture. The representative from rural Missouri would be less likely to be linked with issues surrounding public transportation, which is much more usual in cities.

Disputes associated with Borders

- Several border disputes take place when there is a fight among people over natural resources. For example, Sudan and Egypt have quarrelled for decades over an area called Hala'ib. This triangle of land along the Red Sea is rich in the mineral manganese, which is necessary for the production of iron and steel. It is also used as an additive in unleaded gasoline. As per the Sudanese government, the land rightfully belongs to Sudan, however as of now it currently belongs to Egypt.
- On several occasions, political borders divide groups of people who share a common religion, culture, ancestry or language. The border between North Korea and South Korea, for example, is a purely political one; the Korean people have a united history, culture and language. The nation of Germany was divided between East Germany and West Germany from 1949 to 1989. Like the Korean border, this was a purely political division, between the democratic West and the communist East. In 1990, Germany reunified, and the border disappeared.
- On several occasions, one ethnic group wishes to break off and form its own, independent state. This can lead to a civil war.
- Border issues often arise when foreign powers draw borders in regions they colonize, with or without the consent of the people who already live there. During the 1800s and 1900s, European countries colonized much of Africa. These European colonists created the borders of most African countries. The divisions usually did not reflect the existing ethnic or political groups that lived in those areas. The so-called 'Scramble for Africa' was a conflict between European powers on African soil. European nations, led by the United Kingdom, France, and Belgium, competed to amass the most land and resources in Africa, with little regard for natural boundaries or cultural borders.
- By the late 1960s, most African nations had gained independence. As colonial powers withdrew from the continent, they often left a power vacuum that allowed old tribal conflicts to resurface. For example, after Belgian troops withdrew from Central Africa, two tribes—the Hutus and Tutsis—began fighting. In 1962, two new countries were created. Rwanda was led by Hutus, while Burundi was led by Tutsis. Fighting continued till it came to a head in 1994 with a devastating civil war in Rwanda that left hundreds of thousands of Tutsis and moderate Hutus dead. The Tutsis took control, forcing millions of Hutus to flee into nearby Democratic Republic of Congo (then called Zaire) and Tanzania.
- Border disputes can also develop as communities seek to establish their own city. This process is called incorporation. Many rural or suburban residents resist incorporation. They prefer to be an unincorporated part of a county, instead of affiliated with a town or

city. They say it will lead to more taxes and government rules. Other residents support incorporation and setting their own borders. They say incorporating as a town or city will allow them more independence on issues of law enforcement, education and land use.

Land boundary disputes of India with her neighbours

- India consists of about 15,000 kms of land border running through 92 districts in 17 States and a coastline of 5,422 kms touching 12 States and Union Territories (UTs). India also has a total of 1,197 islands accounting for 2,094 kms of additional coastline. There are 51 Bangladeshi enclaves (area involved 7,110.02 acres) in India and 111 Indian enclaves (area involved 17,158.13 acres) in Bangladesh. In fact, apart from Madhya Pradesh, Chhattisgarh, Jharkhand, Delhi and Haryana, all other States in the country have one or more international borders or a coastline and can be considered as frontline States from the point of view of managing border.
- Disputed borders are both a reason and an indication of tensions between big neighbours in South Asia. At the point when the provincial power, Britain, pulled back from India it left a dangerous heritage of carelessly or arbitrarily drawn borders. Tensions between India and China flare off and on, particularly along India's far north-eastern border, along the state of Arunachal Pradesh. Of late, Chinese officials have taken to calling part of the same area 'South Tibet', to Indian fury, as that seems to imply a Chinese claim to the territory. A failure to agree the precise border, and then to demarcate it, ensures that future disagreements may flare again. Pakistan, too, is beset by difficult borders. Afghanistan, to the north, has long been a hostile neighbour. This is largely because Afghanistan refuses to recognize the frontier—known as the Durand line—between the countries, drawn by the British.

Border of India and Pakistan

This extends across extreme climatic conditions given that the boundary runs from the hot Thar Desert in Rajasthan to the cold Himalayas in Jammu and Kashmir. India shares 3323 km long and complicated boundary with Pakistan.

The boundary India-Pakistan is classified under three different heads:

1. ***Radcliff line:*** An International boundary also called as the 'Radcliff line'. With a length of about 2308 km, it stretches from Gujarat to parts of Jammu district in Jammu and Kashmir.
2. ***Line of control (LoC) or the Cease Fire Line:*** It came into existence after the 1948 and 1971 wars between India and Pakistan. This line is 776 km long, and runs along the districts of Jammu (some parts), Rajouri, Poonch, Baramula, Kupwara, Kargil along with some parts of Leh.
3. ***Actual ground position line (AGPL):*** It is 110 km long and spreads from NJ 9842 to Indira Col in the North (Siachin Glacier).

The LOC and AGPL have witnessed constant tensions with border skirmishes. The LOC has been vulnerable to relentless infiltration by foreign terrorists, Kashmiri Separatists and Pakistan army.

Besides this, anti-India Jihadist Groups are in collusion with Pakistan Armed forces who on a regular basis tries to send terrorists to Indian Side of LOC. For this, Pakistan launches indiscriminate firing in which Soldiers and citizens get killed.

In the 1990s, India started to fence this large border, of which 550 kms in J&K were accomplished in 2004. By the year 2011, almost all of the border fencing – along J&K, Punjab, Rajasthan and Gujarat – was accomplished.

Of late, Border Security Force is making use of ₹ 4500 crore project, 'Smart Fence' mechanism. In this project, laser walls and heat sensor system will be set up on the boundary. While this may deter terrorists and Pakistan, innocent villagers may fall into the trap.

Integrated Check Post at Attari witnesses busy trade activities as this is only place for cross border trade with Pakistan.

Border of India-China

- India and China share a 3,488 km long boundary. Unfortunately, the whole boundary is disputed. The line, which demarcates the boundary between the India and China, is commonly called the McMahon line, after its author Sir Henry McMahon. In 1913, the British-India government had called a tripartite conference, in which the boundary between India and Tibet was formalized after a discussion between the Indians and the Tibetans. A Convention was adopted, which led to the delimitation of the India-Tibet boundary. This boundary is, however, disputed by China which considers it illegal. It is also in the same agreement, boundary up to Myanmar was resolved, and China accepts Mac Mohan line with Myanmar.
- India and China had never shared a common boundary till; China 'liberated' or occupied Tibet in 1950. It was then that the hitherto India Tibet boundary was modified into an India-China boundary.
- In 1957, China asserted control over Aksai Chin and constructed a road through it. This event was followed by intermittent clashes along the border, which ultimately culminated in the border war of 1962. The boundary, which came into being after the war, was called as Line of Actual Control (LAC). It is a military held line.
- In 1988, after the visit of Prime Minister Rajiv Gandhi to China, the Joint Working Group (JWG) was established to inquire into the border problem. In 1993, the Agreement on the Maintenance of Peace and Tranquility along the Line of Actual Control (LAC) was signed and the India-China Expert Group of Diplomatic and Military Officers was formed in order to assist the JWG.

Border Disputes associated with India, Pakistan and China

- Disputed borders are both a reason and an indication of tensions between big neighbours in South Asia. At the point when the provincial power, Britain, pulled back from India it left a dangerous heritage of carelessly or arbitrarily drawn borders. Tensions between India and China flare off and on, particularly along India's far north-eastern border, along the state of Arunachal Pradesh. Of late, Chinese officials have taken to calling part of the same area 'South Tibet', to Indian fury, as that seems to imply a Chinese claim to the territory. A failure to agree the precise border, and then to demarcate it, ensures that future disagreements may flare again. Pakistan, too, is beset by difficult borders. Afghanistan, to the north, has long been a hostile neighbour. This is largely because Afghanistan refuses to recognize the frontier—known as the Durand line—between the countries, drawn by the British.
- Most contentious of all, however, are the borders in Kashmir, where Pakistan, India and China all have competing claims. Since independence in 1947, it was clear that many Indian Muslims were determined to break off from Hindu-majority India. It fell to a British civil servant, who knew nothing of the region, to draw a line of partition between territory that would become Pakistan and

India. Pakistan was given Muslim dominated areas in the far North West, plus territory in the east (which itself got independence as Bangladesh in 1971). The rulers of some disputed areas, especially Kashmir, were told to join a country of their choice.

- On one hand, Kashmir's Hindu rulers prevaricated, thinking somehow to become an independent country, Pakistan's leaders took a decision to force the issue. Since Kashmir was (and is) a Muslim dominated territory, Pakistan considered it justified when it saw Pushtun warlords charge in from the north-west of Pakistan, late in 1947 so as to assert control on Kashmir. In response, India apparently invited by Kashmir's rulers, deployed its national army and stopped the invaders taking Srinagar, Kashmir's capital, located in the Kashmir valley, the most coveted part of the territory. The resulting line of control, by and large, remains the de-facto international frontier within Kashmir and, in effect, is accepted by Pakistan and India. A large number of Indian and Pakistani soldiers remain in Kashmir today as both countries profess to be the rightful authority for the rest of Kashmir. Complicating matters, China has also asserted its control over parts of Kashmir, largely with the support of its ally Pakistan.

Border of India and Bangladesh

- India shares 4096.7 Km of its land border with Bangladesh. The states which share the border with Bangladesh are West Bengal, Assam, Meghalaya, Tripura and Mizoram. The entire stretch includes plain, riverine, hilly/jungle and has hardly any natural hurdles. The region is thickly populated, and at many stretches, the cultivation is done till the last inch of the border. The Bengal Boundary Commission led by Sir Cyril Radcliffe Border made the drawing of the border.
- The border was thus drawn on the basis of old district maps. This made the boundary random. Instead of following natural barriers, it meanders through villages, agricultural lands, and rivers, rendering the border extremely porous with many disputed pockets. Un-demarcated stretches, existence of enclaves (chhit-mohols), and adverse possessions had been causing constant friction between the border guarding forces of India and Bangladesh.
- As a result, an 'India-Pakistan boundary Dispute Commission' was set up in 1949 as it resolved several disputes but very soon they resurfaced along with new problems of enclaves. To resolve the boundary disputes and to reduce tensions between the two countries, the Nehru-Noon Agreement on India-East Pakistan Border was signed in New Delhi in 1958. These efforts, however failed to end the disputes. In the year 1974, merely 3 years post liberation of Bangladesh that the Indira-Mujibur Agreement laid down the mechanisms for demarcating different disputed stretches of the India-Bangladesh boundary. This was also called 'Land Boundary Agreement' and both the countries, India and Bangladesh, committed to exchange the enclaves and cede the adverse possessions.
- About 111 Indian enclaves in Bangladesh and 51 enclaves of Bangladesh in were present in India. India did not have access to these enclaves in Bangladesh, and therefore, no administrative set-up to provide facilities such as police stations, courts, schools, roads, hospitals, banks, markets, and the like to their residents could be established there. In 2014, bill ratifying Indira-Mujibur or 'land boundary agreement' was passed in Indian Parliament.

Problems with this border

Illegal Immigration—Both push and pull factors were working on this border. Lack of development, religious persecution, environmental concerns etc. forced Bangladeshis to move into India, besides India's huge economy and accommodative society attracted immigrants. As per the 'Task Force on Border management, 2001', about 15 million Bangladeshi illegal immigrants are there in India, rising at rate of 3 lakh per month. Latest eruption of communal violence in Assam has direct link with this immigration.

Different border related issues can be elaborated as below:

- ***Smuggling of Cattle and other Products:*** It has been considered to be a major problem with this border. It is believed that if India prohibits this supply then it can starve Bangladeshis of food. Cattle from as far as Haryana, UP, Bihar is taken to borders for grazing and then smuggled to Bangladesh. Bangladesh also imposes custom duty on these imports. Annually, about one lakh cattle are confiscated on border alone. Thus, government is losing a revenue of about 10000 crore on an annual basis.

  Apart from cattle, smuggling of arms and other essential items such as sugar, salt and diesel, human and narcotics trafficking, counterfeit Indian currency, kidnapping, and thefts are quite common along the border of India and Bangladesh.

- ***Anti-India Elements and Their Bases:*** As of now, the United Liberation Front of Assam (ULFA), the All Tripura Tiger Force (ATTF), the National Liberation Front of Tripura (NLFT), and the National Democratic Front of Bodoland (NDFB) as along with many other insurgent outfits from the Northeast have bases in the Chittagong, Khagrachari, and Sylhet districts of Bangladesh. Incumbent government has, to a large extent, minimized their activities in these bases.

- ***Border Outposts:*** Today, BSF is manning 802 existing border outposts on Indo-Bangladesh border. As per the recommendations of Group of Ministers to decrease the inter-BOP distance to 3.5 km, the Government has given a green signal to the construction of additional BOPs on this border.

- ***Trade across Border:*** Near the India-Bangladesh border, 32 land custom stations are spread over the states of West Bengal, Meghalaya, Assam, Tripura and Mizoram. Petrapole in West Bengal is one of the most notable land customs stations with Bangladesh.

- ***Fencing and Floodlighting:*** These are some of the effective methods of maintaining vigilance along the borders. with a purpose to curb infiltration, smuggling and other anti-national activities from across Indo-Pakistan and Indo-Bangladesh borders, the Government has taken up the work of fencing, floodlighting and roads along these borders.

Talking of Bangladesh, out of the 3326 kilometre border only 501 kilometres is left without fence of which 130 kilometres is land where barbed wire fencing is in progress and the remaining portion is covered with rivers and water bodies. On rivers, Border Security Force is making a plan to install 'floating fence'. (As on Aug. 2014).

Integrated Check Posts

Many designated entry and exit points on the international borders of the country are present through which cross border movement of persons, goods and traffic occurs. Conventional infrastructure for discharge of various sovereign functions at these points is neither adequate or integrated nor coordinated and no single agency is responsible for coordination of different Government functions and services at these points. These functions are associated with those of security, immigration, customs, human, plant and animal quarantine etc., as also the provision of support facilities for both the Government personnel and the immigrants such as warehousing, parking etc.

In a response to the situation of inadequate infrastructure for cross border movement of persons, vehicles and goods, it was decided to establish Integrated Check Posts (ICPs) at important entry points on our land borders. These ICPs would house all regulatory agencies such as Immigration, Customs, Border Security, Quarantine etc., along with support facilities in a single complex equipped with all modern amenities.

The first ICP of India was at Attari border, Amritsar with Pakistan and the second one was opened at Bangladesh border at Agartala in 2013.

Boundary along India and Myanmar

- For the first time, frontiers of British India and Myanmar came together in 1826 when British won 1st Anglo Burmese war. Post-Independence, in 1967, the boundary was demarcated as per an agreement signed by both countries. Many border agreements between these two years took place in which borders were fluctuating which led to lots of confusion.
- The region of the Indo-Myanmar boundary throws up many problems to manage the border effectively. Despite the boundary being properly demarcated, there are a few pockets that are disputed. The rugged terrain makes movement and the overall development of the area really challenging. The internal dynamics of the region in terms of the clan loyalties of the tribal people, inter-tribal clashes, insurgency, and trans-border ethnic ties also negatively affect the security of the border areas.
- Practically, there is no physical barrier along the border either in the form of fences or border outposts and roads for strict vigil. Insurgents make use of the poorly guarded border and flee across when pursued by Indian security forces. Close ethnic ties among the tribes such as Nagas, Kukis, Chin, etc., who live on either sides of border, the border helps these insurgents in finding safe haven in Myanmar. These cross-border ethnic ties have facilitated in creating safe havens for various northeast insurgent groups in Myanmar.
- The region of the boundary at the edge of the 'Drugs golden triangle' facilitates the unrestricted illegal flows of drugs into Indian Territory. Heroin is one of the important items of drug trafficking. The major part of heroin enters India through the border town of Moreh in Manipur. As per some reports, the local insurgent groups are actively involved in drugs and arms trafficking. Human trafficking also exists along the border. The provision of allowing the tribal communities of both countries to travel up to 16 kms across the border without any passport or visa is called 'Free Movement Regime' and has also been significantly responsible for increased smuggling in the area.

Border of India and Nepal

- India and Nepal share an open border since 1950. The conception of such a border can be seen in the Treaty of Peace and Friendship that the two countries signed that year. Provisions in the treaty, wherein citizens of both countries are given equal rights in matters of residence, acquisition of property, employment and movement in each other's territory, provide for an open border between the two countries. On one hand, open border has been a great facilitator of strong and unique bilateral relations, at the same time, it has given rise to many irritants and problems that gave rise to several serious concerns.

- Open border has been considered to be a great facilitator of strong and unique bilateral relations. But it has given rise to many irritants and problems too. Allegations of excesses such as intimidation, and forcible grabbing of land by either side along the disputed border also come to light from time to time.
- All terrorist organizations, be it from Punjab, Kashmir, northeast or those of Maoists have fully exploited open borders with Nepal. It has been reported that many terrorists have sneaked into India through the porous and poorly guarded Indo-Nepal border. Apart from insurgents and terrorists, many hard-core criminals pursued by Indian and Nepalese security forces escape across the open border. These anti-national elements involve in illegal activities, for example, smuggling of essential items and fake Indian currency, gun-running, and drugs and human trafficking.
- The existing problem is further aggravated by intelligence inputs that Pakistani Inter-Services Intelligence (ISI) has been using Nepalese territory to execute anti-India activities since the 1990s. As per the revelations of WikiLeaks documents, the ISI has established a number of terrorist fronts in Nepal and has also pushed in men and explosives through the border to carry out terror attacks in India.
- Of late, police forces have accomplished some successes in capturing all types of criminals from these borders. This shows that cooperation from Nepal is increasing in this regard. In 2013, two Terrorists – Abdul Karim Tunda and Yasin Bhatkal, were arrested from this border.
- Nepal is a country surrounded by and its closest access to the sea is through India. As a result, most of its imports pass through India. Keeping this in consideration, India has granted Nepal 15 transit and 22 trading points along the border.

Border along India and Bhutan

- India and Bhutan have a 669 km long boundary in common. The boundary is demarcated except along the tri-junction with China. The demarcation process of the India-Bhutan border began in 1961 and got completed in 2006. As with Nepal, India's boundary with Bhutan is also an open boundary. The border was peaceful till Indian insurgent groups formed camps in the southern districts of Bhutan. This menace has been effectively dealt with during the Bhutanese government's 'Operation All Clear', which saw the destruction and uprooting of all insurgent camps in Bhutanese territory.
- Goods made in China, Bhutanese cannabis, liquor and forest products are some of the important items smuggled into India. Livestock, grocery items and fruits are smuggled out of India to Bhutan.

Border Area Development Programme

- Development of border areas has not been achieved much and has been a matter of concern for the country. The Border Area Development Programme (BADP) was initiated in western region, which at that point of time was the most volatile border, during the Seventh Five Year Plan period for ensuring balanced development of border areas through development of infrastructure and promotion of wellbeing and a sense of security among the border population. The programme has been expanded since to cover the border blocks of the 17 States (including 8 North Eastern States), which have international land borders with Pakistan,

China, Nepal, Bhutan, Myanmar and Bangladesh. The development of border areas is now viewed as a part of the comprehensive approach to the Border Management, which focuses on socio-economic development of the people and promotion of wellbeing and a security environment in the border areas.

- The programme is supplemental in nature to fill the gaps and the funds under BADP are provided to the States as a 100% non-lapsable Special Central Assistance for execution of projects relating to infrastructure, livelihood, education, health, agriculture and allied sectors to achieve the special developmental aspirations of the people living in remote and inaccessible areas located near the international border.
- The BADP is being executed by the Department of Border Management, Ministry of Home Affairs through the State Governments. Guidelines of the programme are designed by the Ministry of Home Affairs in consultation with Planning Commission (or now NITI Aayog), Ministry of Finance and concerned State Governments. Preparation of schemes/projects and their approval and execution are some of the important responsibilities of the State Governments. Execution of the Programme is monitored and reviewed by the State Governments and Ministry of Home Affairs.
- As already mentioned, Group of Ministers recommended principle of 'One Border One Force', because of which the government has raised Paramilitary Forces Border Security Force, Sashastra Seema Bal, Indo Tibetan Border police etc. which have specialized area responsibility. These will be discussed in next article under the topic 'Various Security forces and agencies and their mandate'.

Maritime Boundaries

There are five countries with which India has maritime boundaries. These countries are Sri Lanka, the Maldives, Myanmar, Indonesia and Thailand and two adjacent nations (Pakistan and Bangladesh).

The agreements on Maritime boundary were amicably concluded with:

(a) Sri Lanka in 1974 and 1976.

(b) Indonesia in 1974.

(c) The Maldives in 1976.

(d) Thailand and Indonesia, on the trijunction point, in 1977.

(e) Myanmar in 1982.

Indian Coastal/Maritime Security

- India, having a vast coastal border of 7516 kms, includes nine coastal States and four Union Territories, poses serious security threats and challenges. After the Mumbai terror attacks of 26/11, the whole coastal security scenario of the country has been thoroughly reviewed by the Government at different levels. The National Committee on Strengthening Maritime and Coastal Security (NCSMCS) against threats for the coastal security has been constituted under the chairmanship of the Cabinet Secretary.
- In order to secure the coastline, police of all coastal States/UTs, State administrations, Indian Navy, Ministry of Home Affairs (MHA) and other Central Ministries have been working in coordination. Nevertheless the task of securing India's vast coastline is immense. The proposal of the Coastal Security Scheme (Phase-II), formulated on the basis of vulnerability/gap analysis carried out by the coastal States and UTs in consultation with the Coast Guard was approved by the Government on 24 September 2010 for

implementation from 1 April 2011 for a period of five years. The Scheme is expected to provide support to coastal States/Union Territories to upgrade their coastal security apparatus.

- From Nov 2008 onwards, several measures have been taken by the Government to strengthen security of the coastal areas against threat of non-state actors from the sea. One of the most significant achievements has been the integration of all maritime stakeholders, including several State and Central agencies into the new coastal security mechanism. Indian Navy has established four Joint Operations Centres (JOC) at Mumbai, Visakhapatnam, Kochi and Port Blair. As a result of this there is good coordination, synergy and understanding between all agencies. All coastal security operations are now coordinated from the Joint Operations Centre, which are manned round the clock by Naval and Coast Guard teams. In addition, the State Marine Police and other agencies such as Customs, Intelligence Bureau and Ports etc. are also networked with these centres.

Awareness Campaigns

In a concentrated drive, to integrate the fishermen community into the coastal security structure, awareness campaigns have been put in place in coastal villages across the country since 2009. Navy, Coast Guard and State Police teams have visited coastal villages and fishermen have been made aware of possible security threats from the sea and their important contributions towards strengthening coastal security. This has paid rich dividends in last few years as there have been many incidents, reported by them, leading to successful interceptions.

Surveillance Patrols

A significant rise in the coastal surveillance patrols by Naval and Coast Guard ships and aircraft has been observed. Patrols by the Indian Navy and Coast guard are closely coordinated so as to optimize their efforts and keep the whole of coast under surveillance. Marine Police of each coastal state and CISF units deployed in major ports are also helping in performing patrols near the coast and in harbours.

Exercises to Ensure Coastal Security

With a purpose to periodically review the readiness of the security agencies and the state administrations in averting threats from inimical forces, the Indian Navy has undertaken the lead in performing coastal security exercises in every coastal state and in the Island territories in collaboration with the Coast Guard, Marine Police, Customs and Immigration and Port Authorities etc. During these exercises, many contingency scenarios are simulated, including hijacking of fishing crafts, landing of terrorists on the coast, stowaways on ships etc. All agencies with stake in coastal security participate in these exercises with a view to improve coordination, achieve integration and finally improve the coastal security mechanism. Due to these exercises and drills, there has been a significant improvement in the coordination between all the agencies.

Challenges in Managing Border

- Because of the proclivity of India's neighbours to exploit the country's nation-building difficulties, India's internal security challenges are inextricably associated with the management of border. This is so because Indian insurgent groups have for long been provided shelter across the borders of our country by inimical neighbouring countries.
- The challenge of coping with long-standing territorial and boundary disputes with China and Pakistan, along with porous borders

along some of the most difficult terrain in the world, has led to design an effective and efficient border management as part of a national priority.

- External threats to India's territorial integrity are not the only complex border management issue that the national security decision makers need to deal with. India's rate of growth has far outpaced that of most of its neighbours and this has generated peculiar problems like mass migrations into India.
- Illegal migration from Bangladesh over several decades has completely redrawn the demographic map of Lower Assam. There has been an emergence of other threats and challenges. The border security scenario is identified by increased cross-border terrorism; infiltration and ex-filtration of armed militants; emergence of non-state actors; nexus between narcotics traffickers and arms smugglers; left-wing extremism; separatist movements aided and abetted by external powers; and the setting up of madrasas, some of which are potential security threats.
- Management of borders in an effective way is crucial for national security. Different parts of our extensive borders have a variety of problems specific to them which have to be suitably addressed. These problems have become aggravated in recent times with Pakistan's policy of cross-border terrorism, along with its intensely hostile anti-India propaganda designed to mislead and sway the loyalties of the border population. The intensification of cross-border terrorism, targeted to destabilize India, has given rise to new challenges for our border management policy.
- The interpretation of the term border management must be made in its widest sense and should denote co-ordination and concerted action by political leadership and administrative, diplomatic, security, intelligence, legal, regulatory and economic agencies of the country to secure our frontiers and discharge the best interests of the country. The management of borders involves several challenging problems.
- Cross border smuggling of drugs, cattle, humans, artefacts, fake currency note etc. have been some of the common problems. Unfortunately, in this scenario our border forces appear to be severely undermanned and under-equipped which is taking heavy toll on economic, social and political stability of our country.
- The diverse problems associated with the management of borders are brought out by the manner in which the sensitivity of India-Nepal border has altered over a period of time. This border, which has been an open one, was once peaceful and trouble-free. However, with the rise in the activities of Pakistan's Inter-Services Intelligence (ISI) in Nepal, the nature of the border has altered completely over time.
- The concept of border security has shown a drastic change with the rising vulnerability of the coastline along with its airspace. In response to the gradual expansion and strengthening of security so far, mainly along what has long been perceived as a sensitive land border, the transgressor is already on the look-out for soft gaps, either on the land or along the coast and if need be, from the air. The Purulia incident of 1995 has already demonstrated our vulnerability from the air. The transgressors, with unprecedented money power, access to latest technology, organizational strength, manoeuvrability and scope for strategic alliances with other like-minded groups, can select their theatre of action for surprise strikes. While land borders

have from time to time received Government's attention primarily because of the wars with Pakistan and China and the problems of insurgency, illegal migration from Bangladesh and smuggling activities, the same cannot be said of our coastal areas or of our airspace.

- Insurgent groups present in different parts of the country are getting foreign support and motivation. Illegal infiltration and smuggling of arms and explosives, narcotics and counterfeit currency are major problems associated with security. The porosity of our borders in several parts makes the task of the anti-national forces much easier. All this underlines the need for utmost vigilance on the borders and strengthening the border guarding forces.
- While doing an in-depth review of the management of our borders, the Kargil Review Committee had in mind only our land borders. The Group of Ministers (GoM), however, experienced that the scope of such a review should be wider and should not just be limited to land borders and should also include management mechanisms to ensure the safety of our coastal areas and airspace. While undertaking this exercise, the GoM was assisted by a multi-disciplinary task force under Dr. Madhav Godbole. As per the report of the task force and the ensuing deliberations, the GoM made a number of recommendations to better manage our borders, coastlines and airspace.
- Some of the major problems currently affecting the management of our borders are maritime boundaries. Some of our maritime boundaries are still undefined and much of our land borders are not demarcated on the ground. The disputed and unsettled nature of our boundaries has made them a source of tension with their policing much more difficult.
- Since many of our borders are man-made artificial boundaries and not based on natural features such as rivers and watersheds, they are extremely porous and easy to cross. Multiplicity of forces on the same borders has inevitably led to the lack of accountability as well as problems of command and control.
- Border Guarding Forces have to be differentiated from central police organizations. Being more akin to the Army and different from central police organizations which are called to assist civil power from time to time, they need to be suitably strengthened both in terms of equipment as well as manpower.
- The forces which are hostile to India have endeavoured to occupy the vacuum caused by inadequate reach of the national media. To combat terrorism and insurgency, quite often security forces are called upon to take tough measures. These measures may sometime cause inconvenience and annoyance to the local people. This sense of discontent is exploited by hostile elements to create a feeling of ill will against the security forces and the Government. Timely release of information to the media would help in combating such invidious propaganda of the elements hostile to India. Due to the sensitive nature of their duties, the interaction of the officials of the security agencies and security forces with the media has necessarily to remain restricted. However, specialized officers, properly equipped and trained may impart information to the media.
- The concept of Village Volunteer Forces (VVFs) assists in managing border and has worked successfully in regions where it has been tried so far.

Methods to Ensure Effective Management of Border

Some of the techniques that would help in managing and securing the border are as follows:

- Fencing as well as floodlighting of borders
- Constructing of additional border outposts (bops):
- Developing integrated check posts
- Setting up infrastructure development, like construction of roads
- Effective patrolling and constructing observation post towers
- Installing CCTV and thermal imaging equipment

The observations of the Kargil Review Committee Report on Border Management

- On July 29, 1999 a committee led by Sri K. Subramanian, a defence studies expert, was constituted by the Indian Government to go into the details as what went wrong at Kargil, with the following terms of reference:
  - (a) To review the events that led to the Pakistani aggression in the Kargil District of Ladakh in Jammu & Kashmir; and
  - (b) To suggest such measures which are considered essential to protect national security against such armed intrusions
- In the backdrop of the security lacunae brought to light by Kargil war, the Prime Minister constituted a Group of Ministers (GoM) to review the national security system in its entirety, to consider the recommendations of the Kargil Review Committee's (KRC) Report and formulate specific proposals for implementation. The management of internal security is extremely complex as it is influenced by many factors including its historical legacy, geography, population size, quality of governance, sense of national unity and pride, economic development, poverty, socio-economic disparities and socio-cultural as well as ethno-religious traditions. Regional and global developments also affect the country's security interest. To strengthen the internal security scenario of the country, the Group of Ministers (GoM) deliberated at length on the challenges faced by India and on the efficacy of the measures required for an effective strategy for internal security management.
- The Group of Ministers (GOM) in a report submitted to PM on February 26, 2001 recommended a comprehensive systemic overhaul of the country's security and intelligence apparatus in keeping with the technological revolution and the need for integrated management structures. The GOM had been set up in April 2000 to review the national security system in its entirety and in particular to consider the recommendations of the Kargil Review Committee and formulate specific proposals for implementation. The GOM under the Chairmanship of Shri L.K. Advani also included the Defence Minister, External Affairs Minister and Finance Minister.
- In all, the GOM held 27 meetings. With a purpose to facilitate its work, it had set up 4 Task Forces, one each on Intelligence Apparatus, Internal Security, Border Management and Management of Defence. These Task Forces were multi-disciplinary in character and were constituted of acknowledged experts.
- According to the recommendation of GOM, Border Management is to be re-constituted on a one-border-one-force principle in order to obviate problems of conflict in command and control and Sack of accountability arising from a multiplicity of forces on the same border. They are to be used exclusively for border guarding activities and not, as a rule, withdrawn for internal security disturbances etc. They are furthermore to be appropriately

strengthened, trained and equipped with weapons on par with related army units when deployed on similar tasks. The Coast Guard is to be strengthened and a specialized Marine Police to be raised in all coastal States and island territories. Sanctity of Indian airspace is to be safeguarded inter-alia through procurement of additional low level transportable radars, integrated air command and control systems, integration of national radar resources, revamp of airspace management of coastal and island territories etc.

- The report of the Group of Ministers (GoM) on the feasibility of recommendations made by the Kargil review committee headed by Mr. K. Subramanian, has made recommendations such as (i) the fencing of the entire Indo-Pakistan border along the Line of Control (LoC) and (ii) the creation of a post of Chief of Defence Staff (CDS) to have direct liaison with the Prime Minister on sensitive national security issues.
- The 137-page report has given the suggestion to use Israeli technology and cat wiring for fencing the borders to control infiltration from Pakistan and the occupied Kashmir (PoK).
- This is on the line of the recommendations made by the task force on border management led by former Home Secretary Madhav Godbole.

Approach to Managing Border

The approach as applied by the Government to managing the borders has four important components, namely, guarding, regulation, development of border areas, and constituting bilateral institutional mechanisms for resolving disputes and ironing out conflicts with neighbours.
Guarding the Borders

The BSF has been assigned responsibility for the India-Pakistan and India-Bangladesh borders, Assam Rifles (AR) for the India-Myanmar border, the Indo-Tibetan Border Police (ITBP) for the India-China border, and the Sashastra Seema Bal (SSB) for the India-Nepal and India-Bhutan borders. To house these border guarding personnel, to send regular patrols and to interact with the nearby villages, border out posts (BOP) have been set up all along the borders. For securing the riverine and creek areas, the water wing of the BSF is deployed (Creek Crocodiles). Night Vision Devices, Hand Held Thermal Imagers, Battle Field Surveillance Radars, Direction Finders, Unattended Ground Sensors, High Powered Telescope are used by the border guarding forces as force multipliers for greater surveillance.

Regulation

Fencing, flood-lighting, border roads, Integrated Check Posts (ICPs) – In 2008, the Land Port Authority of India Bill was introduced and passed for the establishment of these ICPs. These ICPs would house all regulatory agencies like Immigration, Customs, border security, etc. together with support facilities like parking, warehousing banking, hotels etc. in a single complex equipped with all modern facilities. A Statutory Authority called Land Ports Authority of India (LPAI) has been set up to oversee and regulate the construction, management and maintenance of the ICPs.

Developing Border Areas

Reduced economic opportunities make the border population more susceptible to take up smuggling and trafficking. BADP schemes include development of community-based infrastructure like forestry, pasture land, fishery ponds, floriculture parks, community centres, mobile dispensaries, mini marketing yards, etc. Funds are provided to the States as a non-lapsable Special Central Assistance

National Highway Development Programme, Special Accelerated Road Development Programme for the Northeast Region.

Bilateral Institutional Mechanisms

Meetings of home secretaries, area commanders of border guarding forces and the Joint Working Group on Border Management, Border Liaison Meetings (BLMs) are carried out between local Area Army Commanders at designated places on a periodic basis after every six months.

The Surveyor Generals of India and Myanmar also carry out meeting to deliberate the work plan for joint inspection, repairs, restoration and maintenance of boundary pillars on the border, similar institutional mechanisms with Bangladesh.

Recommendations

Guarding:

- Recognize sensitive areas along the border and raise the number of border posts in these regions. Also boost the strength of the border guarding personnel in sensitive border outposts.
- Provide training to the border guarding forces and equip them with modern gadgets and weapons for better surveillance of the border. Install alarm systems to detect breach of fence and respond quickly.
- Introducing improvements in the working and living conditions of the border guarding personnel to enhance their morale.
- Ensure improved coordination among all agencies indulged in border management such as the border guarding forces, Customs, intelligence agencies and state police.
- Sensitize the people living along the borders and motivate them to work as eyes and ears for the border guarding forces.

Regulation

- Do not permit human habitation or cultivation in the intervening regions between the border and the fence.
- Legalize trade in essential items so as to prevent smuggling. Open markets in the vicinity of the border where people can buy and sell goods without paying any duties.
- Provide multipurpose identity cards to the people residing near the borders to differentiate between Indian citizens and illegal migrants.

Development

- Work for the all-round development of the border regions to prevent the border people from indulging in illegal activities and dispel the feeling of alienation in them.

Bilateral Mechanisms

- Bolster bilateral mechanisms by convening meetings of concerned officials on a periodic basis to iron out tensions as well as to resolve border disputes.

Challenges associated with Coastal Security and Island Territories

- The coastline is highly indented with a number of creeks, rivulets and streams along with inhabited and uninhabited islands, sandbars and mangrove forests. These water channels, most of which are interconnected and run deep inside the land, render the coastline porous and hence vulnerable to cross-border infiltration, smuggling, and arms and drugs trafficking and provide deal hideaways for infiltrators, criminals and contraband. E.g. 1993 Mumbai serial blasts and the November 2008 attack on Mumbai.
- The matter is made worse by the existence of several high value targets like oil refineries, atomic power plants, space stations, ports and naval bases along the coastline. While it is obvious that these installations would face a conventional threat from Pakistan in the event of war, there are growing worries about non-conventional threats as well as terrorist attacks, sabotage, etc.

- The terrorist's strategic location, i.e. proximity to the important Sea Lanes of Communication (SLOC) and Southeast Asian and African countries combined with considerable distance from the mainland add to the Island Territories vulnerabilities.
- Intelligence reports have suggested that many uninhabited islands are being misused by terrorist groups and criminal gangs as transit points for smuggling arms and narcotics e.g. Lashkar-e-Taiba in Lakshadweep.
- There has been a manifold increase in instances of piracy in the Malacca straits.
- The Andaman and Nicobar islands have witnessed large scale influx of illegal migrants from Bangladesh, Sri Lanka (Tamils) Myanmar, Thailand and Indonesia.
- String of Pearls: Of late, China has been quite active in the Indian Ocean region. With an aim to contain its potential adversary in the region, China has assisted Myanmar to construct a naval base at Haingyi and built up listening posts in Coco Island, close to Andaman and Nicobar. It has also assisted Pakistan, Bangladesh and Sri Lanka to construct ports, which could be utilized by China during adverse times.

Response of the Government

- At the outermost layer, the Indian Navy patrols the high seas and carries out aerial reconnaissance with ship-based aircraft. The intermediate layer comprising of the Exclusive Economic Zone (between 12 and 200 nautical miles) is patrolled by the Coast Guard. And the territorial waters are patrolled by the Coastal Police.
- The fishermen intentionally cross the international border for a good catch. To keep tracking the fishing vessels, the state governments of Maharashtra and Gujarat have made it mandatory for all the fishing vessels to install Global Positioning System (GPS) and high frequency wireless system. The equipment assists the fishing vessels in ascertaining the international borders and remains within the Territory of India.
- Automated Identification System (AIS) aimed to improve the security of the Port by watching the movement of vessels have also been installed in these ports.
- To make a distinction between local people and foreign elements, various coastal states have issued identity cards to all villagers residing along the coast.
- Fast delivery of 204 interceptor boats, easing of environmental norms for setting up coastal police stations, issuance of multipurpose identity cards to all fishermen sea-faring personnel and coastal villages, implementation of uniform licensing of fishing boats across the country, installation of special transponders and Global Positioning System on registered boats for identification and tracking, deployment of commando units of Central Industrial Security Force in all ports, constituting unified command for coastal districts to counter terrorist threats from sea.
- For the security of the Island Territories, the Indian Government has constituted a joint command in Andaman and Nicobar called the Andaman and Nicobar Command (ANC) comprising personnel of the Army, the Navy, the Air Force and the Coast Guard.

Recommendations

- Address the shortage of manpower (biggest problem) for the coastal police by recruiting retired Coast Guard and Navy personnel.
- Make a list of people from coastal villages in the Coastal Police Force. Their maritime experience is going to be an asset.

- Provide incentives like special allowances and insurance to overcome the reluctance of police personnel for efficient coastal patrolling.
- Provide extensive and specialized training to the Coastal Police personnel to alter their indifferent attitude towards coastal security.
- Impose high fines on fishermen who violate the international boundary. Cancel the licenses of offending fishing boats on repeated violation.

Chapter thirteen

Challenges to Internal Security Posed by Organized Crime

Significance of Organized Crime

- Organized crime is an illegal activity committed by any group having some manner of a formalized structure to obtain money through illegal ways. These types of groups uphold their position by using actual or threatened violence, dishonest public officials, graft or extortion as they usually have a major impact on the people in their locales, region or the nation as a whole.
- 'Organized crime means any continuing unlawful activity by an individual, singly or jointly, either as a member of an organized crime syndicate or on behalf of such syndicate, by use of violence or threat of violence or intimidation or coercion, or other unlawful means, with the objective of gaining pecuniary benefits, or gaining undue economic or other advantage for himself or any person or promoting insurgency' (Maharashtra Control of Organised Crime Act, 1999).
- Organized crime exists in many forms, including as dealing in drugs, firearms and even persons. Organized crime groups simultaneously abuse human mobility to traffic migrants and destabilize financial systems through money laundering.

Transnational Organized Crime

- Transnational organized crime comprises the scheduling and implementation of illegal business ventures by groups or networks of individuals functioning in more than one country. These groups employ systematic violence and corruption to reach the desired goals. These crimes commonly consist of money laundering, human trafficking, cyber-crime and trafficking of drugs, weapons, endangered species, body parts or nuclear material.
- These crimes affect economy and financial systems in a negative way while undermining democracy. These groups often work with governments that are not authoritative enough to oppose them, flourishing on illegal actions, such as drug trafficking, that give them humongous profits. In executing illegal activities, they disturb the peace and stability of nations globally, often using bribery, violence, or terror to achieve their goals.
- The political chaos of the 21st century and developments in technology make transnational crime a concern for the United States. Surging travel and trade and developments in IT have had the unplanned

effect of offering opportunities for the speedy extension of transnational organized crime activities. Policing objectives in the United States must extend beyond national borders to seek out and target this type of crime. The United States can form effective protocol and policies for tackling these crimes and mount a serious opposition only by international collaboration and information exchange.

- 'Transnational criminal rings are becoming more and more powerful and universal, and their mobility is growing. The means and resources of any state are not enough to seriously harm them'.
- The United Nations Convention against Transnational Organized Crime (UNTOC) does not have a specific definition of 'transnational organized crime'. Nor does it define the types of crimes that might constitute it.
- This dearth of definition was intended to permit for a wider applicability of the Organized Crime Convention to new forms of crime that arise constantly as global, regional and local circumstances change over time.

The Convention contains a definition of 'organized criminal group'. In Article 2(a):

- a group of three or more persons that was not randomly formed;
- existing for a period of time;
- acting in concert with the aim of committing at least one crime punishable by at least four years' incarceration;
- in order to obtain, directly or indirectly, a financial or other material benefit.

Because most 'groups' of any sort have three or more people employed in concert and most remain for a period of time, the true outlining features of organized crime groups under the Convention are their profit-driven nature and the gravity of the offences they conduct.

The UNTOC covers only crimes that are 'transnational', a term used broadly. The terminology includes not only offences occurred in more than one state, but even those that happen in one state but are scheduled or managed in another. Also included are crimes in one State committed by groups that operate in more than one State, and crimes committed in one State that has considerable effects in another State.

The understood meaning 'transnational organized crime' then covers virtually all profit-driven serious criminal acts with international consequences. This comprehensive definition is in reference to the global complexity of the issue and permits cooperation on the widest possible range of common concerns.

UNTOC and Protocols

- The United Nations Convention against Transnational Organized Crime, approved by General Assembly resolution on 15 November 2000, is the principal international tool in the contest against transnational organized crime. It was thrown open for signature by Member States at a High-level Political Conference initiated for that purpose in Palermo, Italy, on 12–15 December 2000 and enacted on 29 September 2003. The Convention is further accompanied by three Protocols, which aim specific areas and manifestations of organized crime: the Protocol to Prevent, Suppress and Punish Trafficking in Persons, Especially Women and Children; the Protocol against the Smuggling of Migrants by Land, Sea and Air; and the Protocol against the Illicit Manufacturing of and Trafficking in Firearms, their Parts and Components and Ammunition. Nations must become parties to the Convention itself before they can become parties to any of the Protocols.

- The Convention epitomizes a step further in fighting against transnational organized crime and suggests the acknowledgement by Member States of the gravity of the problems posed by it, as well as the requirement to raise and augment close international cooperation to limit those problems. States that sanction this instrument pledge themselves to implementing a series of measures against transnational organized crime, including the formation of domestic criminal offences (involvement in an organized criminal group, money laundering, corruption and hindrance of justice); the acceptance of new and sweeping outlines for extradition, mutual legal assistance and law enforcement cooperation; and the advancement of training and technical assistance for building or upgrading the necessary capacity of national authorities. (Palermo Conference).
- The Protocol to Prevent, Suppress and Punish Trafficking in Persons, specifically Women and Children, was approved by General Assembly resolution. It came into force on 25 December 2003. It is the primary global legally binding tool with an approved definition on trafficking in persons. The purpose behind this definition is to provide convergence in national approaches in relation to the formation of domestic criminal offences that would aid well-organized international assistance in probing and indicting trafficking in persons cases. An additional objective of the Protocol is to protect and assist the victims of trafficking in persons with full respect for their human rights.
- The Protocol against the Smuggling of Migrants by Land, Sea and Air, approved by General Assembly resolution, came into force on 28 January 2004. It tackles the surging problem of organized criminal groups who traffic migrants, often at high risk to the migrants and at great profit for the offenders. A major accomplishment of the Protocol was that a definition of smuggling of migrants was formed and agreed upon for the first time in a global international instrument. The Protocol aims at preventing and combating the smuggling of migrants, as well as promoting cooperation among States parties, while protecting the rights of smuggled migrants and preventing the worst forms of their exploitation which often characterize the smuggling process.
- The Protocol against the Illicit Manufacturing of and Trafficking in Firearms, their Parts and Components and Ammunition was approved by General Assembly resolution on 31 May 2001. The same came into force on 3 July 2005. The goal of the Protocol, which is the primary legally binding tool on small arms that has been approved at the global level, is to encourage, facilitate and toughen cooperation among States Parties to stop, fight and eliminate the illicit manufacturing of and trafficking in firearms, their parts and components and ammunition. By approving the Protocol, States takes a pledge to embrace a series of crime-control measures and apply in their domestic legal order three sets of normative provisions: the first one includes the establishment of criminal offences in relation to illegal manufacturing of, and trafficking in, firearms on the basis of the Protocol requirements and definitions; the second to a system of government authorizations or licensing intending to ensure legitimate manufacturing of, and trafficking in, firearms; and the third one is to the marking and tracing of firearms.

Connections of Organized Crime with Terrorism

- Organized crime groups and terrorists usually work on same network structures. Terrorists flourish upon the work of transnational organized crime groups. Both organized crime groups and terrorist groups function in regions with minimal government controls, weak implementation of laws and open borders. Both often use akin means of modern technology to talk.
- The modifications between them depend on means and ends. Terrorism targets to take over the mantle from existing government by altering the status quo. Organized crime, in contrast, wishes to form a parallel government while being with the existing one; any alteration in the current situation is only circumstantial and born out of convenience rather than zealous revisionist policy. Secondly, terrorism initially employs fierce means, whereas organized crime chooses to be non-violent notwithstanding odd resort to belligerence. Third, terrorism is motivated solely by political motives despite abuse of regional, national and religious feelings to attain their ends; contrariwise, economic goals are the operational elements of organized crime.
- What are the connections between terrorism and organized crime and how are they significant in the Indian context? Although organized crime includes many activities, its connections with terrorism stem from illicit trading of drugs, arms and human beings and money laundering. Terrorist organizations, whether indigenous or backed by outside states, require arms and money for their struggle against the security forces. Organized crime conglomerates need a clientele and couriers who can smuggle drugs, arms and human beings across the countries and regions.
- In India, the connections between the two are at national and transnational levels. When considered at the national level, both terrorists and those involved in organized crime are within India. On the other hand, at the international level, coordination remains between transnational organizations and terrorists from inside and outside India.

Association between Terrorism and Organized Crime in Kashmir

- In Kashmir, the links between terrorists and organized crime remain at a different level. In contrast to the northeast, dependence on funding from extortion and other related means is minimal. As there is no parallel government in Kashmir, government resources cannot be accessed by militants. However, external funds compensate for insufficient internal mobilization. Militant organizations fighting in Kashmir receive funds from external sources thorough various means. For example, large amount of funds that are mobilized in Pakistan and other Muslim countries, especially in the Gulf, are reach Kashmir through various organizations in Pakistan. Markaz dawa al Arshad, for instance, manages funds from inside and outside Pakistan, to aid its militant wing, Lashkar-e-Toiba. In addition, external funds are also channelled through specific organizations and individuals in Kashmir, which finally reach the militants. Money laundering plays a significant role. Hawala (money laundering) transactions take place swiftly and effectively in Kashmir. Additionally, it is also thought that the ISI uses drug money to fund militant activities in Kashmir.

- Another noteworthy association between organized crime and terrorism, specifically in Kashmir, is via the spread of counterfeit currency. Terrorists are the main agents of Indian counterfeit currency inside Kashmir, which then goes all over India. Even guides for the militants from the other side of the border are rewarded with counterfeit money. In fact, when some of the 'indigenous' militants were also paid with counterfeits, it resulted in squabble between them and the so-called guest militants.

Connection between Terrorism and Organized Crime in the North-East

- In northeast states in India, nearly all the militant organizations run a parallel government or have their areas of influence and are involved in collecting money directly from the people. Considerable amounts of the government funds are channelled to militants indirectly due to misgovernance. Government employees in conflict areas are either threatened or bribed to allot contracts to those patronized by the militant groups. Leave contracts, main commodities like rice and kerosene reach the militant groups directly, which are then given to public at much higher rates. This hidden cycle, which is unnoticed in other parts of India, is a clear example of the connection between organized crime and terrorism inside India.
- The money collected by extortion, kidnap, contracts and black marketing fall short of financing the evil activities of the militants, making a way for transnational drugs and arms syndicates. Terrorist groups in India, specifically in the northeast, generate funds by becoming couriers of illegal drugs and arms and at times even human beings from one point to another within the nation. Some of the infamous entry points from Southeast Asia are Moreh and the entire Chittagong Hill tracts, especially Cox's Bazaar. Primarily, international criminal groups had their own network; however, with these routes being taken over by various terrorist groups in the northeastern states, the groups started using these groups instead of bribing them to let their consignments get through.

Relation between Terrorism and Organized Crime in Other Parts of India

In addition to Kashmir and the northeast, periodic incidents in other parts of India, like the Bombay blasts, for instance, have revealed the connection between terrorism and organized crime. This is different from the traditional connections thriving between organized crime syndicates and local criminals.

CASE STUDY: 2008 MUMBAI ATTACKS

The terror attacks in Mumbai in 2008 comprise 12 synchronized shooting and bombing attacks across Mumbai by members of Lashkar-e-Toiba, the Pakistan-based militant group. The assailants purportedly received reconnaissance assistance before the attacks. Ajmal Kasab, the only accused who was captured alive, later acknowledged upon questioning that the attacks were piloted with the support of Pakistan's ISI. The attacks, which drew extensive global criticism, began on 26 November and lasted until 29 November 2008, taking lives of 166 people and wounding at least 308. Pakistan has repeatedly utilized substitute terrorists organizations to accomplish its foreign policy goal, in this case emphasizing the issue of jurisdiction over Kashmir. Eight of the attacks were done in South Mumbai: at Chhatrapati Shivaji Terminus, the Oberoi Trident, the Taj Mahal Palace & Tower, Leopold Cafe, Cama Hospital (a women and children's hospital),

Contd...

the Nariman House Jewish community centre, the Metro Cinema and a lane behind the Times of India building and St. Xavier's College. There was also an explosion at Mazagaon, in Mumbai's port area, and in a taxi at Vile Parle. By the early morning of 28 November, all sites except for the Taj hotel had been secured by Mumbai Police and security forces. On 29 November, India's National Security Guards (NSG) initiated Operation Black Tornado to kill the remaining attackers; it led to the deaths of the last remaining attackers at the Taj hotel. Kasab revealed that the attackers belong to Lashkar-e-Taiba, considered a terrorist group by India, Pakistan, the United States, the United Kingdom and the United Nations, among others. The Indian government also stated that the attackers came from Pakistan, and the whole process was managed from the soil of Pakistan. On 7 January 2009, Pakistan's Information Minister Sherry Rehman officially accepted Ajmal Kasab's nationality as Pakistani. On 12 February 2009, Pakistan's Interior Minister Rehman Malik asserted that parts of the attack had been planned in Pakistan. A trial court on 6 May 2010 sentenced Ajmal Kasab to death on all the 86 charges for which he was convicted. Listening to his appeal against this verdict, Bombay High Court on 21 February 2011 and Supreme Court of India on 29 August 2012 upheld his death sentence. Lastly, Kasab was hanged at Yerwada Jail in Pune on 21 November 2012.

Background

Mumbai has been a regular victim of terror attacks since the 13 coordinated bomb explosions that killed 257 people and injured 700 on 12 March 1993. The 1993 attacks are believed to be a retaliation of the Babri Mosque demolition. On 6 December 2002, a blast in a BEST bus near Ghatkopar station claimed the lives of two people and injured 28. The bombing was conducted on the 10th anniversary of the demolition of the Babri Mosque in Ayodhya. A bicycle bomb exploded near the Vile Parle station in Mumbai, killing one person and injuring 25 on 27 January 2003, just a day ahead of the visit of the Prime Minister of India Atal Bihari Vajpayee to the city. On 13 March 2003, a day after the 10th anniversary of the 1993 Bombay bombings, a bomb

Contd...

exploded in a train compartment near the Mulund station, claiming lives of 10 people and injuring 70. On 28 July 2003, an explosion in a BEST bus in Ghatkopar claimed lives of 4 people and injured 32. On 25 August 2003, two bombs exploded in South Mumbai, one near the Gateway of India and the other at Zaveri Bazaar in Kalbadevi. At least 44 people died and 150 injured in the attack. On 11 July 2006, seven bombs exploded within 11 minutes on the Suburban Railway in Mumbai, claiming the lives of 209 people, including 22 foreigners, and over 700 were injured. As per the Mumbai Police, the bombings were carried out by Lashkar-e-Taiba and Students Islamic Movement of India (SIMI).

Training

It was reported that a group of recruits, sometimes stated as 24, at other times 26, got training in marine warfare at a remote camp in mountainous Muzaffarabad, Azad Kashmir in Pakistan. It is also said that a part of the training conducted on the Mangla Dam reservoir.

These men got the training in the following stages of training, according to the Indian and US media:

- *Psychological:* Brainwashing for Islamist propaganda, including descriptions of alleged violence suffered by Muslims in India, Chechnya, Palestine and across the globe.
- *Basic Combat:* Lashkar's elementary combat training and terror methodology course, the Daura Aam.
- *Advanced Training:* They have undergone advanced combat training at a camp near Mansehra, a programme the organization calls the Daura Khaas. As per an unnamed source at the US Defense Department, it includes advanced weapons and explosives training overseen by retired personnel of the Pakistan Army, along with survival training and further brainwashing.
- *Commando Training:* Lastly, an even smaller group selected for specialized commando tactics training and marine navigation training given to the Fedayeen unit selected in order to target Mumbai.

Contd...

Among all the recruits, 10 were selected for the Mumbai mission. They were also taught swimming and sailing, in addition to the use of high-end weapons and explosives under the supervision of LeT commanders. As per a media report referring to an unnamed former Defence Department Official of the US, the intelligence agencies of the USA had reported that ex officers from Pakistan's Army and Inter-Services Intelligence agency helped actively and continuously in training. They were given blueprints of all the four targets – Taj Mahal Palace & Tower, Oberoi Trident, Nariman House and Chhatrapati Shivaji Terminus.

Drug Smuggling and Funding of Terrorism

Symbiotic Relationship

Generally, there exists a nexus between terrorism and organized crime, including drug trafficking. Associations between terrorist organizations and drug traffickers have various forms, spanning from facilitation – protection, transportation and taxation – to direct trafficking by the terrorist organization itself to fund its activities. Smugglers and terrorists have alike logistical requirements in terms of material and the covert movement of goods, people and money.

Dealings between drug traffickers and terrorists prove beneficial for both. Drug traffickers take the advantage in terms of terrorists' military skills, weapons trade and access to clandestine institutions. Terrorists gain a source of revenue and expertise in illicit transfer and laundering of proceeds from illicit transactions. Both groups bring corrupt officials whose services provide mutual benefits, such as greater access to fake documents, including passports and customs papers. Drug traffickers may also gain significant freedom of movement when they operate in conjunction with terrorists who control large amounts of territory.

The UNODC's World Drug Report 2007 stated that the total probable value of Afghanistan's 2006 opium harvest accruing to farmers, laboratory owners and Afghan traffickers reached about $US3.1 billion. Besides, it was revealed that in the year 2004, approximately 400 tonnes of cocaine was exported from one Latin American nation, with a projected domestic value of US$ 2 billion. What amount of this money is utilized for executing acts of terrorism? Estimates vary. But even a small percentage would be more than sufficient for some individuals or groups to plan, finance and carry out terrorist acts.

Actually, drug smuggling has offered funding for insurgency and those who use terrorist ferocity in various regions throughout the world, including in transit regions. In some situations, drugs were treated as the currency to execute terrorist attacks, such as in the Madrid bombings.

Effective tools do, however, exist which can eradicate the – and finally help to breaking – the links. For instance, at the international arena, there is a common legal guideline consisting of 16 global anti-terrorist instruments, as well as relevant UN Security Council resolutions. Included in the latter is a series of UN resolutions forcing sanctions – such as the freezing of assets, a travel embargo and an arms embargo, on members of the Taliban, Al-Qaida and their acquaintances. There are presently 124 groups and 226 individuals on this list.

Illegal drug brokers and terrorists are not some covert entity, rather, they are commonly groups and networks that work in ways that can be understood, recognized, followed and ultimately unsettled. We need to incorporate our work to set up more effective and efficient frameworks so that we may perish these illegal networks that spread so much destruction throughout the world.

❑❑❑

Chapter fourteen

Challenges to Internal Security Posed by Money Laundering and Terrorism Financing

Money Laundering

Money laundering is a process of converting black money into white money, that is, converting money from crime, or 'dirty money', into money that seems to come from an authentic source.

This act lets criminals to camouflage their criminal activities and relish the benefits of their crimes, including investing their profits for future criminal acts.

It also makes it tough for authorities to track the origins of money from crime, punish offenders and seize their proceeds.

Money laundering can be defined in the following three stages:

- *Placement:* Adjusting cash generated from crime into the financial system. For instance, depositing the money in a bank.
- *Layering:* Splitting the criminal capitals into different deposit accounts to hide their origin.
- *Integration:* Withdrawing the layered money and depositing them back together in one account or multiple accounts so that they seem authentic.

There are various tactics to launder money, some of which are sophisticated and complex. The most common examples are 'smurfing' or structuring, currency smuggling, exchanging transactions, purchasing assets and gambling.

- *'Smurfing' or structuring:* Dumping cash at various institutions in amounts less than the amount that must be conveyed to government, and subsequently shifting them to a central account.
- *Currency smuggling:* Physically transferring funds across borders to camouflage their source and ownership, often to nations with strict bank secrecy laws. The funds may be moved by mail, courier or body packing.
- *Exchanging transactions:* Purchasing foreign currency that can be shifted to offshore banks.
- *Purchasing assets:* Buying cars, boats and real estate in someone else's name, then selling them and depositing the funds.
- *Gambling:* Purchasing gambling chips, then redeeming them in a different currency or denomination.

Impactful anti-money laundering rules make it easier to spot and examine money laundering actions by instituting links between criminal activity and the funds they generate.

Funding of Terrorism

The method of funding of terrorism operates like money laundering, but in reverse. Instead of camouflaging criminal proceeds as authentic funds, funding of terrorism seeks to camouflage the origin of authentic funds for use in terrorist activities.

People who fund terrorism utilize similar methods and tools as those used for money laundering.

Money laundering is a course by which the illegal source of assets attained or produced by criminal activity is hidden to obscure the connection between the funds and the original criminal activity. Terrorist backing involves the raising and processing of assets to supply terrorists with resources to pursue their activities. While these two occurrences differ in many ways, they often abuse the same vulnerabilities in financial systems that allow for an inappropriate level of anonymity and non-transparency in the execution of financial transactions.

Money Laundering and Terrorist Funding as Threat to Economic and Financial Stability

The global community has prioritized the struggle money laundering and terrorist financing. The IMF is specifically apprehensive about the likely consequences money laundering, terrorist funding and related governance issues have on the integrity and stability of the financial sector and the broader economy. These actions can dent the integrity and stability of financial organizations and systems, disappoint foreign investment and distort global capital flows. They may have negative consequences for a country's financial stability and macroeconomic performance, resulting in welfare losses, draining resources from more productive economic activities, and even have destabilizing spill over effects on the economies of other countries. In an increasingly interconnected world, the negative effects of these activities are global, and their impact on the financial integrity and stability of countries is widely recognized. Masterminds in money laundering and terrorist financing use both the complexity inherent in the global financial system and differences between national AML/CFT laws and systems, and they are especially allured to jurisdictions with weak or ineffective controls where they can more easily move their funds without detection. Moreover, problems in one country can quickly spread to other countries in the region or in other parts of the world.

Tough AML/CFT regimes boost financial sector integrity and stability, which in turn assist countries' integration into the global financial system. They also reinforce governance and fiscal administration. The uprightness of national financial systems is important to financial sector and macroeconomic stability both at the national and international levels.

Global Criteria Guide: Effective AML/CFT Regimes

The Financial Action Task Force on Money Laundering (FATF), a 36-member intergovernmental agency formed by the 1989 G-7 Summit in Paris, has principal aim of devising a global guidelines for AML and CFT. It operates in close cooperation with other key global organizations, including the IMF, the World Bank, the United Nations and FATF-style regional bodies (FSRBs).

To aid national governments in executing effective AML/CFT regimes, the FATF developed a list of sanctions which set out an elementary, globally applicable framework of measures covering the criminal justice system, the financial sector, certain non-financial businesses and professions, transparency of legal persons and arrangements, and mechanisms of international cooperation. In February 2012, these sanctions were reviewed and updated (The FATF Recommendations). In February 2013, the FATF embraced a revised common Methodology for Assessing Technical Compliance with the FATF Recommendations and the Effectiveness of AML/CFT Systems. The first valuations under the new Methodology have now started. The effort of the FATF, as well as the IMF's AML/CFT labours, has been endorsed by the G-7 and the G-20, most recently in relation to initiatives to address the 2008–2009 international financial crisis and its aftermath.

The FATF Plenary, FATF's decision-making body, meets three times every year.

Money Laundering and Terrorist Funding Related to Counterfeiting of Currency

The threat of counterfeit currency is a global spectacle. Related criminal act has the ability to produce high profits and is usually connected to other types of criminal activities such as trafficking in drugs and racketeering. Currency counterfeiters continue to invent and take advantage of new technologies to be at par with regular periodical changes in currency design and security features.

Making counterfeit currency has always been a high profit crime and one that exists ever since money was introduced as a means of exchange. The exchange of counterfeit currency can seriously weaken a country's currency and as such represents a serious risk to national economies.

The FATF has piloted a study of the money laundering methods utilized for placing the proceeds of the illegal trade in counterfeit currency into the regular financial system. The research also emphasizes on how counterfeit currency is utilized for the aim of terrorist funding and other crimes. The report recognizes relevant AML/CFT measures and red flag indicators for detecting counterfeit currency, in particular as it relates to money laundering and terrorist financing.

Trade-Based Money Laundering

- Trade-based money laundering is a substitute transmittal system that permits illegal institutions the chance to earn, move and store proceeds disguised as legitimate trade. Money can be transferred through this method by false-invoicing, over-invoicing and under-invoicing merchandises that are imported or exported around the globe.
- There are three main approaches by which criminal officialdoms and terrorist sponsors move money for the purpose of concealing its origins and assimilating it into the formal economy. The first involves using the financial system; the second includes the physical movement of money (e.g. using cash couriers); and the third is via the physical movement of goods via the trade system. In recent years, the Financial Action Task Force has concentrated significantly on the first two of these methods. By comparison, the opportunity for abuse of the international trade system has received relatively little attention.
- The global trade system is clearly subject to a widespread risks and vulnerabilities that can be abused by criminal institutions and terrorist sponsors. In part, these emanate from the large volume of trade flows, which disguises individual transactions; the complications linked with the use of multiple foreign exchange transactions and diverse trade financing arrangements; the commingling of authentic and illicit funds; and the restricted resources that most customs

agencies have available to detect suspicious trade transactions.

- For the sake of this research, trade-based money laundering can be understood as the method of masquerading the proceeds of crime and moving value through the use of trade dealings to legitimize their illegitimate origins. In practice, this can be attained by the falsification of the price, quantity or quality of imports or exports. Furthermore, trade-based money laundering methods differ in complexity and are often utilized in combination with other money laundering methods to further obscure the money trail. This study delivers a number of case studies that show how the global trade system has been misused by criminal establishments. It also has made use of a comprehensive questionnaire to collect information on the current practices of more than 30 nations. This information focuses on the ability of various government organizations to recognize suspicious activities related to trade transactions, to share this information with domestic and foreign partner agencies and to act on this information.
- The study determines that trade-based money laundering signifies a vital channel of criminal activity and, provided the growth of world trade, an increasingly important money laundering and terrorist funding susceptibility.
- Furthermore, as the principles applied to other money laundering skills become increasingly effective, the utilization of trade-based money laundering can be expected to become increasingly striking.

Prevention of Money Laundering

- The chief initiative to stop money laundering was United Nations convention against illicit traffic in Narcotic Drugs and Psychotropic substances in 1988. But major revolution came with the institution of Financial Action Task Force (FATF) in 1989. The FATF is an intergovernmental agency formed in 1989 by G-7 Summit in Paris, primarily to inspect and develop measures to fight money laundering.
- The objects of the FATF are to fix guidelines and encourage effective application of legal, regulatory and operational measures for fighting money laundering, terrorist funding and other related threats to the integrity of the international financial system.
- The FATF observers the growth of its members in employing essential methods, analyses money laundering and terrorist financing practices and counter-measures, and endorses the adoption and implementation of appropriate measures globally.
- The FATF currently consists of 34 member jurisdictions and 2 regional institutions, representing most major financial centres in all parts of the globe. India became member of FATF in 2010.

40+9 Recommendations

Forty Recommendations were made by the FATF in 1990, which were last amended in 2003. Some of them are applying the international conventions of this relevance and criminalizing money laundering and permitting authorities to seize the proceeds of money laundering. 8 Special Recommendations on Terrorist Financing were made by the FATF in the wake of 9/11 attacks. A 9th Special Recommendation on Terrorist Financing was made in October 2004. In total, there are 49 recommendations by the FATF to fight the money laundering.

The Prevention of Money Laundering Act, 2002 (PMLA)

- The Prevention of Money Laundering Act, 2002 (PMLA) is the basis of the legal framework devised by India to fight money laundering. It came into effect in 2005. PMLA explains money laundering offence and offers the freezing, seizure and confiscation of the proceeds of crime. Prominent characteristics of this act are as follows:

- RBI, SEBI and IRDA were put under the PMLA; therefore, the provisions of this act apply to all financial organizations, banks, mutual funds, insurance companies and their financial intermediaries.
- The body observing the anti-Money laundering actions in India is the Financial Intelligence Unit (FIU-IND). This agency has the responsibility of receiving, processing, analysing and distributing information regarding suspect financial transactions. FIU-IND is also liable for coordinating and boosting efforts of national and international intelligence, investigation and enforcement bodies in trailing the global efforts against money laundering and related crimes. FIU-IND is an autonomous body under the Economic Intelligence Council (EIC) headed by the Finance Minister.
- Sentence for offence of money laundering: There can be penalty of sentence up to 3 to 7 years with fine up to 5 lakh rupees. In case of violations under Narcotic Drugs and Psychotropic Substance Act 1985, maximum punishment can be extended to 10 years rather than 7 years.

Responsibility of Banking Companies, Financial Institutions and Intermediaries

- Banking corporations have to follow the practice of KYC Norms (Know your customer)
- Retain records for nature and value of the deal to be transacted.
- Whether such deal was singly transacted or series of transaction taken place in a month.
- Preserve record for a period of 10 years from the date of cessation of transaction between the clients and the banking company or financial institution or intermediary as the case may be.
- Provide information of above transaction to director within the fixed timeframe.
- Verify and keep the records of identity of all clients in respect of such transactions to Director within the fixed time.

The Prevention of Money Laundering (Amendment) Act 2012

- The PMLA was formed in 2002, but was revised thrice, that is in 2005, 2009 and 2012. The 2012 form of the amendment received president's assent on 3 January 2013, and the law became effective from February 15, when the finance ministry notified it. The PMLA (Amendment) Act, 2012, has widened the definition of money laundering by including actions such as concealment, acquisition, possession and use of proceeds of crime as criminal activities. Some other features include the following:
- The revision has presented the concept of Corresponding law to join the provisions of Indian law with the laws of foreign nations and to offer for transfer of the earnings of foreign predicate offence committed in any manner in India.
- It also includes the approach of 'reporting entity', which would involve a banking company, financial organization, intermediary or a person carrying on a nominated business or profession.
- The Prevention of Money Laundering Act, 2002, had a fine up to ₹ 5 lakh. The amendment act has removed this upper limit.
- The act has offered conditional attachment and seizure of property of any person (for a

period not exceeding 180 days). This step may be taken by the authority if it has purpose to believe that the offence of money laundering has taken place.

- The act has vested the Director with a power to call for records of transactions or any additional information that may be required for investigation. The Director may also make investigations for non-compliance of the obligations of the reporting entities.
- Part B of the Schedule in the previous Act included only those wrongdoings that are above ₹ 30 lakh or more, whereas Part A did not state any monetary limit of the offence. The revised act has brought all the offences under Part A of the Schedule to ensure that the monetary thresholds do not relate to the offence of money laundering.

India has been Classified as High-risk Zone in relation to Money Laundering

Among 140 nations, India was ranked 70th in 2013 and 93rd in 2012, by the Anti-Money Laundering (AML) Basel Index.

This clearly states that India, in the present-day situation, is very at risk money laundering activities.

There are ample of acts in India to curb money laundering activities.

A few of such acts are:

- The Conservation of Foreign Exchange and Prevention of Smuggling Activities Act, 1974
- The Income Tax Act, 1961
- The Benami Transactions (Prohibition) Act, 1988
- The Indian Penal Code and Code of Criminal Procedure, 1973
- The Narcotic Drugs and Psychotropic Substances Act, 1985

Instead of so many acts, money laundering matters are still happening unabated. To limit the examples of Money Laundering, the PMLA Act was presented in the Lok Sabha on 4 August 1998 and was ultimately passed on 17 January 2003.

Besides the PMLA, there are other initiatives taken by the government to confirm that the instances of money laundering are stopped.

Financial Intelligence Unit (FIU)

- The Financial intelligence Unit (FIU) works in the legal charter recognized by the PMLA. FIU executes the basic roles of receipt, analysis and dissemination of information in accordance with the global standards set up by the FATF and Egmont Group of FIUs.
- As provisioned under the PMLA, FIU accepts reports on cash transactions, doubtful transactions, counterfeit currency transactions and funds received by non-profit institutions.
- These reports are done by reporting entities, that is, banks, financial organizations and capital market intermediaries, casinos, private locker operators, registrar to an issue of shares and dealers in precious metals.
- FIU keeps a database and shares these reports with various agencies.

Know Your Customer (KYC) Guidelines

- The aim of KYC framework is to avert banks from being used, deliberately or accidentally, by criminals for money laundering or terrorist funding activities.
- To prevent identity theft, identity fraud, money laundering, terrorist financing, etc., the RBI ordered all banks and financial institutions to make a policy framework to know their customers before opening any account.
- The KYC framework was introduced by RBI in 2002, and all banks were instructed comply the same by 31 December 2005.

- This includes authenticating customers' identity and address by requesting them to submit documents that are accepted as relevant proof. Compulsory details needed under KYC norms are proof of identity and proof of address.
- KYC norms have been flouted many a times, and there is requirement for the RBI to make the system more efficient.

A few examples of such instances are:

- An individual investor, Roopalben Panchal, had around 6,315 demat accounts with the National Securities Depository Ltd (NSDL) in benami names.
- She received 150 shares each from 6,315 allottees through off-market transactions, 9,47,250 shares in aggregate, which were then removed to six accounts, five of which sold the shares on listing to make a handsome profit of ₹ 1.37 crore.
- Similar modus operandi was applied by some investors during the IPO of Infrastructure Development Finance Company (IDFC).

Recent Variations in Prevention of Money Laundering Act (PMLA)

- Description of 'Activities of Terrorism' was not given in PMLA 2002; but, the same was incorporated in 2010 as 'Transaction involving financing of the activities relating to terrorism includes transaction involving funds suspected to be linked or related to, or to be used for terrorism, terrorist acts or by a terrorist, terrorist organization or those who finance or are attempting to finance terrorism'.
- Till 2010, the enactment permitted guarding identity of beneficial owners, who could be represented by lawyers and accountants. However, it has been eliminated as a part of the recent revisions made to the act in 2013.
- RBI and IRDA did not have any rule to tackle cases for filling Suspicious Transaction Report to Financial Monitoring Unit. Circulars were released by both establishments to address the issue.
- The prior provisions of the Act lacked the competence for due law-making act. Hence, the range was widened in 2013 to embrace concealment, possession, acquisition or use of property, and projecting or claiming it as clean property. Commodity future brokers were been brought under the scope of the Act now.
- The recent revisions in the PMLA are welcome as a report from Global Financial Integrity, published in December 2013, which stated that the total black money outflow from India was approximately $343 billion during 2002–2011.

Black Money

- There is no constant description of black money in the literature or economic concept. In reality, some terms with similar meanings have been in trend, namely 'unaccounted income', 'black income', 'dirty money', 'black wealth', 'underground wealth', 'black economy', 'parallel economy', 'shadow economy', and 'underground' or 'unofficial' economy. All these expressions usually mean any income on which the taxes levied by government or public establishments have not been paid. Such wealth may comprise revenue produced from authentic activities or activities which are illegal per se, like trafficking, illicit trade in banned substances, counterfeit currency, arms trafficking, terrorism and corruption. 'Black money' can be regarded as assets or resources that have neither been informed to the public establishments at the time of their generation nor revealed at any point of time during their possession.

- Approximations of black money in India vary wildly. A World Bank report positions India's shadow economy at close to one-fifth of economic output. Another study on illegal financial movements by Global Financial Integrity (GFI), a non-profit institution, places these at 3% of economic output for India between 2002 and 2011. This difficulty in measurement is because black money is generated through a raft of complex, sophisticated activities for the purposes of tax evasion, crime and corruption. This makes it inherently difficult to measure black money accurately. Some studies exclude certain sources of black money. For example, the GFI excludes criminal activities and a part of corporate tax evasion, both massive sources of black money. Hence, its estimates are naturally more conservative. This study also declares that in the developing world, including India, corporate tax evasion is liable for 60% of overall black income; criminal actions are responsible for 35%, while corruption, which has caused much havoc in India, accounts for only 5%. Although the drop in personal income tax rate from nearly 100% in the 1970s to under 30% now has reduced tax evasion, it has been offset by higher rates of corporate taxation.

Prevailing Legal Outline to Check Black Money in India

- Remarkably, Indian tax laws do not have any clear meaning of the term 'black money'. Mostly, money can be referred to as black money in two circumstances. First is where it has been attained by illegitimate actions like the drug trade, terrorism, corruption, etc. The second includes a situation where wealth has been created out of money on which taxes have not been paid.
- The term is not easy to define as it might have the characteristics of a chameleon, changing its colour to suit the purpose. It includes 'unaccounted income', 'black income', 'dirty money', 'black wealth', 'underground wealth', 'black economy', 'parallel economy', 'shadow economy', and 'underground' or 'unofficial' economy, says Vidya Rajarao, partner, forensic services, Grant Thornton India LLP.
- Corporate law specialists say tax establishments are progressively expected to authenticate whether foreign currency accounts held by resident and non-resident Indians conform with the foreign exchange regulations, and were revealed properly in annual tax returns.
- As per Deep Roy, associate partner, Economic Laws Practice, no person resident in India is allowed to open any foreign currency account without approval of the Reserve Bank of India (RBI).
- However, an individual who is resident in India is permitted to open a bank account in a foreign bank if he or she has to conduct any current or capital account transaction, and must dispatch the money from India as approved under the Foreign Exchange Management Act (FEMA) of 1999.
- There is a definite money-laundering regulation–the Prevention of Money Laundering Act, 2002. It has provisions for penalty in the case of money laundering and for keeping black money. Corporate attorneys say if any foreign account holder infringes Indian laws regulating the flow of foreign currency, tax establishments can impose deportation of such funds, including funds needed to recuperate the unpaid taxes, besides the penalty under FEMA.
- Besides this act, various rules under the Income Tax Act, 1961; Prevention of Corruption Act, 1988; and the Narcotic Drugs and Psychotropic Substances Act (NDPS) of 1985 could also be used if the case demands.

- An NRI can to be tried under FEMA if there has been any concealment of income. Any non-payment or under-payment of tariff is subject to interest and penalty. The penalty could go up to three times the amount of tax evaded.
- The civil and criminal liabilities for hoarding black money vary from severe imprisonment for not less than three years and up to seven to 10 years, plus a fine.
- As per the Income Tax Act, any Indian citizen who has stashed money out of the country on which tax was owed but not paid has to pay tax, interest and penalty.
- 'The penalty could be as high as 300 per cent of the tax that was avoided. The interest would be 15 per cent per annum since the time the tax authorities believe the tax was evaded', says Rajarao.
- If case is filed under the provisions of NDPS, the maximum sentence could extend up to 20 years; the death penalty is also an option. India's struggles to bring back black money stashed abroad in foreign currency accounts are disrupted by bilateral Double taxation Avoidance Agreements (DTAAs) signed with various countries.
- Corporate tax specialists say the privacy provisions of these DTAAs generally permit revelation or use of information only for tax purposes.
- Most nations have normally declined to accept India's appeal to totally eradicate the confidentiality requirements. A majority of nations feel the evidence should not be revealed unless a tax case comes up before a court of law. Corporate tax legal representatives feel there is bound to be a step-up in scrutiny by tax authorities of any money held by Indians and NRIs in foreign bank accounts. As per Milind S Kothari, managing partner & head - direct tax, BDO India LLP, 'the new tax return form requires information to be provided in relation to various assets held by an individual outside India, including bank accounts in which one is a signatory. However, there are no such provisions applicable to NRIs. However, NRIs are required to report income that is sourced, and therefore liable to be taxed, in India'.
- When the discussed NRI becomes a resident in India, he or she needs to guarantee that global income is offered to tax in India (subject to some exceptions), and also reveal information in relation to assets held outside India.

Plan to Tackle Black Money

- FICCI in his analysis titled 'Widening of tax base and tackling black money' has revealed a plan for solving the frustrating problem of black money and sent it to the PM Narendra Modi government.
- The document recognizes the main reasons for generation of black money in India, segments where black money generation is widespread and proposals to expose the generation, accumulation and distribution of black money within the Indian economy.

Some of the important proposals forming part of the document are as follows:

1. ***Incentivised dealings through credit/debit cards and other banking tools:*** It is suggested that Government may offer some incentives so that dealers (particularly of high valued items like jewellery, FMCG etc.) are cheered to receive payments through credit card/ debit card and other banking instruments. These incentives could take the form of an additional deduction from income related to the transaction value for computing the tax liability or a reduced Value Added Tax (VAT).
2. ***Set-up central database to store invoices:*** It is recommended that a central database should

be constituted to assist storing of invoices issued by Fast Moving Consumer Goods (FMCG) companies to small businesses across the nation. The database can be then utilized to successfully observe the purchases made by these small businesses from FMCGs stores and the equivalent sales reported by them. This will aid in spotting any inconsistency in sales reported by small businesses and probable chain of generation of black money.

3. *Develop the range of Presumptive Taxation:* The Government can think of implementing a presumptive profit estimation scheme by integrating rules and regulations in the income tax law to arrest professionals who work through transactions in cash and stay out of the tax net.
4. *Tax on Agricultural Income:* State governments should be promoted to initiate appropriate instrument (while providing rationally high level of thresholds to avoid small farmers being burdened) for widening the scope and quantum of agricultural income tax.
5. *Changes in real estate:* As the registration charges and taxes are reliant on the value of the transaction, purchasers under-report the value to evade paying higher taxes and charges (by making a portion of the payment in cash). This lets the parties indulged to declare lower transaction values.

   Taxes and charges during the process of registration can be divided into two parts – a fixed component and a variable component. Regardless of the reported value of the property, a fixed amount should be paid to civic authorities, whereas the variable amount may be reliant on the current market prices of the property. The market price of a property may be determined by an sovereign government-approved unit. The value of the property reported by the agency may form the basis for calculating the taxes and charges to be paid by the buyer.
6. *Constitute IT infrastructure to track tax evasion:* It is vital to set up and utilize robust IT Infrastructure to combine and exchange information related to different streams of taxes, i.e., income tax, service tax, sales tax, excise duty, etc. by common means such as PAN of an assesse. This will help in monitoring cases pertaining to tax evasion resulting in accumulation of black money.
7. *Develop the provisions of Tax Deduction at Source/Tax Collection at Source:* It is recommended that the rules and regulations of the Income Tax Act, 1961, be revised to enlarge the scope of TDS and TCS by including uncovered sectors where black money develops.
8. *Develop tax base by detecting non-filers of income tax returns:* To boost the tax base and augment tax collection, it is important for the government to emphasize on non-filers and unearth black money within the economy. The Income-Tax (IT) department should execute tougher instruments to trace persons who resorted to tax evasion and bring them under the tax net.
9. *Simplify the tax structure:* The government should streamline the tax structure, and possibly decrease tax rates. This would dissuade tax evasion by leading to reporting of full transaction value. The step would be instrumental to discourage black money generation.

Influence of Demonetization on the Internal Security of India

On 8th November, 2016, Indian Prime Minister Mr. Narendra Modi addressed the public about eliminating the bane of black money and other problems from the Indian society, economy and polity. In a historic change, he declared that the ₹ 500 and one ₹ 1,000 notes will cease to be legal tender from the night of 8th November 2016. Besides, ₹ 2,000 notes and new notes of ₹ 500 will be circulated. He said that the move help in fighting against corruption, black money, money laundering, terrorism and financing of terrorism as well as Fake Indian Currency Notes (FICN). Fully sensitive to some of the difficulties the common citizens may face in the coming days, the Prime Minister also announced a series of steps that will help overcome the potential problems. Persons holding old notes of five hundred or one thousand rupees were allowed to deposit these notes in bank or post offices from 10th November onwards till 30th December. There were also some limits placed on the withdrawals from ATMs and bank for the very short run. Shri Modi stated that on humanitarian grounds notes of five hundred and one thousand rupees will be accepted at government hospitals, pharmacies in government hospitals (with prescription of a doctor), booking counters for railway tickets, government buses, airline ticket counters, petrol, diesel and gas stations of PSU oil companies, consumer cooperative stores authorized by the state or central government, milk booths authorized by state government and crematoria, burial grounds. During his address, the Prime Minister expressed about how the level of cash in circulation is linked to inflation and how the inflation condition is deteriorated due to the cash organized through corrupt means. The Prime Minister added that it adversely shakes the poor and the neo-middle class people. He referred to the problems being faced by the honest citizens while buying houses.

Demonetization refers to the removal of old ₹ 500 and ₹ 1,000 notes, as official means of payment, by the Reserve Bank of India. According to Investopedia, demonetization is an act of stripping a currency of its status as a legal tender. Following it, the notes of ₹ 500 and ₹ 1,000 won't be utilized as a medium of exchange of goods and service in India. The total worth of old ₹ 500 and ₹ 1,000 notes in the circulation is around ₹ 14.2 trillion, which is approximately 85% of the total value of currency in circulation. This presents a situation where the total cash has to now go through the formal banking channels to get legitimacy. The World Bank in July 2010 projected that the size of the shadow economy for India is at 20.7% of the Gross Domestic Product (GDP) in 1999 and is surging to 23.2% in 2007. Supposing that this figure has not risen since then (quite unlikely though) and that the cash factor of the shadow economy is also proportional (it could be higher), the projected unaccounted value of the currency could be to the tune of ₹ 3.3 trillion. Now, after the declaration of demonetization by the government, this money would have to either accounted for by paying the relevant tax and penalties or would get eliminated. There are greater chances of larger proportion of this unaccounted currency getting eliminated as the tax rate and successive legal issues could be prohibitively high for such money.

Analysing the Impact on Money Laundering and Terrorism Financing: Terrorist groups are mainly funded by the supply of Fake Indian Currency Notes (FICN) and money laundering. The movement of money to the terrorist organizations goes through the following media:

- Transferring proceeds by financial system including transfers by hawala or other similar tool of illegal, informal transfer of funds in bulk.
- Physical transfer of money by cash couriers and use of FICN.
- Utilization of international trade system in high-valued items like diamonds and gold through money laundering.

Normally, the money used by the terrorist groups is the illegal or black money, and those involved in transferring cannot disclose their source to the law enforcement agencies. The maximum amount of money with the terrorist groups is in the form of old ₹ 500 and ₹ 1,000 notes. After demonetization, all the wealth with these organizations has become null and void. As a result, funding became difficult. This approach has also cramped future financing of terrorist organizations. The demonetization step made all the unaccounted money invalid after 30th December 2016. Government also executed adequate steps to observe the movement on new currency notes through the banking channel. Any doubtful deal involving a large amount of money without disclosing the income source were being tracked by the law enforcement agencies. Agencies like Enforcement Directorate, banks and Financial Intelligence Unit were geared up to trace any new transaction apprehensive to be aimed at terror financing. By the step, the old FICN notes became invalid and were no longer used for terror financing. It is also known that the security features of the new notes are difficult to copy. Moreover, the responsible agencies are well prepared to fight counterfeiting of these new notes and their trafficking into the Indian economy. Once money laundering is curbed, terrorists won't be able to use the international trade system in high value items as the money movement would be curbed in the manner described above.

Analysing the Influence of Demonetization on Black Money: Post demonetization, all the black money holders were not able to deposit their old ₹ 500 and ₹ 1,000 notes in the banks, as they were not in a position to give an account of that to the Income Tax authorities. Thus, the black money held by them lost its worth, and India is expected to come out from the problem of black money in the long run.

Analysing the Impact of Demonetization on Criminal Activities and Corruption: As the amount of black and unaccounted money was expected to decrease post demonetization, the funding of illegal activities became costlier. Thus, it became tough to commit illegal actions like drugs trafficking, organized crime and human trafficking. It also made collusive corruption most costly as unaccounted and black money was no longer available to be used in it. Likewise, the rate of corruption is expected to decrease in the long run.

Following impacts were estimated on the Indian economy after the demonetization process:

- It is likely to increase the liquidity position of banks, which can be used further for lending purposes, decreasing the lending interest rates.
- With cash dealings facing a reduction, alternative procedures of payment is thought to see a surge in demand. Digital transaction procedures, E-wallets and apps, online transactions using E-banking, usage of Plastic money (Debit and Credit Cards), etc. are likely to see considerable increase in demand.
- It is likely to increase the demand for gold as people may start having more faith on gold than Indian currency notes.
- As the amount of currency in hand is likely to decrease, the inflation is expected to go down in short run.
- The property prices will come down as the real estate sector involves circulation of a large sum of black money at present.

The approach of demonetization intended at generating many long lasting positive impacts, but in the short run, the nation has suffered and will suffer from certain negative effects. There will be a trouble in the current liquidity condition as households are expected to get affected by the note exchange terms set by the government. Unorganized sector measures including small trade market actions will continue to be volatile in the short-term. It is vital to note that a substantial percentage of the Indian workforce is working in this sector which is likely to be affected by immediate liquidity issues. Overall, negative impact on disposable income is expected along with likely disruption in the consumption patterns of the general populace.

The government has acknowledged the troubles faced due to the demonetization and has presented great dynamism in dealing with it. The government machinery is constantly checking the ground realities and taking daily decisions in tackling them. Some of the vibrant steps taken by the government in tackling the hardships are:

- Old notes can still be substituted at the Reserve Bank of India.
- Government has extended the date (considering the ground realities) for the use of old ₹ 500 note at petrol pumps, government hospitals, and some other public utilities till a prescribed date.
- Seeing the liquidity crunch, government also relieved the citizens from paying toll taxes till a prescribed date.
- Government allowed old currency in school fees, colleges, pre-paid mobile top-ups, purchases at consumer cooperative stores, at international airports, etc.
- Government eliminated withdrawal charges at all ATMs.
- Seeing the situation, government augmented the daily withdrawal limit in ATM from ₹ 2,000 to ₹ 2,500.
- Government constituted a task force under the chairmanship of RBI deputy governor S. S. Mundra to make sure ATMs across the country become ready to dispense higher denomination notes in the shortest time.

The above and other steps were implemented daily after reviewing the ground reality of demonetization. This determined the seriousness of government in executing this breakthrough reform. ❑❑❑

Chapter fifteen

India's Security Forces, Security Organizations and Their Mandates: An Overview

Like a number of federal structures, the nature of the Constitution of India mandates law and order as a subject of the state, therefore the most of the policing lies with the respective states and territories of India. At the federal level, many agencies are part of the Union Ministry of Home Affairs and assist the states in their duties. Larger cities also operate metropolitan police forces under respective state governments. All senior police officers in the state police forces, as well as those in the federal agencies, are members of the Indian Police Service (IPS) and Indian Revenue Service (IRS), one of the civil services.

Central (Federal) Agencies

- The federal police are controlled by the central Government of India. The majority of federal law enforcement agencies are controlled by the Ministry of Home Affairs. The head of each of the federal law enforcement agencies is always an Indian Police Service (IPS). The constitution assigns responsibility for maintaining law and order to the states and territories, and almost all routine policing—including apprehension of criminals—is carried out by state-level police forces. The constitution also permits the central government to participate in police operations and organization by authorizing the maintenance of the Indian Police Service. Police officers are recruited by the Union Public Service Commission through a competitive nationwide examination. On completion of a nationwide basic public-service course, police officer candidates attend the National Police Academy at Hyderabad, Andhra Pradesh. They are then assigned to particular state or union territory forces, where they usually remain for the rest of their careers. About 50 per cent of the officers are regularly assigned to states or territories other than their own in an effort to promote national integration.
- The constitution also gives power to the central government to maintain forces that are required to ensure national security. Under the terms of the constitution, Central Police forces can be legally detailed to help the states but only if so requested by the state governments. In practice, the central government has largely observed these limits.

In isolated instances, the central government has deployed its armed police units to protect central government institutions over the protest of a state government. During the Emergency of 1975-77, the constitution was amended (effective 1 February 1976) to permit the central government to dispatch and deploy its Central Armed Police forces without regard to the wishes of the states. This action proved unpopular, and the use of the Central Police Forces was controversial. After the Emergency was lifted, the constitution was amended in December 1978 to make deployment of central Police forces once again dependent on the consent of the state government. According to apologists for the central government, this amendment prevented the government from sending in Central Armed Police Forces to protect the Babri Masjid (Babri Mosque) in Ayodhya, Uttar Pradesh, in December 1992.

Ministry of Home Affairs

The major national-level organization connected with law enforcement is the Ministry of Home Affairs, which supervises a large number of government functions and agencies operated and administered by the central government. The ministry is associated with all matters pertaining to maintaining public peace and order, the staffing and administration of the public services, the delineation of internal boundaries and the administration of union territories. Besides managing the Indian Police Service, the Ministry of Home Affairs maintains several agencies and organizations dealing with police and security. Police in the union territories are the responsibility of the Police Division, which also runs the National Police Academy and the Institute of Criminology and Forensic Science. The Central Bureau of Investigation investigates crimes that might involve public officials or have ramifications for several states. The ministry also is the parent organization of the Border Security Force.

Central Armed Police Forces

- Central Armed Police Forces (CAPF) were earlier known as Central Paramilitary Forces (CPMF). The new terminology was introduced in 2011 on the request of Army.
- Eight forces that exist officially are termed as 'Central Armed Police Forces', namely: BSF, CRPF, ITBP, CISF, SSB, NSG, SPG, and RPF.
- The first six, i.e., BSF, CRPF, ITBP, CISF, SSB and NSG are administered by the Ministry of Home Affairs, while the SPG is under the Cabinet secretariat and the RPF is under the Ministry of Railways.

Border Security Force

- The Border Security Force (BSF) has a duty to safeguard India's land borders during peacetime and preventing trans-border crimes. It was set up on 1 December, 1965. It is a central police force operating under the Union Ministry of Home Affairs. The Indo-Pakistani War of 1965 demonstrated the inadequacies of the existing border management system and led to the formation of the Border Security Force as a unified central agency with the specific mandate of guarding India's international boundaries.
- The BSF's policing capabilities were used in the Indo-Pakistani War of 1971 against the Pakistani Armed Forces in areas where the Indian Armed Forces was thinly spread; BSF troops took part in the Battle of Longewala. When the insurgency in Jammu and Kashmir broke out in 1989, the Jammu and Kashmir state police and the thinly-deployed Central Reserve Police Force (CRPF) struggled to cope

with the spiralling violence, and the Indian government deployed the BSF to Jammu and Kashmir to combat Islamic militants. The BSF had trained, supported and formed part of 'MUKTI VAHINI'.

- It consists of 2,50,000 personnel in 186 battalions. Some battalions of the BSF are deployed with CRPF in Naxal affected region of Dandakaranya and Jammu and Kashmir.

Duties of the BSF

The functions of the BSF are classified below as:

Peace time:

- Boost a sense of security among the people living in the border areas.
- Overcome Trans-border crimes, unauthorized entry into or exit from the territory of India.
- Check smuggling and any other illegal activities.

In the last few years, the BSF, apart from their duties, has been deployed to counter insurgency and ensure internal security.

War Time:

- Holding ground in less threatened sectors so long as the main attack does not develop in a particular sector and it is felt that the local situation is within the capacity of BSF to deal with. The BSF units can continue to remain deployed in specific sector even in a war-like situation to release the Army for offensive tasks. In the event of a major attack developing, which is not within the capacity of the BSF to deal with, the Army can be expected either to reinforce the BSF with Artillery or other support, or relieve the BSF from its role in particular sector.
- Safe-guarding vital installations, especially air-fields against enemy commandoes/para troopers or raids. The role can be entrusted to the BSF Units which are placed under the Army's operational Control.
- Offering extension to the flanks of main defence line by the holding of strong points in conjunction with other units.
- Limited Aggressive action against para military or irregular forces of the enemy within the overall plan of the Armed Forces.
- Performing special duties associated with intelligence including raids. These are duties which might be entrusted to BSF Units by the Army in a war situation according to local necessity. It would, however, be expected that the state of training and equipment of the particular BSF Units would be kept in view in assessing their adequacy for the tasks.
- Working as guides in an area of responsibility where routes are known. This is a task which the BSF should be able to perform.
- Maintaining law and order in enemy territory administrated under the control of Army. Usually, ordinary civil police force would be used for this task but the BSF could be used to supplement the civil police or to act in lieu thereof in a situation where civil police is not readily available.
- Provision of escorts.
- Guarding prisoners of war cages.
- Assistance in control of refugees. It is the motto to use civil police force and armed Home Guards etc. for these operations but again depending upon local exigencies, the BSF might be entrusted with these tasks.
- Anti-infiltration duties in particular regions. This is a remarkable responsibility which will have to be executed by security forces. The exact responsibility of the BSF in this matter is still being considered and separate instructions are expected to be issued.

Some instances of important contributions of BSF

- The BSF creates a number of personnel for services for UN Mission every year.
- At the time of the Kargil conflict in May–July 1999, the BSF stayed at greater heights of the mountains and defended the integrity of the country with all the might at its command in coordination with the Army.
- BSF personnel have been performing Internal Security Duty in Manipur for the last two years and have been fighting insurgency in those regions successfully.
- When the earthquake occurred in Gujarat on 26th January 2001, the BSF was the first to reach out to help the distressed people.
- When the communal disturbances took place in Gujarat, BSF personnel went all out to restore amity and brotherhood among the people.
- The BSF carried out the work of erecting the border fencing in Jammu and Kashmir and it was successful in its task despite all efforts of Pakistan to scuttle our work.
- The BSF along with the army has been defending the borders and checking infiltration on the borders during the current standoff with Pakistan.
- The air wing of the BSF also contributed immensely to the relief work in Uttarakhand during the Kedarnath disaster in 2013.

Central Industrial Security Force

- In 1969, CISF came into being. At the time of its formation, it had strength of about 3000 men. Today the CISF is known to have carried out a multi-faceted role whereby in addition to its traditional role of Industrial Security, it has also moved into new areas such as Airport Security, Security of Government Buildings, Monument Security, Disaster Management, VIP Security, Delhi Metro Rail etc.
- Now the Force is offering security cover to 294 units (including 57 domestic & international airportsm79 Fire units and 03 Pvt. sector units) spread all across the country with a strength of over 1,22,000 officers and men. It is a matter of great pride for the Force that as of now 22 of its units are ISO certified for Quality Management Systems.
- The mandate of the force has been widened to offer security cover to the private sector also-Infosys being the first one to get the security cover of CISF in 2009. Reliance Refinery, Jamnagar and Delhi metro airport Express Line are the recent additions to the list of private sector establishment to be positioned under CISF cover.

Central Reserve Police Force

- The CRPF is the biggest police force in the world. The Central Reserve Police Force (CRPF) is the largest paramilitary force in the country. On 27 July 1939, it came into being as the Crown Representative's Police. After India's Independence, it became the Central Reserve Police Force on enactment of the CRPF Act on 28 December 1949.
- Its primary motto is to assist and help state and union territories' law enforcement agencies in maintaining law and order and to contain insurgency. It is also deployed as anti-terrorist unit in different areas. It is actively looking after the internal security of every part of India and is even operating abroad as part of United Nations peacekeeping missions. It is performing a wide range of duties ranging from VIP security to election duties, from guarding of vital installations to the counter-naxal operations.

Broad spectrum of duties carried out by the CRPF is:

- Controlling crowd
- Controlling riot
- Countering Militancy or Insurgency operations
- Countering Left Wing Extremism
- Ensuring overall co-ordination of large scale security arrangement particularly at the time of elections in disturbed regions of country.
- Safe-guarding VIPs and important installations.
- Controlling environmental de-gradation and protecting local flora and fauna
- Confronting aggression during war time
- Taking part in UN Peace Keeping Mission
- Indulging in rescue and relief operations at the time of natural calamities

Specialized forces associated with CRPF

Rapid Action Force (RAF)

RAF is a highly specialized force, formed by converting 10 unattached battalions of CRPF in Oct. 1992. These units were formed to combat riots or riot-like situations to instil confidence amongst all sections of the society and also, handle internal security duty. RAF is a zero response force which gets to the crisis situation within a short span of time, thus enthusing an immediate sense of security and confidence amongst the common masses.

Commando Battalion for Resolute Action (COBRA)

- In 2009, the MHA gave a green signal for raising of 10 COBRA (Combat Battalion for Resolute Action) with a purpose to meet the challenges posed by Naxalites. This specialized CRPF unit is one of the few units of the Central Armed Police Forces in the country that are particularly trained in guerilla warfare. This elite fighting unit has been trained to track, hunt and wipe out small Naxalite group.

Special Duty Group (SDG) and Parliamentary Duty Group (PDG)

- SDG is an elite CRPF unit whose duty is to provide armed protection to SPG protected areas.
- Parliament Duty Group (PDG) has been created out of the Central Reserve Police Force and it was first mooted to be raised in the backdrop of the 2001 Parliament terror attack. Parliament Duty Group is an elite CRPF unit tasked to provide armed protection to Parliament House. It consists of 1,540 personnel drawn from different units of Central Reserve Police Force (CRPF). PDG members are provided training in combating nuclear and bio-chemical attacks, rescue operations and behavioural management.
- The Parliament House complex is protected by four layers of security, each under teams from Delhi police, CRPF, ITBP and personnel of Parliament Security Service.

Women in the CRPF

- The CRPF comprises of three battalions staffed completely by women. The first battalion No. 88 was formed in 1986 with its headquarters at New Delhi. The second battalion 135 came into its formation in 1996 at Gandhinagar, Gujarat. The third battalion, Number 213 is situated at Ajmer, Rajasthan.

The Green Force

- The Green Force is another specialized outfit of the CRPF. The force has been able to keep an effective control on environmental degradation and sustain the regeneration of local flora and fauna. Green Force personnel plant hundreds of thousands of trees in different regions of the country on an annual basis.

Commando 469

- CRPF Commandos are specialized in counter-terrorism, reconnaissance and sabotage and have the honour of being the most elite among the forces. They undergo extremely rigorous training for years sometimes, before they are ready and when their training is over, they can be easily categorized as among the toughest and most competent men in the forces.

Indo-Tibetan Border Police

- ITBPF was formed on 24 Oct, 1962. Of late, ITBP is placed on border for guarding the Indian territories from Karakoram Pass in Ladakh to Jachep La in Arunachal Pradesh stretched over a distance of 3488 km of Indo-China Border. It is involved in manning border outposts on altitudes ranging from 9000 to 18700 in the Western, Middle and Eastern Sector of the Indo-China Border.
- ITBPF is known to be a specialized mountain Force and most of the officers and men are professionally trained mountaineers and skiers. Being the first responder for natural disaster in the Himalayas, ITBPF has been performing a number of rescue and relief operations.

  ITBP is a force known for its multi-dimensional functions and carries out a number of functions which can be classified under the following broad categories:

  - ❖ Alertness on the northern borders, detection and prevention of border violations, and promotion of the sense of security among the local populace.
  - ❖ Keep a watch on illegal immigration, trans-border smuggling and crimes
  - ❖ Securing sensitive installations, banks and protected persons.
  - ❖ Restore and preserve law and order in any region in case of disturbance.
- In border vigil task ITBP man's forward border posts at altitudes ranging from 9000' to 18000'. During winter, most of the forward posts remain cut off by the surface route. The border posts are exposed to the fury and violence of the nature such as snow blizzards, avalanches, landslides, besides the hazards of high altitude and extreme cold where temperature usually remains below 40 degrees Celsius.
- The force apart from guarding the border is heavily engaged in fighting terrorism in the State of J and K, where it has shown exemplary nerve and gallantry.
- The 'Himveers', as the personnel are fondly called, also provide security cover to installation and to VIPs in Delhi. Every year ITBP Personnel are positioned to UN Peace Keeping Missions in Kosovo, Angola and Western Sahara and Sierra Leone. Crest of the Force epitomizes the Force motto Shaurya Drindhdta Karamnishta has Ashoka Chakra on Top with two rifles. It inspires men to put duty before self.
- ITBP is in the forefront of movement in preserving Himalayan environment and ecology. ITBP has taken up in a significant way the task of greening the Himalayan areas particularly in Inner Himalayas. Being the only human presence on forward regions, it has taken on itself the task of maintaining the delicate balance of flora and fauna.
- ITBP being deployed in mountains has developed the expertise in rescue and relief operations in mountains, which entail different

specialized skills of very high standard. It is always first in extending rescue and relief in case of natural calamity. Two major rescue and relief operations conducted by ITBP were at the time of massive land slide at Malpa village in the Kumaon Hills in Aug - Sep '98 and in the major earthquake in Chamoli and Rudraprayag regions of Garhwal in the State of U.P in Mar - Apr '99.

- ITBP carries out a huge number of medical civic action programmes in remote border and terrorist affected regions to provide free and expert medical, health and hygiene care to the civilian population in remote villages.
- It is the only police force in the country, which has the expertise to police the most formidable mountains of the Himalayas. The annual pilgrimage to MOUNT KAILAS and HOLY MANSAROVAR LAKE in Tibet (China) is conducted under the wings of ITBP.
- The motto of the ITBP 'SHAURYA - DRIDATA - KARM NISHTHA' (VALOUR - DETERMINATION - DEVOTION TO DUTY) has always inspired its personnel in accepting challenges to bring glory to the nation and honour to the force. In the course of active duties, the force has earned a number of Civil and Service honours, and decorations.

National Security Guards

The National Security Guard (NSG) was formed in 1984 as a Federal Contingency Deployment Force to handle all forms of terrorism in the country. Thus, the main task of this Force is to combat terrorism in whatever form an area may have and where activity of terrorists may assume serious proportions, and the State Police and other Central Police Forces cannot adapt with the situation. The NSG is a Force particularly equipped and trained to deal with specific situations and is therefore, to be used only in exceptional situations. The Force is not designed to carry out the functions of the State Police Forces or other Para Military Forces of the Union of India.

It is a task-oriented Force with two complementary elements in the form of the Special Action Group (SAG) that comprises of Army personnel and the Special Ranger Groups (SRG), comprising personnel drawn from the Central Para Military Forces/State Police Force.

Tasks

- It neutralizes specific terrorist threat in any given region, building, vital installation etc.
- It engages terrorists or suspected terrorists in specific situations with a purpose to neutralize them.
- It is equipped to handle hijacks situations comprising of piracy in the air and/ or land.
- Ensuring rescue of hostages in kidnapping incidents.

Additional Tasks

The following were the additional tasks entrusted in 1986-87:

- To provide security for high risk VIPs
- Anti-sabotage checks of venues of visits/public meetings of VVIPs.
- Anti-hijack duties in domestic and international flights.
- Immediate back up security operations.
- Collecting data on bomb explosions
- Training of State Police personnel in anti-terrorism, VIP security.
- PSO duties and Bomb Detection and Disposal.

Some of the NSG's known tasks include:

- April 30, 1986 – attack on Khalistani militants who took over the Golden Temple during Operation Black Thunder I

- May 12, 1988 — attack on Khalistani militants hiding in the Golden Temple during Operation Black Thunder II
- April 25, 1993 — rescue of hijacked plane Indian Airlines Boeing 737 by Islamic militants during Operation Ashwamedh
- October, 1998 — important combat missions in Jammu and Kashmir
- July 15, 1999 — rescue of 12 hostages held by armed terrorists who had stormed an apartment complex in Kashmir and killed 4 people
- September 25, 2002 — Operation Vajra Shakti to free hostages held by terrorists who had killed 26 worshippers at the Akshardham temple in Ahmedabad, Gujarat. They suffered their first combat death in this operation. A second commando, who was seriously injured and was in a coma, died after 18 months.
- November 26 2008 Mumbai attacks — Operation Black Tornado and Operation Cyclone to clear out terrorists and rescue hostages after several attacks across Mumbai, India.

Railway Protection Force

The Railway Protection Force (RPF) is a security force of India entrusted with protecting railway passengers, passenger area and railway property of the Indian Railways. The Force is under the authority of Ministry of Railways (India). The strength of RPF is about 65,000. RPF is headed by Director General who is usually an Indian Police Service officer.

The Mission of the Railway Protection Force include:

- Protecting and safeguarding railway passengers, passenger area and railway property
- Ensuring the safety, security of the passengers in the Indian Railways and boost their confidence
- The origin of this force was 'Watch & Ward' and functioned under the administrative control of railway administration. Later on, this force was renamed as Railway Protection Force and its members were provided with the power of arrest without warrant for the unlawful possession of railway property.
- The term railway property comprised of only the properties owned by the railway administration. In due course of time, the definition for the term Railway Property was extended and it included the properties owned by, or in the charge of or entrusted with the railways. The offenders are booked under the Railway Property (Unlawful Possession) Act 1966 which is shortly known as RP (UP) Act 1966. Now the Railway Protection Force has a separate administrative system and functions under the general supervision of the Railway Administration.

Special Protection Group

- The Special Protection Group (SPG) is the executive protection agency of the Government of India. It is mainly responsible for the protection of the Prime Minister of India, other top officials and their immediate families. The force came into existence in 1985. The force is controlled by the Cabinet secretariat.
- The Special Protection Group comprises of about 3,000 personnel. Recruits are drawn from police forces and National Security Guards commandos, who undergo training similar to that conducted by the United States Secret Service. The officer cadre is mainly Indian Police Service (IPS) officers from various state/central cadres.
- The Special Protection Group performed its function as a security group purely on the strength of an Executive Order for three years without legislation from 1985 to 1988.

Sashastra Seema Bal (SSB)

- SSB is a Border Guarding Force (BGF) which is administratively controlled by the Ministry of Home Affairs.
- SSB was constituted in early 1963 in the backdrop of the Indo-China conflict to infuse feelings of national belonging in the border population and develop their capabilities for resistance through a continuous process of motivation, training, development, welfare programmes and activities in the then NEFA, North Assam, North Bengal, hills of Uttar Pradesh, Himachal Pradesh and Ladakh. The programme was later spread up to Manipur, Tripura, Jammu (1965), Meghalaya (1975), Sikkim (1976), border areas of Rajasthan and Gujarat (1989), Manipur, Mizoram and some more regions of Rajasthan and Gujarat (1988), South Bengal, Nagaland (1989) and Nubra Valley, Rajouri and Poonch district of Jammu and Kashmir (1991).
- In the fifty years of its existence, SSB has been able to present a benign face of the government among border populace in the far-flung and inaccessible areas subscribing to the ETHOS of Service, Security and Brotherhood. The local populace always found SSB standing always with them during adverse situations.

Central Paramilitary Forces

Assam Rifles

- Assam Rifles is the oldest Para-Military force in the country. Assam Rifles is the only para-military force to have participated in both the World Wars and all operations in Independent India. Apart from ensuring a favourable security situation in the North-East, the force is also the fountain-head of several developmental activities in the rural, far-flung and backward areas of the North east. Since its humble birth in 1835 as a civil protection force, known as the 'Cachar Levy' during the British Colonial rule, the Assam Rifles has metamorphosed into a tough paramilitary force, ensuring peace and political stability in the insurgency-ravaged region along with safeguarding tenuous frontiers.
- The Assam Rifles has performed different roles in its glorious past, even as its main task is to ensure peace and internal security. During the two World Wars, the force exhibited exemplary military prowess, courage and agility while performing assigned tasks with the Gorkha Battalion, including helping in evacuating the fleeing British and Indian refugees from Burma at the advance of the Japanese Army and indulging them in special operations during the Burma campaign.
- Post-independence, the Assam Rifles got its new task as the vanguard for internal security, helping set up administration in remote frontiers. Simultaneously, the force was deployed to overcome the spreading separatist violence in the region, a task which still a reality. It faced the real test in the wake of the Chinese aggression in 1962, when the Force was at the forefront of receiving the full brunt of the attack.
- Based on the recognition to its military and jungle warfare skills and experience in controlling military in the region, the Assam Rifles was sent to Sri Lanka on the Indian peace keeping mission. It was also indulged in counter- insurgency operation in J&K.
- With the passage of several years, the Force's strength has increased and so has its significance as a stabilizing authority in the Northeast. Apart from its operational roles, the Assam Rifles has played a very crucial role in enhancing ethnic peace and harmony in the diverse multi-ethnic region and

socio-economic development of the region. In the process, it has also made adjustment to local culture and environment so that it can gain local support and co-operation. It has always made efforts to become truly a 'Friend of the Hill People', providing different opportunities to the local youth for jobs, social welfare, sports and adventure. In times of natural calamity, the Assam Rifles was called to provide succour to the affected people.

- 'It is absolutely geared up to meet any future challenges and capable of delivering and multitasking anytime, anywhere', asserts Director General of Assam Rifles, Lt Gen Rameshwar Roy. He believes that in the near future, as India opens up the region to neighbourhood in pursuits of its 'Look East policy' the Assam Rifles will have multi-dimensional roles to play—defending its frontiers and safeguarding internal security of the region.

Special Frontier Force

- The Special Frontier Force (SFF) is a paramilitary unit of India which was conceived in the post Sino-Indian war period as a guerrilla force formed primarily of Tibetan refugees whose main purpose was to conduct covert operations behind Chinese lines in case of another war between the People's Republic of China and India. Based in Chakrata, Uttarakhand, SFF is also called as the Establishment 22. The force was put under the direct supervision of the Intelligence Bureau, and afterwards, the Research and Analysis Wing, India's external intelligence agency.

Indian Coast Guard

- The Indian Coast Guard is a branch of the Indian Armed Forces whose mission is to ensure the protection of India's maritime interests and maritime law enforcement with jurisdiction over both territorial and international waters. ICG was formally constituted on 18 August 1978 as an armed force of the Union by the Coast Guard Act, 1978. It functions under the Department of Defence of the Union Ministry of Defence. The Coast Guard works in close cooperation with the Indian Navy, Department of Fisheries, Department of Revenue (Customs) and the Central and State police forces. The ICG is often and presently headed by a naval officer of the rank of Vice-Admiral on deputation, although one of the Director Generals (the 16th), Prabhakaran Paleri, was a Naval officer on permanent secondment to the Coast Guard. Subsequent Director Generals have again all been from the Indian Navy.
- To ensure effective command and control, the Maritime Zones of India are divided into five Coast Guard Regions, namely, North-West, West, East, North-East and Andaman & Nicobar, with the respective Regional Headquarters located at Gandhinagar, Mumbai, Chennai, Kolkata and Port Blair. The Coast Guard Regions are commanded by Officers of the rank of Inspector General.

Different Security Forces, Central Intelligence Agencies and Their Mandate

Intelligence Bureau

- IB was constituted on 23 December 1887, by the then British Secretary of State as a sub-sect of the Central Special Branch but there is no act of the Indian parliament nor executive order pertaining to the functioning of the IB. In 2012, a PIL was filed challenging the legality of IB. There are different ranks of executives which adhere to managing and executing the goals of the organization. Occasionally, executives are compared with state police service ranks which are different from the ranks in IB.

- The Intelligence Bureau (IB) is internal intelligence agency of India and is considered the world's oldest intelligence agency. It was modified as the Central Intelligence Bureau in 1947 under the Ministry of Home Affairs.

Activities and Accountabilities

- Shrouded in secrecy, the IB is used to garner intelligence from within India and also execute counter-intelligence and counter-terrorism tasks. The Bureau comprises employees from law enforcement agencies, mostly from the Indian Police Service (IPS) and the military. However, the Director of Intelligence Bureau (DIB) has always been an IPS officer. In addition to domestic intelligence responsibilities, the IB is particularly tasked with intelligence collection in border areas, following the 1951 recommendations of the Himmat Sinhji Committee (also known as the North and North-East Border Committee), a task entrusted to military intelligence organizations prior to independence in 1947. All spheres of human activity within India and in the neighbourhood are allocated to the charter of duties of the Intelligence Bureau. The IB was also tasked with other external intelligence responsibilities as of 1951 until 1968, when the Research and Analysis Wing was formed. The current chief of the organization is Syed Asif Ibrahim.
- Understanding of the arcane workings of the IB is largely speculative. Many a times even their own family members are unaware of their whereabouts. One known task of the IB is to clear licences to amateur radio enthusiasts. The IB also passes on intelligence between other Indian intelligence agencies and the police. The Bureau also grants the necessary security clearances to Indian diplomats and judges before they take the oath. On rare occasions, IB officers interact with the media during a crisis situation. The IB is also rumoured to intercept and open around 6,000 letters daily. It also has an email spying system similar to FBI's Carnivore system. The Bureau is also authorized to conduct wiretapping without a warrant.

Multi-Agency Centre (MAC)

- MAC is a multi-agency centre for Counter Terrorism whose mandate is to share terrorism related inputs on a regular basis.
- Post-incursion of Pakistan in Kargil in 1999, the Government of India formed the Kargil Review Committee and subsequently created a Group of Ministers (GoM) to review the National Security Apparatus in its entirety. One of the relevant recommendations of the Group of Ministers presented in the year 2001 was creation of Multi agency Centre.
- According to the GoM recommendation, Multi Agency Centre (MAC) was constituted at Delhi and Subsidiary Multi Agency Centres (SMACs) in different states comprising representatives from different security agencies, for streamlining intelligence efforts. Later Union Home Minister of India reviewed the security situation and issued Multi Agency Centre (functions, powers and duties) order, 2008 was issued on December 31, 2008. MAC-SMAC is functioning since 2002 and has been re-operationalized with effect from 2009. As a follow up of the above order, 24x7 Control Rooms have been set up at Multi Agency Centre (MAC) at New Delhi and the Subsidiary Multi Agency Centres (SMACs) at State Level and at Headquarters of Intelligence Wings of other agencies to ensure timely sharing of information and

better co-ordination between intelligence agencies Daily meetings of Nodal Officers of 25 member agencies are being conducted on every working day. Currently, MAC-SMAC network has 416 nodes spread across the country and connected to MAC HQ at New Delhi. This includes 31 SMAC HQs & 32 SSBs located at State Capitals. These nodes are connected by 2 Mbps leased lines of BSNL/MTNL. As of March 14, 2013, 362 nodes out of total 416 have been installed and made functional.

National Investigation Agency

- National Investigation Agency (NIA) is a federal agency constituted by the Indian Government to fight against terror in India. It acts as the Central Counter Terrorism Law Enforcement Agency. The agency is empowered to deal with terror related crimes across states without special permission from the states. The Agency came into existence with the enactment of the National Investigation Agency Act 2008 by the Parliament of India on 31 December 2008. NIA was created after the 2008 Mumbai terror attacks as need for a central agency to combat terrorism was realized. The founding Director-General of NIA was Radha Vinod Raju.

Vision

- Agency works with an aim to be a thoroughly professional investigative agency matching the best international standards. It aims to set the standards of excellence in counter terrorism and other national security related investigations at the national level by developing into a highly trained, partnership oriented workforce. It also aims at creating deterrence for existing and potential terrorist groups/individuals. It aims to develop as a storehouse of all terrorist related information.

Jurisdiction

- The Agency has been given power to conduct investigation and prosecution of offences under the Acts specified in the Schedule of the NIA Act. A State Government may request the Central Government to hand over the investigation of a case to the NIA, provided the case has been registered for the offences as contained in the schedule to the NIA Act. Central Government can also order NIA to take over investigation of any scheduled offence anywhere in the India.

Special NIA Courts

- Different Special Courts have been notified by the Central Government of India for trial of the cases registered at different police stations of NIA under Section 11 and 22 of the NIA Act 2008. Any question as to the jurisdiction of these courts is decided by the Central Government. These are presided over by a judge appointed by the Central Government on the recommendation of the Chief Justice of the High Court with jurisdiction in that region. Supreme Court of India has also been empowered to transfer the cases from one special court to any other special court within or outside the state if the same is in the interest of justice in light of the prevailing circumstances in any particular state.
- They are endowed with all powers of the court of sessions under Code of Criminal Procedure, 1973 for trial of any offence. Trial by this courts are held on day-today basis on all working days and have precedence over the trial of any other case against the accused in any other court (not being a Special Court) and have to be concluded in preference to the trial of such other case. An appeal from any judgment, sentence or order, not being an interlocutory order, of a Special Court lies to the High Court both on facts and on law.

Such an appeal is heard by a bench of two Judges of the High Court.

- Presently, there are 38 Special NIA Courts. State Governments have also been given power to appoint one or more such special courts in their states.

NATGRID

- The National Intelligence Grid or NATGRID is an integrated intelligence grid that will link the databases of many departments and ministries of the Government of India so as to gather comprehensive patterns of intelligence that can be readily accessed by intelligence agencies. It was first proposed in the backdrop of the terrorist attacks on Mumbai in 2008 and is to become functional in 2013.

Reason for Establishment

- The 26/11 attacks on Mumbai brought to the surface many weaknesses in India's intelligence gathering and action networks. NATGRID is part of the radical overhaul of the security and intelligence apparatuses of India that was mooted by the then Home Minister P. Chidambaram.
- The National Investigating Agency and the National Counter Terrorism Centre are two organizations formed in the backdrop of the Mumbai attacks of 2008. Before the attacks, the American Lashkar operative David Coleman Headley had visited India many times and had made a recce of different places that came under attack on 26/11. In spite of having travelled to India many times and having returned to the US through Pakistan or West Asia, his trips failed to raise the suspicion of Indian agencies as they lacked a system that could reveal a pattern in his unusual travel itineraries and trips to the country. It is said that if a system like the NATGRID been in place, Headley would have been apprehended much before the attacks.

Structure and Functions

- NATGRID is an intelligence sharing network that collates data from the standalone databases of the different agencies and ministries of the Indian government. It is a counter terrorism measure that collects and collates a number of information from government databases which include tax and bank account details, credit card transactions, visa and immigration records and itineraries of rail and air travel. This combined data will be made available to 11 central agencies consisting of the RAW, the National Investigation Agency, the CBI, the Directorate of Revenue Intelligence, the Intelligence Bureau, the Narcotics Control Bureau and the Enforcement Directorate.

Opposition

- NATGRID got opposition on charges of probable violations of privacy and leakage of confidential personal information. Its efficacy in overcoming terrors has also been questioned provided that no state agency or police force has access to its database, thereby decreasing chances of immediate, effective action. NATGRID claims to be protected by a number of structural and procedural safeguards and oversight mechanisms including that of external audits and technology safeguards.

Narcotics Control Bureau

- The NCB is responsible for anti-narcotic operations all over the country. It checks the spread of contraband as well as the cultivation of drugs. The officers in this organization are drawn from both the IRS and the IPS.

Bureau of Police Research & Development (BPR&D)

- The Bureau of Police Research and Development (BPR&D) was formed on 28

August 1970 in achieving the objective of the Government of India for the modernization of Police Forces. It is indulged in doing research on problems confronting the Indian police, the training of various ranks of Police in India, and the introduction of technology at both federal and state levels.

National Crime Records Bureau (NCRB)

- The National Police Commission in 1979 made a recommendation in creating a 'Nodal Agency' which would suggest a common format for maintaining Crime-Criminal records at all the police stations in the country, with the same common format being used to design shareable databases at police stations and districts and at state and federal Level. On this recommendation NCRB was constituted in 1986 with amalgamation of the Directorate of Coordination Police Computers, Central Finger Print Bureau, Data Section of Coordination Division of Central Bureau of Investigation and Statistical Section of the Bureau of Police Research and Development.

Central Forensic Institutions

Central Forensic Science Laboratory

- The Central Forensic Science Laboratory (CFSL) is a wing of the Indian Ministry of Home Affairs, which satisfies the forensic requirements in the country. It houses the only DNA repository in South and Southeast Asia. There are many central forensic laboratories in India, at Hyderabad, Kolkata, Mumbai, Rajkot, Chandigarh, Pune and New Delhi. CFSL Hyderabad is known to be a centre of excellence in chemical sciences, CFSL Kolkata in biological sciences and CFSL Chandigarh in physical sciences. These laboratories are administered by the Directorate of Forensic Science (DFS) of the Ministry of Home Affairs. The laboratory in New Delhi is controlled by the Central Bureau of Investigation (CBI) and investigates cases on its behalf.

National Institute of Criminology and Forensic Sciences (NICFSC)

- The National Institute of Criminology and Forensic Science (earlier called the 'Institute of Criminology and Forensic Science') came into being on 4 January 1972 on the recommendations of a Committee appointed by the UGC to inquire into the applied aspects of education, training and research in the fields of Criminology and Forensic Science to commensurate with the growing needs of the country in general and the Criminal Justice System in India in particular. In September 1976, the Institute was modified as a separate department under the Ministry of Home Affairs headed by a full-time Director.

Indian Armed Forces

- The Indian Armed Forces are the military forces of the Republic of India and comprise of the Army, Navy and Air Force supported by Paramilitary forces (Indian Coast Guard, Assam Rifles and Special Frontier Force) and many other inter-service institutions like the Strategic Forces Command.
- The Supreme Commander of the Indian Armed Forces is the President of India. The Indian Armed Forces are managed by the Ministry of Defence (MoD), which is led by the Union Cabinet Minister of Defence.
- The Indian armed forces have been indulged in several important military operations, including the Indo-Pakistani wars of 1947, 1965 and 1971, the Sino-Indian War, the 1987 Sino-Indian skirmish, the Kargil War,

and the Siachen conflict among others. India pays respect to its armed forces and military personnel every year on Armed Forces Flag Day, 7 December.

- From 1962, the IAF has maintained intimate military relations with Russia, including cooperative development on programs like the Fifth Generation Fighter Aircraft (FGFA) and the Multirole Transport Aircraft (MTA). The Indian armed forces are steadily undergoing modernization, with investments in such areas as a missile defence system and a nuclear triad.
- The Department of Defence Production of the Ministry of Defence is accountable to the indigenous production of equipment utilized by the Indian Armed Forces. It consists of the 41 Indian Ordnance Factories under control of the Ordnance Factories Board and 8 Defence PSUs namely, HAL, BEL, BEML, BDL, MDL, GSL, GRSE and Midhani. The Indian Armed Forces are presently the world's largest arms importer, with Russia, Israel, and to some extent, France and United States being the major foreign suppliers of military equipment.

History

Dating back several millennia, India has one of the longest military histories. The first reference of armies is found in the Vedas along with the epics like Ramayana and Mahabharatha. Classical Indian texts on archery in particular, and martial arts in general are known as Dhanurveda.

From Ancient to Medieval Era

The history of Indian maritime dates back 5,000 years. The first tidal dock is considered to have been built at Lothal around 2300 BC during the Indus Valley Civilization, near the present day Mangrol harbour on the Gujarat coast. The Rig Veda written around 1500 BC, credits Varuna with knowledge of the ocean routes and describes naval expeditions. There is reference to the side wings of a vessel called Plava, which give stability to the ship under storm conditions. A compass, Matsya yantra was utilized for navigation in the fourth and fifth century AD. The earliest known reference to an organization devoted to ships in ancient India is the Mauryan Empire from the 4th century BC. Emperor Chandragupta Maurya's Prime Minister Kautilya's Arthashastra consists of a full chapter on the state department of waterways under navadhyaksha (Sanskrit for Superintendent of ships). The term, nava dvipantaragamanam (Sanskrit for sailing to other lands by ships, i.e. Exploration) is seen in this book besides appearing in the Buddhist text, Baudhayana Dharmasastra as the interpretation of the term, Samudrasamyanam. Sea lanes between India and neighbouring lands were the usual form of trade for many centuries, and are liable for the widespread influence of Indian Culture on other societies. Powerful navies comprised those of the Maurya, Satavahana, Chola, Vijayanagara, Kalinga, Mughal and Maratha empires. The Cholas excelled in foreign trade and maritime activity, widening their influence overseas to China and Southeast Asia. During the 17th and 18th centuries, the Maratha and Kerala fleets were expanded, and became the most powerful Naval Forces in the subcontinent, defeating European Navies at different times. The fleet review of the Maratha navy took place at the Ratnagiri fort in which the ships Pal and Qalbat participated. The Maratha Kanhoji Angre and Kunjali Marakkar, the Naval Chief of Saamoothiri were two notable naval chiefs of the period.

British India (1857 to 1947)

- The Royal Indian Navy was first constituted by the British while much of India was controlled by the East India Company. The first Indian to be granted a commission was Sub Lieutenant D. N. Mukherji, who joined the Royal Indian Marine as an engineer officer in 1928.

- Indian sailors began a rebellion called as the Royal Indian Navy mutiny in 1946, on board ships and in shore establishments which spread all over India. A total of 78 ships, 20 shore establishments and 20,000 sailors were indulged in the rebellion.

Republic of India (1947 to present)

After India became a republic on 26 January 1950, the navy was called as the Indian Navy, and its vessels as Indian Naval Ships (INS). On 22 April 1958 Vice Admiral R. D. Katari was appointed as the first Indian Chief of the Naval Staff. India underwent four big wars with its neighbour Pakistan in 1949, 1965, 1971 and 1999, and with China in 1962. The starting of the 21st century witnessed reorientation for India on the global stage from a regional role in the subcontinent to a major role in the Indian Ocean region stretching from Gulf of Aden to the Malacca Strait.

Sketch of Defence Structure in India

- In New Delhi (the capital city of India), the headquarters of the Indian Armed Forces is situated. The President functions as de jure Commander in chief of the Armed Forces. While de facto control exists with the executive, the Ministry of Defence (MoD) is the ministry charged with the responsibilities of confronting insurgency and maintaining external security of India.
- Administratively, the Indian Army is divided into 7 tactical commands, each controlled by different Lieutenant Generals. The Indian Air Force is divided into five operational and two functional commands. Each Command is headed by an Air Officer Commanding-in-Chief with the rank of Air Marshal.
- The operation of Indian Navy comprises of three Commands. Each Command is administered by a Flag Officer Commanding-in-Chief in the rank of Vice Admiral. There are two joint commands whose head can be from any of the three services. These are the Strategic Forces Command and the Andaman and Nicobar Command. The lack of an overall military commander has managed to keep the Indian Armed Forces under civilian control, and has averted the rise of military dictatorships (unlike in neighbouring Pakistan).

Six main tasks of the Armed Forces are:

1. To maintain the territorial integrity of India at any cost.
2. To safeguard the nation in case of attacks by a foreign nation.
3. To send own amphibious warfare equipment with an aim to take the battle to enemy shores.
4. To follow the Cold Start doctrine, which means that the Indian Armed Forces are in a position to mobilize rapidly and take offensive actions without crossing the enemy's nuclear-use threshold.
5. To provide assistance to the civil community at the time of disasters (e.g. flooding).
6. To take part in United Nations peacekeeping activities in consonance with India's commitment to the United Nations Charter.

- The details of the code of conduct of the Indian military are in a semi-official book called 'Customs and Etiquette in the Services', composed by retired Major General Ravi Arora, which details how Indian personnel are often expected to conduct themselves.
- The significant deployments of the Indian army comprise of the border regions of India, especially Jammu and Kashmir, Ladakh and the Northeast India, with an aim to engage in counter-insurgency and anti-terrorist operations. The most important

commitments of the Indian Navy comprise of patrol missions, anti-piracy operations off the coast of Somalia, the 'Singapore Indian Maritime Bilateral Exercise' with the Republic of Singapore Navy in the Straits of Malacca, maintaining a military presence in Southeast Asia's waters, and joint exercises with other countries, such as Brazil, South Africa, the United States and Japan, France (Varuna naval exercises), People's Republic of China, the Russian Navy (INDRA naval exercises) and others. At present, India has the 7th largest defence budget in the world. In 2011 the budget was at $48.9 billion ($112 billion PPP), which comprised of 2.5% of GDP. Extra spending is provided separately by the government to be spent on infrastructure in border areas and for paramilitary organizations.

- An ample part of India's defence budget is focused to the modernization of the country's armed forces, from the period 2007 to 2012. India was expected to spend about $50 billion on new equipment. In 2009, India raised the defence expenditure by 21%. Contemporary criticisms of the Indian military have brought attention to different issues, like lack of political reform, obsolete equipment, and lack of adequate ammunition, discipline problems and inadequate Research and Development due to over-reliance on foreign imports.
- Besides, the lack of a 'strategic culture' among the political class in India is believed to have held up the efficiency of the Indian military. These issues are believed by critics to falter the progress and modernization of the military. However, analysis of the Central Intelligence Agency shows that India is projected to possess the fourth most capable concentration of power by 2015. According to a report published by the US Congress, India is among the world's leading arms purchaser. India is investing 99.7 billion (US$1.8 billion) to construct a dedicated and secured optical fibre cable (OFC) network for exclusive use of the Army, Navy and Air Force. This will be one of the world's largest closed user group (CUG) networks.

Personnel

- The Param Vir Chakra (PVC) is the highest wartime gallantry award given by the Military of India which is followed by the Maha Vir Chakra (MVC) and the Vir Chakra (VrC). the Ashoka Chakra Award is its peacetime equivalent.
- The Param Vishisht Seva Medal is the highest decoration for meritorious service. During 2012, the Indian Armed Forces has a reported strength of 1.45 million active personnel and 2.20 million reserve personnel.
- Besides, there are about 1.40 million paramilitary personnel, making it one of the world's largest military forces. A total of 1,567,390 ex-servicemen are registered with the Indian Army, most of them coming from Uttar Pradesh (271,928), Punjab (191,702), Haryana (165,702), Maharashtra (143,951), Kerala (127,920), Tamil Nadu (103,156), Rajasthan (100,592) and Himachal Pradesh (78,321). Many of them are re-employed in various Central government sectors. ❑❑❑

Chapter sixteen

Model Questions/Answers and Previous Years' Questions

To answer problems in 'Internal Security' portion of UPSC syllabus GS Paper III, a comprehensive understanding is sought across different themes, such as border security, IT security-related questions, Maoism, insurgence in the North East and the means in which it has been tackled in states like Tripura, Manipur, etc. Naxalism and Maoism are hot subjects today, and they require a noble understanding as far as related elements and trends are concerned. The entire problem has to be envisioned in the context of the nature of progresses taking place in the nation. Besides, one also requires to address the question that how the lack of development can encourage extremism. For addressing internal security concerns, the examinee should keep a broad mind, in addition to a good knowledge of the facts and the history of the problem. After that, one must also consider the grievances of the group and the circumstances which led to embracing of violence as means to accomplish the said goals. Further, the facts associated with State's response also required to be considered logically. There remain varied kinds of tactics for undertaking internal security problems in various parts of India. It is recommended herein that it would be better to have a solution-centric attitude to all internal security problems.

Probable Questions from Internal Security Section for UPSC Mains and Their Answers:

1. Analyse the statement and validate your arguments. 'Poor development and lack of growth opportunities is the primary reason for spread of extremism in India'.

Ans.: In Indian scenario, extremism activities are increasing rapidly. The scale of the extremists operations is massive and consequently these activities have perilous impact on nation's social, economic and political development. There are numerous of reasons for the development of Extremism in India. Priority of Government bodies is to focus on industrialization and do not give much importance to people living in tribal areas. Tribal have been denied their constitutional rights and justice. Most of these people who are entering into the movement of extremism are lacking primary education, basic amenities and infrastructure facilities. Economic discontent is a prevailing factor which led to the growth of the militant nationalism. It is a truism that underdevelopment often creates the conditions for insurgency and spread of extremist ideologies among the people, who perceive that their needs are not being taken care of by the government.

While it has been the policy of governments around the world today to emphasize on 'inclusive development', there are always groups in every state who feel alienated because they perceive that they are left out of the developmental efforts. Such perceptions coupled with inefficient and corrupt governance create an ideal condition for extremism and militancy. More than lack of development, it is the perception of injustice, bad governance and inability of the system to engage the disaffected lot that lead people to violence and extremism. It is established that extremism became a major philosophy of Indian nationalism. There are several grounds for development of extremism in India such as joblessness, ignorance of weaker section of society by government. After thorough review of causes and issues for the development of extremism, it is revealed that extremism is viewed differently by dissimilar sections of the society. On one side, there are passionate supporters and, at the other extreme, some others hold the view that the movement should be crushed cruelly. It is difficult to classify the opinion in the middle path. It can be said that some of the demands of the extremists are genuine and cannot be ignored. Therefore, the Government must seriously consider such demands and make policies and execute them, either voluntarily or subsequent to negotiations with the protestors.

2. In addition to external factors, India's security is challenged equally by internal factors. Make a critical evaluation.

Ans.: As India strives to emerge as a strong regional power it faces formidable security challenges which may cause obstacles in its progress. The most formidable of these stems from terrorism, in both its external and internal dimensions — the trans-national and home-grown, against which India has long waged a relentless fight. The former originates from Pakistan, which faced a crisis of identity after Partition. It sought to compensate for its diminishing conventional military clout after 1971 through a quest for nuclear parity and deterrence. It also pursued the option of asymmetric power, through use of non-state actors, first during the Khalistan movement in east Punjab and then in Jammu & Kashmir. The Lashkar-e-Taiba (LeT) or 'Army of the Pure', founded in 1990 by Hafez Mohd Saeed and Zafar Iqbal in Kunar, Afghanistan started functioning from Muridke, near Lahore, with increasing state patronage. Though its primary focus for militant operations was initially the Kashmir Valley, its professed goal now extends to destabilizing other parts of India. As the U. S. and International/NATO forces withdraw from Afghanistan, Pakistan's Inter-Services Intelligence Directorate (ISI) could assign a new role for the LeT there, as seen in the recent attack on the Indian Consulate in Herat. Indian diplomatic premises and developmental support workers there will remain targets in the foreseeable future. India has been in the ideological crosshairs of al-Qaeda and its affiliates. Both Osama-bin-Laden and Ayman-al-Zawahiri spoke of a 'Zionist-Crusader alliance' which was extended after 9/11, to a 'Zionist-Crusader-Hindu alliance' when al-Qaeda developed links with Pakistan-based militant organizations like the Harkat-ul-Mujahideen (HuM) and Lashkar-e-Taiba (LeT). In a video which surfaced on September 04, 2014 al-Qaeda chief Zawahiri announced formation of al-Qaeda in the Indian Subcontinent (AQIS). He threatened to 'liberate our brothers' in Myanmar, Kashmir, Bangladesh 'from injustice and oppression'. One objective of this declaration could be intended to compete for leadership, influence and legitimacy with the Islamic State (IS) in Iraq and Syria, but as the suicide bomb attack near the Wagah border, inside Pakistan (November 2, 2014) revealed, it brought the spectre of an AQIS threat that much nearer to India. The Burdwan blasts (Oct 02, 2014) revealed a sinister linkage developing with the Jamaat-ul-Mujahideen Bangladesh (JMB), for possible terrorist operations in West Bengal and Bangladesh. This brings another perspective to the fragile security situation in Bangladesh, which has been plagued by gun running trails and linkages to disgruntled militant factions of our North Eastern insurgents. Till lately, India has not provided a fertile ground for establishing an al-Qaeda base though newly motivated Indian jihadists have started seeking global affiliations. The Tanzim Islahul Muslimeen (TIM) was formed in 1985 after the communal riots in Maharashtra. Its message found resonance among young members of the Students Islamic Movement of India (SIMI), founded in Aligarh, Uttar Pradesh in April, 1977. SIMI was banned in 2001. But its followers regrouped under Indian Mujahideen (IM), which was successful in plotting and executing several bombings between 2002 and 2008, with logistic help from across the border. IM operated through several networks — the Azamgarh module in Uttar Pradesh, recruits in Beed, Maharashtra and Bhatkal in Karnataka. Two other modules surfaced later, one from Pune in 2009 and the other from Darbhanga in 2011. IM sleeper cells have been seen also in Hyderabad and Ranchi. Despite recent arrests of some of its prominent leaders, IM remains a potentially powerful disruptive force. Despite all their grievances, unhappiness and anger against the Government, Indian Muslims have kept away from pernicious pan-Islamic ideologies advocated by jihadi terrorist organizations so far. However, even as AQIS becomes increasingly interested in India, it could try to tap the wellsprings of discontent among young Islamists in India. China's rapidly enhancing clout as a major power in our vicinity impinges directly on India's geo-political space. In the near term, the power differential with India, in terms of its economic and military capability will widen. Long-standing disagreements on the Line of Actual Control (LAC) are unlikely to be resolved quickly but India must accelerate gradation of its border infrastructure, putting in place military operational concepts and capabilities to deter big incursions from the north, while nuancing the posture of political exchanges with China in a calibrated manner. On the internal front, left wing extremism (LWE) in the so- called Naxalite corridor, extending to five/six States—Jharkhand, Bihar, Odisha, Andhra Pradesh/ Telangana and Maharashtra — poses the most serious threat. In 2014, there was a declining trend of fatalities, though violence continued. A mix of force-centric and development-oriented approach by the establishment has not curtailed its ability to carry out periodic attacks resulting in high casualties among the security forces. Expediting police reforms, plugging manpower shortages, enhancing rapid response capabilities and equipment modernization should be essential facets of our strategy to cope with these threats in the near term.

3. What is the role of Civil Society in combating terrorism? Elaborate.

Ans.: The stalemate of terrorism has always been a threat to humans of this world in one form or the other, radiating from number of causes such as insensitive religious emotions, sectarian divergences, disparity of power among leftist and rightist schools of thought, communism vs. capitalism, exploitation of the ignorant and deprived ones and lust for acquisition of resources entailing in invasions etc. However, this problem emerged as a flash point after a tragic incident of 9/11 which drew attention of world towards uprooting this cancer by taking certain counter measures. Military solution, when crucial, plays its roles to some extent but cannot fully figure out the intricacies of terrorism without taking all the communities and nation onboard. This not only educates masses about issues in 'war against terror' but plays a key role in boosting morale of forces on frontlines. These have included the introduction of anti-terror laws; changes in reporting requirements for civil society organizations; and the increasing use of new border security technologies. In many countries, the impact of these measures on civil society and on citizens has been a source of great concern. The meaning of involving civil society in a wide-ranging and multidimensional response to the threat of terrorism has been stressed by various international platforms. 'Civil society' covers a vast range of societal groups, interests, representations, inbuilt tensions and conflicts. It is very much obvious by a series of intended associations together with biased parties, skilled unions and specialized bodies, classified fundamentals, learned and research foundations, pious, strong believers, and community-based societies, social and environmental groups. An energetic civil society can show a strategic role in countering extremist ideologies, sectarian / social violence in the society. Civil society can promote the voice of diverse social groups and causes, which endow with a channel of expression for the unimportant and can encourage an atmosphere of patience and pluralism. As a matter of fact, civil societies can also play a momentous role in building local support for counterterrorism through education, entrancing government establishments to adopt a pragmatic response that respects human rights, supervising execution of counterterrorism procedures, considering and broadcasting abuses committed in the name of fighting terrorism, backing and support to sufferers, sponsoring the significance of harmony and safety, and providing capacity- building training. This paper will address this aspect of countering the terrorism to see where and how civil society comes into action for countering terrorism. Civil society can play a significant role in helping states increase awareness of the threat and the impact of an attack on local communities, and in deepening public support for government action to address it, which is an essential component of any effective long-term strategy. Terrorism is obviously the state of extreme in human conflict that occurs when the violence enters in the matter. The terrorism is the result of failure in conflict resolution which can occur anywhere in the world. It is the crucial social problem of the society as well. The generally classified and unified roles of civil society in order to preventing and reducing of terrorism are as follows:-

- Counselling and Educational Role
- Community Services
- Sponsorship and Research
- Legal Facets

Although, there are numerous measures that could be taken by civil societies and governments at short/long term levels to overcome the obstacles for deeper engagement, however, a meticulous model has to be crafted by remaining cognize to the peculiar needs of our society in dealing terrorism. More so, a model applied at any point in time should remain flexible to absorb new capacities enabling an all- encompassing approach instead of inducing rigidity and inertia. The civil society in close ranks must stand to understand and materialize its due role in combating terrorism. Given simply, civil society is the core ingredient in creating conducive environment for all elements of national power to tackle the menace of terrorism with a cohesive and unified approach. Task is indeed gigantic than the words can describe given the peculiar order of our society vis-à-vis deeply seated, fundamentally porous and widely divergent perceptions of the masses to accept their responsibilities. However, a start even with primitive designs will eventually prove fruitful in shaping our society's landscape to mitigate those potentials and indicators that presents opportunity for terrorism to make ground. On the whole, civil society should work as a catalyst to curtail terrorism. They should endeavour to identify the region, specific causes of terrorism through in depth social researches and should work with the masses, social groups and governments to diminish the terrorism from the society.

4. Why money laundering a big threat to present day Indian economy? What possible steps by the Government can control it?

Ans.: According to estimates put forth by international accounting firms, India is estimated to have a parallel economy of nearly 40 per cent of its $600 billion Gross Domestic Product. That's some serious parallel banking system. Money laundering constitute a serious threat to national economies, and respective governments. Economic crimes can have a devastating effect on a national economy since potential victims of such crimes are far more numerous than those in other forms of crime. Economic crimes also have the potential of adversely affecting people who do not, prima-facie, seem to be the victims of the crime. For example, tax evasion results in loss of government revenue, thus affecting the potential of the government to spend on development schemes thereby affecting a large section of the population who could have benefited from such government expenditure. A company fraud not only results in cheating of the people who have invested in that company but may also adversely impact investors' confidence thereby affecting the growth of the economy. There have also been instances of manipulation of stock markets resulting in the loss of a substantial amount of assets of the small investors. Corruption not only results in loss of citizens' rights but also has the potential of ruining the moral fabric of the society. Therefore, economic crimes constitute a serious threat to the national economy and system of governance. Indian companies are reportedly misusing public trusts for money laundering. India has no centralized repository, like the registrar of companies for corporates, of information on public trusts. For preventing money laundering, one needs to refer to RBI Guidelines and directives issued by the Finance Ministry. The Prevention of Money Laundering Act (PMLA), 2002, provides that the properties of corrupt public servants shall be confiscated. However, the Government is considering incorporating provisions for confiscation or forfeiture of the property of corrupt public servant in the Prevention of Corruption Act, 1988 to make it more self-contained and comprehensive. PMLA, 2002 and subsequent amendments in the year of 2005, which mandates that in addition to client identity verification, banks and financial institutions need to maintain and furnish records to the various regulatory authorities as defined by the Indian government. It also allows regulatory authorities to freeze, seize and confiscate suspect accounts. Besides these two important laws, there are other laws and guidelines formulated by the government or regulatory bodies such as the Securities and Exchange Board of India (SEBI). PMLA, 2002, provides for mutual legal assistance in India by making enabling provisions for agreements with foreign countries to enforce this Act, assistance to a contracting State in the investigation of an offence, reciprocal arrangements for processes and assistance for transfer of accused persons and attachment, seizure and confiscation of property in a contracting State or India. Recent amendments have been made to the FEMA Act, which are relevant to understand the apparatus of monitoring and preventing money laundering. The economic and social impact of money laundering and its distinction with black money must be clearly understood. Joint efforts made by each country, in developing a reliable strategy of a vigorous domestic enforcement of law as well as international cooperation, is the most effective means to cope with problems related to economic crime, including money laundering. It would also be beneficial to adopt some of the following measures:

- First and foremost it is important that the number of state parties to the TOC convention should be increased.
- Given the fact that the TOC convention gives due consideration to diversities of the legal and financial system of member states and allows each state party to exercise discretionary power to a certain degree, it is feared that those committing economic crimes, including money laundering, may target countries with lenient legal provisions and international criminal organizations may end up setting a strong foothold in these countries, even if every State accedes to the Convention. In order to dispel such concerns States Parties should be encouraged to apply article 34 paragraph 3 of the TOC convention which stipulates each State Party may adopt more strict or severe measures than those provided for by this Convention for preventing and combating transnational organized crime", since a thorough revision of the convention, increasing the mandatory provisions, is not possible in near future.
- Borderless criminal justice is essential in order to deal with borderless economic crimes including money laundering. Group 2 considers it necessary that any sense of turfdom embedded in the criminal justice system of each country be removed.
- It should be recognized that information sharing is important in order to suppress cross-border crimes. Items of information to be shared are as follows: suspicious transaction reports; information relating to offences and suspects modus operandi and others. Despite some countries' efforts to exchange information on economic crimes, including money laundering, it has become more evident that information sharing instead of information exchange is more necessary.
- To have a unified standard for Criminalization of common criminal offences occurring in each country. Grant authority for universal jurisdiction on the above offences to all countries.
- The adaptation in local legislation of legal criteria applicable to an increase in scope of predicate offences, which would enable the successful combating of organized economic crime, including money laundering.
- The establishment of viable practices on confiscation and seizure measures, through the renewed legal concepts that enhance the powers of prosecuting authorities.
- The financial institutions, telephone carriers and internet service providers should take responsibility for preventing their services from being misused as criminal tools. In view of this, the following will be in order:

  a. Reinforce personal identification in financial institutions through know your customer

     I. Identification norms: Impose sanctions on financial institutions when this is neglected.

     II. Criminalize the selling, purchasing and transferring of bank accounts.

  b. Create regulations to prevent the use of cell phones for criminal acts. Impose sanctions on cell phone companies when the above regulations are violated.

  c. Create regulations to prevent the use of the Internet for criminal acts. Impose sanctions on Internet service providers when these regulations are violated.

5. Management of security challenges in border areas is not only a delicate issue but also a crucial one. Suggest practical measures in this regard.

Ans.: India shares 15,106. 7 km of its boundary with six nations, Pakistan, China, Nepal, Bhutan,

Myanmar and Bangladesh. Its coastal boundary of 7,516 km includes 5,422 km of coastline in the mainland and 2,094 km of coastline bordering the islands. The border runs through 92 districts in 17 states and the coastline touches 13 states and union territories. The complexities of guarding our borders are further enhanced due to varying degree of ground realities and a number of agencies guarding the borders. Actual Ground Position Line (AGPL) in Siachen glacier, Line of Control (LC) in J&K, International Boundary (IB) with Pakistan from J&K to Gujarat, Line of Actual Control (LAC) with China are the varying nomenclatures based on the ground situation as well as different claim lines. There are various forces looking after the border that include the Indian Army, Assam Rifles, Border Security Force (BSF), Indo-Tibetan Border Police (ITBP) and the Sashastra Seema Bal (SSB). The Indian Navy and the Coast Guard looks after the maritime frontiers. The dynamics of the border and the forces deployed keeps changing with the place and with time. Each border has its own nuances based on perceived threat, terrain and local population. The approach to border management must vary from one border to other. India needs to formulate and promulgate its policy on border management. The policy must enunciate clear cut response mechanisms and issues of command and control. The border management policy must take into account the peculiarities of each border and evolve a comprehensive strategy to amalgamate all available resources for effective border management. The management of disputed and unresolved border must be the responsibility of Indian Army functioning under the MoD. The management of other borders must be with the CAPFs, functioning under MHA. All organizations involved in border management must seek directions from and be accountable to one nodal agency during peace and war. In event of more than one force on a particular border, the chain of command must be clearly laid down. The nodal ministry for management of unresolved and disputed should be MoD. The MHA should be the nodal ministry for all borders other than unresolved and disputed borders. Presently, the resolution of border disputes is the responsibility of MEA. Low staffing levels and limited leverage of MEA with state governments, restricts its ability to effectively resolve border disputes. The responsibility for border resolution must hence be re-allocated to MoD for unresolved borders and to the MHA for other borders. MEA functionaries can however be part of border resolution committees. Each ministry must have a dedicated section working on resolution of border disputes. It can be composed of experts from various fields. There must be continuity in the dialogue process with one thought process. It can be the nodal agency for issuing guidelines, directions and illustrations to all the stakeholders. Border guarding responsibility is recommended to be changed as under:

- ***Indian Army:*** To be given the responsibility to manage all unresolved and disputed borders, i. e, AGPL, LC and LAC. CAPFs deployed on such borders should be under the army's operational control.
- ***Assam Rifles:*** To retain the responsibility of guarding the Myanmar border. The present proposal to hand over the responsibility of guarding the Myanmar to the BSF is NOT RECOMMENDED.
- ***BSF:*** To guard the Bangladesh border and the IB section of the border with Pakistan. It is recommended that the BSF be constituted into two wings, East and West, for better management due to different nuances of each border.
- ***ITBP:*** To be placed under the Operational Control of the Indian Army for border guarding duties on the India-China border.

The ITBP should be reconstituted as a para military force on the lines of the Assam Rifles and not be a CAPF.

- *SSB:* To continue to guard the Nepal and Bhutan borders as hitherto fore.

Composition of Units deployed on border guarding duties is recommended as under:

- The battalions deployed on border guarding duties should have a significant proportion of local youth in its ranks to exploit their knowledge of terrain, language and most importantly, cultural and historic links to the region. The local troops can also be utilized as acclimatized quick reaction forces in case of unforeseen transgressions/ intrusions in high altitude areas.
- Territorial Army battalions based on ex-servicemen should be raised, which can form part of border guarding CAPF. As army soldiers retire at a relatively younger age profile, a significant number can be re-enrolled in border guarding forces.

The management of India's international border along its North Eastern States has remained a critical and complex issue. In period of growing interdependence, threats from eccentric sources pose challenge to the country's security. Due to the tendency of India's neighbours to exploit the country's nation-building problems, India's internal security challenges are indistinguishably related with border management. Indian rebellious groups have for long been provided shelter across the nation's borders by hostile neighbours.

6. Why India is so prone to repeated cyber-attacks? Identify India's inherent vulnerability.

Ans.: India along with China, Russia, Saudi Arabia and South Korea is most vulnerable nation when it comes to cyber-attack. India is increasingly on the radar of cybercriminals from countries like China, Russia and the US, who are using advanced persistent threat (APT) attacks to steal data from consumers and enterprises. The safest in terms of cyber security are Scandinavian countries like Denmark, Norway and Finland. Damaging cyber-attacks on a global scale continue to surface every day. Some nations are better prepared than others to deal with online threats from criminals, terrorists and rogue nations. As more and more devices get connected to the Internet, the level of sophistication of these attacks is also on the rise. Experts believe while PM Narendra Modi-led Digital India initiative is an ambitious move, in which a number of crucial sectors of the economy embraces the Internet to foster growth, expansion, and accessibility, it also increases the risks of cyber threats. Studies show that the cyber-security awareness and efforts continue to lag behind the curve. Therefore, it is important that security vendors, and the government take proactive measure to prevent the country from various advanced cyber- attacks. Websites which are identified or are associated with the government need to be extra careful and take necessary precautionary measures to protect them from cyber-attacks. The following preventative strategies are intended to help our public and private partners proactively look for emails attempting to deceive users into 'clicking the link' or opening attachments to seemingly real websites:

- Never click on links in emails. If you do think the email is legitimate, whether from a third party retailer or primary retailer, go to the site and log on directly. Whatever notification or service offering was referenced in the email, if valid, will be available via regular log on.
- Never open the attachments. Typically, retailers will not send emails with attachments. If there is any doubt, contact the retailer directly and ask whether the email with the attachment was sent from them.
- Do not give out personal information over the phone or in an email unless completely

sure. Social engineering is a process of deceiving individuals into providing personal information to seemingly trusted agents who turn out to be malicious actors. If contacted over the phone by someone claiming to be a retailer or collection agency, do not give out your personal information. Ask them to provide you their name and a call-back number. Just because they may have some of your information does not mean they are legitimate!

Other practical tips to protect yourself from cyberattacks:

- Set secure passwords and don't share them with anyone. Avoid using common words, phrases, or personal information and update regularly.
- Keep your operating system, browser, anti-virus and other critical software up to date. Security updates and patches are available for free from major companies.
- Verify the authenticity of requests from companies or individuals by contacting them directly. If you are asked to provide personal information via email, you can independently contact the company directly to verify this request.
- Pay close attention to website URLs. Pay attention to the URLs of websites you visit. Malicious websites sometimes use a variation in common spelling or a different domain (for example, .com instead of .net) to deceive unsuspecting computer users.
- For e-Mail, turn off the option to automatically download attachments.
- Be suspicious of unknown links or requests sent through email or text message. Do not click on unknown links or answer strange questions sent to your mobile device, regardless of who the sender appears to be.

7. Is India equipped enough to combat a terrorist attack like the one in Pathankot recently? Discuss India's preparedness.

Ans.: In early hours of January 2, terrorists attacked the Indian Air Force base in Pathankot, killing seven Indian soldiers. Timely retaliation by Indian forces resulted in all six terrorists killed, preventing the greater devastation that could have occurred if the terrorists had been able to reach the high-value strategic assets they were targeting. Media reports in the wake of the attack suggested that the terrorists received clandestine support from Pakistan. India Today has claimed that 'the brazen attack was carried out on the behest of Pakistani's intelligence agency Inter-Services Intelligence (ISI)'. Other reports have suspected the involvement of Pakistan-based Jaish-e-Muhammad. The Hindustan Times and other Indian newspapers have reported that phone calls made by the terrorists were intercepted, and were made to Bahawalpur in Pakistan, the hometown of Jaish chief Maulana Nasood Azhar. Experts in India feel that the heavily armed terrorists would not have been able to carry out the attack without the full knowledge and support of the Pakistani military and the ISI and it would be naïve to believe the argument that the attackers were rogue elements or non-state actors. In fact, while welcoming Prime Minister Narendra Modi's surprise visit to Lahore, many security experts and former diplomats had cautioned India to be ready to deal with an adverse situation like the Kargil War, which took place following the Lahore Summit of 1999. At the same time, there was apprehension among the Indian strategic community that the Pakistani Army would not have taken kindly to Modi's oblique reference to Pakistani as a sponsor of terrorism in Afghanistan in his address to the Afghan parliament on December 25. The fears may well have been justified, given Pathankot and the subsequent attack on the Indian consulate in the city of

Mazar-i-Sharif. At any rate, the incidents refute any belief that the Pakistani military is supporting Prime Minister Nawaz Sarif in his endeavour to improve ties with India. Only an investigation by the National Investigating Agency will enable India to conclusively establish the identity of the terrorists and ascertain the role of the Pakistani military and ISI. But what is clear from the Pathankot attack is the fact that the terrorists had two main aims. The first was to destroy MiG-21, Mi-25, Mi-35, and other military hardware, while the second was to derail the peace process, which received a boost with Modi's surprise stopover in Lahore. While the Indian forces neutralized the terrorists before they could reach their target area, the Indian government has taken care in dealing with the attack, trying to ensure that it does not cast a cloud over the peace process, especially given that a meeting of foreign secretaries is scheduled in mid-January. This is evident from the fact that New Delhi has been cautious about naming Pakistan with regard to this terrorist attack. Commenting on the attack, Modi said, 'Today, enemies of humanity who can't see India progress tried to strike at our strategic area, a prominent airbase at the Pathankot'. Meanwhile, in an unprecedented move, the Pakistani government has condemned the attack, and offered its cooperation to India. In a brief press statement, Pakistan's Foreign Office said India and Pakistan will continue with a 'sustained dialogue process'. A spokesperson went on to say that, 'In line with Pakistan's commitment to effectively counter and eradicate terrorism, the government is in touch with the Indian government and in working on the leaders provided by it'. Yesterday, NDTV reported that Pakistani authorities have carried out raids in relation to the attack, leading to some arrests, and has formed a joint investigation team. These are welcome steps. Understandably, the Pathankot airbase attack has put the Indian government in a difficult situation, especially at a time when Modi is ready to travel miles to forge a durable peace with Pakistan. In fact, the attack has given opponents the opportunity to criticize Modi's overtures towards Pakistan. However, it is equally true that New Delhi has very limited options as far its relations with Islamabad are concerned. It is only through talks that India and Pakistan will be able to move towards building a peaceful environment in South Asia. The renewed dialogue process provides India with an opportunity to place all the evidence relating to the Pathankot attack before Pakistan and ask it to show its commitment to fighting terrorism. Meanwhile, India can call on the United States to take serious note of the growing terrorist activity in South Asia and to pressure Islamabad to step up its efforts to eliminate the threat. India should also seek help from Russia and Japan in building pressure on Pakistan. What makes the current phase in India-Pakistan relations different is the fact that both sides have refrained from attacking and counter-attacking each other, preventing the relationship from dropping to its nadir, as has happened after past terrorist attacks on India. There is reason to hope then that the two countries can work around the vested interests that do not want to see them live together in peace and prosperity. The Pathankot attack reflects a new template of terrorism and is a reminder that India needs a well-coordinated approach to security emergencies. This is particularly necessary as the country has embarked on a bold foreign policy path under Prime Minister Narendra Modi. The approach of the Pakistan-based terrorist groups in Pathankot is evidence that this template of terrorism is aimed to expose Indian weaknesses and harm strategic military assets. The new template has moved beyond the frequent infiltration by low-level terrorist cadres and movement into civilian areas (Jammu and Kashmir-style), into a more sophisticated, meticulously-planned, long-term, detailed operation, hitting at military targets, with local support networks and exploitation of social vulnerabilities such as drugs. This new format has made the cross-border challenge the gravest ever, especially because our response is entrapped within old doctrines and conventional thinking. By all measures, Pathankot was a meticulously-planned terrorist attack, with the clear stamp of military precision. Our security agencies treated it initially like a traditional terrorist assault. It took two days to recognize that it needed a far more sophisticated response, and act on it. India should expect more such emboldened attacks, and this is the time to frame and roll out a well-coordinated approach to security emergencies like Pathankot, hijackings and hostage-taking. A file image of security personnel taking position near the first base of IAF in Pathankot. AFPA file image of security personnel taking position near the first base of IAF in Pathankot. Some improvements have already been put in place since December 1989, when the daughter of then union home minister Mufti Mohammad Sayeed was kidnapped and released in exchange for five terrorists. In the 1999 Kandahar hijacking, the national response was also weak. The home ministry learned from the two incidents and framed guidelines on hostage-taking and a strong anti-hijacking policy, which emphasized that India will not negotiate with terrorists. India has not faced another hijacking since then, so it is unclear how the policy will work when tested. The 2008 Mumbai attacks were again a long-planned, successful military-precision terrorist operation. Our excruciatingly slow response resulted in heavy losses and exposed the lack of a meaningful policy framework. Post-Mumbai, a substantial region-wise National Security Guard (NSG) presence was established – untested till Pathankot. At Pathankot, the vacuum was not in the NSG's actions, but in the political decision-making which was ad hoc and un- institutionalized.

A well-conceived and organized policy framework would have put into action a series of steps from political decisions to operational procedures. These include:

- A well-defined chain of command, both political and operational;
- Inter-agency co-ordination, spanning civilian agencies like the National Disaster Management Authority, law and order enforcement machinery like the city and state police, the paramilitary and central and military intelligence agencies;
- Standard Operating Procedures or SOPs – the crucial determinant of a well- institutionalized policy;
- Channels of communications both internal and external. Internally, the use of encrypted communication networks during on-going operations, as well as data collection and real-time monitoring; externally, a code of conduct for the news media; and
- Regular review and updating of the SOPs and test drills to determine their functionality.

Institution-wise, India has some agencies which act as decision-making bodies during crises. One is the Cabinet Committee on Security (CCS), chaired by the PM, and the China Study Group (CSG) comprising the National Security Advisor and secretaries of home, defence and external affairs ministries. What is required is a crisis management mechanism which will bring in the political vision of the CCS, the administrative experience of the bureaucrats in the CSG, and the operational experience of the armed forces. The National Security Council which was established in 1999, was to be that mechanism, but its authority has been negated because of the lack of an institutionalized policy framework as outlined above. India does have a well-organized intelligence system that sniffs out terrorist conspiracies. After the 2008 Mumbai attacks,

India set up the Multi Agency Centre (MAC), which brought together over 25 security agencies for analysis and dissemination of terror threat inputs, to ensure co-ordination on actionable intelligence. The MAC is still an experiment; it has not moved to the next level of operationalization because of opposition from the states to establish the National Counter Terrorism Centre (NCTC)—a central agency mandated to perform the functions of intelligence, investigation, and operations. Several chief ministers including PM Modi as the Gujarat Chief Minister, wouldn't sign up, fearing that the NCTC's operational powers will encroach upon the powers of the state and thereby affect the federal distribution of power. Nor does India have sufficient intellectual capacity on Pakistan, our perennial security challenge and national media obsession. There are no dedicated research centres which study and analyse the social, economic, political and security developments in that country. Research emanating from these studies would have been a valuable input for the policy makers. The only entity with some research capability is the Centre for Pakistan Studies in New Delhi's Jamia Milia Islamia- but its role in policy-making remains opaque. The Pathankot attack is an opportune time to put in place a well-coordinated approach for future emergency security situations. The task becomes urgent as PM Modi continues on his bold foreign policy path, raising India's profile and broadening our sphere of influence even as he hopes to functionalize a dysfunctional bilateral like Pakistan.

Questions Asked in 2016

1. 'Increasing cross-border terrorist attacks in India and growing interference in the internal affairs of several member-states by Pakistan are not conducive for the future of SAARC (South Asian Association for Regional Cooperation)'. Explain with suitable example.
2. The terms 'Hot Pursuit' and 'Surgical Strikes' are often used in connection with armed action against terrorist attacks. Discuss the strategic impact of such actions.
3. 'Terrorism is emerging as a competitive industry over the last few decades'. Analyse the above statement.
4. Border management is a complex task due to difficult terrain and hostile relations with some countries. Elucidate the challenges and strategies for effective border management.
5. Use of Internet and social media by non-state actors for subversive activities is a major concern. How these have misused in the recent past? Suggest effective guidelines to curb the above threat.

Questions Asked in 2015

1. Human right activists constantly highlight the fact that the Armed forces (Special Powers) Act, 1958 (AFSPA) is a draconian act leading to cases of human right abuses by security forces. What sections of AFSPA are opposed by the activists? Critically evaluate the requirement with reference to the view held by Apex Court.
2. Religious indoctrination via social media has resulted in Indian youth joining the ISIS. What is ISIS and its mission? How can ISIS be dangerous to the internal security of our country?
3. The persisting drives of the government for development of large industries in backward areas have resulted in isolating the tribal population and the farmers who face multiple displacements. With Malkangiri and Naxalbari foci, discuss the corrective strategies needed to win the Left Wing Extremism (LWE) doctrine affected citizens back into mainstream of social and economic growth.
4. Considering the threats cyberspace poses for the country, India needs a 'Digital Armed

Forces' to prevent crimes. Critically evaluate the National Cyber Security Policy, 2013 outlining the challenges perceived in its effective implementation.

5. China and Pakistan have entered into an agreement for development of an economic corridor. What threat does this pose for India's security? Critically examine.

Questions Asked in 2014

1. 'The diverse nature of India as a multi-religious and multi-ethnic society is not immune to the impact of radicalism which is seen in her neighbourhood?' Discuss along with strategies to be adopted to counter this environment.
2. International civil aviation laws provide all countries complete and exclusive sovereignty over the airspace above their territory. What do you understand by 'airspace'? What are the implications of these laws on the space above this airspace? Discuss the challenges which this poses and suggest ways to contain the threat.
3. How does illegal transborder migration pose a threat to India's security? Discuss the strategies to curb this, bringing out the factors which give impetus to such migration.
4. In 2012, the longitudinal marking for high-risk areas for piracy was moved from 65 degrees east to 78 degrees east in the Arabian Sea by the International Maritime Organization. What impact does this have on India's maritime security concerns?

Questions Asked in 2013

1. Money laundering poses a serious threat to country's economic sovereignty. What is its significance for India and what steps are required to be taken to control this menace?
2. What are social networking site and what security implications do these sites present?
3. Cyber warfare is considered by some defense analysts to be a larger threat than even Al Qaeda or terrorism. What do you understand by Cyber warfare? Outline the cyber threats which India is vulnerable to and bring out the state of the country's preparedness to deal with the same.
4. Article 244 of Indian Constitution relates to Administration of Scheduled areas and tribal areas. Analyse the impact of non-implementation of the provisions of fifth schedule on the growth of Left Wing Extremism.
5. How far are India's internal security challenges linked with border management, particularly in view of the long porous borders with most countries of South Asia and Myanmar?

❑❑❑

Appendix one

The Armed Forces (Special Powers) Act, 1958 (Act No. 28 of 1958)

[11th September, 1958.]

An Act to enable certain special powers to be conferred upon members of the armed forces in disturbed areas [1][in the States of [2][3][Arunachal Pradesh, Assam, Manipur, Meghalaya, Mizoram, Nagaland and Tripura]]].

BE it enacted by Parliament in the Ninth Year of the Republic of India as follows:

1. *Short title and extent.* (1) This Act may be called [4][the Armed Forces (Special Powers) Act, 1958].

   [5][(2) It extends to the whole of the States of [2][3][Arunachal Pradesh, Assam, Manipur, Meghalaya, Mizoram, Nagaland and Tripura]]].

2. *Definitions.* In this Act, unless the context otherwise requires,
   - (a) "armed forces" means the military forces and the air forces operating as land forces, and includes any other armed forces of the Union so operating;
   - (b) "disturbed area" means an area which is for the time being declared by notification under section 3 to be a disturbed area;
   - (c) all other words and expressions used herein, but not defined and defined in the Air Force Act, 1950 (45 of 1950), or the Army Act, 1950 (46 of 1950), shall have the meanings respectively assigned to them in those Acts.

[6][3. *Power to declare areas to be disturbed areas.* If, in relation to any State or Union territory to which this Act extends, the Governor of that State or the Administrator of that Union territory or the Central Government, in either case, is of the opinion that the whole or any part of such State or Union territory, as the case may be, is in such a disturbed or dangerous condition that the use of armed forces in aid of the civil power is necessary, the Governor of that State or the Administrator of that Union territory or the Central Government, as the case may be, may, by notification in the Official Gazette, declare the whole or such part of such State or Union territory to be a disturbed area.]

4. *Special powers of the armed forces.* Any commissioned officer, warrant officer, non-commissioned officer or any other person of equivalent rank in the armed forces may, in a disturbed area,
   - (a) if he is of opinion that it is necessary so to do for the maintenance of public order,

after giving such due warning as he may consider necessary, fire upon or otherwise use force, even to the causing of death, against any person who is acting in contravention of any law or order for the time being in force in the disturbed area prohibiting the assembly of five or more persons or the carrying of weapons or of things capable of being used as weapons or of fire-arms, ammunition or explosive substances;

(b) if he is of opinion that it is necessary so to do, destroy any arms dump, prepared or fortified position or shelter from which armed attacks are made or are likely to be made or are attempted to be made, or any structure used as a training camp for armed volunteers or utilized as a hide-out by armed gangs or absconders wanted for any offence;

(c) arrest, without warrant, any person who has committed a cognizable offence or against whom a reasonable suspicion exists that he has committed or is about to commit a cognizable offence and may use such force as may be necessary to effect the arrest;

(d) enter and search without warrant any premises to make any such arrest as aforesaid or to recover any person believed to be wrongfully restrained or confined or any property reasonably suspected to be stolen property or any arms, ammunition or explosive substances believed to be unlawfully kept in such premises, and may for that purpose use such force as may be necessary.

5. ***Arrested persons to be made over to the police.*** Any person arrested and taken into custody under this Act shall be made over to the officer in charge of the nearest police station with the least possible delay, together with a report of the circumstances occasioning the arrest.

6. ***Protection to persons acting under Act.*** No prosecution, suit or other legal proceeding shall be instituted, except with the previous sanction of the Central Government, against any person in respect of anything done or purported to be done in exercise of the powers conferred by this Act.

---

1. Subs. by Act 7 of 1972, s. 2, for "in the State of Assam and the Union territory of Manipur" (w.e.f. 5-4-1972).

2. Subs. by Act 34 of 1986, s. 40, for "Meghalaya, Nagaland and Tripura and the Union territories of Arunachal Pradesh and Mizoram" (w.e.f. 20-2-1987).

3. Subs. by Act 69 of 1986, s. 43, for "Assam, Manipur, Meghalaya, Mizoram, Nagaland and Tripura and the Union territory of Arunachal Pradesh" (w.e.f. 20-2-1987).

4. Subs. by Act 7 of 1972, s. 3, for "the Armed Forces (Assam and Manipur) Special Powers Act, 1958" (w.e.f. 5-4-1972).

5. Subs. by s. 3, ibid. for sub-section (2) (w.e.f. 5-4-1972).

6. Subs. by s. 4, ibid. for section 3 (w.e.f. 5-4-1972).

7. [Repeal and Saving.] Rep. by the Repealing and Amending Act, 1960 (58 of 1960), s. 2 and the First Schedule (w.e.f. 26-12-1960).

Appendix two

The National Investigation Agency Act, 2008 (Act No. 34 of 2008)

[31st December, 2008.]

An Act to constitute an investigation agency at the national level to investigate and prosecute offences affecting the sovereignty, security and integrity of India, security of State, friendly relations with foreign States and offences under Acts enacted to implement international treaties, agreements, conventions and resolutions of the United Nations, its agencies and other international organizations and for matters connected therewith or incidental thereto.

BE it enacted by Parliament in the Fifty-ninth Year of the Republic of India as follows:

Chapter I: Preliminary

1. ***Short title, extent and application:*** (1) This Act may be called the National Investigation Agency Act, 2008. (2) It extends to the whole of India and it applies also—
   (a) to citizens of India outside India;
   (b) to persons in the service of the Government wherever they may be; and
   (c) to persons on ships and aircrafts registered in India wherever they may be.
2. ***Definitions:***
   (a) In this Act, unless the context otherwise requires,—
   (i) "Agency" means the National Investigation Agency constituted under section 3;
   (ii) "Code" means the Code of Criminal Procedure 1973 (2 of 1974);
   (iii) "High Court" means the High Court within whose jurisdiction the Special Court is situated;
   (iv) "prescribed" means prescribed by rules;
   (v) "Public Prosecutor" means a Public Prosecutor or an Additional Public Prosecutor or a Special Public Prosecutor appointed under section 15;
   (vi) "Schedule" means the Schedule to this Act;
   (vii) "Scheduled Offence" means an offence specified in the Schedule;
   (viii) "Special Court" means a Special Court constituted under section 11 or, as the case may be, under section 22;
   (ix) Words and expressions used but not defined in this Act and defined in the Code shall have the meanings respectively assigned to them in the Code.

(b) Any reference in this Act to any enactment or any provision thereof shall, in relation to an area in which such enactment or such provision is not in force, be construed as a reference to the corresponding law or the relevant provision of the corresponding law, if any, in force in that area.

Chapter II: National Investigation Agency

3. *Constitution of National Investigation Agency.*

(a) Notwithstanding anything in the Police Act, 1861 (5 of 1861), the Central Government may constitute a special agency to be called the National Investigation Agency for investigation and prosecution of offences under the Acts specified in the Schedule.

(b) Subject to any orders which the Central Government may make in this behalf, officers of the Agency shall have throughout India in relation to the investigation of Scheduled Offences and arrest of persons concerned in such offences, all the powers, duties, privileges and liabilities which police officers have in connection with the investigation of offences committed therein.

(c) Any officer of the Agency of, or above, the rank of Sub-Inspector may, subject to any orders which the Central Government may make in this behalf, exercise throughout India, any of the powers of the officer-in-charge of a police station in the area in which he is present for the time being and when so exercising such powers shall, subject to any such orders as aforesaid, be deemed to be an officer-in-charge of a police station discharging the functions of such an officer within the limits of his station.

4. *Superintendence of National Investigation Agency.*

(a) The superintendence of the Agency shall vest in the Central Government.

(b) The administration of the Agency shall vest in an officer designated as the Director-General appointed in this behalf by the Central Government who shall exercise in respect of the Agency such of the powers exercisable by a Director-General of Police in respect of the police force in a State, as the Central Government may specify in this behalf.

5. ***Manner of constitution of Agency and conditions of service of members.*** Subject to the provisions of this Act, the Agency shall be constituted in such manner as may be prescribed and the conditions of service of persons employed in the Agency shall be such as may be prescribed.

Chapter III: Investigation by the National Investigation Agency

6. *Investigation of Scheduled Offences.*

(a) On receipt of information and recording thereof under section 154 of the Code relating to any Scheduled Offence the officer-in-charge of the police station shall forward the report to the State Government forthwith.

(b) On receipt of the report under sub-section (1), the State Government shall forward the report to the Central Government as expeditiously as possible.

(c) On receipt of report from the State Government, the Central Government shall determine on the basis of information made available by the State Government or received from other sources, within fifteen days from the date of receipt of the report, whether the offence is a Scheduled Offence or not and also whether, having regard to the gravity of the offence and other relevant factors, it is a fit case to be investigated by the Agency.

(d) Where the Central Government is of the opinion that the offence is a Scheduled Offence and it is a fit case to be investigated by the Agency, it shall direct the Agency to investigate the said offence.

(e) Notwithstanding anything contained in this section, if the Central Government is of the opinion that a Scheduled Offence has been committed which is required to be investigated under this Act, it may, suo moto, direct the Agency to investigate the said offence.

(f) Where any direction has been given under sub-section (4) or sub-section (5), the State Government and any police officer of the State Government investigating the offence shall not proceed with the investigation and shall forthwith transmit the relevant documents and records to the Agency.

(g) For the removal of doubts, it is hereby declared that till the Agency takes up the investigation of the case, it shall be the duty of the officer-in-charge of the police station to continue the investigation.

7. ***Power to transfer investigation to State Government.*** While investigating any offence under this Act, the Agency, having regard to the gravity of the offence and other relevant factors, may:

(a) if it is expedient to do so, request the State Government to associate itself with the investigation; or

(b) with the previous approval of the Central Government, transfer the case to the State Government for investigation and trial of the offence.

8. ***Power to investigate connected offences.*** While investigating any Scheduled Offence, the Agency may also investigate any other offence which the accused is alleged to have committed if the offence is connected with the Scheduled Offence.

9. ***State Government to extend assistance to National Investigation Agency.*** The State Government shall extend all assistance and co-operation to the Agency for investigation of the Scheduled Offences.

10. ***Power of State Government to investigate Scheduled Offences.*** Save as otherwise provided in this Act, nothing contained in this Act shall affect the powers of the State Government to investigate and prosecute any Scheduled Offence or other offences under any law for the time being in force.

Chapter IV: Special Courts

11. ***Power of Central Government to constitute Special Courts.***

(a) The Central Government shall, by notification in the Official Gazette, for the trial of Scheduled Offences, constitute one or more Special Courts for such area or areas, or for such case or class or group of cases, as may be specified in the notification.

(b) Where any question arises as to the jurisdiction of any Special Court, it shall be referred to the Central Government whose decision in the matter shall be final.

(c) A Special Court shall be presided over by a judge to be appointed by the Central Government on the recommendation of the Chief Justice of the High Court.

(d) The Agency may make an application to the Chief Justice of the High Court for appointment of a Judge to preside over the Special Court.

(e) On receipt of an application under sub-section (4), the Chief Justice shall, as soon as possible and not later than seven days, recommend the name of a judge for being appointed to preside over the Special Court.

(f) The Central Government may, if required, appoint an additional judge or additional judges to the Special Court, on the recommendation of the Chief Justice of the High Court.

(g) A person shall not be qualified for appointment as a judge or an additional judge of a Special Court unless he is, immediately before such appointment, a Sessions Judge or an Additional Sessions Judge in any State.

(h) For the removal of doubts, it is hereby provided that the attainment, by a person appointed as a judge or an additional judge of a Special Court, of the age of superannuation under the rules applicable to him in the service to which he belongs shall not affect his continuance as such judge or additional judge and the Central Government may by order direct that he shall continue as judge until a specified date or until completion of the trial of the case or cases before him as may be specified in that order.

(i) Where any additional judge or additional judges is or are appointed in a Special Court, the judge of the Special Court may, from time to time, by general or special order, in writing, provide for the distribution of business of the Special Court among all judges including himself and the additional judge or additional judges and also for the disposal of urgent business in the event of his absence or the absence of any additional judge.

12. ***Place of sitting.*** A Special Court may, on its own motion, or on an application made by the Public Prosecutor and if it considers it expedient or desirable so to do, sit for any of its proceedings at any place other than its ordinary place of sitting.

13. ***Jurisdiction of Special Courts.***

(a) Notwithstanding anything contained in the Code, every Scheduled Offence investigated by the Agency shall be tried only by the Special Court within whose local jurisdiction it was committed.

(b) If, having regard to the exigencies of the situation prevailing in a State if,—

(i) it is not possible to have a fair, impartial or speedy trial; or

(ii) it is not feasible to have the trial without occasioning the breach of peace or grave risk to the safety of the accused, the witnesses, the Public Prosecutor or a judge of the Special Court or any of them; or

(iii) it is not otherwise in the interests of justice, the Supreme Court may transfer any case pending before a Special Court to any other Special Court within that State or in any other State and the High Court may transfer any case pending before a Special Court situated in that State to any other Special Court within the State.

(c) The Supreme Court or the High Court, as the case may be, may act under this section either on the application of the Central Government or a party interested and any such application shall be made by motion, which shall, except when the applicant is the Attorney-General for India, be supported by an affidavit or affirmation.

14. ***Powers of Special Courts with respect to other offences.***

(a) When trying any offence, a Special Court may also try any other offence with which the accused may, under the Code be charged, at the same trial if the offence is connected with such other offence.

(b) If, in the course of any trial under this Act of any offence, it is found that the accused person has committed any other offence under this Act or under any other law, the Special Court may convict such person of such other offence and pass any sentence or award punishment authorized by this Act or, as the case may be, under such other law.

15. ***Public Prosecutors***

(a) The Central Government shall appoint a person to be the Public Prosecutor and may appoint one or more persons to be the Additional Public Prosecutor or Additional Public Prosecutors:

Provided that the Central Government may also appoint for any case or class or group of cases a Special Public Prosecutor.

(b) A person shall not be qualified to be appointed as a Public Prosecutor or an Additional Public Prosecutor or a Special Public Prosecutor under this section unless he has been in practice as an Advocate for not less than seven years or has held any post, for a period of not less than seven years, under the Union or a State, requiring special knowledge of law.

(c) Every person appointed as a Public Prosecutor or an Additional Public Prosecutor or a Special Public Prosecutor under this section shall be deemed to be a Public Prosecutor within the meaning of clause (u) of section 2 of the Code, and the provisions of the Code shall have effect accordingly.

16. ***Procedure and powers of Special Courts.***

(a) A Special Court may take cognizance of any offence, without the accused being committed to it for trial, upon receiving a complaint of facts that constitute such offence or upon a police report of such facts.

(b) Where an offence triable by a Special Court is punishable with imprisonment for a term not exceeding three years or with fine or with both, the Special Court may, notwithstanding anything contained in sub-section (1) of section 260 or section 262 of the Code, try the offence in a summary way in accordance with the procedure prescribed in the Code and the provisions of sections 263 to 265 of the Code shall, so far as may be, apply to such trial:

Provided that when, in the course of a summary trial under this sub-section, it appears to the Special Court that the nature of the case is such that it is not desirable to try it in a summary way, the Special Court shall recall any witnesses who may have been examined and proceed to re-hear the case in the manner provided by the provisions of the Code for the trial of such offence and the said provisions shall apply to, and in relation to, a Special Court as they apply to and in relation to a Magistrate:

Provided further that in the case of any conviction in a summary trial under this section, it shall be lawful for a Special Court to pass a sentence of imprisonment for a term not exceeding one year and with fine which may extend to five lakh rupees.

(c) Subject to the other provisions of this Act, a Special Court shall, for the purpose of trial of any offence, have all the powers of a Court of Session and shall try such offence as if it were a Court of Session so far as may be in accordance with the procedure prescribed in the Code for the trial before a Court of Session.

(d) Subject to the other provisions of this Act, every case transferred to a Special Court under sub-section (2) of section 13 shall be dealt with as if such case had been transferred under section 406 of the Code to such Special Court.

(e) Notwithstanding anything contained in the Code, but subject to the provisions of section 299 of the Code, a Special Court may, if it thinks fit and for reasons to be recorded by it, proceed with the trial in the absence of the accused or his pleader and record the evidence of any witness, subject to the right of the accused to recall the witness for cross-examination.

17. ***Protection of witnesses***

(a) Notwithstanding anything contained in the Code, the proceedings under this Act may, for reasons to be recorded in writing, be held in camera if the Special Court so desires.

(b) On an application made by a witness in any proceeding before it or by the Public Prosecutor in relation to such witness or on its own motion, if the Special Court is satisfied that the life of such witness is in danger, it may, for reasons to be recorded in writing, take such measures as it deems fit for keeping the identity and address of such witness secret.

(c) In particular, and without prejudice to the generality of the provisions of sub-section (2), the measures which a Special Court may take under that sub-section may include—

(i) the holding of the proceedings at a place to be decided by the Special Court;

(ii) the avoiding of the mention of the names and addresses of the witnesses in its orders or judgments or in any records of the case accessible to public;

(iii) the issuing of any directions for securing that the identity and address of the witnesses are not disclosed; and

(iv) a decision that it is in the public interest to order that all or any of the proceedings pending before such a Court shall not be published in any manner.

(d) Any person who contravenes any decision or direction issued under sub-section (3) shall be punishable with imprisonment for a term which may extend to three years and with fine which may extend to one thousand rupees.

18. ***Sanction for prosecution.*** No prosecution, suit or other legal proceedings shall be instituted in any court of law, except with the previous sanction of the Central Government, against any member of the Agency or any person acting on his behalf in respect of anything done or purported to be done in exercise of the powers conferred by this Act.

19. ***Trial by Special Court to have precedence:*** The trial under this Act of any offence by a Special Court shall be held on day-to- day basis on all working days and have precedence over the trial of any other case against the accused in

any other court (not being a Special Court) and shall be concluded in preference to the trial of such other case and accordingly the trial of such other case shall, if necessary, remain in abeyance.

20. ***Power to transfer cases to regular courts.*** Where, after taking cognizance of any offence, a Special Court is of the opinion that the offence is not triable by it, it shall, notwithstanding that it has no jurisdiction to try such offence, transfer the case for the trial of such offence to any court having jurisdiction under the Code and the Court to which the case is transferred may proceed with the trial of the offence as if it had taken cognizance of the offence.

21. ***Appeals***

(a) Notwithstanding anything contained in the Code, an appeal shall lie from any judgment, sentence or order, not being an interlocutory order, of a Special Court to the High Court both on facts and on law.

(b) Every appeal under sub-section (1) shall be heard by a bench of two Judges of the High Court and shall, as far as possible, be disposed of within a period of three months from the date of admission of the appeal.

(c) Except as aforesaid, no appeal or revision shall lie to any court from any judgment, sentence or order including an interlocutory order of a Special Court.

(d) Notwithstanding anything contained in sub-section (3) of section 378 of the Code, an appeal shall lie to the High Court against an order of the Special Court granting or refusing bail.

(e) Every appeal under this section shall be preferred within a period of thirty days from the date of the judgment, sentence or order appealed from:

Provided that the High Court may entertain an appeal after the expiry of the said period of thirty days if it is satisfied that the appellant had sufficient cause for not preferring the appeal within the period of thirty days:

Provided further that no appeal shall be entertained after the expiry of period of ninety days.

22. ***Power of State Government to constitute Special Courts.***

(a) The State Government may constitute one or more Special Courts for the trial of offences under any or all the enactments specified in the Schedule.

(b) The provisions of this Chapter shall apply to the Special Courts constituted by the State Government under sub-section (1) and shall have effect subject to the following modifications, namely:

(i) references to "Central Government" in sections 11 and 15 shall be construed as references to State Government;

(ii) reference to "Agency" in sub-section (1) of section 13 shall be construed as a reference to the "investigation agency of the State Government";

(iii) reference to "Attorney-General for India" in sub-section (3) of section 13 shall be construed as reference to "Advocate-General of the State".

(c) The jurisdiction conferred by this Act on a Special Court shall, until a Special Court is constituted by the State Government under sub-section (1) in the case of any offence punishable under this Act, notwithstanding anything contained in the Code, be exercised by the Court of Session of the division in which such offence has been committed and it shall have all the powers and follow the procedure provided under this Chapter.

(d) On and from the date when the Special Court is constituted by the State Government the trial of any offence investigated by the State Government under the provisions of this Act, which would have been required to be held before the Special Court, shall stand transferred to that Court on the date on which it is constituted.

Chapter V: Miscellaneous

23. ***Power of High Courts to make rules.*** The High Court may, by notification in the Official Gazette, make such rules, as it may deem necessary for carrying out the provisions of this Act relating to Special Courts within its territory.

24. ***Power to remove difficulties***

(a) If any difficulty arises in giving effect to the provisions of this Act, the Central Government may, by order published in the Official Gazette make such provisions, not inconsistent with the provisions of this Act, as may appear to it to be necessary or expedient for removing the difficulty:

Provided that no order shall be made, under this section after the expiration of two years from the commencement of this Act.

(b) Every order made under this section shall be laid, as soon as may be after it is made, before each House of Parliament.

25. ***Power to make rules.***

(a) The Central Government may, by notification in the Official Gazette, make rules for carrying out the provisions of this Act.

(b) In particular, and without prejudice to the generality to the foregoing power, such rules may provide for all or any of the following matters, namely:—

(i) the manner of constitution of the Agency and the conditions of service of persons employed in the Agency under section 5;

(ii) any other matter which is required to be, or may be, prescribed.

26. ***Laying of rules:*** Every rule made by the Central Government under this Act shall be laid, as soon as may be after it is made, before each House of Parliament, while it is in session, for a total period of thirty days which may be comprised in one session or in two or more successive sessions, and if, before the expiry of the session immediately following the session or the successive sessions aforesaid, both Houses agrees in making any modification in the rule or both Houses agree that the rule should not be made, the rule shall thereafter have effect only in such modified form or be of no effect, as the case may be; so, however, that any such modification or annulment shall be without prejudice to the validity of anything previously done under that rule.

The Schedule

[See section 2(1) (f)]

1. The Atomic Energy Act, 1962 (33 of 1962);
2. The Unlawful Activities (Prevention) Act, 1967 (37 of 1967);
3. The Anti-Hijacking Act, 1982 (65 of 1982);
4. The Suppression of Unlawful Acts against Safety of Civil Aviation Act, 1982 (66 of 1982);
5. The SAARC Convention (Suppression of Terrorism) Act, 1993 (36 of 1993);

6. The Suppression of Unlawful Acts Against Safety of Maritime Navigation and Fixed Platforms on Continental Shelf Act, 2002 (69 of 2002);
7. The Weapons of Mass Destruction and their Delivery Systems (Prohibition of Unlawful Activities) Act, 2005 (21 of 2005);
8. Offences under—
   (a) Chapter VI of the Indian Penal Code (45 of 1860) [sections 121 to 130 (both inclusive)];
   (b) Sections 489-A to 489-E (both inclusive) of the Indian Penal Code (45 of 1860).

❑❑❑

Appendix three

MCOCA, 1999

Government of Maharashtra, Law and Judiciary Department Maharashtra Act No. XXX of 1999

The Maharashtra Control of Organised Crime Act, 1999

(As modified up to the 29th October 2012)

(This Act received the assent of the President on the 23rd April 1999; assent was first published in the Maharashtra Government Gazette, Part IV, Extraordinary, on the 24th April 1999.)

To make special provisions for prevention and control of, and for coping with, criminal activity by organized crime syndicate or gang, and for matters connected therewith or incidental thereto.

WHEREAS it was expedient to make special provisions for prevention and control of, and for coping with, criminal activity by organized crime syndicate or gang, and for matters connected therewith or incidental thereto;

AND WHEREAS both Houses of the State Legislature were not in session;

AND WHEREAS the Governor of Maharashtra was satisfied that circumstances existed which rendered it necessary for him to take immediate action to make a law, for the purposes aforesaid; and therefore, promulgated the Maharashtra Control of Organized Crime Ordinance, 1999, on the 24th February 1999;

AND WHEREAS it is expedient to replace the said Ordinance by an Act of the State Legislature; It is hereby enacted in the Fiftieth Year of the Republic of India as follows:—

1. ***Short title, extent and commencement:***
   (a) This Act may be called the Maharashtra Control of Organized Crime Act, 1999.
   (b) It extends to the whole of the State of Maharashtra.
   (c) It shall be deemed to have come into force on the 24th February 1999.
2. ***Definitions:***
   (i) In this Act, unless the context otherwise requires:
      (a) "abet", with its grammatical variations and cognate expression, includes,
         - the communication or association with any person with the actual knowledge or having reason to believe that such person is engaged in assisting in any manner, an organized crime syndicate ;
         - the passing on or publication of, without any lawful authority, any

information likely to assist the organized crime syndicate and the passing on or publication of or distribution of any document or matter obtained from the organized crime syndicate ; and

❖ the rendering of any assistance, whether financial or otherwise, to the organized crime syndicate;

(b) "Code" means the Code of Criminal Procedure, 1973;

(c) "Competent Authority" means the Competent Authority appointed under section 13;

(d) "continuing unlawful activity" means an activity prohibited by law for the time being in force, which is a cognizable offence punishable with imprisonment of three years or more, undertaken either singly or jointly, as a member of an organized crime syndicate or on behalf of such syndicate in respect of which more than one charge-sheets have been filed before a competent Court within the preceding period of ten years and that Court has taken cognizance of such offence;

(e) "organized crime" means any continuing unlawful activity by an individual, singly or jointly, either as a member of an organized crime syndicate or on behalf of such syndicate, by use of violence or threat of violence or intimidation or coercion, or other unlawful means, with the objective of gaining pecuniary benefits, or gaining undue economic or other advantage for himself or any other person or promoting insurgency;

(f) "organized crime syndicate" means a group of two or more persons who, acting either singly or collectively, as a syndicate or gang indulge in activities of organized crime ;

(g) "Special Court" means the Special Court constituted under section 5.

(ii) Words and expressions used but not defined in this Act and defined in the Code shall have the meanings respectively assigned to them in the Code.

3. ***Punishment for organized crime:***

(a) Whoever commits an offence of organized crime shall,—

(i) if such offence has resulted in the death of any person, be punishable with death or imprisonment for life and shall also be liable to a fine, subject to a minimum fine of rupees one lac;

(ii) in any other case, be punishable with imprisonment for a term which shall not be less than five years but which may extend to imprisonment for life and shall also be liable to a fine, subject to a minimum fine of rupees five lacs.

(b) Whoever conspires or attempts to commit or advocates, abets or knowingly facilitates the commission of an organized crime or any act preparatory to organized crime, shall be punishable with imprisonment for a term which shall be not less than five years but which may extend to imprisonment for life and shall also be liable to a fine, subject to a minimum fine of rupees five lacs.

(c) Whoever harbours or conceals or attempts to harbour or conceal, any member of an organized crime syndicate shall be punishable with imprisonment for a term which shall not be less than five years but which may extent to imprisonment for life, and shall also be liable to a fine, subject to a minimum fine of rupees five lacs.

(d) Any person who is a member of an organized crime syndicate shall be punishable with imprisonment for a term which shall not be less than five years but which may extend to imprisonment for life and shall also be liable to a fine, subject to a minimum fine of rupees five lacs.

(e) Whoever holds any property derived or obtained from commission of an organized crime or which has been acquired through the organized crime syndicate funds shall be punishable with a term which shall not be less than three years but which may extend to imprisonment for life and shall also be liable to fine, subject to a minimum fine of rupees two lacs.

4. ***Punishment for possessing unaccountable wealth on behalf of member of organized crime syndicate:*** If any person on behalf of a member of an organized crime syndicate is, or, at any time has been, in possession of movable or immovable property which he cannot satisfactorily account for, he shall be punishable with imprisonment for a term which shall not be less than three years but which may extend to ten years and shall also be liable to fine, subject to a minimum fine of rupees one lac and such property shall also be liable for attachment and forfeiture, as provided by section 20.

5. ***Special Courts:***

(a) The State Government may, by notification in the Official Gazette, constitute one or more Special Courts for such area or areas, or for such case or class or group of cases, as may be specified in the notification.

(b) Where any question arises as to the jurisdiction of any Special Court, it shall be referred to the State Government whose decision shall be final.

(c) A Special Court shall be presided over by a judge to be appointed by the State Government, with the concurrence of the Chief Justice of the Bombay High Court. The State Government may also appoint, with the concurrence of the Chief Justice of the Bombay High Court, additional judges to exercise jurisdiction in a Special Court.

(d) A person shall not be qualified for appointment as a judge or an additional judge of a Special Court, unless he immediately before such appointment, is a sessions judge or an additional sessions judge.

(e) Where any additional judge is or additional judges are appointed in a Special Court, the judge of the Special Court may, from time to time, by general or special order in writing, provide for the distribution of the business of the Special Court among himself and the additional judge or additional judges and also for the disposal of urgent business in the event of his absence or the absence of any additional judges.

6. ***Jurisdiction of Special Court:*** Notwithstanding anything contained in the Code, every offence punishable under this Act shall be triable only by the Special Court within whose local jurisdiction it was committed, or as the case may be, by the Special Court constituted for trying such offence under sub-section (1) of section 5.

7. *Power of Special Court with respect to other offences:*

   (a) When trying any offence punishable under this Act, a Special Court may also try any other offence with which the accused may, under the Code, be charged at the same trial, if the offence is connected with such other offence.

   (b) If, in the course of any trial of any offence under this Act, it is found that the accused person has committed any other offence under this Act or under any other law, the Special Court may convict such person of such other offence and may pass any sentence authorized by this Act or, as the case may be, such other law, for the punishment thereof.

8. *Public Prosecutor:*

   (a) For every Special Court, the State Government shall appoint a person to be the Public Prosecutor and may appoint one or more persons to be the Additional Public Prosecutor or Additional Public Prosecutors :

   Provided that, the State Government may also appoint for any case or group of cases, a Special Public Prosecutor.

   (b) A person shall not be qualified to be appointed as a Public Prosecutor, an Additional Public Prosecutor or a Special Public Prosecutor unless he has been in practice as an Advocate for not less than ten years.

   (c) Every person appointed as a Public Prosecutor or Additional Public Prosecutor or Special Public Prosecutor under this section shall be deemed to be Public Prosecutor within the meaning of clause (u) of section 2 of the Code, and the provisions of the Code shall have effect accordingly.

9. *Procedure and powers of Special Court:*

   (a) A Special Court may take cognizance of any offence without the accused being committed to it for trial, upon receiving a complaint of facts which constitute such offence or upon a police report of such facts.

   (b) Where an offence triable by a Special Court is punishable with imprisonment for a term not exceeding three years or with fine or with both, the Special Court may, notwithstanding anything contained in sub-section (1) of section 260 or section 262 of the Code, try the offence in a summary way in accordance with the procedure prescribed in the Code and the provisions of section 263 to 265 of the Code shall, as far as may be, apply to such trial:

   Provided that, where in the course of a summary trial under this sub- section, it appears to the Special Court that the nature of the case is such that it is undesirable to try in a summary way, the Special Court shall recall any witnesses who may have been examined and proceed to re-hear the case in the manner provided by the provisions of the Code for the trial of such offence and the said provisions shall apply to and in relation, to a Special Court as they apply to and in relation, to a Magistrate :

   Provided further that, in case of any conviction in a summary trial under this section, it shall be lawful for a Special Court to pass a sentence of imprisonment for a term not exceeding two years.

   (c) A Special Court may, with a view to obtaining the evidence of any person, supposed to have been directly or indirectly concerned in or privy to an offence, tender a pardon to such person on condition of his making a full and true disclosure of the whole circumstances within his knowledge relative to the offence and to every other person concerned, whether as principle or abettor, in the commission thereof, and any pardon so tendered shall, for the purposes of section 308 of the Code, be deemed to have been tendered under section 307 thereof.

(d) Subject to other provisions of this Act, a Special Court shall, for the purpose of trial of any offence, have all the powers of a Court of Session and shall try such offence as if it were a Court of Session, so far as may be, in accordance with the procedure prescribed in the Code for the trial before a Court of Session.

10. *Trial by Special Courts to have precedence:* The trial of any offence under this Act by a Special Court shall have precedence over the trial of any other case against the accused in any other Court (not being a Special Court) and shall be concluded in preference of the trial of such other cases and accordingly the trial of such other cases shall remain in abeyance.

11. *Power to transfer cases to regular Courts:* Where, after taking cognizance of an offence, a Special Court is of the opinion that the offence is not triable by it, it shall, notwithstanding that it has no jurisdiction to try such offence, transfer the case for trial of such offence to any Court having jurisdiction under the Code and the Court to which the case is transferred may proceed with the trial of the offence as if it had taken cognizance of the offence.

12. *Appeal:*

(a) Notwithstanding anything contained in the Code, an appeal shall lie from any judgement, sentence or order, not being an interlocutory order, of a Special court to the High Court.

(b) Every appeal under this section shall be preferred within thirty days from the date of the judgement, sentence or order.

13. *Appointment of Competent Authority:* The State Government may appoint any of its officer, in Home Department, not below the rank of Secretary to Government, to be the Competent Authority for the purposes of section 14.

14. *Authorization of interception of wire, electronic or oral communication:*

(i) A police officer not below the rank of Superintendent of Police supervising the investigation of an organized crime under this Act may submit an application in writing to the Competent Authority for an order authorizing or approving the interception of wire, electronic or oral communication by the investigating officer when such interception may provide or has provided evidence of any offence involving an organized crime.

(ii) Each application shall include the following information:—

(a) the identity of the investigative or law enforcement officer making the application, and the head of the department authorizing the application;

(b) a statement of the facts and circumstances relied upon by the applicant, to justify his belief that an order should be issued, including—

- ❖ details as to the offence of organized crime that has been, is being, or is about to be committed;

- ❖ a particular description of the nature and location of the facilities from which or the place where the communication is to be intercepted;
- ❖ a particular description of the type of communications sought to be intercepted; and
- ❖ the identity of the person, if known, committing the offence of organized crime whose communications are to be intercepted;

(c) a statement as to whether or not other modes of enquiry of intelligence gathering have been tried and failed or why they reasonably appear to be unlikely to succeed if tried or to be too dangerous or is likely to expose the identity of those connected with the operation of interception;

(d) a statement of the period of time for which the interception is required to be maintained. If the nature of the enquiry is such that the authorization for interception should not automatically terminate when the described type of communication has been first obtained, a particular description of facts establishing probable cause to believe that additional communications of the same type will occur thereafter;

(e) a statement of the facts concerning all previous applications known to the individual authorizing and making the application, made to the Competent Authority for authorization to intercept, or for approval of interceptions of, wire, electronic or oral communications involving any of the same persons, facilities or places specified in the application and the action taken by the Competent Authority on each such application; and

(f) where the application is for the extension of an order, a statement setting forth the results thus far obtained from the interception, or a reasonable explanation of the failure to obtain such results.

(iii) The Competent Authority may require the applicant to furnish additional oral or documentary evidence in support of the application.

(iv) Upon such application, the Competent Authority may after recording the reasons in writing reject the application, or issue an order, as requested or as modified, authorizing or approving interception of wire, electronic or oral communications, if the Competent Authority determines on the basis of the facts submitted by the applicant that—

(a) there is a probable cause for belief that an individual is committing, has committed, or is about to commit a particular offence described and made punishable under sections 3 and 4 of this Act;

(b) there is a probable cause for belief that particular communications concerning that offence will be obtained through such interception;

(c) normal modes of enquiry and intelligence gathering have been tried and have failed or reasonably appear to be unlikely to succeed if tried or to be too dangerous or is likely to expose the identity of those connected with the operation of interception ;

(d) there is probable cause for belief that the facilities from which, or the place where, the wire, electronic or oral communications are to be intercepted or be used or are about to be used, in connection with the commission of such offence, leased to, or are listed in the name of or commonly used by such person.

(v) Each order by the Competent Authority authorizing or approving the interception of any wire, electronic or oral communication under this section shall specify—

(a) the identity of the person, if known, whose communications are to be intercepted;

(b) the nature and location of the communication facilities as to which, or the place where, authority to intercept is granted;

(c) a particular description of the type of communication sought to be intercepted, and a statement of the particular offence to which it relates;

(d) the identity of the agency authorized to intercept the communications, and of the person authorizing the application; and

(e) the period of time during which such interception is authorized, including a statement as to whether or not the interception shall automatically terminate when the described communication has been first obtained.

(vi) The Competent Authority shall immediately after passing the order under sub-section (4), but in any case not later than seven days from the passing of the order, submit a copy of the same to the Review Committee constituted under section 15 along with all the relevant underlying papers, record and his own findings, etc., in respect of the said order, for consideration and approval of the order by the Review Committee.

(vii) An order authorizing the interception of a wire, electronic or oral communication under this section shall, upon request of the applicant, direct that a provider of wire or electronic communication service, landlord, custodian or other person shall furnish to the applicant forthwith all information, facilities, and technical assistance necessary to accomplish the interception unobtrusively and with a minimum of interference with the services that such service provider, landlord, custodian, or person is providing to the person whose communications are to be intercepted.

(viii) No order issued under this section may authorize or approve the interception of any wire, electronic or oral communication for any period longer than is necessary to achieve the objective of the authorization, nor in any event longer than sixty days. Such sixty days period shall begin on the day immediately preceding the day on which the investigative or law enforcement officer first begins to conduct an interception under the order or ten days after the order is issued, whichever is earlier. Extension of an order may be granted, but only upon an application for an extension is made in accordance with sub- section (1) and the Competent Authority making the findings required by sub-section (4). The period of extension shall be no longer than the Competent Authority deems necessary to achieve the purposes for which it was granted and in no event for longer than sixty days at a time. Every order and extension thereof shall contain a provision that the authorization to intercept shall be executed as soon as practicable and shall be conducted in such a way or manner as to minimize the interception of communications not otherwise subject to interception under this section and must terminate upon attainment of the authorized objective, or in any event on expiry of the period of order. In the event the intercepted communication is in a code or foreign language, and an expert in that foreign language or code is not reasonably available during the interception period, minimization may be accomplished as soon as practicable after such interception. An interception under this section may be conducted in whole or in part by public servant, or by an individual operating under a contract with the State Government, acting under the supervision of the investigative or law enforcement officer authorized to conduct the interception.

(ix) Whenever an order authorizing interception is issued pursuant to this section, the order may require reports to be made to the Competent Authority who issued the order showing that progress has been made towards achievement of the authorized objective and the need for continued interception. Such reports shall be made at such intervals as the Competent Authority may require.

(x) Notwithstanding anything contained in any other provision of this section, an Officer not below the rank of Additional Director General of Police who reasonably determines that—

(a) an emergency situation exists that involves—

- ❖ immediate danger of death or serious physical injury to any person;
- ❖ conspiratorial activities threatening the security or interest of the State; or
- ❖ conspiratorial activities, characteristic of organized crime,

that requires a wire, electronic or oral communication to be intercepted before an order from the Competent Authority authorizing such interception can, with due diligence, be obtained, and

(b) there are grounds upon which an order could be issued under this section to authorize such interception, may authorize, in writing, the investigating Police Officer to intercept such wire, electronic or oral communication, if an application for an order approving the interception is made in accordance with the provisions of sub-sections (1) and (2) within forty-eight hours after the interception has occurred, or begins to occur.

(xi) In the absence of an order approving the interception made under sub-section (10), such interception shall immediately terminate when the communication sought is obtained or when the application for the order is rejected, whichever is earlier. In the event where an application for permitting interception is rejected under sub-section (4) or an application under sub-section (10) for approval is rejected, or in any other case where the interception is terminated without an order having been issued, the contents of any wire, electronic or oral communication intercepted shall be treated as having been obtained in violation of this section.

(xii) (a) The contents of any wire, electronic or oral communication intercepted by any means authorized by this section shall, if possible, be recorded on tape or wire or other comparable device. Recording of the contents of any wire, electronic or oral communication under this sub-section shall be done in such a way as will protect the recording from editing or other alterations. Immediately upon the expiration of the period of order, or extension thereof, such recordings shall be made available to the Competent Authority issuing such order and shall be sealed under his directions. Custody of the recordings shall be wherever the Competent Authority orders. They shall not be destroyed except upon an order of the Competent Authority and in any event shall be kept for ten years.

(b) Applications made and orders issued under this section shall be sealed by the Competent Authority. Custody of the applications and orders shall be wherever the Competent Authority directs, and shall not be destroyed except on an order of the Competent Authority, and in any event shall be kept for ten years.

The Competent Authority upon the filing of a motion, may in his discretion make available to such person or his counsel for inspection such portions of the intercepted communications, applications and orders as the Competent Authority determines to be in the interest of justice.

(xiii) Notwithstanding anything in the Code or in any other law for the time being in force, the evidence collected through the interception of wire, electronic or oral communication under this section shall be admissible as evidence against the accused in the Court during the trial of a case:

Provided that, the contents of any wire, electronic or oral communication intercepted pursuant to this section or evidence derived therefrom shall not be received in evidence or otherwise disclosed in any trial, hearing or other proceeding in any Court unless each party, not less than ten days before trial, hearing or proceeding, has been furnished with a copy of the order of the Competent Authority, and accompanying application, under which the interception was authorized or approved:

Provided further that, this ten days period may be waived by the judge, trying the matter, if he finds that it was not possible to furnish the party with the above information ten days before the trial, hearing or proceeding and that the party will not be prejudiced by the delay in receiving such information.

Explanation. For the purposes of this section—

(a) 'wire communication' means any aural transfer made in whole or part through the use of facilities for the transmission of communications by the aid of wire, cable or other like connection between the point of origin and the point of connection, between the point of origin and point of reception (including the use of such connection switching station) and such term includes any electronic storage of such communication;

(b) 'oral communication' means any oral communication uttered by a person exhibiting an expectation that such communication is not subject to interception under circumstances justifying such expectation but such term does not include any electronic communication;

(c) 'electronic communication' means any transfer of signs, signals, writings, images, sounds, data or intelligence of any nature transmitted in whole or in part by a wire, radio, electromagnetic, photo electronic or photo optical system that affects inland or foreign commerce but does not include,—

❖ the radio portion of a cordless telephone communication that is transmitted between the wireless telephone hand-set and the base unit;

❖ any wire or oral communication;

❖ any communication made through a tone only paging device; or

❖ any communication from a tracking device;

(d) 'intercept' means the aural or other acquisition of the contents by wire, electronic or oral communication through the use of any electronic, mechanical or other device.

15. Constitution of Review Committee for review of authorisation orders-

(a) There shall be a Review Committee to review every order passed by the Competent Authority under section 14.

(b) The Review Committee shall consist of the following ex officio members, namely:

(i) the Chief Secretary to Government Chairman

(ii) the Additional Chief Secretary or the Member senior most Principal Secretary, as the case may be, in the Home Department.

(iii) Principal Secretary or Secretary and Member

Remembrancer of Legal Affairs, Law and Judiciary Department.

(c) Every order passed by the Competent Authority under section 14, placed before the Review Committee, shall be considered by the Review Committee within ten days after its receipt, to decide whether the order, authorizing or approving the application under sub-section

(d) Of section 14, for interception or disapproving the interception made under sub-section (10) of that section in emergency situation, passed by the Competent Authority was necessary, reasonable and justified.

(e) The Review Committee, after examining the entire record and holding such enquiry, if any, deemed necessary may, by order in writing, either approve the order passed by the Competent Authority or may issue order disapproving the same. On issue of an order of disapproval by the Review Committee, the interception, if any, already commenced shall be forthwith discontinued. The intercepted communication, if any, in the form of tape, wire or other device shall, thereupon, not be admissible as evidence in any case and shall be directed to be destroyed.

16. ***Interception and disclosure of wire, electronic or oral communications prohibited:***

Except as otherwise specifically provided in section 14, any police officer who:

(a) intentionally intercepts, endeavours to intercept or procures any other person to intercept or endeavour to intercept any wire, electronic or oral communication;

(b) intentionally uses, endeavours to use, or procures any other person to use or endeavours to use any electronic, mechanical or other device to intercept any oral communication when—

(i) such device is affixed to, or otherwise transmits a signal through a wire, cable, or other like connection used in wire communication; or

(ii) such device transmits communications by radio, or interferes with the transmission of such communication;

(c) intentionally discloses, or endeavours to disclose, to any other person the contents of any wire, electronic or oral communication, knowing or having reason to know that the information was obtained through the interception of a wire, electronic or oral communication in violation of this sub-section ;

(d) intentionally uses, or endeavours to use, the contents of any wire, electronic or oral communication, knowing or having reason to know that the information was obtained through the interception of a wire, electronic or oral communication in violation of this sub-section ; or

(e) (i) intentionally discloses, or endeavours to disclose, to any other person the contents of any wire, electronic or oral communication, intercepted by means authorized by section 14;

(ii) knowing or having reason to know that the information was obtained through the interception of such a communication in connection with a criminal investigation under this Act;

(iii) having obtained or received the information in connection with a criminal investigation; and

(iv) with intent to improperly obstruct, impede, or interfere with a duly authorized criminal investigation; or

(f) intentionally continues the interception of wire, electronic or oral communication after the issue of an order of disapproval by the Review Committee under sub-section (4) of section 15, shall for such violation be punishable with imprisonment for a term which may extend to one year and with fine up to rupees fifty thousand.

17. ***Special Rules of evidence:***

(a) Notwithstanding anything to the contrary contained in the Code, or the Indian Evidence Act, 1872, for the purposes of trial and punishment for offences under this Act or connected offences, the Court may take into consideration as having probative value, the fact that the accused was,—

(i) on any previous occasion bound under section 107 or section 110 of the Code;

(ii) detained under any law relating to preventive detention; or

(iii) on any previous occasion was prosecuted in the Special Court under this Act.

(b) Where it is proved that any person involved in an organized crime or any person on his behalf is or has at any time been in possession of movable or immovable property which he cannot satisfactorily account for, the Special Court shall, unless contrary is proved, presume that such property or pecuniary resources have been acquired or derived by his illegal activities.

(c) Where it is proved that the accused has kidnapped or abducted any person, the Special Court shall presume that it was for ransom.

18. ***Certain confessions made to police officer to be ta en into consideration:***

(a) Notwithstanding anything in the Code or in the Indian Evidence Act, 1872, but subject to the provisions of this section, a confession made by a person before a police officer not below the rank of the Superintendent of Police and recorded by such police officer either in writing or on any mechanical devices like cassettes, tapes or sound tracks from which sounds or images can be reproduced, shall be admissible in the trial of such person or co-accused, abettor or conspirator :

Provided that, the co-accused, abettor or conspirator is charged and tried in the same case together with the accused.

(b) The confession shall be recorded in a free atmosphere in the same language in which the person is examined and as narrated by him.

(c) The police officer shall, before recording any confession under sub-section (1), explain to the person making it that he is not bound to make a confession and that, if he does so, it may be used as evidence against him and such police officer shall not record any such confession unless upon questioning the person making it, he is satisfied that it is being made voluntarily. The concerned police officer shall, after recording such voluntary confession, certify in writing below the confession about his personal satisfaction of the voluntary character of such confession, putting the date and time of the same.

(d) Every confession recorded under sub-section (1) shall be sent forthwith to the Chief Metropolitan Magistrate or the Chief Judicial Magistrate having jurisdiction over the area in which such confession has been recorded and such Magistrate shall forward the recorded confession so received to the Special Court which may take cognizance of the offence.

(e) The person from whom a confession has been recorded under sub- section (1) shall also be produced before the Chief Metropolitan Magistrate or the Chief Judicial Magistrate to whom the confession is required to be sent under sub-section (4) along with the original statement of confession, written or recorded on mechanical device without unreasonable delay.

(f) The Chief Metropolitan Magistrate or the Chief Judicial Magistrate shall scrupulously record the statement, if any, made by the accused so produced and get his signature and in case of any complaint of torture, the person shall be directed to be produced for medical examination before a Medical Officer not lower in rank than of an Assistant Civil Surgeon.

19. ***Protection of witnesses:***

(a) Notwithstanding anything contained in the Code, the proceedings under this Act may be held in Camera, if the Special Court so desires.

(b) A Special Court may, on an application made by a witness in any proceeding before it or by the Public Prosecutor in relation to such witness or on its own motion, take such measures as it deems fit for keeping the identity and address of any witness secret.

(c) In particular, and without prejudice to the generality of the provisions of sub-section (2), the measures which a Special Court may take under that sub-section may include:

(i) the holding of the proceedings at a place to be decided by the Special Court;

(ii) the avoiding of the mention of the names and addresses of the witnesses in its orders or judgements or in any records of the case accessible to public;

(iii) the issuing of any directions for securing that the identity and addresses of the witnesses are not disclosed;

(iv) that, it is in the public interest to order that all or any of the proceedings pending before such a Court shall not be published in any manner.

(d) Any person who contravenes any direction issued under sub-section (3) shall be punishable with imprisonment for a term which may extend to one year and with fine which may extend to one thousand rupees.

20. ***Forfeiture and attachment of property:***

(a) Where a person has been convicted of any offence punishable under this Act, the Special Court may, in addition to awarding any punishment, by order in writing, declare, that any property, movable or immovable or both, belonging to the accused and specified in the order, shall stand forfeited to the State Government, free from all encumbrances.

(b) Where any person is accused of any offence under this Act, it shall be open to the Special Court trying him, to pass an order that all or any properties, movable or immovable or both, belonging to him, shall, during the period of such trial, be attached, and where such trial ends in conviction, the properties so attached shall stand forfeited to the State Government, free from all encumbrances.

(c) (i) If, upon a report in writing made by an investigating police officer with the approval of the supervisory officer referred to in sub-section (1) of section 14, any Special Court has reason to believe that any person, who has committed an offence punishable under this Act has absconded or is concealing himself so that he may not be apprehended, such Court may, notwithstanding anything contained in section 82 of the Code, publish a written proclamation requiring him to appear at a specified place and at a specified time not less than fifteen days but not more than thirty days from the publication of such proclamation :

Provided that, if the investigating police officer concerned fails to arrest the accused, who has absconded or is concealing himself, within a period of three months from the date of registering the offence against such person, the officer shall, on the expiry of the said period, make a report to the Special Court for issuing the proclamation.

(ii) The Special Court issuing a proclamation under clause (a) may, at any time, order the attachment or any property, movable or immovable or both, belonging to the proclaimed person, and thereupon the provisions of sections 83 to 85 of the Code shall apply to such attachment as if such attachment were made under that Code.

(iii) If, within six months from the date of attachment, any person, whose property is, or has been, at the disposal of the State Government under sub-section (2) of section 85 of the Code, appears voluntarily or is apprehended and brought before the Special Court by whose order the property was attached, or the Court to which such Court is subordinate, and proves to the satisfaction of such Court that he did not abscond or conceal himself for the purpose of avoiding apprehension and that he had not received such notice of the proclamation as to enable him to attend within the specified time therein, such property or, if the same has been sold, the net proceeds of the same and the residue of the property, shall, after satisfying therefrom all costs incurred in consequence of the attachment, be delivered to him.

21. ***Modified application of certain provisions of the code:***

(a) Notwithstanding anything contained in the Code or in any other law, every offence punishable under this Act, shall be deemed to be a cognizable offence within the meaning of clause (c) of section 2 of the Code and "cognizable case" as defined in that clause shall be construed accordingly.

(b) Section 167 of the Code shall apply in relation to a case involving an offence punishable under this Act subject to the modifications that, in sub-section (2),—

(i) the references to " fifteen days ", and " sixty days ", wherever they occur, shall be construed as references to "thirty days " and " ninety days", respectively ;

(ii) after the proviso, the following proviso shall be inserted, namely:—

"Provided further that if it is not possible to complete the investigation within the said period of ninety days, the Special Court shall extend the said period up to one hundred and eighty days, on the report of the Public Prosecutor indicating the progress of the investigation and the specific reasons for the detention of the accused beyond the said period of ninety days.".

(c) Nothing in section 438 of the Code shall apply in relation to any case involving the arrest of any person on an accusation of having committed an offence punishable under this Act.

(d) Notwithstanding anything contained in the Code, no person accused of an offence punishable under this Act shall, if in custody, be released on bail or on his own bond, unless—

(i) the Public Prosecutor has been given an opportunity to oppose the application of such release; and

(ii) where the Public Prosecutor opposes the application, the Court is satisfied that there are reasonable grounds for believing that he is not guilty of such offence and that he is not likely to commit any offence while on bail.

(e) Notwithstanding anything contained in the Code, the accused shall not be granted bail if it is noticed by the Court that he was on bail in an offence under this Act, or under any other Act, on the date of the offence in question.

(f) The limitations on granting of bail specified in sub-section (4) are in addition to the limitations under the Code or any other law for the time being in force on the granting of bail.

(g) The police officer seeking the custody of any person for pre- indictment or pre-trial interrogation from the judicial custody shall file a written statement explaining the reason for seeking such custody and also for the delay, if any, in seeking the police custody.

22. ***Presumption as to offences under section 3:***

(a) In a prosecution for an offence of organized crime punishable under section 3, if it is proved:

(i) that unlawful arms and other material including documents or papers were recovered from the possession of the accused and there is reason to believe that such unlawful arms and other material including documents or papers were used in the commission of such offence ; or

(ii) that by the evidence of an expert, the finger prints of the accused were found at the site of the offence or on anything including unlawful arms and other material including documents or papers and vehicle used in connection with the commission of such offence, the Special Court shall presume, unless the contrary is proved, that the accused had committed such offence.

(b) In a prosecution for an offence of organized crime punishable under sub-section (2) of section 3, if it is proved that the accused rendered any financial assistance to a person accused of, or reasonably suspected of, an offence of organized crime, the Special Court shall presume, unless the contrary is proved, that such person has committed the offence under the said sub-section (2).

23. ***Cognizance of, and investigation into, an offence:***

(a) Notwithstanding anything contained in the Code,—

(i) no information about the commission of an offence of organized crime under this Act, shall be recorded by a police officer without the prior approval of the police officer not below the rank of the Deputy Inspector General of Police;

(ii) no investigation of an offence under the provisions of this Act shall be carried out by a police officer below the rank of the Deputy Superintendent of Police.

(b) No Special Court shall take cognizance of any offence under this Act without the previous sanction of the police officer not below the rank of Additional Director General of Police.

24. ***Punishment for public servants failing in the discharge of their duties:*** Whoever being a public servant renders any help or support in any manner in the commission of organized crime as defined in clause (e) of section 2, whether before or after the commission of any offence by a member of an organized crime syndicate or abstains from taking lawful measures under this Act or intentionally avoids to carry out the directions of any Court or of the superior police officers in this respect, shall be punished with imprisonment of either description for a term which may extend to three years and also with fine.

25. ***Overriding effect:*** The provisions of this Act or any rule made thereunder or any order made under any such rule shall, have effect notwithstanding anything inconsistent therewith contained in any other law for the time being in force or in any instrument having the force of law.

26. ***Protection of action ta en in good faith:*** No suit, prosecution or other legal proceeding shall lie against the State Government or any officer or authority of the State Government for anything which is in good faith done or intended to be done in pursuance of this Act or any rule made thereunder or any order issued under any such rule.

27. ***Annual Report of Interceptions***

(a) The State Government shall cause an annual report to be prepared giving a full account of,—

(i) the number of applications for authorization of interceptions received by the Competent Authority from the Police Department in which prosecutions have been launched;

(ii) the number of such applications permitted or rejected;

(iii) the number of interceptions carried out in emergency situations and the number of ex-post-facto authorizations or approvals granted or rejected in such matters;

(iv) the number of prosecutions launched based on such interceptions and convictions resulting from such interceptions, along with an explanatory memorandum giving general assessment of the utility and importance of the interceptions authorized.

(b) Such annual report shall be laid by the State Government before each House of the State Legislature within three months of the completion of every calendar year:

Provided that, if the State Government is of the opinion that the inclusion of any matter in the annual report would be prejudicial to the security of the State or to the prevention or detection of any organized crime, the State Government may exclude such matter from being included in such annual report.

28. ***Power of High Court to make rules:*** The High Court may, by notification in the Official Gazette, make such rules as it may deem necessary for carrying out the provisions of this Act relating to the Special Courts.

29. ***Powers of State Government to make rules:***

(a) Without prejudice to the powers of the High Court to make rules under section 28, the State Government may, by notification in the Official Gazette, make rules for carrying out the purposes of this Act.

(b) Every rule made under this Act shall be laid, as soon as may be after it is made, before each House of the State Legislature, while it is in session, for a total period of thirty days, which may be comprised in one session or in two or more successive sessions, and if, before the. expiry of the session immediately following the session or the successive sessions aforesaid, both Houses agree in making any modification in the rule or both Houses agree that the rule should not be made, and notify such decision in the Official Gazette, the rule shall, from the date of publication of such notification, have effect only in such modified form or be of no effect, as the case may be, so, however, that any such modification or annulment shall be without prejudice to the validity of anything previously done under that rule.

30. ***Repeal of Mah. Ord. Ill of 1999 and saving:***

(a) The Maharashtra Control of Organized Crime Ordinance, 1999 is hereby repealed.

(b) Notwithstanding such repeal, anything done or any action taken under the said Ordinance shall be deemed to have been done or taken, as the case may be, under the corresponding provisions of this Act.

❑❑❑

Appendix four

List of Indian Intelligence Agencies

National Security Council

- National Security Council
- National Security Advisor
- Joint Intelligence Committee
- National Technical Research Organization

Internal Security

- Intelligence Bureau
- Central Bureau of Investigation
- National Investigation Agency
- All India Radio Monitoring Service
- Narcotics Control Bureau

External Intelligence

- Research and Analysis Wing
- Aviation Research Centre
- Radio Research Center
- Electronics and Technical Services

Defence Intelligence

- Defence Intelligence Agency
- Directorate of Military Intelligence
- Directorate of Naval Intelligence
- Directorate of Air Intelligence
- Image Processing and Analysis Centre
- Directorate of Signals Intelligence
- Joint Cipher Bureau

Economic Intelligence

- Economic Intelligence Council
- Central Economic Intelligence Bureau
- Directorate of Revenue Intelligence
- Directorate General of Income Tax Investigation
- Directorate General of Economic Enforcement

❑❑❑

Previous Years' Questions of IAS GS Mains Exam

UPSC MAINS G.S. PAPER-III – 2017

9. Discuss the potential threats of Cyber attack and the security framework to prevent it.

Ans.: India witnessed more than 27, 000 Cyber Security threat incidents in the first-half of 2017. According to ASSOCHAM, there has been a surge of about 350 percent in Cybercrime cases registered from the year of 2011 to 2014.

The potential threats areas follows:

1. The ransomware attacks like Wannacry and Petya have brought in light the susceptibility of Cyber systems.
2. The Cyber Security incidents such as phishing, scanning, website intrusions and defacementsand virus code have increased in recent years.
3. The Cyber-attack from neighbours like China and Pakistan has put a threat on critical infrastructure. The recent Cyber breach by China in India's naval defence is one such example.
4. With digitization of economy, the cyber-attacks on banks have grown. The joint study by ASSOCHAM and PWC said that an ATM card hack hit the Indian banks in October last year, affecting around 3.2 million debit cards.
5. India remains vulnerable to digital intrusions such as cyber-espionage, cyber crime, digital disruption and Distributed Denial of Service.

Following are the salient features of India's cyber security preparedness: Legal Measures: IT act, Provisions of IPC and Indian Copyright Act are some of the various laws dealing with IT sphere.

1. ***National Cyber Security policy 2013*** aims to protect public and private infrastructure and information from cyber-attacks.
2. ***CERT-IN:*** A dedicated team of professionals to protect major sectors of economy power systems, finance (CERT-IN).
3. ***Cyber Swachhta Kendra:*** MEITY's malware and Botnet cleaning centre.
4. International Cyber Security cooperation Agreements with the USA, Russia, Bangladesh, etc. and Convention on Cyber crime also known as Budapest Convention. They aim to harmonize national laws, improve investigative techniques, and increase cooperation among nations.
5. ***Diverse network*** of specialized bodies to tackle cybercrime like NATGRID, National Cyber Co-ordination Centre, National cyber defense research centre, etc.

UNITU's Global Cyber Security Index measures commitment to protect against cybercrime. India is currently ranked at the 23rd position.

Further, the National Cyber Security Policy was adopted with the mission to protect the information and related infra in cyber space. It aims to build capacities to prevent and respond to cyber threat and also reduce vulnerabilities and damage from cybercrime.

Objectives and features of the policy:

- Create secure Cyber Ecosystem and confidence in IT and promote secure IT adoption in all sectors of economy.

- Assurance framework for design of security policy based on International standard and best practices.
- 24×7 mechanism to obtain threat to ICT infrastructure.
- Protect resilience of critical information by National Critical Information Infrastructure Protection Centre.
- Develop Indigenous security technology through Research and Development.
- Create a workforce of 5 lakh professionals in next 5 years–capacity building, training and skill development.
- Strong law enforcement to enable prevention; investigation and prosecution of cybercrime.
- Develop Public-Private Partnership and global collaboration.
- Mandate appointment for Chief Information Security Officer in each private and public organization.
- Create Awareness about threat, vulnerability and consequence of cybercrime and encourage reporting.
- Create a think-tank for cyber security for policy inputs, discussions and deliberations.

10. The north-eastern region of India has been infested with insurgency for a very long time. Analyse the major reasons for the survival of armed insurgency in this region.

Ans.: The insurgencies in north east are a reflection of its social, cultural, ethnic and linguistic diversity. The lack of socio-economic development, unstable politico-economic conditions, threat to culture by migrants and changes in the environment of the area have altered the way of life of different tribes, and they have demanded regional autonomy and even independence to preserve their traditional way of life.

Reasons for armed insurgency and its survival in north eastern regions are as follows:

Role of the Neighbouring countries: China and Pakistan have supported them with weapons and funding to wage war against Indian state and make the national security unstable and create dissent among people against the government.

- ***Divided into multiple factions:*** The region has presence of several tribes with their own culture and dominance region. They fight among themselves and with Indian state to demand regional autonomy. For example, the National Democratic Front of Bodoland (NDFB) is a separatist group that demands a sovereign state for the Bodo people of North Assam.
- ***Migration problems:*** The major ethnic conflict in the Assam is the grievance against the perceived influx of 'foreigners', i.e., people with a language and culture substantially different from the Assamese from Bangladesh.
- ***Geographical factors:*** The terrain of the region makes it difficult to demarcate borders, and the porous borders help the insurgents to hide in the neighbouring regions of Myanmar and Bangladesh as can be seen in NSCN(K) group insurgents.
- ***Lack of socio-economic development:*** The region has not seen much of development works in terms of infrastructure, health and education, and this has not helped them realize the benefits of independence.
- ***The economic integration has also not occurred:*** The region suffers from unemployment and low per capita income. The ULFA (United Liberation Front of Assam) in Assam blames the government for the economic exploitation of Assamese natural resources, which results in wealth being drained from the region in return for very little investment in development projects and no substantial benefits for the local population.
- ***AFSPA:*** AFSPA has led to military and armed

force presence in the region which has instilled a sense of insecurity among people. Also, the abuses by some of personnel like murder, fake encounter and rapes in Manipur havefurther degraded the authority of government.

The way forward lies in establishing peace in the region and gaining the confidence of the local tribes and population.

- The efforts should be made to provide facilities in health and education.
- Also, northeast has great economic potential and natural resources, and it should be harnessed to provide employment to local youth of the region.
- Talks must be initiated with the dissent faction who wishes to communicate within the ambit of law, and problems must be addressed. The Naga Peace Accord is important in this regard.
- The porous borders must be sealed, security enhanced and agreements must be made with Bangladesh and Myanmar to ensure that the insurgents donot use their lands to spread violence in India.

19. Mob violence is emerging as a serious law and order problem in India. By giving suitable examples, analyse the causes and consequences of such violence.

Ans.: Mob violence is the action taken by crowd by subverting the law and legal institutions and inciting violence. A recent report by India spend concludes that 'In the first six months of 2017, 20 cow-terror attacks were reported–more than 75 per cent of the 2016 figure, which was the worst year for such violence since 2010. The attacks include mob lynching, attacks by vigilantes, murder and attempt to murder, harassment, assault and gang-rape'.

Causes of Mob Violence:

1. ***Political support:*** The mob violence in recent years has been used as a tool to garner votes through muscle power. The Muzzafarnagar riot is attributed to it. An imaginary Hindu fear seems to have overpowered the political class and rendered them paralyzed. Their failure to come forward in support of Muslims and Christians shows that the secular resolve in the Indian body politics has weakened.
2. ***Show religious dominance:*** Majority religions have been used as tool to create fear among the minorities. The violence of cow vigilantism and beef eating has been based on it. The day before Eid, 15-year-old Junaid Khan lost his life after being attacked by fellow passengers on a train. He was mocked for being Muslim and a 'beef-eater' and was knifed to death.
3. ***Weak law and order situation:*** The weakness of police to handle riot and low conviction rate in court has encouraged the mob to violate law.
4. ***High unemployment:*** The youth finding no job and subsistence get attracted and motivated by communal political propaganda and resort to mob violence and rioting.
5. ***Communalism:*** The degrading of secular values and the projection of superiority of one religion over other have led to mob violence. On 22 June, three Muslims were killed in West Bengal state after being accused of cow smuggling. On 27 June, a Muslim dairy owner in the state of Jharkhand was attacked by a mob after being accused of killing a cow.
6. Lack of trust in institutions has also led to people taking law in their own hands.
7. ***Role of media:*** Some of the media groups have used communalism to gain TRP and sensationalized the issue of law and order.

Consequences of Mob Violence:

1. ***Threat to minorities:*** The dominance by majority group has led to fear among the minorities. This is a threat to social fabric

of the country. In 2016, seven members of a dalit family were attacked by cow vigilantes in the state of Gujarat, which led to mass protests by the Dalit community. Attacks on Christians remain under-reported, but incidents involving churches and priests accused of converting Hindus to Christianity continue.

2. ***Threat to ideals of secularism:*** The spread of communalism has led to rift between communities with each religion trying to project itself as dominant and threatening the secular nature of country.
3. ***Loss of life and property:*** The violence causes heavy loss of life and property.
4. ***Shown ineffectiveness of institutions:*** The institutions like police and judiciary have lost trust of people for taking either no action or limited action against the violators of law.
5. ***Moral crisis:*** The mob rioting also raises question on the wisdom of people who accept and choose to participate in such activity. This has undermined the very idea of democracy.
6. ***Loss of economic activity:*** Any region facing such type of activity and subvert law and order situation sees decline in economic activity as companies prefer peaceful regions. This is evident in Kashmir as due to stone pelting the local tourism has declined.

The need of the hour is to preserve and protect the idea of secularism where each community is respected and given space for development. The institutions of police and law must be strengthened, and violators of law must be brought to swift justice. Moreover, the voice must come from within the society to not accept such mob violence. The 'NOT IN MY NAME' Campaign is a good way to start with.

20. The scourge of terrorism is a grave challenge to national security. What solution do you suggest to curb this growing menace? What are the major sources of terrorist funding?

Ans.: In recent years, India has been the victim of state-sponsored terrorism by its neighbouring country which poses a grave threat to national security. It is evident from following:

1. There has been increase in terrorist attacks in India, for example, the Pathankot attack, Mumbai attack, etc.
2. It has become threat to global order and peace due to rise in new terrorism groups like ISIS.
3. The productive youths are brain washed and made to join terrorist organizations by terrorists, which are then used against the nation. This is evident in Jammu and Kashmir where young students are influenced to throw stones and even carry out attack on security force camps.
4. The terrorist threats in India also range from Left Wing Extremism (LWE), ethnic separatism to religious militancy.
5. The cyber-attack is a new tool of terrorists to destabilize the critical infrastructure of the nation.

The solution to terrorism lies in multi-pronged approach involving all the stakeholders. The solution includes:

1. At world level, all the nations should come together to create a common framework to fight terrorism. India's proposedComprehensive convention on international terrorism (CCIT) provides a comprehensive legal framework against terrorism with a universal definition of terrorism.
2. As a solution to cross-border terrorism, India must strengthen its border security. The recently proposed comprehensive integrated border management system involves five layers of security including CCTV cameras, thermal image and night-vision devices, battle field surveillance radar, underground monitoring sensors and laser barriers.

3. Further, India has adopted a policy of isolating and exposing Pakistan at a global level for acting as safe haven and supporting terrorism.
4. For Cyber-attacks, India has adopted Cyber Security Policy in 2013, and CERT-IN has been given responsibility to protect the critical infrastructure from such attacks.
5. Community awareness, economic development and involvement of NGOs are done to prevent youths from joining terrorist organizations and report any such activity.
6. Also, a policy of socio-economic development of region and deploying strong security measures by arming forces with modern weapons has been done to tackle insurgency and naxalite terrorism.

The major sources of terror financing include the following:

1. ***Counterfeit currency:*** A major source of financing constitutes printing fake currency and circulating them in market.
2. ***Black money:*** The black money is brought in through tax havens and used for financing terrorism.
3. ***Drug trafficking:*** India lies between Golden Triangle and Golden Crescent which is major drug route for trafficking drugs. This method is used to both attract youth and generate money for terrorism.
4. ***External support:*** The nations like Pakistan, China and Saudi Arabia are funding terrorism in different nations.
5. ***Extortions:*** The IB report has shown that even the government departments pay extortions for developmental projects in North-Eastern regions to Naxalites.

The efforts need to be made to cut the source of terror financing. Financial Action Task Force is one such effort to prevent terror financing and money laundering.

Bibliography

1. P.R. Chari,—National Counter Terrorism Centre for India‖, Institute of Peace and Conflict Studies, Issue Brief No. 181, March 2012, New Delhi.
2. Sanjay Hazarika & V. R Raghvan (ed.), —Conflicts in the North East: Internal and External Threats‖, New Delhi, 2011, pp. 231-232.
3. Major General RS Choudhary: Intelligence Journal
4. Michael Cunningham: Intelligence Its Organization and Development
5. Nigel West: Secret War
6. Major General RS Choudhary: A Short History of the Intelligence Corps
7. Patrick Howarth: Special Operations
8. Senator Bob Graham: Intelligence Matters
9. Army Training Command: Manual of Military Intelligence Pamphlet No 1, General
10. Principles A Guide to Military Intelligence Army Training Command: Military Security Instructions
11. Andrew Tuky: Central Intelligence Agency
12. Yossi Melman: The Imperfect Spies : The history of Israeli Intelligence
13. Michael N. Demers: Fundamentals of Geographical Information System User Handbook: Geo-media
14. Military Intelligence Training School and Depot Précis
15. Jeff Hawkins: On Intelligence
16. Irving Heymont: Combat Intelligence in Modern Warfare
17. Col Edwin E Schwien: Combat Intelligence
18. Army Training Command: Pamphlet on Sub Conventional Warfare
19. RV Jones: Reflections of Intelligence
20. Alexandria: Artificial Intelligence
21. Jeffery T Richelson: Strategic Intelligence
22. K Johnson: Global Security and Intelligence
23. Girish Bihari: Civil Insurgency and Intelligence Operations
24. Dr. NC Asthana, IPS: Intelligence and Security Management
25. India's National Security: A Reader
26. Challenges to Internal Security of India
27. Bureau of Police Research and Development (2006). Indian police: An introductory and statistical overview.
28. Bureau of Police Research and Development (2009). Police communications.
29. Bureau of Police Research and Development (2012). Data on police organizations in India. New Delhi: BPR&D.
30. Business Standard (2012, 13 June). Contagion: India's vulnerability to cyber-attacks.
31. Crelinsten R. (1978). Terrorism and criminal justice. Massachusetts: Lexington Books.
32. Federal Research Division, US Library of Congress (2002, May). A global overview of narcotics-funded terrorist and other extremist groups.
33. Ganz Kian (2012, 7 June). Supreme Court's battle against backlog in cases. Live Mint.
34. Government of India (2012, January). National Policy on Narcotic Drugs and Psychotropic Substances. New Delhi: Department of Revenue.
35. India Today (2009, 12 November). High level meet reviews coastal security.
36. India Today (2011, 6 June). War on terror: CCS clears NATGRID project.
37. Jha Om Shankar (2007, December). Impact of modernization of Police Force Scheme on Combat Capability of the Police Forces in

Naxal-affected States: A critical evaluation (IDSA Occasional Paper No. 7, pp. 26–28).

38. Lal Chaman (1999). Terrorism and insurgency. Seminar, 483 (November).
39. Maplecroft website (2011). Global risks atlas. Retrieved 1 November 2012, from http://maplecroft.com/about/news/gra_2012.html
40. Ministry of Home Affairs (2003, March). Committee on Reforms of Criminal Justice System (Vol. 1, para 1.3).
41. Ministry of Home Affairs, Bureau of Police Research and Development (2006, 14 November). Draft national policy on police training.
42. National Crime Records Bureau (NCRB) (2010). Crime in India 2009. New Delhi: NCRB.
43. National Crime Records Bureau (NCRB) (2012a). Crime in India 2011. New Delhi: NCRB.
44. National Crime Records Bureau (NCRB) (2012b). Prison statistics India 2011.
45. Office of the White House of the United States of America (2010, 15 September). Presidential memorandum—Major illicit drug transit or major illicit drug producing countries (Presidential Determination No. 2010–16).
46. PRS Legislative Research (2011, 6 July). Pendency of cases in Indian courts.
47. Raghavan R K. (2003, January). Reforming criminal justice systems. Frontline, 20(2), 18–31.
48. Rediff Business (2008, 19 December). How fake currency funds terror.
49. Srinivasulu B. (2009). Pak ISI sponsored counterfeit currency circulation.
50. Subrahmanyam K. (2003). 'External security', in India: Vision 2025. New Delhi: Planning Commission.
51. Swami Praveen (2010, 23 July). India's counter-insurgency conundrum.
52. The Hindu (2005, 6 September). Rs 81 lakhs fake currency seized; gang busted in A.P.
53. The Hindu (2007, 20 December). Communist rebels pose the single biggest threat to India, says PM.
54. The Indian Express (2010, 22 March). Fake currency threat to economy: FM.
55. The Indian Express (2012, 11 June). Rs 16,000 Cr in fakes, 'printed in Pakistan' and circulated all over.
56. The Times of India (2010, 14 April). Dantewada fallout: CRPF to split.
57. US Department of State (2012). Country reports on terrorism 2011 (chap. 2).
58. Wilkinson Paul (2001). Terrorism versus democracy: The liberal state response. Portland: Frank Cass.
59. November 11, 2016, Demonetization and its impact, Event Update, HDFC Bank
60. Vivek Chadha, Demonetization and Beyond: Addressing the Finance of Terrorism, November 18, 2016, Institute of Defense Studies and Analyses.
61. Shashank Kamath, "Unknown facts about Demonetization 1946, 1978 and 2016", 19th November, 2016, A Word to the World.
62. November 11, 2016, Demonetization and its impact, Event Update, HDFC Bank
63. Vivek Chadha, Demonetization and Beyond: Addressing the Finance of Terrorism, November 18, 2016, Institute of Defense Studies and Analyses.
64. Shashank Kamath, "Unknown facts about Demonetization 1946, 1978 and 2016", 19th November, 2016, A Word to the World.

❑❑❑